Microsoft Power BI Performance Best Practices

Learn practical techniques for building high-speed
Power BI solutions

Thomas LeBlanc | Bhavik Merchant

‹packt›

Microsoft Power BI Performance Best Practices

Group Product Manager: Apeksha Shetty

Publishing Product Manager: Nilesh Kowadkar

Book Project Manager: Aparna Nair

Senior Editor: Sushma Reddy

Technical Editor: Kavyashree K S

Copy Editor: Safis Editing

Proofreader: Sushma Reddy

Indexer: Manju Arasan

Production Designer: Prashant Ghare

DevRel Marketing Coordinator: Nivedita Singh

First published: April 2022
Second edition: July 2024
Production reference: 1260724

Published by Packt Publishing Ltd.
Grosvenor House
11 St Paul's Square
Birmingham
B3 1RB, UK

ISBN 978-1-83508-225-6

www.packtpub.com

To my family, Janet, Tyler, and Kaylyn – I love y'all!

Thomas LeBlanc

Foreword

I have known Thomas for close to 15 years. From the very beginning, his desire to pass on his knowledge to those around him was obvious. Today, it is my pleasure to serve with him as a leader in the Baton Rouge User Groups. Thomas co-leads our SQL Server and .NET User Group meetings. He also plays a key role in the organization of our annual SQL Saturday and Analytics events. He understands the value of community and he works hard to bring more people into our community and make them feel welcome.

Thomas is not only a great leader but also a great friend. He is always supportive, generous, and kind to everyone he meets. He has taught me a lot about SQL Server, BI, and community building. I am honored to serve the community with him and to be able to call him a friend.

Kenneth Neal,

President, Baton Rouge User Groups

Contributors

About the author

Thomas LeBlanc is a seasoned Business Intelligence Architect at Data on the Geaux, where he applies his extensive skillset in dimensional modeling, data visualization, and analytical modeling to deliver robust solutions. With a Bachelor of Science in Management Information Systems from Louisiana State University, Thomas has amassed over 30 years of experience in Information Technology, transitioning from roles as a software developer and database administrator to his current expertise in business intelligence and data warehouse architecture and management.

Throughout his career, Thomas has spearheaded numerous impactful projects, including consulting for various companies on Power BI implementation, serving as lead database administrator for a major home health care company, and overseeing the implementation of Power BI and Analysis Service for a large bank. He has also contributed his insights as an author to the Power BI MVP book.

Thomas is recognized as a Microsoft Data Platform MVP and is actively engaged in the tech community through his social media presence, notably as TheSmilinDBA on Twitter and ThePowerBIDude on Bluesky and Mastodon. With a passion for solving real-world business challenges with technology, Thomas continues to drive innovation in the field of business intelligence.

I want to thank all the people who have helped me with the updates to an already great book.

Bhavik Merchant has nearly 18 years of deep experience in Business Intelligence. He is currently the Director of Product Analytics at Salesforce. Prior to that, he was at Microsoft, first as a Cloud Solution Architect and then as a Product Manager in the Power BI Engineering team. At Power BI, he led the customer-facing insights program, being responsible for the strategy and technical framework to deliver system-wide usage and performance insights to customers. Before Microsoft, Bhavik spent years managing high-caliber consulting teams delivering enterprise-scale BI projects. He has provided extensive technical and theoretical BI training over the years, including expert Power BI performance training he developed for top Microsoft Partners globally.

About the reviewer

Devanshu Tayal is a highly accomplished data scientist with a master's degree from BITS, Pilani, India. His extensive expertise in data science is evidenced by his contributions to a wide range of industries. Devanshu is deeply committed to mentoring and guiding aspiring data scientists and is an avid researcher of emerging technologies in the field. He is a strong advocate for diversity and inclusion and has shared his insights through various publications. Devanshu is frequently invited to deliver guest lectures at universities throughout India, and his contributions as a technical reviewer have been acknowledged in multiple books. His comprehensive knowledge and experience in the field make him an asset to any team or project.

Table of Contents

3

Learning the Tools for Performance Tuning   35

Part 2: Performance Analysis, Improvement, and Management

4

Analyzing Logs and Metrics   59

5

Optimization for Storage Modes   81

6

Third-Party Utilities   97

7

Performance Governance Framework   117

Part 3: Fetching, Transforming, and Visualizing Data

8

Part 4: Data Models, Calculations, and Large Semantic Models

10

11

12

Part 5: Optimizing Capacities in Power BI Enterprises

13

14

Performance Needs for Fabric Artifacts   287

15

Embedding in Web Apps   301

Index   309

Other Books You May Enjoy   320

Preface

It is very easy to start building analytical solutions in Power BI. Insightful content can come from many sources imported into a semantic model. The popularity of the model can bring many requests from various people in the organization for additional slicers and filters. If you do not plan for scale appropriately, performance issues will arise at all angles. This book can help by covering performance issues with optimizations for every layer of Power BI, from the report pane to data modeling as well as transformation, storage, and architecture.

Developers and architects working with Power BI will be able to put their knowledge to work with this practical guide to designing and implementing solutions at every step of the development process ending with a deployment. This book is not only a collection of best practices but it also provides a structured process with a hands-on approach to identifying and preventing common issues with using Power BI.

Complete with explanations of essential concepts and practical examples, you'll learn about common design choices that affect the performance and consumption of resources. You'll grasp common architectural patterns and settings that affect most deployments to the service. As you progress through the book, each level will show a typical example at that stage. This will help with the scale and usability of the semantic model and any reports associated with that model. The layers include the report pane, a semantic model, capacities for deployment, and gateway optimizations.

By the end of this book, you will know where to go to get the latest optimization techniques for each layer of design and deployment of Power BI models and reports.

Who this book is for

This book is for a range of users. These can be data analysts who use Power BI for analytical reporting. They could be architects who are deploying a shared model to a host of report developers. As far as Power BI administrators are concerned, there are chapters for the gateway and capacities assisting with configurations. Other titles include business intelligence developers, report writers, application developers, and Power Platform administrators. These titles do not include beginner levels because an intermediate level of business intelligence implementation should be already part of their experience.

What this book covers

Chapter 1, Setting Targets and Identifying Problem Areas, describes a Power BI solution as a stream of data from multiple sources reaching consumers in a consolidated fashion. We look at how data can be stored in Power BI and the different paths it can take before reaching a user. Many of the initial architectural design choices made in the early stages of the solution are very difficult and costly to switch later. That's why it's important to have a solid grasp of the implications of those choices and how to decide what's best at the start.

Chapter 2, Exploring Power BI Architecture and Configuration, looks at data storage modes in Power BI and how the data reaches the data model while giving some general guidance to improve throughput and latency. The storage mode chosen can limit size and data freshness. It also covers how to best deploy Power BI gateways, which are commonly used to connect to external data sources. This is important because users often demand up-to-date data, historical data, and aggregated data.

Chapter 3, Learning the Tools for Performance Tuning, explores how the easiest way to see where time is being spent in reports is to use the desktop Performance Analyzer to get detailed breakdowns for every user action, on a per-visual basis. Queries from this tool can be run in DAX Studio for server timing breakdown and better analysis. In addition, Tabular Editor can be used to examine measures for properties and syntax for performance tuning.

Chapter 4, Analyzing Logs and Metrics, describes how performance can only be improved if it can be measured objectively. Therefore, this chapter covers all the sources of performance data and how to make sense of the information provided to identify the parts of the solution that are bottlenecks. This includes useful native and third-party utilities. We also provide guidelines to help monitor and manage performance continuously.

Chapter 5, Optimization for Storage Models, describes how, with the proliferation of data lakes, more options are available for performance improvements with DirectQuery or DirectLake. Synapse has brought **Massively Parallel Processing** (**MPP**) from big data to analytical databases. DirectQuery can use the column store type tables in Synapse and other MPPs in the cloud. The use of aggregations with DirectQuery external data sources has become a common choice for large fact tables. There are optimizations that can be made in both Power BI and external sources to avoid hitting limits too quickly.

Chapter 6, Third-Party Utilities, covers a few popular third-party utilities that are effective in performance investigation and tuning and walks through typical use cases around connecting them to Power BI, collecting metrics, and what to look for when diagnosing performance problems.

Chapter 7, Performance Governance and Framework, talks about how the metrics and tools covered in earlier chapters are essential building blocks for performance management. However, success is more likely with a structured and repeatable approach to build performance-related thinking into the entire Power BI solution lifecycle. This chapter provides guidelines to set up data-driven processes to avoid sudden scale issues for new content and prevent degradations for existing content.

Chapter 8, Loading, Transforming, and Refreshing Data, explains how loading data periodically is a critical part of any analytical system, and in Power BI, this applies to Import mode semantic models. Data refresh operations in Import mode are CPU- and memory-intensive, which can lead to long delays or failures, especially with large semantic models. This can leave users with stale data or slow down development significantly, which is why it should be designed with performance in mind.

Chapter 9, Report and Dashboard Design, covers reports and dashboards, which are the "tip of the iceberg" in a Power BI solution since they are what consumers interact with regularly. This chapter covers important considerations and practices to apply regarding visual layout, configuration, and slicing/filtering. It also looks at paginated reports, which behave differently from interactive reports and have special performance considerations.

Chapter 10, Dimensional Modeling and Row-level Security, describes how the Power BI semantic model is where data lands after being shaped, and where data is retrieved for analysis. Hence, it is arguably the most critical piece, at the core of a Power BI solution. Power BI's feature richness and modeling flexibility provide alternatives when modeling data. Some choices can make development easier at the expense of query performance and/or semantic model size. This chapter provides guidance on model design, size reduction, and faster relationships.

Chapter 11, Improving DAX, covers DAX formulas, which allow BI developers to add a diverse range of additional functionality into the model. The same correct result can be achieved by writing different DAX formulas without realizing that one version may be significantly slower in certain query or visual configurations. This chapter highlights common DAX issues and recommended practices to get calculations performing at their best. It will also contain the definitions and examples for computed columns and measures with a dive into the filter context.

Chapter 12, High-Scale Patterns, explains how the amount of data organizations collect and process is increasing all the time. Even with Power BI's data compression technology, it isn't always possible to load and store massive amounts of data in an Import mode model in a reasonable amount of time. This problem is worse when you must support hundreds or thousands of users in parallel. This chapter covers the options available to deal with such issues by leveraging Azure technologies and Power BI aggregations and composite models. In addition, Fabric and Synapse will be utilized for speed improvements in data sources including the lakehouse.

Chapter 13, Working with Capacities, covers working with and monitoring capacity. Power BI offers dedicated capacity, higher limits, and many additional capabilities such as paginated reports and AI. This does, however, require diligent capacity management to prevent resource exhaustion. This chapter covers each of the available workload settings in detail. We then look at ideal to extreme usage/load scenarios and how the capacity manages its memory in each case. We also look at the Microsoft-provided template apps to monitor capacities.

Chapter 14, Performance Needs for Fabric Artifacts, talks about how Fabric options bring new artifacts into the capacity and some that are updated. Performance of the capacity will be affected by pipelines, Lakehouse/warehouse structures, as well as a destination added for Dataflow Gen2. These all have resource requirements and many people will be guided toward a different capacity for using Fabric features.

Chapter 15, Embedding in Web Apps, teaches how embedding Power BI content in a custom web app is a great way to expose data analytics within a completely customized UI experience, along with other no-Power BI-related content. This pattern does introduce additional considerations since the Power BI application is hosted externally via API calls. This chapter looks at how to do this efficiently and then measure performance.

To get the most out of this book

Some chapters in this book come with sample files that you can open in Power BI Desktop to explore the concepts and enhancements we provide. The examples largely show designs before and after performance improvements have been implemented. Therefore, it is not mandatory to review these examples, but they do provide useful context and can help teach new concepts through hands-on experience.

Software/hardware covered in the book	Operating system requirements
Power BI Desktop	Windows
DAX Studio 3.0.11	
Tabular Editor 2.x	
Power BI Pro license	
Premium Capacity or Fabric (can be trial version)	

We always recommend having the latest version of Power BI Desktop available due to the monthly release cycle.

If you are using the digital version of this book, we advise you to type the code yourself or access the code from the book's GitHub repository (a link is available in the next section). Doing so will help you avoid any potential errors related to the copying and pasting of code.

Download the example code files

You can download the example code files for this book from GitHub at `https://github.com/PacktPublishing/Microsoft-Power-BI-Performance-Best-Practices-Second-Edition`. If there's an update to the code, it will be updated in the GitHub repository.

The example files included with the book are of various types. The PBIX files are Power BI desktop examples used in each chapter. The other file types are as follows:

1.   .bak - SQL Server database backup file, to be used when data is needed.

2.   .json - Exports from monitoring tools or configuration file examples.

3.   .xlsx - Example Excel files.

4.   .ps1 - PowerShell scripts for monitoring.

5.   .txt - Tabular Editor rules for best practices.

6.   .csv - Example data.

7.   .gitattributes - GitHub configuration file.

Each file has a use for following a specific example in the related chapter.

We also have other code bundles from our rich catalog of books and videos available at `https://github.com/PacktPublishing/`. Check them out!

Conventions used

There are a number of text conventions used throughout this book.

`Code in text`: Indicates code words in text, database table names, folder names, filenames, file extensions, pathnames, dummy URLs, user input, and Twitter handles. Here is an example: "We exported this data and then worked on it in the sample Analyzing Desktop Performance Logs.pbix file."

A block of code is set as follows:

```
{
    "version":"1.1.0",
    "events":[
      {
        "name":"User Action",
        "component":"Report Canvas",
        "start":"2021-09-03T03:53:22.139Z",
        "id":"a702542d7cbbcd9b37a0",
        "metrics":{
          "sourceLabel":"UserAction_StartedMonitoring"
          }
      },
```

Any command-line input or output is written as follows:

```
$json = Get-PowerBIActivityEvent -StartDateTime $StartDate-EndDateTime
$EndDate | ConvertFrom-Json
```

Bold: Indicates a new term, an important word, or words that you see onscreen. For instance, words in menus or dialog boxes appear in **bold**. Here is an example: "Initial architectural choices can help with the cost, but the **Software as a Service (Saas)** structure of Power BI enables many easy and fast ways to adjust the service behind reports or dashboards"

Tips or important notes
Appear like this.

Get in touch

Feedback from our readers is always welcome.

General feedback: If you have questions about any aspect of this book, email us at customercare@ packtpub.com and mention the book title in the subject of your message.

Errata: Although we have taken every care to ensure the accuracy of our content, mistakes do happen. If you have found a mistake in this book, we would be grateful if you would report this to us. Please visit www.packtpub.com/support/errata and fill in the form.

Piracy: If you come across any illegal copies of our works in any form on the internet, we would be grateful if you would provide us with the location address or website name. Please contact us at copyright@packt.com with a link to the material.

If you are interested in becoming an author: If there is a topic that you have expertise in and you are interested in either writing or contributing to a book, please visit authors.packtpub.com.

Share Your Thoughts

Once you've read *Microsoft Power BI Performance Best Practices*, we'd love to hear your thoughts! Scan the QR code below to go straight to the Amazon review page for this book and share your feedback.

https://packt.link/r/1-835-08225-4

Your review is important to us and the tech community and will help us make sure we're delivering excellent quality content.

Download a free PDF copy of this book

Thanks for purchasing this book!

Do you like to read on the go but are unable to carry your print books everywhere?

Is your eBook purchase not compatible with the device of your choice?

Don't worry, now with every Packt book you get a DRM-free PDF version of that book at no cost.

Read anywhere, any place, on any device. Search, copy, and paste code from your favorite technical books directly into your application.

The perks don't stop there, you can get exclusive access to discounts, newsletters, and great free content in your inbox daily

Follow these simple steps to get the benefits:

1. Scan the QR code or visit the link below

https://packt.link/free-ebook/978-1-83508-225-6

2. Submit your proof of purchase
3. That's it! We'll send your free PDF and other benefits to your email directly

Part 1: Architecture, Bottlenecks, and Performance Targets

In this part, we will review high-level Power BI architecture and identify areas where performance can be affected by design choices. We will explain how to define realistic performance targets.

This part has the following chapters:

- *Chapter 1, Setting Targets and Identifying Problem Areas*
- *Chapter 2, Exploring Power BI Architecture and Configuration*
- *Chapter 3, Learning the Tools for Performance Tuning*

1

Setting Targets and Identifying Problem Areas

Many people would consider report performance as the most critical area to focus on when trying to improve the speed of an analytics solution. This is largely true, because it is the most visible part of the system used by pretty much every class of user, from administrators to business executives. However, you will learn that there are other areas of the solution that should be considered if performance is to be managed comprehensively. For example, achieving good performance in the reporting layer might be of no consequence if the underlying dataset that powers the report takes a long time to be refreshed or is susceptible to failures due to resource limits or system limits being reached. In this case, users may have great-looking, fast reports that do not provide value because the data is stale.

The authors of this book have experienced the effects of poor report performance firsthand but have also enjoyed the fruits of improving performance or a great dimensional model. In multiple projects, large companies have tried to migrate from one reporting system to another without much planning. They just wanted to duplicate the existing system in a new reporting application. Copying the old reporting system was not functionally equivalent. This led to poor design choices and resulted in some slow reports. Some end users were reluctant to adopt the new system after lots of money was spent on licensing and consulting. While this example is on the extreme side, it does demonstrate the potential ramifications when you do not use a good design for great performance.

This chapter begins the journey to achieving good and consistent performance in Microsoft Power BI. To introduce the full scope of performance management, we will describe a Power BI solution as a stream of data from multiple sources. These streams will be consolidated and presented to a data analyst. Data will be looked at to examine and understand the storage process and how it gets to the report viewer. Initial architectural choices can help with the cost, but the **Software as a Service (Saas)** structure of Power BI enables many easy and fast ways to adjust the service behind reports or dashboards. Hence, it is important to have a solid grasp of the implications of the path to implementation and see a data-driven approach to help us decide what is the best start.

An area of performance management that is easily overlooked is that of setting performance targets. How do you know whether the experience you are delivering is great, merely acceptable, or poor? We will begin by exploring this theoretical area first to define our goal before diving into technical concepts.

The chapter is broken into the following sections:

- Defining good performance
- Considering areas that could slow you down
- Choices that affect performance

Defining good performance

With the advent of ever-faster computers and the massive scale of processing available today by way of cloud computing, business users expect and demand analytical solutions that perform well. This is essential for competitive business decision-making. **Business Intelligence** (**BI**) software vendors echo this need and tend to promise quick results in their sales and marketing materials. Their expectations mean that it is uncommon to find users getting excited about how fast reports are or how fresh data is because it is something implicit to them having a positive experience.

Conversely, when users must wait a long time for a report to load, they are quite vocal and tend to escalate such issues via multiple channels. When these problems are widespread, they can damage the reputation of both software platforms and the teams involved in building and maintaining those solutions. In the worst possible case, users may refuse to adopt these solutions and management may begin looking for alternative platforms. It's important to think about performance from the onset because it is often very costly and time-consuming to fix performance after a solution has reached production, potentially affecting thousands of users.

Reporting performance goals

Today, most BI solutions are consumed via a web interface. A typical report consumption experience involves not just opening a report, but also interacting with it. In Power BI terms, this translates to opening a report and then interacting with filters, slicers, and report visuals, plus navigating to other pages explicitly or via a bookmark and drill through. With each report interaction, the user generally has a specific intention, and the goal is to not interrupt their flow. A term commonly used in the industry is analysis at the speed of thought. This experience and the related expectations are very similar to navigating regular web pages or interacting with a web-based software system.

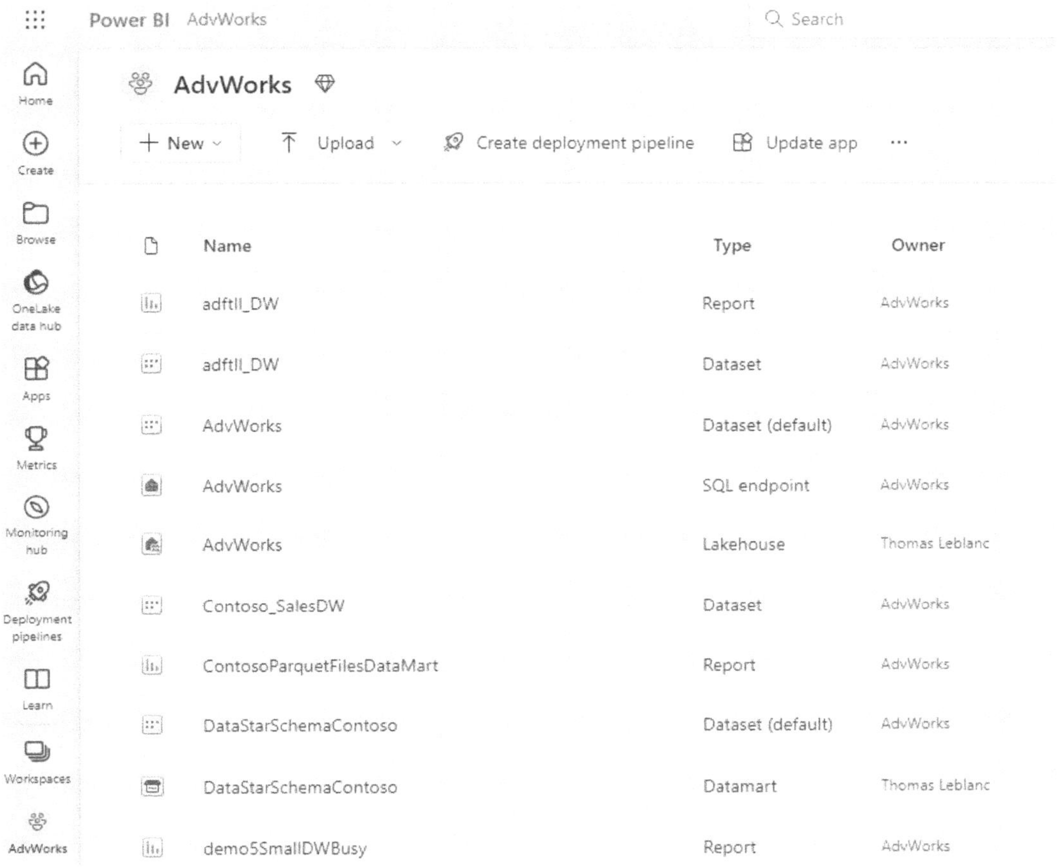

Figure 1.1 – Power BI portal (app.powerbi.com)

Therefore, defining good performance for a BI solution can take some cues from the many studies on web and user interface performance that have been performed over the past two or three decades: it is not a complex task. *Nah F. (2004)* conducted a study focusing on **tolerable wait time** (**TWT**) for web users. TWT was defined as how long users are willing to wait before abandoning the download of a web page. Nah reviewed many previous studies that explored the thresholds at which users' behavioral intentions get lost and when their attitudes begin to become negative. From this research, we can derive that a well-performing Power BI report should completely load a page or the result of an interaction, ideally, in less than 4 seconds and in most cases not more than 12 seconds. We should always measure report performance from the user's perspective, which means we measure from the time they request the report (for example, click a report link on the Power BI portal) until the time the last report visual finishes drawing its results on the screen.

Setting realistic performance targets

Now that we have research-based guidance to set targets, we need to apply it to real-world scenarios. A common mistake is to set a single performance target for every report in the organization and to expect it to be met every single time a user interacts with a report. For example, very large dataset sizes (tens of GBs) combined with complex nested DAX calculations that are displayed on multiple hierarchical levels of granularity in a table visual will naturally need significant time to be processed and displayed. This would generally not be the case with a report working on a small data model (tens of MBs) containing a row of simple sum totals, each displayed within a **Card** visual.

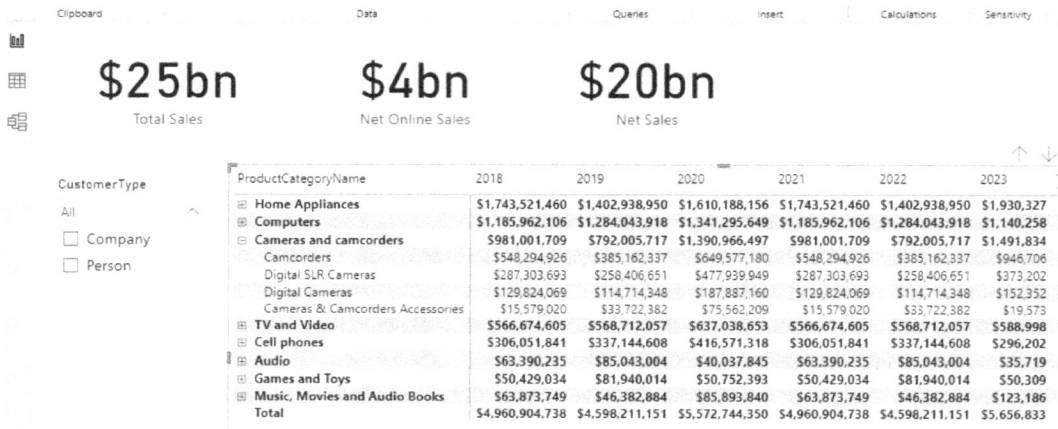

Figure 1.2 – Card and table visuals

Due to the variability of the solution complexity and other factors beyond the developer's control (such as the speed of a user's computer or which web browser they use), it is recommended that you think of performance targets in terms of typical user experience and acknowledge that there may be exceptions and outliers. Therefore, the performance target metric should consider what most users experience. We recommend report performance metrics that use the 90th percentile of the report load or interaction duration, often referred to as P90. Applying the research guidance on how long a user can wait before becoming frustrated, a reasonable performance target would be a P90 report load duration of 10 seconds or less. This means 90% of report loads would occur in under 10 seconds.

However, a single target such as P90 is still not sufficient and we will introduce further ideas about this in *Chapter 7, Performance Goverance Framework* . For now, we should consider that there may be different levels of complexity, so it is recommended to set up a range of targets that reflect the complexity of solutions and the tolerance levels of users and management alike. The following table presents an example of a performance target table that could be adopted in an organization:

	Typical Report	Complex Report
P90 Duration Target	Under 5 Seconds	Under 15 Seconds

Figure 1.3 – Example report performance targets

Next, we will look at Power BI from a high level to get a broad understanding of the areas that need to be considered for performance improvement.

Considering areas that could slow you down

The next step in our performance management journey is to understand where time is spent. A Power BI solution is ultimately about exposing data to a user and can be thought of as a flow of data from source systems to data stores. Through these various components, eventually, the visual will reach a user through a browser or mobile device. A simplified view of a Power BI solution is presented in the following figure.

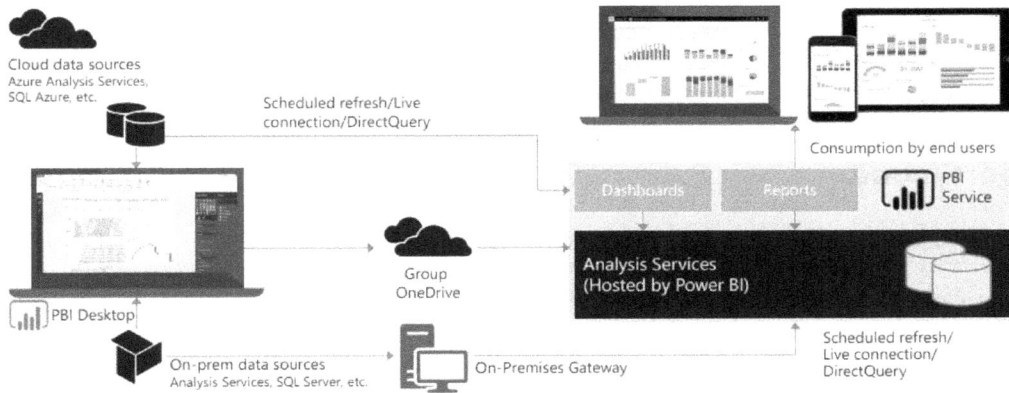

Figure 1.4 – Power BI solution overview

Here, we will briefly focus on the different paths of a typical solution to explain why each piece has important considerations for users and the effect poor performance can have on each process. Some of these areas will be covered in more detail in *Chapter 2, Exploring Power BI Architecture and Configuration*.

Connecting data sources

The following diagram highlights the areas of the solution that are affected when data sources and connectivity methods do not perform well:

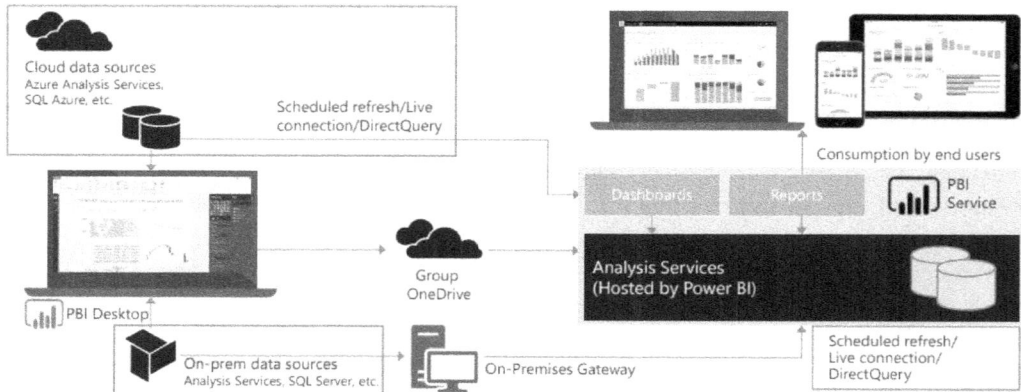

Figure 1.5 – Areas affected by data source and connectivity issues

Import mode

When using **Import mode** datasets, developers can experience sluggish user interface responsiveness when working with **Power Query** or **M** on the desktop. In extreme cases, this can extend data transformation development from hours to days. Once the solution is deployed, problems in this area can cause refresh times to time out or fail. The Power BI service has a refresh limit of 2 hours, while Premium and Fabric capacities can extend this to 5 hours. Any refresh hitting this limit will be canceled by the system.

DirectQuery mode

DirectQuery mode leaves the data at the source and needs to fetch data and process it for measures when users interact with a report page. Issues with this part of the configuration most often cause slow report responses. Visuals will take a longer time to load because the source data must be accessed and transformed. Users will get frustrated and, in turn, interrupt the current page, and interact with another view that has a similar response time. This itself will issue more queries to the data source and, ironically, slow down the report even further by placing an additional load on the external data system.

Live connection mode

Live connection mode originally referred exclusively to connections to external Analysis Services deployments. These could be cloud-native (Azure Analysis Services) or on-premises (SQL Server Analysis Services). More recently, this mode was extended to more use cases with the introduction of shared datasets deployed to the Power BI service. Now, the desktop can connect to a published dataset and build a report separate from the data or have a composite mode with a dataset connection and import mode for more data sources. The connected dataset can be Import, DirectQuery, or DirectLake (see the next subsection), so performance can vary.

DirectLake mode

DirectLake is a Fabric (or Premium) capacity data source that uses the Delta Lake structure from a Fabric warehouse or lakehouse. The performance is somewhere between an Import and DirectQuery mode connection. The structure of the Parquet files underlying the Delta tables plus the processing of a big data system can help increase performance with a single source data. This is called OneLake in the Fabric documentation.

Summary

As we have seen in this chapter, interacting with analytical reports is very similar to other web applications, so the user's level of engagement and satisfaction can be measured in similar ways. Studies of use interfaces and web browsing suggest that a report that is generated in less than 5 seconds is ideal. They also suggest that reports completing in 10-second durations or higher should be considered carefully as this is the point of user frustration.

You should set performance targets and be prepared for outliers by measuring against baselines. Success may still require setting the right expectations by having different targets if you have highly complex reports.It is impotant to remember that each component of Power BI along with system resources can contribute to performance issues. Therefore, performance issues cannot be solved in isolation of just the report.

In the next chapter, we will focus on data conectivity with various storage modes of the semantic model. We will also look at gateway optimization and general architectural advice to make sure the environment does not become a bottleneck.

2

Exploring Power BI Architecture and Configuration

In the previous chapter, we established guidelines for setting reasonable performance targets and gained an understanding of the major solution areas and Power BI components that should be considered for holistic performance management.

In this chapter, we will dig deeper into specific architectural choices, learning how and why these decisions affect your solution's performance. You will learn to consider broad requirements and make informed decisions to design a solution that meets the needs of different stakeholders. Ultimately, this chapter will help you choose the best components to host your data within Power BI. We will focus mainly on the efficient movement of data from the source system to end users by improving data throughput and minimizing latency.

We will begin by looking at data storage modes for the tabular engine and how data reaches the Power BI dataset. We will cover how to best deploy Power BI gateways, which are commonly used to control external data sources. These aspects are important because users often demand up-to-date data, or historical data, and there can be thousands of parallel users in very large deployments.

This chapter is broken down into the following sections:

- Understanding data connectivity and storage modes
- Deploying Power BI data gateways
- General architectural guidance

Understanding data connectivity and storage modes

Choosing a data connectivity and storage mode is usually the first major decision that must be made when setting up a brand-new solution in Power BI. Today, this decision is based on what is available in Power BI or Fabric, plus the underlying data sources. This means choosing between **Import**, **DirectQuery**, and **Direct Lake**, which we introduced in the previous chapter. Within Power BI Desktop or the Power BI service, you need to make this decision as soon as you connect to a data source and before you can see a preview of the data to begin modeling.

A few notes here:

- DirectQuery mode does not support all data sources. Most only offer **Import** mode. Be aware of this for data freshness and when combining different data sources.

- Direct Lake supports the Delta Table format in Fabric. An extract, transform, and load method would need to be implemented in Fabric or another Lakehouse tool to have the Delta Table support needed for this storage mode.

- Direct Lake is only supported by developing in the Power BI service or a third-party tool such as Tabular Editor. It is not supported by the Power BI Desktop application.

Figure 2.1 shows a SQL Server data connector in Power BI Desktop showing both **Import** and **DirectQuery** modes:

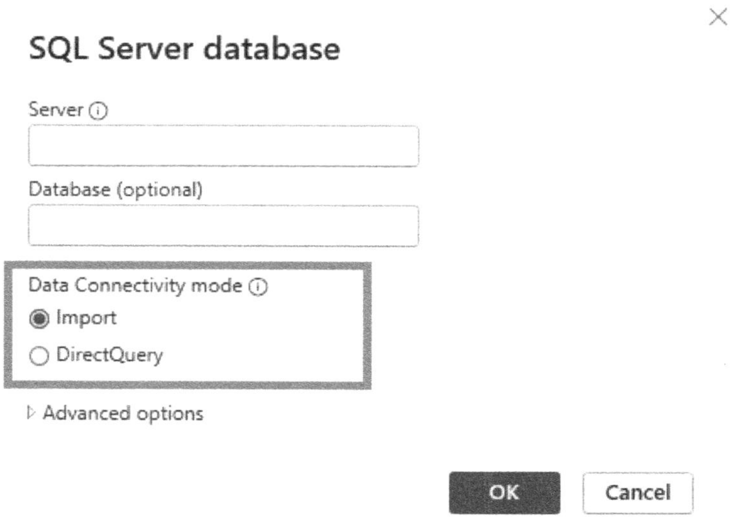

Figure 2.1 – Data connectivity options for a SQL Server source

Excel workbooks can only be configured with **Import** mode. *Figure 2.2* demonstrates this, where we can only see a **Load** button without any choices for data connectivity mode. This implies that it is **Import** mode.

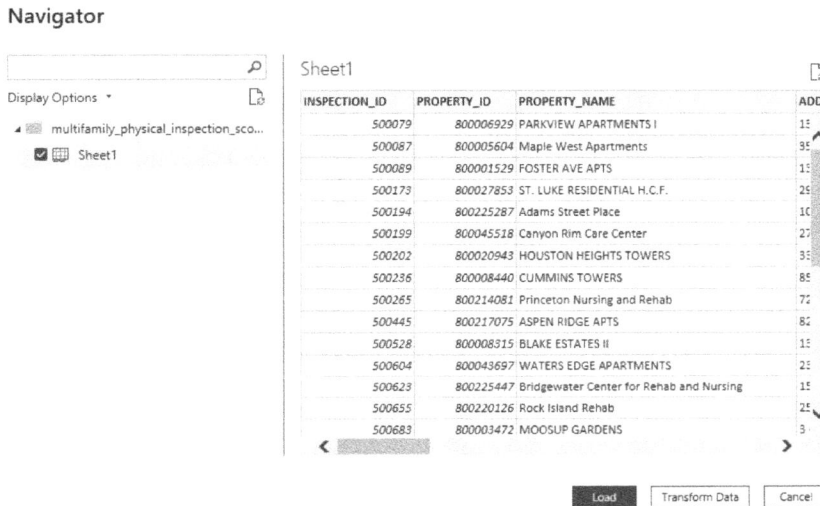

Figure 2.2 – Data connection for Excel showing no Import or DirectQuery choice

The **Direct Lake** mode is created in a *Lakehouse* or *Warehouse* in Fabric. *Figure 2.3* shows the creation of a **semantic model** in a *Lakehouse*.

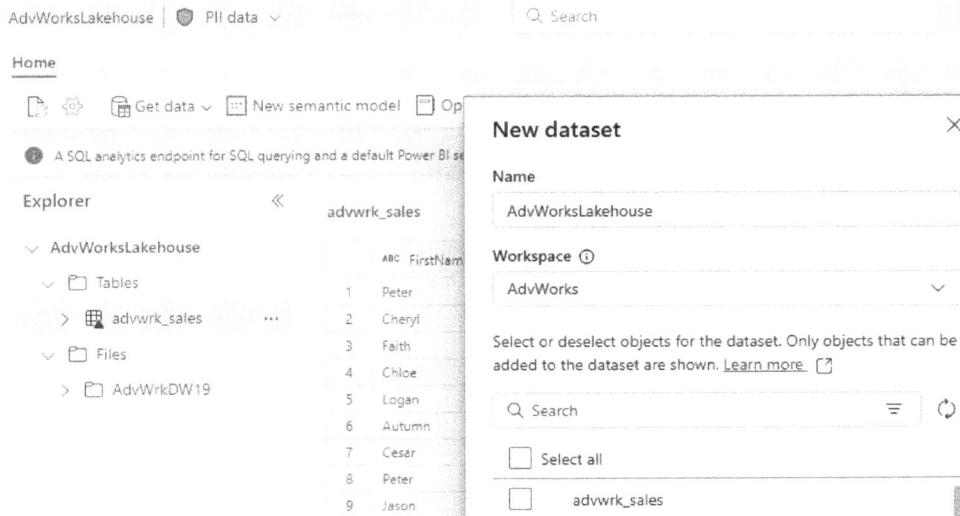

Figure 2.3 – Data connection to Direct Lake Delta Table(s) in Fabric Lakehouse

The *Warehouse* model is shown in *Figure 2.4* as the **Model** tab. There is no **DirectQuery** or **Import** mode in this area of the Power BI service. The storage mode is like DirectQuery to a data source except there is only one type of data source: *Delta Tables*. Fabric workspaces can be created in a Premium capacity.

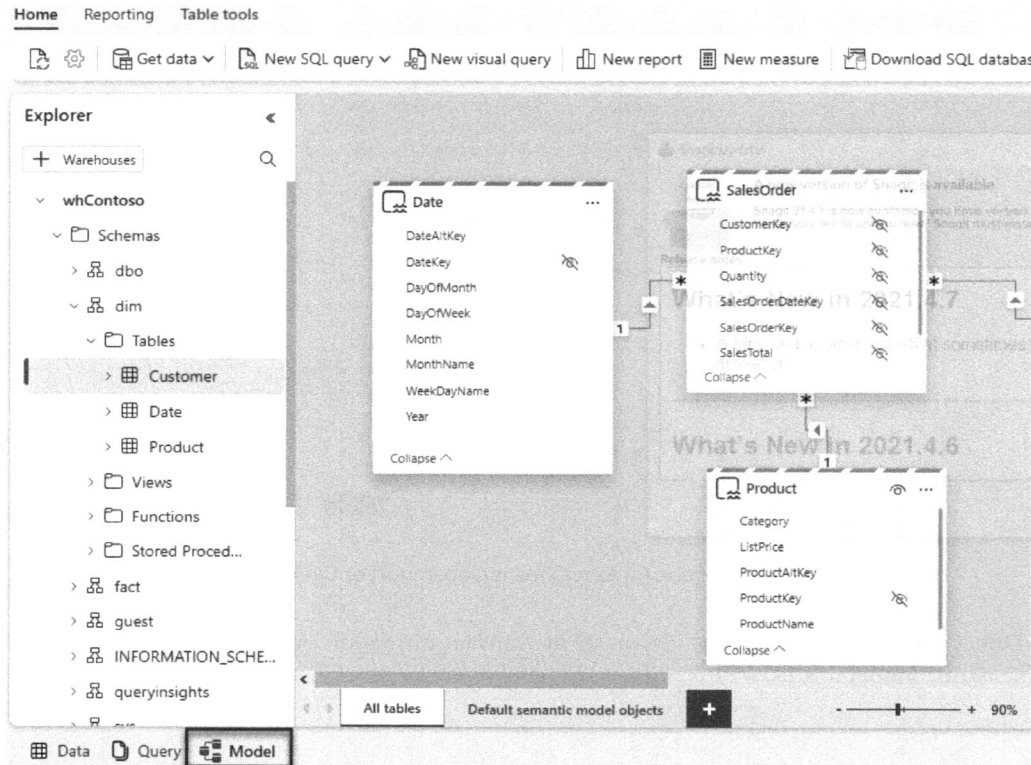

Figure 2.4 – Data connection to Direct Lake Delta Table(s) for Fabric Warehouse

The following section will dig deeper into the storage modes of data for a tabular model. The tabular engine from SQL Server Analysis Services is the underlying storage for Power BI semantic models. This engine uses *xVelocity* technology to create a compressed, column storage structure that is fast for analytical reporting. It also places the data in-memory, which is faster than disk storage.

Choosing between Import, DirectQuery, and Direct Lake mode

When using Power BI Desktop, import data connectivity mode is the default choice because it is faster than DirectQuery, sometimes by orders of magnitude. **Import** mode tables store data in a tabular database, which is effectively an in-memory cache. With the advent of *Fabric*, Power BI datasets will now be called **semantic models**. The use of the term dataset and semantic model refers to the same object.

The different modes offer different speeds and capabilities, listed as follows:

- *Fastest* – **Import** mode: Data is imported into an in-memory cache
- *Acceptable* – **Direct Lake** mode: DirectQuery to Parquet supported with Delta Table structure
- *Slowest* – **DirectQuery** mode: Connection to a data source with queries retrieving the data

Import mode

From a purely performance-oriented standpoint, the recommendation is **Import** mode to take advantage of the tabular engine. The column-store compressed structure will help satisfy the analytical reporting needed from Power BI. The downside is data must be refreshed to be current. Composite models with aggregate tables can help.

The other reason why Import models are much faster is that they use Microsoft's proprietary *xVelocity* storage known as *VertiPak*. xVelocity is a **column-based storage** engine, as opposed to **row-based storage** found in relational databases. Column-based storage came about to deal with how badly row-based transactional databases handle queries from reporting applications. They do many aggregations, potentially over large volumes of data while also offering detailed data exploration capability.

Figure 2.5 shows the imported semantic models (datasets) in a data warehouse workspace with their imported data sizes.

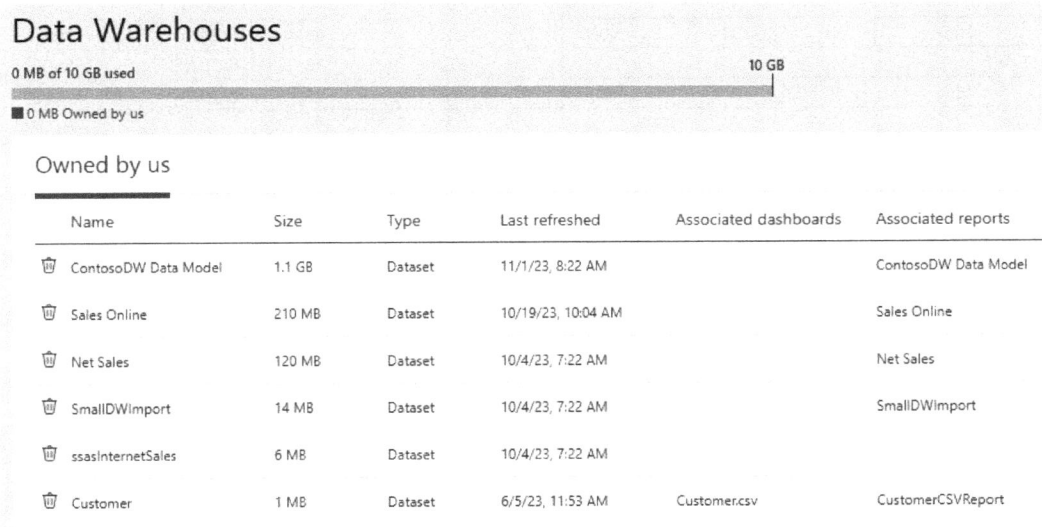

Data Warehouses

0 MB of 10 GB used   10 GB

■ 0 MB Owned by us

Owned by us

Name	Size	Type	Last refreshed	Associated dashboards	Associated reports
🗑 ContosoDW Data Model	1.1 GB	Dataset	11/1/23, 8:22 AM		ContosoDW Data Model
🗑 Sales Online	210 MB	Dataset	10/19/23, 10:04 AM		Sales Online
🗑 Net Sales	120 MB	Dataset	10/4/23, 7:22 AM		Net Sales
🗑 SmallDWImport	14 MB	Dataset	10/4/23, 7:22 AM		SmallDWImport
🗑 ssasInternetSales	6 MB	Dataset	10/4/23, 7:22 AM		
🗑 Customer	1 MB	Dataset	6/5/23, 11:53 AM	Customer.csv	CustomerCSVReport

Figure 2.5 – Import mode models and sizes

Row-based data storage engines physically store information in groups of rows. This works well when used by transaction systems because they frequently read and write individual or small groups of rows. They end up using most or all columns in the underlying table and were traditionally optimized to save and retrieve whole rows of data. Consider a sales management system where a new order is entered into a system – this would require writing a few complete rows in the database. Now consider the same system being used to view an invoice onscreen – this would read a few rows from various tables and likely use most of the columns in the underlying tables.

Now, let's consider typical reporting and analytical queries for the same sales management system. Business staff would most often be looking at aggregate data such as sales and revenue figures by month, broken down into various categories or being filtered by them. These queries need to look at large volumes of data to work out the aggregates, and they often ignore many columns available in the underlying tables. This access pattern led to column-based storage engines, which store columns physically instead of rows. They are optimized to perform aggregates and filtering on a column of data without having to retrieve entire rows with many redundant columns that do not need to be displayed or filtered.

The following diagram shows a simplified view of a table stored in a row-based relational database versus column-based storage of analytical databases.

ROW-BASED STORAGE

SalesOrderID	CustomerID	DateOfSale	SalesAmount
556	34	1/12/2021	5000
113	45	30/6/2021	7000
523	16	15/8/2020	5500
767	16	6/2/2021	12800

COLUMN-BASED STORAGE

SalesOrderID	CustomerID	DateOfSale	SalesAmount
556	34	1/12/2021	5000
113	45	30/6/2021	7000
523	16	15/8/2020	5500
767	16	6/2/2021	12800

Figure 2.6 – Comparison of row and column storage

They also recognize that there is often significant repetition within a column of data; that is, the same values can be found many times. This fact can be leveraged to apply compression to the columns by not storing the same physical values many times. The xVelocity engine does exactly this – it applies different compression algorithms to columns depending on their data type and the number of unique values. This concept of reducing repetition to reduce data size is not new and is the same technique you end up using when you compress or zip files on a computer to make them smaller.

In summary, xVelocity's **column-based compression** technology gives you the best speed by bringing the data close to reports and squeezes that data down to significantly less than the original size. In *Chapter 10, Data Modeling and Row-Level Security*, you will learn how to optimize import models.

Keeping import models as small as possible will help you avoid hitting system limits such as the per-workspace storage limit, which varies depending on shared capacity (1 GB) versus dedicated capacity (10 to 100s of GB).

> **Important note**
>
> A good rule of thumb is that Import mode tables using xVelocity are about 5 to 10 times smaller. For example, 1 GB of raw source data could fit into a 100 to 200 MB semantic model. It is often possible to get even higher compression depending on the data's **cardinality** (uniqueness of values in a column).

Next, we will talk about when **DirectQuery** mode is more appropriate than Import mode.

DirectQuery mode

From a *near* real-time reporting perspective, DirectQuery would be the go-to for this requirement. DirectQuery does not import data into the VertiPaq engine. The DAX measure sends a structured query to the data source engine to gather data for visuals. Each interaction with the visuals will send a new query to the data source for execution. The downside is slower results with administrative requirements for the source data. If this were a relational database as a source, then a database administrator would be needed for any performance tuning at the source.

The advantage of DirectQuery over Import mode is the query gets current data from the data source whereas the Import mode would have to perform a refresh to get current data. While Import mode offers great benefits in terms of model size and query speed, there are some good reasons to choose DirectQuery instead. The main point is that it gets current data from a data source. Sometimes, you will not have a choice and requirements will dictate the use of DirectQuery. The model is smaller because only the metadata about tables, columns, relationships, and measures is stored.

> **Important note**
>
> Import versus DirectQuery is a trade-off. Import gives you the best query performance while needing data refresh management and potentially not having the latest data available. DirectQuery can get you the latest data and allow you to have data sizes beyond Power BI's model size limits. DirectQuery sacrifices some queries and can add optimization work to the source system. Direct Lake offers current data but relies on the storage and compute engines of OneLake for data retrieval.

Here are the main reasons why you would use DirectQuery mode:

- **Large data volumes**: A model published to a workspace in a capacity can vary in size limit according to the available memory capacity. So, a P1 is 25 GB while a P5 is 400 GB. The 10 GB limit is for publishing a pbix file to the service. If you have more data than this, it may be impractical or simply impossible to move it into the service and have a refresh run successfully. DirectQuery does have a 1 million row limit per query. The row limit is because Power BI is an analytical tool for aggregation, not row-level detail reporting.

- **Near real-time access to source data**: If business requirements stipulate near real-time results from the data source, then DirectQuery is the right choice between the Import and DirectQuery models. Direct Lake is also a possibility for near real-time queries.

- **Existing data platform investment**: Some organizations may already have significant investments in a *data warehouse* or *data mart(s)* that stores data in a centralized database. These already contain clean data, modeled in a form that is directly consumable by analysts and business users, and act as a single source of truth. These data sources are likely to be accessed by different reporting tools and a consistent, up-to-date view is expected across these tools. You may want to use DirectQuery here to fit into this central source of truth model and not have older copies in a Power BI model.

- **Regulatory or compliance requirements**: Laws or company policies that restrict where data can be stored and processed may require source data to remain within a specific geographical or political boundary. This is often referred to as data sovereignty. If you cannot move the data into Power BI because it would break compliance, you may be forced to use DirectQuery mode.

- **Frequently changed data**: If the source of data changes frequently, such as in a matter of seconds or minutes, the visuals might change aggregations after applying a filter and then returning to the non-filtered data. The user might see different results from the previous non-filtered total and believe the reports are working correctly and then not want to return to the report again.

- **Single sign-on (SSO)**: This is the only security used for connecting DirectQuery to SQL Server data sources. There is no alternative in DirectQuery mode.

More details about using DirectQuery mode are discussed in *Chapter 5*, *Optimization for Storage Modes*.

Direct Lake mode

Direct Lake is the latest capability for analyzing large data sources. Direct Lake performance is somewhere between DirectQuery and Import mode levels but leans more toward the performance of Import mode. All data is stored in **Delta Table** (**Parquet** file format) collectively in **OneLake**. Since the data is not imported into the in-memory structure, you achieve some of the near real-time reporting. In addition to that, the Parquet file format is a column store compressed **big data** structure. Just like Databricks and Synapse, the compute performance is achieved by the Spark cluster(s) engine. Here, like other Lakehouse structures, the storage is separated from the compute engine, so scaling can be increased for speed and decreased for cost savings.

The Direct Lake engine also has some caching options for storing some query results in memory for quicker access when needed. The data is based on column segments and has a temperature (hot to cold) that eventually determines what gets paged out of memory. The **column segment data** is compressed data held in the Vertipaq engine. The downside of Direct Lake is the semantic model must be designed in the service in a Fabric-enabled workspace as well as the data structure in Delta Table(s). A plus with this is that OneLake can share these Delta Tables with other workspaces through **Shortcuts**.

Figure 2.7 does a comparison between Import, DirectQuery, and Direct Lake modes. The OneLake model eliminates an intermediate step that is involved with the Import and DirectQuery modes.

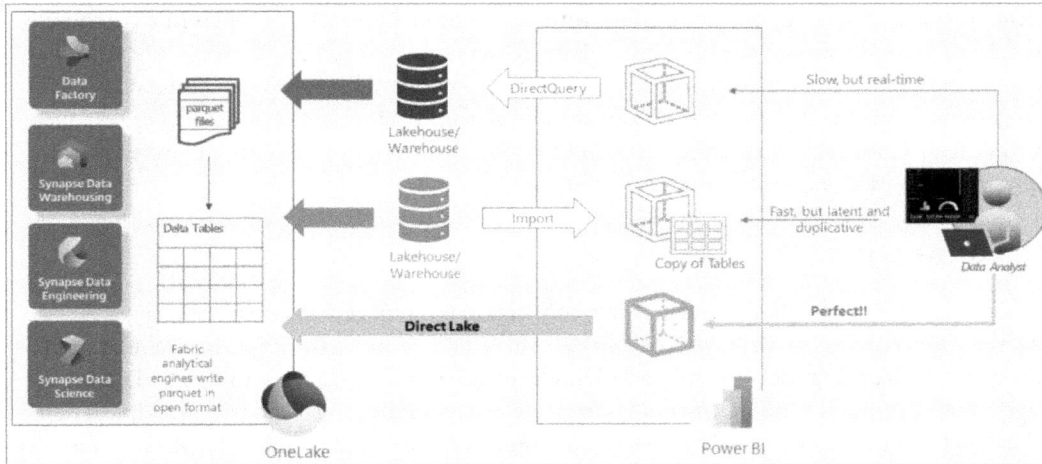

Figure 2.7 – Comparing Import, DirectQuery, and Direct Lake

If the caching of the Direct Lake query results in too much memory being requested, beyond the capacity, the DAX will not fail. The engine will default to using DirectQuery to the SQL endpoint in the lakehouse structure.

> **Important note**
> Unlike Import mode, which requires memory to be available in the right capacity for a full refresh, the Direct Lake structure does not require this. Since the whole semantic model for Direct Lake does not have this memory requirement, the memory limit capacity does not need to be as high as in the Import mode.

Now that we have discussed the three primary storage mode options and understand the trade-offs, we recommend bearing the following considerations in mind when choosing between them:

- How much source data do you have and at what rate will it grow?
- How compressible is your source data?

- Is there a capacity option that allows larger Import models to be hosted?

- Can you move or create the data warehouse in a lakehouse in Fabric?

- Will a blended architecture suffice? See the following *Composite models* section.

From purely a performance standpoint, the recommendation is Import mode.

Composite models

Power BI does not limit you to using only a single mode for a dataset or `.pbix` file. It is possible to combine one or more Import mode tables with one or more DirectQuery tables in a **composite model**. In a composite model, the Import and DirectQuery tables would be optimized the same way you would in a strictly Import-only or strictly DirectQuery-only model. However, combined with the **Aggregations** feature, composite models allow you to strike a balance between report performance, data freshness, dataset size, and dataset refresh time. You will learn how to leverage aggregations in *Chapter 10*, *Data Modeling and Row-level Security*.

Live connection

Live connection is not a storage model. A live connection is a report that instead of using a storage mode, the connection is to a deployed data model. This could be an Analysis Service's tabular model or a Power BI semantic model. The connected model could be a DirectQuery, Import, or DirectLake storage mode. The idea behind this method is to create one semantic model and have multiple reports get the data from the same set of data. This is commonly called a single source of truth data model. This method of connecting eliminates multiple pbix files having the same or similar data imported, which can cause issues with size or capacity limitation.

The Power BI report will issue native DAX queries to the external dataset. A live connection is used in the following scenarios:

- Creating reports from a dataset available in a Power BI workspace from Power BI Desktop or Power BI on the web.

- Your organization has invested in Azure Analysis Services or SQL Server Analysis Services, and this is the primary central data source for Power BI reports. The top reasons for choosing this are as follows:

  - You need a high level of control around partitions, data refresh timings, scale-out, and query/ refresh workload splitting

  - Integration with **CI/CD** or similar automation pipelines

  - Granular Analysis Services auditing and diagnostics are required

  - The initial size of the dataset cannot fit into Premium capacity

  - Previous investment in using SQL Server Analysis Services and training for developers

Figure 2.4 highlights the scenarios that use a live connection:

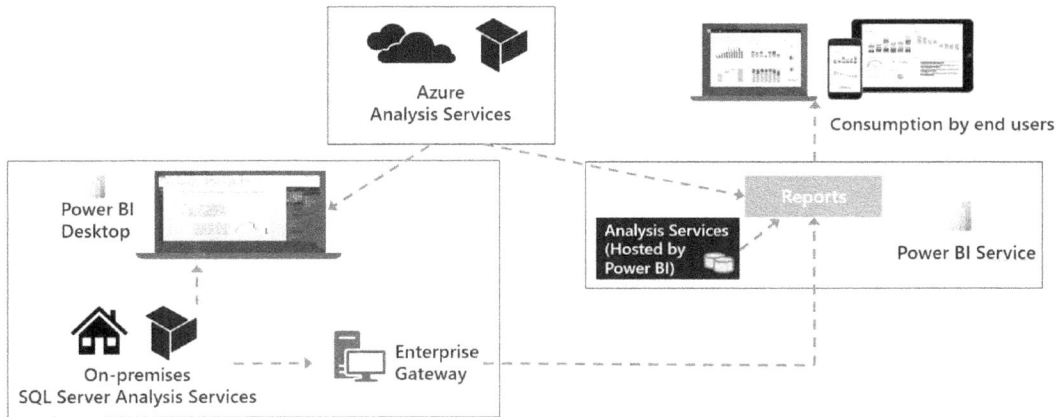

Figure 2.8 – Live connection scenarios

> **Important note**
>
> Connections to Analysis Services or Power BI semantic models also support Import mode, where data is copied and only updated when a data refresh is executed. The external Analysis Services semantic model may itself be in Import mode, so you should consider whether a live connection is indeed a better option to get the latest data. Import can be a good choice if you are simply building lookup tables for a smaller data mart or temporary analysis (for example, a list of products or customers).

The way a report connects to its data source depends on where the report is being run. A connection from Power BI Desktop from a work office may take a completely different route than a connection from the Power BI service initiated by a person using the Power BI web portal or mobile app. When organizations need a way to secure and control communications from Power BI to their on-premises data sources (data that is not in the cloud), they deploy Power BI gateways. In the next section, we will discuss Power BI gateways, their role in data architecture optimization, and specific tips on getting the most out of gateways.

Deploying Power BI gateways

The **on-premises data gateway** provides a secure communications channel between on-premises data sources and various Microsoft services in the Power Platform domain. These cloud services include Power BI, Power Apps, Power Automate, Azure Analysis Services, and Azure Logic Apps. **Gateways** allow organizations to keep sensitive data sources within their network boundaries on-premises and then control how Power BI and users can access them. The gateway is available in Enterprise, Personal, and cloud versions. The remainder of this section focuses on the Enterprise version.

When a gateway is heavily loaded or undersized, this usually means slower report loading and interactive experiences for users. Worse, an overloaded gateway may be unable to make more data connections, which will result in failed queries and some empty report visuals. What can make matters worse is that the user's first reaction is often to refresh the failed report, which can add even more loads to a gateway or on-premises data source.

How gateways work

Gateways are sometimes thought of as just a networking component used to channel data. While they are indeed a component of the data pipeline, gateways do more than just allow data movement. The gateway hosts Power BI's **Mashup Engine** and supports Import, DirectQuery, and live connections. The gateway service must be installed on a physical or virtual server. It is important to know that the gateway executes PowerQuery/M as needed, performing the processing locally on the gateway machine. In addition, the gateway compresses and encrypts the data streams it sends to the Power BI service. This design minimizes the amount of data sent to the cloud to reduce the refresh and query duration. However, since the gateway supports such broad connectivity and performs potentially expensive processing, it is important to configure and scale gateway machines, so they perform well.

Figure 2.5 shows a simplified view of the gateway architecture. The dotted line is the layers of processing that are hidden for a normal user.

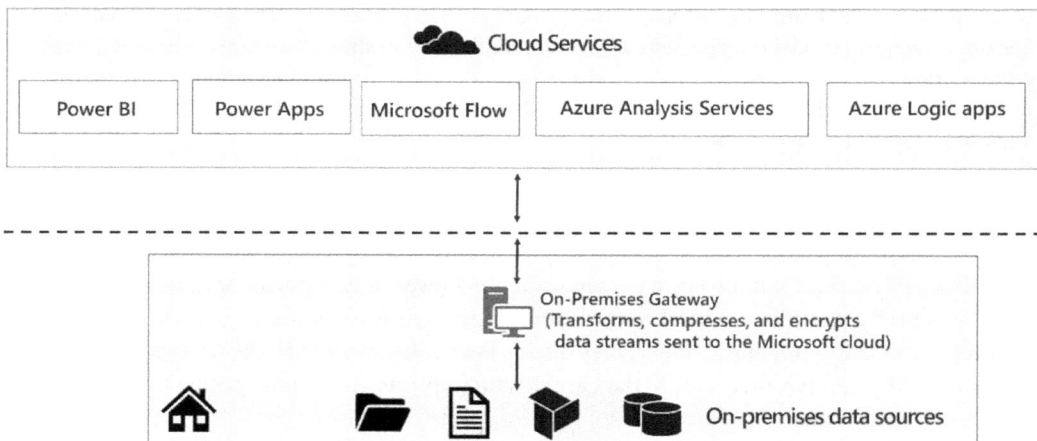

Figure 2.9 – The on-premises gateway performs mashup processing locally

Good practices for gateway performance

Some general guidelines should be applied whenever gateways are deployed. We will discuss each one in the following list and provide reasons to explain how this design will benefit you:

- **Place gateways close to data sources**: Gateways should be as physically close to the data source as possible. The physical distance can add to network latency due to more infrastructure and network paths. We want to remove as many *hops* as possible. For data sources on *virtual machines* in the cloud, try to place them in the same region as your Power BI home region.

- **Remove network throttling**: Some network firewalls or proxies may be configured to throttle connections to optimize internet connectivity. This may slow down transfers through the gateway, so it is a good idea to check this with network administrators.

- **Avoid running other applications or services on the gateway**: This ensures that loads from other applications cannot unpredictably impact queries and users. This could be relaxed for development environments.

- **Separate DirectQuery and scheduled refresh gateways**: Import mode connections would only be used during data refresh operations and are often used more after hours, when data refreshes are scheduled. Since they often contain Power Query/M data transformations, refresh operations consume both CPU and memory and may require significant amounts for complex operations on large datasets. For DirectQuery connections, the gateway acts as a pass-through for query results from a data source. DirectQuery connections generally consume much less CPU and memory than Import mode. Significant bursts in CPU can occur for datasets with lots of transformations and calculations. By separating DirectQuery from Import datasets to different gateways, the servers can be created with the proper resources on the VM or physical server.

- **Use sufficient and fast local storage**: The gateway server buffers data on the disk before it sends it to the cloud. It is saved to the `%LOCALAPPDATA%\Microsoft\On-premises data gateway\Spooler` location. If you are refreshing large datasets in parallel, you should ensure that you have enough local storage to temporarily host those datasets. We highly recommend using high-speed, low-latency storage options such as solid-state disks to avoid storage becoming a bottleneck.

- **Understand gateway parallelism limits**: The gateway will automatically configure itself to use reasonable default values for parallel operations based on the CPU cores available. We recommend monitoring the gateway. If advised by an expert to change parallelism settings, consulting with Microsoft is the best option due to the advanced nature of parallelism and servers.

Sizing gateways

Most organizations start with a single gateway server and then scale up and/or out based on their real-world data needs. It is very important to follow the minimum specifications suggested by Microsoft for a production gateway. At the time of writing, Microsoft recommends a machine with at least 8 CPU cores, 8 GB RAM, and multiple gigabit network adapters. Regular monitoring is recommended to understand what load patterns the gateway experiences and which resources are under pressure. We will cover monitoring later in this chapter.

We have already learned that the gateway supports different connection types. The type and number of connections will largely determine resource usage on the gateway server. Therefore, you should keep the following questions in mind when planning a gateway deployment:

- How many concurrent dataset refreshes will the gateway need to support?

- How much data is going to be transferred during the refresh?

- Is the refresh performing complex transformations?

- How many users would hit a DirectQuery source in parallel?

- How many visuals are in the most used DirectQuery reports? Each data-driven visual will generate at least one query to the data source.

- How many reports use **Automatic Page Refresh** and what is the refresh frequency?

In the next section, we will look at how to monitor a gateway and gather data to inform sizing and scaling to ensure consistent performance.

Configuring gateway performance logging

The on-premises gateway has performance logging enabled by default. There are two types of logs captured – **query executions** and **system counters**. The gateway configuration file has many configuration options that can fine-tune the individual gateway.

Administrative access must be enabled to look at the raw logs. They can be exported from the gateway service application as well.

Figure 2.6 shows the diagnostic setup and configuration for log files in the gateway.

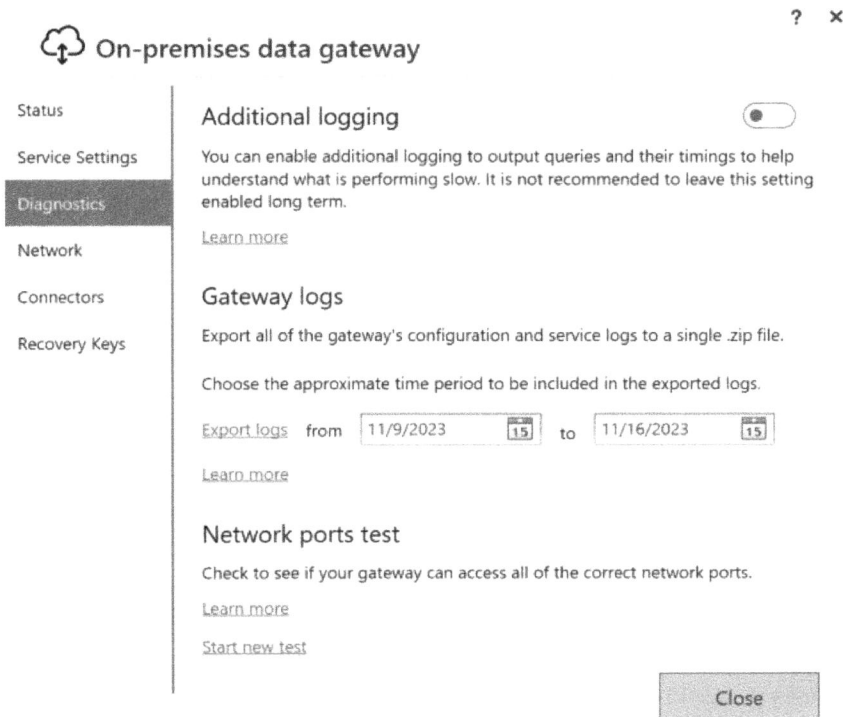

Figure 2.10 – The gateway application Diagnostics screen to export logs

Things such as turning the logs on and off are controlled in the configuration file by the **DisableSystemCounterReport** setting. Other settings include **ReportFileCount** and **ReportFileSizeInBytes**, as well as **QueryExecutionAggregarionTimeInMinutes**. Due to the monthly updates for the gateway application, it is better to reference Microsoft's help online than to list the options and values in this book. The default as well as the suggested range can change frequently, as well as the type of log files.

When logging is enabled, you will start to collect information in four sets of files with the `.log` extension and numerical suffixes in the filename. The log file group names are provided in the following list. This is explained in more detail in the Microsoft documentation for monitoring and optimizing gateways – `https://learn.microsoft.com/en-us/data-integration/gateway/service-gateway-performance`:

- **Query execution report:** These logs contain detailed information on every query execution. They tell you whether the query was successful, the data source information, the type of query, how long is spent executing and processing data, how long it took to write data to the disk, how much data was written, and what the average speed was of the disk operations. This information can be used to work out where bottlenecks are at a query level.

- **Query start report**: These are simpler query logs that provide the actual query text, data source information, and when the query started. You can see the exact query that was sent to data sources, which can be useful for performance troubleshooting, especially with DirectQuery data sources.

- **Query execution aggregation report**: These logs contain aggregated query information in buckets of 5 minutes by default. They provide useful summary information such as the number of queries within the time window, the average/minimum/maximum query execution duration, and the average/minimum/maximum data processing duration.

- **System counter aggregation report**: This log contains aggregated system resource information from the gateway server. It aggregates average/minimum/maximum CPU and memory usage for the gateway machine, gateway service, and the mashup engine.

Parsing and modeling gateway logs

Microsoft has provided a basic Power BI *report template* to help you analyze gateway data. This template can be found at the following link: (`https://learn.microsoft.com/en-us/data-integration/gateway/service-gateway-performance`). The template will scan your log folder and process all the files it finds that match the default naming pattern. It parses and expands complex columns such as JSON.

Figure 2.8 demonstrates one of the default views in the gateway performance template:

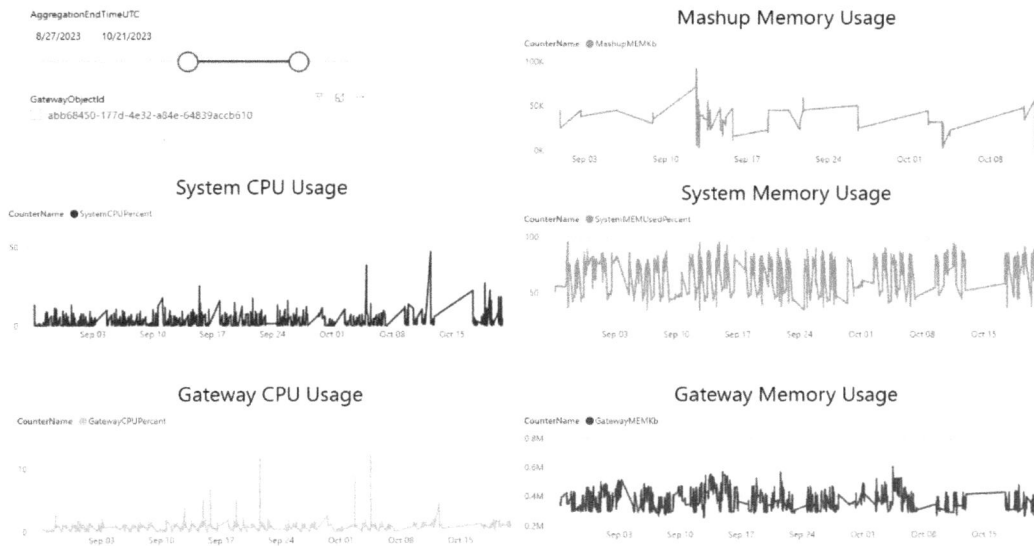

Figure 2.11 – Example of gateway performance visualization from the template

The Microsoft-provided template does a reasonable job of giving you visibility of some aggregate and detailed operations on the gateway. However, to extract further value from it, you will likely need to make some changes to the transformations, data model, and calculations. This could take some work to perfect, so it may be worth considering whether a pre-built option is feasible.

If your organization uses Microsoft Premier or Unified support, you may have access to Power BI performance assessments. These are run by experienced customer engineers who have enhanced templates to analyze gateway logs. Another option is to engage consultants who have a professional solution on the market.

If you choose to build on the Microsoft template yourself, do consider the following improvements:

- Examine the PowerQuery transformations in the template to see how to parse the log files.
- Automate the retrieval and storage of logs from the gateway server, for example, with *PowerShell* scripts.
- Build separate date and time dimensions and connect them to all the log tables so that you can build reports that can look at time-correlated activity across every log.
- Build common *dimension tables* for Query Status, Query Type, and Data Source from the log files and connect them to each log table. This will allow you to slice report pages using the same filter across different logs.

- Add a dimension table containing details of all your gateways, such as the environment, gateway ID, name, memory size, and CPU core count. Use the gateway ID to connect it to the *fact tables* log.

- Build report views that focus on trends and aggregates to highlight spikes in CPU or memory while able to distinguish between DirectQuery and Refresh queries. Further details are provided in the next section.

Next, we'll look at gateway logs.

Analyzing gateway logs

We suggest that the initial views you build on gateway logs will help you to answer high-level questions and spot problem areas quickly. Here are some important questions you should be able to answer:

- Are there any spikes in overall gateway resource usage and do the spikes recur regularly? When I reach high or maximum resource usage, what is the workload pattern?

- What datasets, dataflows, or reports consume the most gateway resources?

- What is the gateway throughput in terms of queries per second and bytes processed per second? When I see throughput drops, what operations were running in that time slice, and which contributed most from a resource perspective?

- Is the gateway performing many refresh and DirectQuery operations in parallel? This is likely to create pressure on CPU and memory at the same time, so consider dedicated DirectQuery and refresh gateways, spreading out refresh operations and scaling.

- What is the average query duration over time and what contributes to increases – gateway resource limits or growing data volume/query complexity?

- What are the slowest queries? Are they consistently slow or does the performance vary greatly? The former may suggest query or model design issues, or that optimization may be needed at the data source or even the network. The varying performance of the same queries suggests unpredictable loads on the gateway or data source are the issue.

Next, we will look at when you should consider scaling and how to do so.

Scaling up gateways

It is possible to manage a gateway well but still begin to reach resource limits due to data and usage growth. **Scaling up** is simply adding more resources or replacing them with faster components. You know it is time to scale when your analysis shows you are hitting a memory, CPU, or disk limit and have no more room to import refresh schedules or optimize other layers of the solution. We will cover such optimizations in detail in subsequent chapters.

For now, let's assume that the deployed solutions are perfect, yet you are seeing performance degradation and an increase in query failures caused by excessive loads. The first choice here should be to scale up. You may choose to increase the number of CPU cores and memory independently if your analysis identified only one as the problem and you see enough headroom in the other. While CPU and memory are the common candidates for scaling up, do keep an eye on disk and network performance too. You may need to scale those up too or scale out if this is not an option.

Scaling out with multiple gateways

When you can no longer effectively scale up a single gateway machine, you should consider adding a node or nodes to the cluster. When an enterprise gateway is created, a **cluster** is automatically created when the initial node is created. This will allow you to load balance across more than one gateway machine, referred to as a node. Clusters also provide high availability through redundancy in case one machine goes down for whatever reason.

To create a **gateway cluster**, you simply run the gateway installer on a different server. At the time of installation, you will be given the option of connecting the gateway to an existing gateway cluster, which acts as the primary instance. This is shown in the following figure.

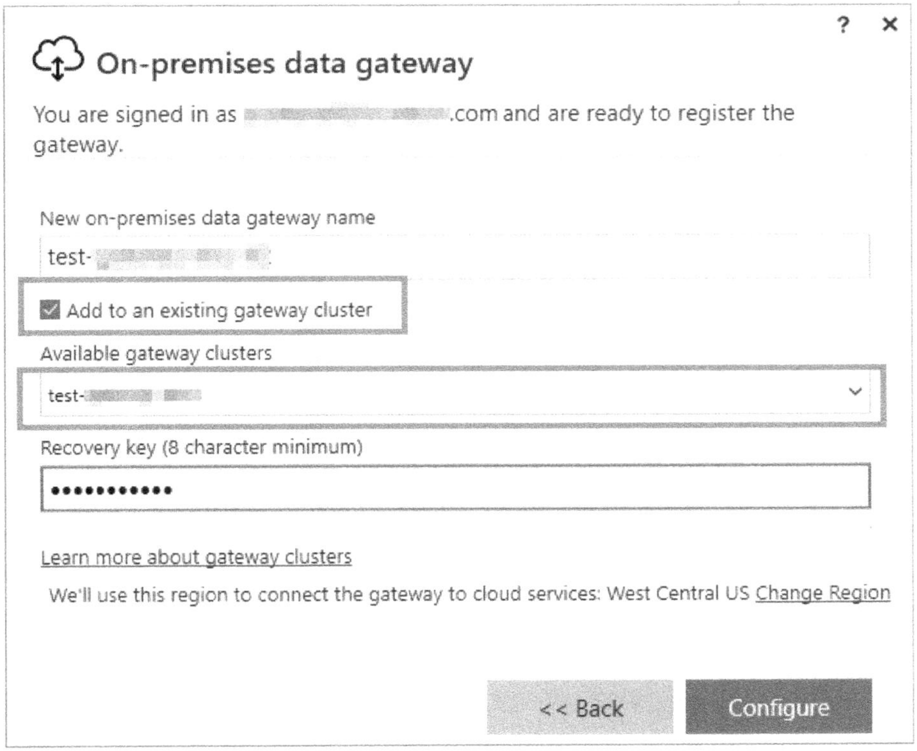

Figure 2.12 – Adding a gateway to a cluster by selecting the primary instance

All requests are routed to the primary instance of a gateway cluster. The request is routed to another gateway instance in the cluster only if the primary gateway instance is offline.

> **Tip**
>
> If a gateway member server goes down, you should remove it from the cluster using the `Remove-OnPremisesDataGateway` PowerShell command. If not, query requests may still be sent to it, which can reduce performance.

Load balancing on the gateway is random by default. You can change this to balance the load based on CPU or memory thresholds. This will change the behavior so that when a member is at or over the throttling limit, another member within the cluster is selected. The request will fail only if all members within the cluster are above the limits.

A gateway admin must update settings in the config file introduced earlier.

The following settings can be adjusted to control load balancing:

- `CPUUtilizationPercentageThreshold`: A value between 0 and 100 that sets the throttling limit for the CPU. 0 means the configuration is disabled.

- `MemoryUtilizationPercentageThreshold`: A value between 0 and 100 that sets the throttling limit for memory. 0 means the configuration is disabled.

- `ResourceUtilizationAggregationPeriodInMinutes`: The time window in minutes for which CPU and memory system counters of the gateway machine are aggregated. These aggregates are compared against the thresholds defined beforehand. The default value is 5.

Now that we have a good grasp of storage modes and gateway optimization, we will consider broader factors that come into play and can slow down operations in these areas.

General architectural guidance

This section presents general architectural items for using Power BI.

Capacities

There are different capacities for Power BI architecture. They can be grouped under two categories – shared and dedicated:

- **Shared capacity**: Power BI Pro license or **Premium Per User** (PPU) license not in a tenant with a Premium or Fabric capacity

- **Dedicated**: Premium, Fabric, and Embedded capacities purchased through a subscription

Shared capacities

The Power BI Pro and PPU licenses allow individuals to publish datasets and reports to shared capacity. You share the capacity with other Pro and PPU users. There is no administration for controlling or adjusting the resources for your reports and datasets. Limits for dataset sizes to import as well as the number of refreshes (8) are tighter than dedicated capacity. To ensure everyone on shared capacity plays together, there are certain limits and throttling done behind the scenes.

Dedicated capacity

Dedicated capacity is either a Premium, Embedded, or Fabric subscription. This capacity is reserved just for a single Power BI company. In the admin portal, there are tenant settings as well as adjustments for capacity to help set the resources for the workload's needs. There are features such as more refreshes a day and refresh size increases than for shared capacity. These capacity nodes are like individual virtual machines for each capacity purchased with a few vCPUs and memory size.

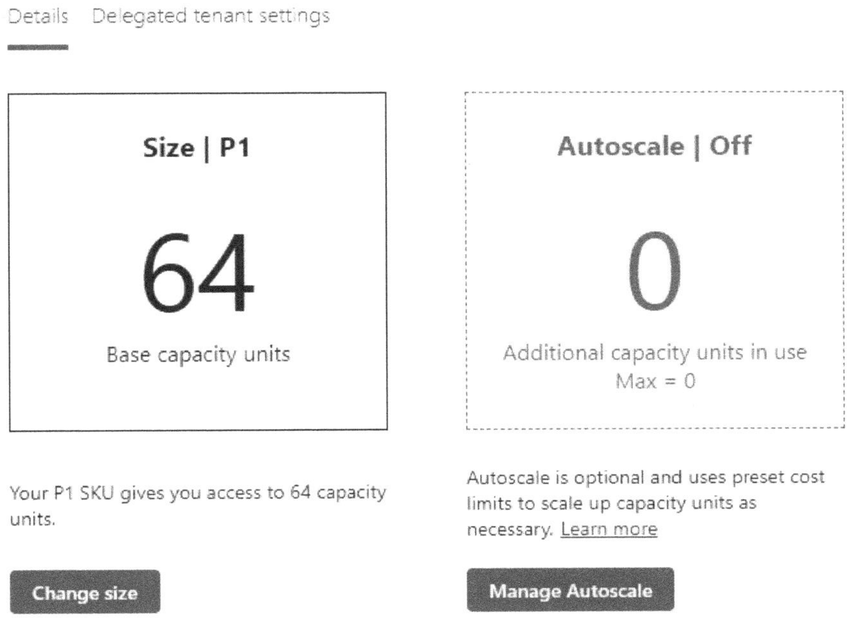

Details   Delegated tenant settings

Size | P1	Autoscale | Off
64	0
Base capacity units	Additional capacity units in use Max = 0
Your P1 SKU gives you access to 64 capacity units.	Autoscale is optional and uses preset cost limits to scale up capacity units as necessary. Learn more
Change size	Manage Autoscale

Figure 2.13 – Capacity administration

Figure 2.10 shows the capacity administration and the option to manage autoscale for this capacity.

Other options for capacities are the ability to split the capacity node(s) into individual other capacities within the company tenant. A **P2 capacity** can be purchased and split into a developement and test capacity and different security groups can manage each capacity separately. Additionally, an A1 or higher SKU can be created in your Azure environment to assign to the **Autoscale** option. *Figure 2.11* shows the **Enable Autoscale** option.

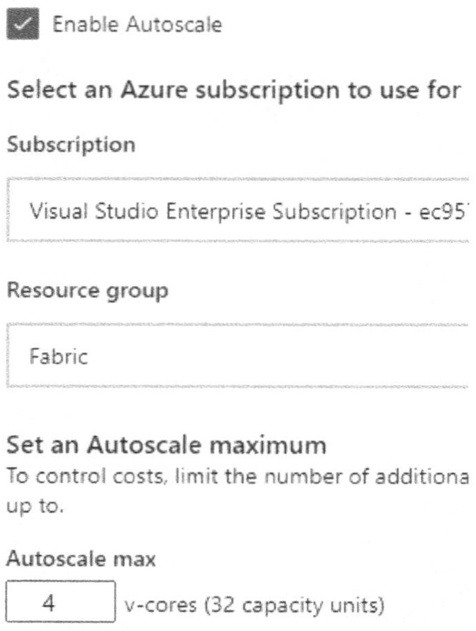

✓ Enable Autoscale

Select an Azure subscription to use for

Subscription

Visual Studio Enterprise Subscription - ec95

Resource group

Fabric

Set an Autoscale maximum
To control costs, limit the number of additiona
up to.

Autoscale max

4   v-cores (32 capacity units)

Figure 2.14 – Autoscale settings

Autoscaling enables an additional set of compute to be turned on and used while a large load is running to prevent a timeout. The autoscale function will turn off the additional compute when the load returns below the Premium capacity and a configurable amount of time has elapsed. This is configured in the **Manage Autoscale** settings.

The embedded and Fabric subscriptions can have their capacities paused. This allows for pay-as-you-go type billing, whereas Premium has a fixed cost per month. Fabric allows a fixed cost per month as well as the ability to be pay-as-you-go.

Power BI Report Server

The Power BI Report Server license is for a version of SQL Server Report Server with Power BI support that can be installed on a physical or virtual server. The limits are the resources in the physical or virtual server. The releases for updates to this version are every three to five months and some features such as AutoML, AI functions, and dashboards are not available. Tuning is the job of an administrator with the infrastructure for CPU, memory, and disk speeds.

Planning data and cache refresh schedules

A sometimes-overlooked consideration is how fresh an Import dataset's sources are. There is no point refreshing a dataset multiple times a day if it relies on an external data mart that is only refreshed nightly. This adds an unnecessary load on data sources and the Power BI service.

Look at your environment to see when refresh operations are happening and how long they take. If many are happening in parallel, this could slow down other operations due to intense CPU and memory usage. The effect can be larger with Power BI Premium. Consider working with dataset owners to remove unnecessary refreshes or change timings so that they do not occur altogether but are potentially staggered instead. A data refresh in progress can require as much additional memory as the dataset itself – sometimes more if the transformations are complex or inefficient. A general rule of thumb is that a refreshing dataset consumes twice the memory.

Reducing network latency

In an earlier section, we discussed how reducing the physical distance and hops between data sources helps to reduce network latency. Here are additional considerations:

- *Co-locate* your data sources, gateways, and other services as much as possible, at least for production. If you relied on Azure, for example, it would be recommended to use the same Azure Region as your Power BI home tenant region.

- Consider a *cloud replica* of on-premises data sources. This incurs some cloud costs but can significantly reduce latency for Power BI if the cloud region is far from the on-premises data center.

- If your data is in the cloud, consider performing Power BI development through a *remote desktop* into cloud virtual machines. Those virtual machines should ideally be in the same region as the data sources.

- Use Azure *ExpressRoute* to have a secure, dedicated, high-speed connection from your on-premises network to the Azure cloud.

Now that you have a good understanding of the architectural choices that affect performance in Power BI, let's summarize what we've learned before we explore the next area of performance in Power BI.

Summary

In this chapter, we saw how the different storage modes in Power BI work. Import mode datasets create an in-memory data cache in the Power BI service. DirectQuery mode datasets pass queries to the external data sources. Delta Lake allows connections to Delta Table structures in a Fabric lakehouse or warehouse. Generally, import mode is the fastest because it is local to Power BI, in-memory, a column-based analytical database, and compresses data. However, DirectQuery mode provides a way to always have the latest data returned from the source and avoid managing refreshes. Fabric's Direct Lake is somewhere in between. There is a trade-off between all three options. There is also the composite model if the data is large, but you can provide some aggregate tables in import mode.

You also learned about the role of on-premises gateways for enterprises to allow Power BI to connect securely with on-premises data sources. Gateways host Power BI's mashup engine, where data transformations are performed locally. These can be resource-hungry, especially with hundreds or thousands of users, which could translate to many connections per second. This means gateways need to be sized, monitored, and scaled. Hence, we looked at the high-level questions that should be asked, for example, relating to simultaneous refreshes or user counts. An introduction to gateway logs drifted to the Microsoft-provided template for monitoring. Patterns were revised to help if a scale-up or scale-out approach is needed.

The last section looked at other performance features such as parallel activity, refresh scheduling, and capacity options through subscription. The next chapter will start to review the different free tools to use for performance tuning and management. These tools will be used throughout the book to help with best practices in Power BI performance tuning.

3

Learning the Tools for Performance Tuning

Until now, we have looked at **Power BI** performance from a relatively high level. You have learned which areas of Power BI performance can be impacted by your design decisions and what to consider when making these choices. Those decisions were architectural, so were about choosing the right components to ensure the most efficient movement of data to suit your data volume and freshness requirements.

However, this knowledge alone is not sufficient and will not guarantee good performance. With the gateways in the previous chapter, we saw how a single component of the solution can be configured and optimized quite heavily. This applies to most of the other areas of Power BI, so now we will begin to look at performance tools that can help us pinpoint issues.

In *Chapter 2, Exploring Power BI Architecture and Configuration*, we looked at storage modes for Power BI datasets and learned about **Import**, **DirectQuery** (**DQ**), and **Direct Lake** (**DL**). For **Power BI reports**, we often need to know whether visuals, queries, or combinations thereof are slow. Using these tools can help with slow model calculations, slow reports, or slow model refreshes.

Some of this granularity is not available from the Power BI service in production at the time of writing. However, you can get much more granular performance information using desktop and external tools. As we progress through this book, you will learn how the performance experience is affected by varied factors. An effective way to pinpoint these is to analyze report behavior at the level of each user interaction, and the behavior of each visual in response to that action.

This chapter will cover the following topics:

- Overview of data engine architecture
- Learning about the performance analyzer
- Using the Optimize ribbon
- Adapting external tools

Technical requirements

There are samples available for some parts of this chapter. We will mention which files to refer to in the relevant sections. Please check out the `Chapter03` folder on GitHub to get these assets: `https://github.com/PacktPublishing/Microsoft-Power-BI-Performance-Best-Practices-Second-Edition`.

Overview of data engine architecture

Whenever you launch Power BI Desktop, an **Analysis Service** process is launched on your local machine. *Figure 3.1* shows the service running in **Task Manager**.

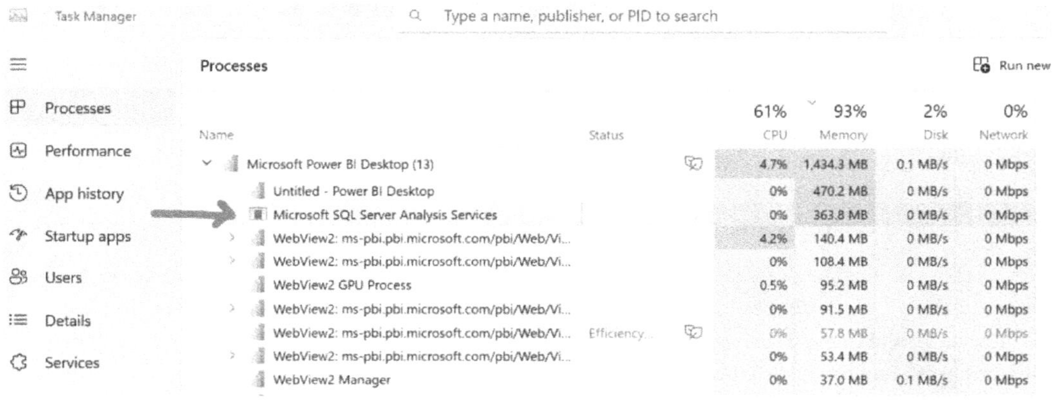

Figure 3.1 – Analysis Services service in Task Manager

This engine, referred to as **VertiPaq**, is where the imported and transformed data resides for a Power BI dataset. The term dataset has been switched for semantic model, which was the original name for SQL Server Analysis Services. This process or service stores the data in the column structure in a compressed mode. Included with the structure are column indexes, dictionaries, and hierarchies. We will see more on this in the sections on DAX Studio. DAX Studio can display the actual storage structure for column data and all the subsets of the column structure.

There are two engines that process queries and return data in visualizations in Power BI. The *formula engine* processes the query request, and the *storage engine* returns the data. *Figure 3.2* shows a common flow of using the VertiPaq service to submit DAX query processing to the data source.

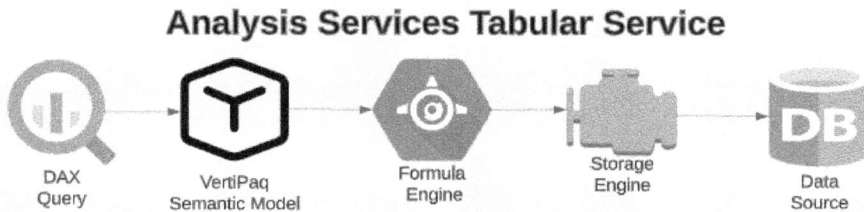

Figure 3.2 – VertiPaq service processing a query

The processing is either a query to retrieve data for a visual or the import process to format the source data into the in-memory structure. This structure for import mode is a column store and is compressed as explained in *Chapter 2*. The storage engine can aggregate some data for the formula engine, such as the DAX measures SUM or SUMX. The reference to calculations can mean calculated columns, measures, or queries in a semantic model.

The following two sections will explain the difference between the semantic model storing the data versus a query running against the semantic model.

Import mode

The **tabular semantic model** needs to be processed to store data in the VertiPaq in-memory structure. This is different than a DAX query that retrieves data for a visualization. Storing and retrieving analytical measures is a powerful aspect of tabular data. Aggregations can be as simple as SUM or COUNT, but can be as complicated as computing a rolling average using the CALCULATE function with other DAX functions.

In addition to column-store compressed data, the storage engine can create indexes and dictionaries for faster lookups. These are created for each column in a table if necessary. Some numeric-based columns do not need an index or dictionary based on the low cardinality of data in a column. Storing this data is more CPU intensive than requiring larger memory sets.

Consider an example: The following steps reflect a semenatic model refresh that has transformations in Power Query as well as dimension tables with one-to-many relationships:

1. Process refresh initiated.
2. Semantic model structure requests source data.
3. Transformations from Power Query processed on data.
4. Table data is stored in column structure with compression.
5. Dictionary, hierarchies, and indexes created on columns.
6. In-memory structure recalculated for all measures and relationships.

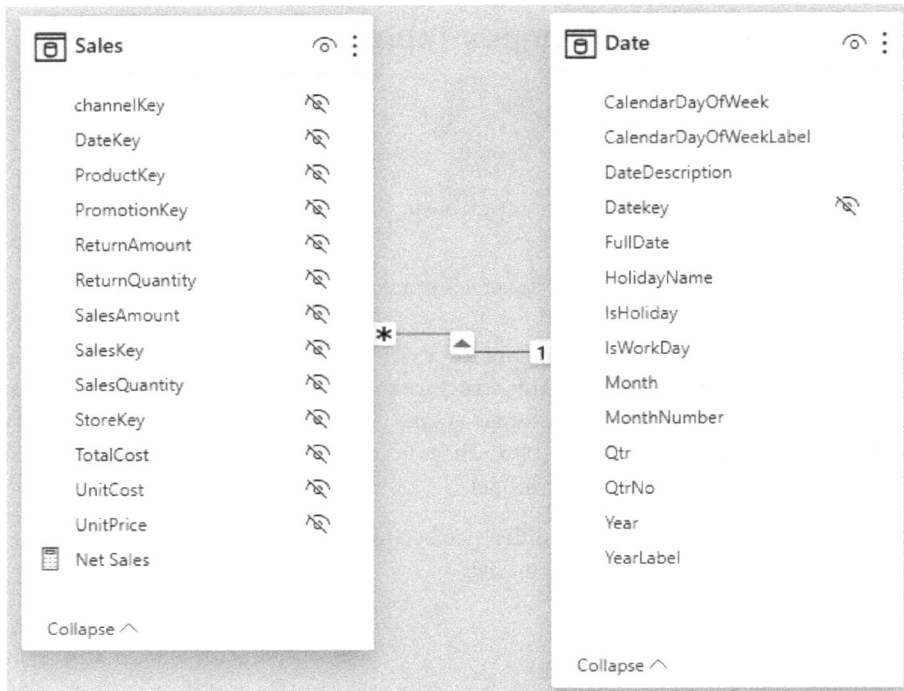

Figure 3.3 – Semantic model of Sales related to Date

Figure 3.3 shows the model view of the semantic model for this example.

Executing a query

To be able to optimize the calculation, it is important to know what is happening with these engines for query requests. When the query is processed by the semantic model, the formula engine receives the request and creates a query plan. The plan has steps for performing the calculations and child steps that request data from the storage engine. The formula engine is single-threaded, while the storage can have multiple threads based on a single request from the formula engine. The storage engine will then retrieve and aggregate the data from the semantic model.

One note to remember is this process is for import mode. If using DirectQuery or Direct Lake, there is no storage of data in memory, only retrieval from the data source and aggregated for returning the data to the formula engine. The speed of the data retrieval is dependent on the data source service.

There is a cache that can have data from queries recently run that can answer subsequential queries that return the same data.

Term definitions

- **VertiPaq**: Contains the in-memory data formatted by the metadata from the semantic model designed in Power Query through transformations. This model must be refreshed periodically.

- **Formula engine**: Generates a query plan for formatting the data requested by a visualization or slicer in a report or DAX query request. Part of the query plan is requests to the storage engine.

- **Storage engine**: Retrieves data from the VertiPaq in-memory data for Import model semantic models or sends query requests to the data source system for DirectQuery or Direct Lake semantic models.

- **Tabular model**: Set of tables, columns, relationships, transformations, calculated columns, and measures in your semantic model. This is called the metadata about the semantic model.

- **Cardinality**: The number of unique values in a column.

Year	Net Sales
2019	$3,740,483,119
2020	$4,561,940,955
2021	$4,111,233,535
2022	$3,729,767,671
Total	**$16,143,425,280**

Figure 3.4 – Table visual

Consider the following example. The steps here reflect running a DAX query from a table visual in a PowerBI report like *Figure 3.4*. *Figure 3.4* above shows the tables and relationships for the semantic model.

1. The query is generated from the visual to retrieve the table from the visual.

2. The tabular semantic model has metadata for the table:

   A. `Date` table related to `Sales` table by `OrderDateKey`

   B. `Net Sales` is a DAX measure – `SUM(Sales[SalesAmount])`

3. The formula engine does calculations for total sales by year (more advanced calculations):

   A. Calculates the grand totals (row or column)

   B. Table visual data is sorted by year

4. The storage engine is requested for each row with a year and related total sales for the intersection of `date` with `sales`:

    A. Calculates the aggregate of `Sales by Year` – returns this data.

    B. xmSQL – the language for requests made to the VertiPaq engine.

5. Data is returned to the formula engine for query requests and results are sent to the requestor (report).

The next section will go through the use of the performance analyzer to assist with performance tuning a report.

Learning about the performance analyzer

The **performance analyzer** is an excellent tool for analyzing the reports in a pbix file. In this section, we will spend some time learning about its features. We will also learn when and how to use the tool to diagnose performance problems.

The performance analyzer lets you record user actions and break down report behavior by each report visual, including DAX and DirectQuery queries. The tool provides durations for phases of a report visual's internal operations, in milliseconds. The following screenshot shows how the **Performance analyzer** pane displays statistics for a single-page refresh operation that's initiated from the tool itself.

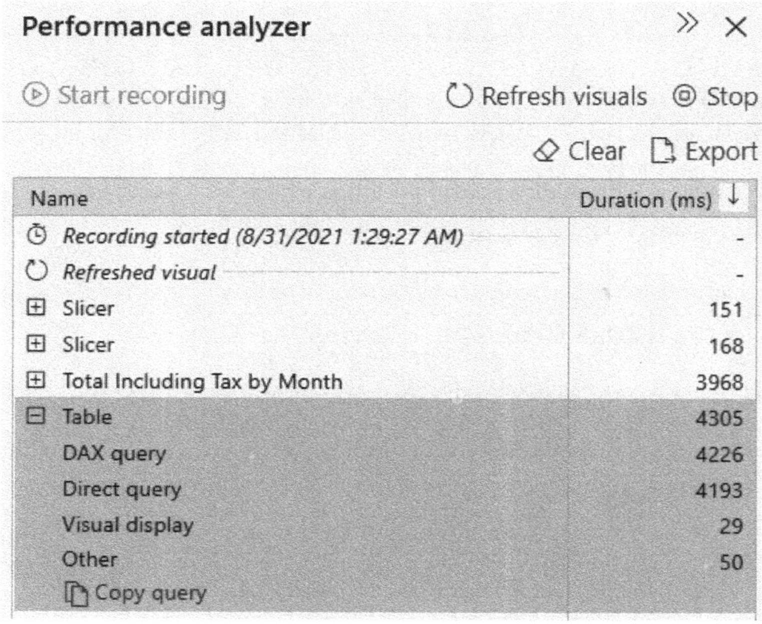

Figure 3.5 – Performance analyzer results with an expanded visual

Take note of the action that's been captured, and the duration breakdowns provided. The **Copy query** functionality is especially useful when you're debugging performance related to DAX and data model design. It allows you to extract a DAX query or the external DirectQuery command that the visual generated. These queries can be analyzed in other tools, which we will cover in *Chapter 6, Third-Party Utilities*.

This chapter will focus on practical examples of using the tool and nuances in Power BI's behavior that should be considered when running performance testing. If you do need an introduction to using the performance analyzer, please review the product documentation: `https://docs.microsoft.com/power-bi/create-reports/desktop-performance-analyzer`.

> **Important note**
>
> The performance analyzer measures durations from its perspective – that is, the Power BI Desktop client. Be aware that development conditions in Power BI Desktop may be very different from those in production. Many things can differ, such as data volume, source load, user concurrency, security enforcement, location, and the inclusion of on-premises gateways. Always keep this in mind when assessing benchmarks from the performance analyzer. Power BI Desktop development conditions are often ideal and may not represent reality for most users.

Actions and metrics in the performance analyzer

The performance analyzer captures the following user actions:

- **Changed page**: This covers changing pages using the tabs provided by Power BI and custom page navigation buttons that you place in the report.

- **Cross-highlighted**: This captures typical cross-highlight activities such as selecting points or bars in visuals. Note, however, that most clicks in Power BI report visuals trigger at least a visual refresh. For example, when you click an empty space in a visual to deselect a cross-highlighted item, the visuals refresh as expected. If you click the same empty space again, you will notice a visual refresh, and this will be captured by the performance analyzer.

- **Changed a slicer**: This triggers when a slicer value is changed and is applied to the other visuals. If you are using the **Query Reduction** settings in the report to place an **Apply** button on slicers, you need to click the **Apply** button to trigger the **Changed a slicer** event. Even if you do not use **Apply** buttons, interacting with slicers can trigger visual updates that the analyzer will capture.

- **Changed a filter**: This triggers when a report filter value is applied. Query reduction with **Apply** buttons on filters behaves the same way as with slicers.

The following figure shows the changes in items captured, such as page changes and **Cross-highlighted**.

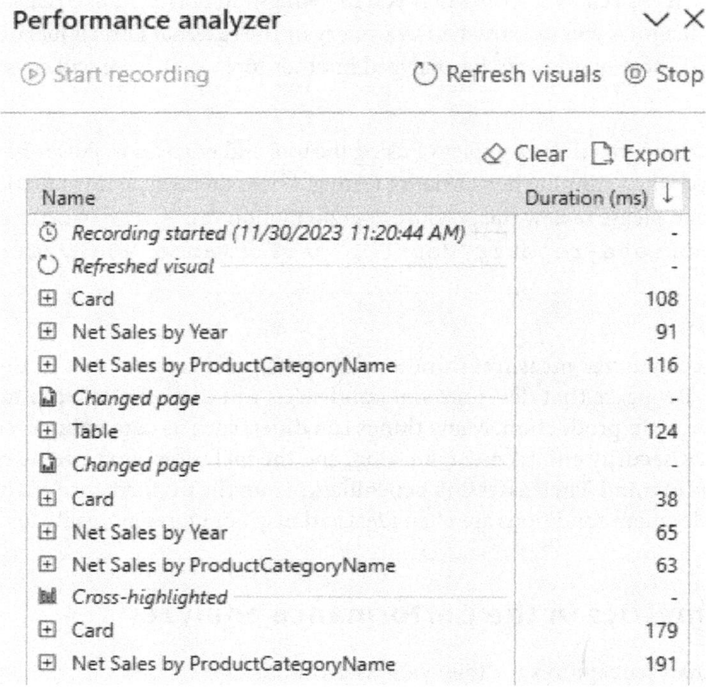

Performance analyzer ∨ ✕

▷ Start recording   ↻ Refresh visuals   ◎ Stop

                                            ◇ Clear   🗋 Export

Name	Duration (ms) ↓
⏱ *Recording started (11/30/2023 11:20:44 AM)*	-
↻ *Refreshed visual*	-
⊞ Card	108
⊞ Net Sales by Year	91
⊞ Net Sales by ProductCategoryName	116
📄 *Changed page*	-
⊞ Table	124
📄 *Changed page*	-
⊞ Card	38
⊞ Net Sales by Year	65
⊞ Net Sales by ProductCategoryName	63
📊 *Cross-highlighted*	-
⊞ Card	179
⊞ Net Sales by ProductCategoryName	191

Figure 3.6 – Performance analyzer additional captured items

The performance analyzer contains the following breakdowns per visual:

- **DAX query**: This is only shown if a query is required. It measures the time from when the visual issues the query to when it receives the results from the Analysis Services engine (VertiPaq). This time is expected to be a bit longer than the DAX query time that's reported by the Analysis Services engine because it includes communication and other overhead. It can be affected by users' physical distance from data sources.

- **Direct query**: This is only shown for DirectQuery data storage if a query was required. It measures the time from when the Analysis Services engine issued an external query to when it received the results. This number should correspond to DirectQuery class event timings from the Analysis Services engine.

- **Visual display**: This is the time spent by the visual drawing results on the screen. It includes the time taken fetching external assets such as images or performing geocoding. Poorly implemented or complex custom visuals tend to take more time here.

- **Other:** This is a general category for any non-display-related activities that are performed by the visual, such as preparing queries or other background processing. It also includes time spent waiting for other visuals. This is because visuals all share a single user interface thread and, in very simplistic terms, they all get a sequential slice of the CPU. Every time you add a new visual to a page, the higher this *other* number becomes for *every* visual. This isn't necessarily bad, but it can make visual-heavy reports more sluggish. We will explore this topic in more detail in *Chapter 9, Report and Dashboard Design*.

> Tip
>
> A visual refresh does not necessarily trigger a query in the underlying data source. The Power BI client has a local query result cache, so it can avoid re-running queries when switching back and forth between recently used filtered views. This explains why it is possible to see no DAX query for a data-driven visual. To force the query, you can use the **Refresh visuals** button in the **Performance analyzer** pane.

Determining user actions

At the time of writing, there are some interesting behaviors to note when viewing captured activity in the performance analyzer. Some user interactions will not be logged at the action level by the performance analyzer. If you have a slicer configured as a dropdown, for example, not all your interactions with it will be captured at the same granularity. This can make it difficult to work out what the user was doing after a long series of report interactions. The following screenshot shows a simple case as an example:

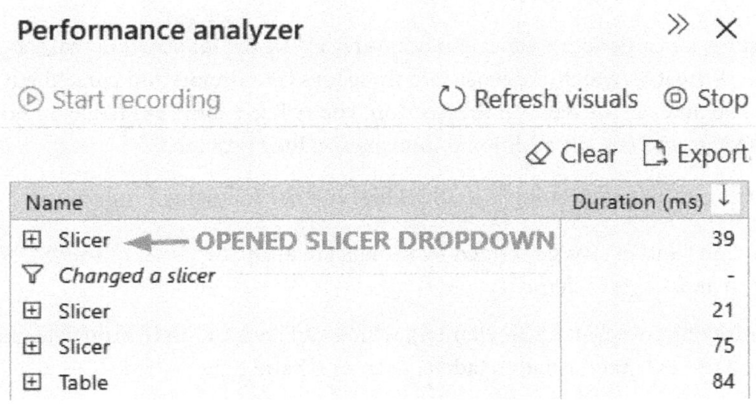

Figure 3.7 – The Slicer dropdown is opened, then a selection is made

Here, first, the **Slicer** dropdown is opened, then the slicer value is selected, denoted by **Changed a slicer**. It is not obvious that the first item was a user action since it looks like a generic visual update. If we extend this example by opening the **Slicer** dropdown again, it becomes even less clear. The following screenshot shows how the analyzer simply appends the drop-down action to the visuals from the previous **Changed a slicer** action:

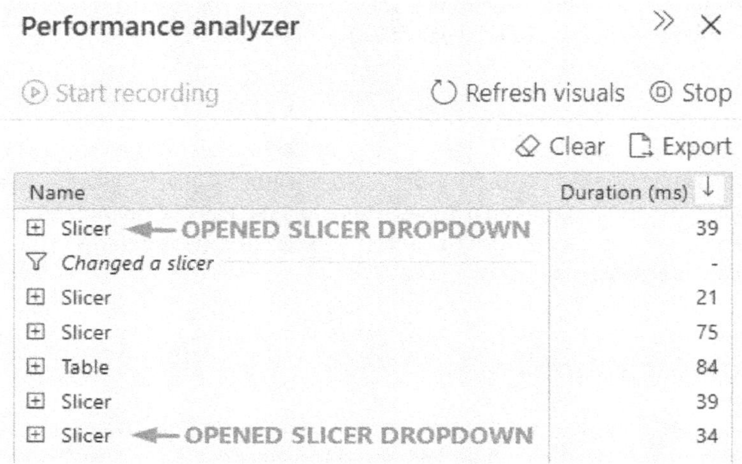

Figure 3.8 – The Slicer dropdown opened a second time

Exporting and analyzing performance data

Earlier in this chapter, we came across a few limitations regarding the information that the performance analyzer provides. A great way to dive deeper into these logs is to import and parse them in Power BI itself so that you can analyze the data. In this section, you will get some guidance on how to import and transform the logs and use the additional information they provide.

The Power BI performance analyzer log is a JSON file with the following properties:

- All user actions and events generated by visuals are at the top level of the JSON document, contained in an events element

- Some events contain a metrics element, which can have multiple properties such as query duration, query text, and visual metadata, such as ID and type

- Events have an id and a parentid, both of which can be used to define a parent-child hierarchy of events, allowing you to visualize the tree

The following screenshot shows the first few entries in an exported performance analyzer log file (PowerBIPerformanceData.json):

```
{
    "version": "1.1.0",
    "events": [
        {
            "name": "User Action",
            "component": "Report Canvas",
            "start": "2021-09-03T03:53:28.246Z",
            "id": "cc7f4683c7eae2856ba2",
            "metrics": {
                "sourceLabel": "UserAction_ChangePage"
            }
        },
        {
            "name": "Visual Container Lifecycle",
            "component": "Report Canvas",
            "start": "2021-09-03T03:53:28.420Z",
            "end": "2021-09-03T03:53:30.665Z",
            "id": "0aeda8bb1e877969ee3f-9ab27e40bdc010c9196c",
            "metrics": {
                "status": 1,
                "visualTitle": "Slicer",
                "visualId": "0aeda8bb1e877969ee3f",
                "visualType": "slicer",
                "initialLoad": true
            }
        },
        {
            "name": "Query",
            "component": "Report Canvas",
            "start": "2021-09-03T03:53:28.422Z",
            "end": "2021-09-03T03:53:30.636Z",
            "id": "393e8e690c654094ca0c",
            "parentId": "0aeda8bb1e877969ee3f-9ab27e40bdc010c9196c"
        },
```

Figure 3.9 – The first few elements of the performance analyzer log file

Some transformation work is required before you can get value out of the data. We mentioned earlier that the user actions and visual events are at the same level in the file. Events themselves are not associated with the user action because user actions have no children. First, we must assume that, after a user action, the next few events in the time sequence are the visual changes caused by that action. To visualize the events like a tree, we must derive some new columns to group each user action's events together and parent them to that action. We can also calculate a duration by subtracting the start and end timestamps.

The following screenshot shows a simple DirectQuery report that we will use to analyze the log files:

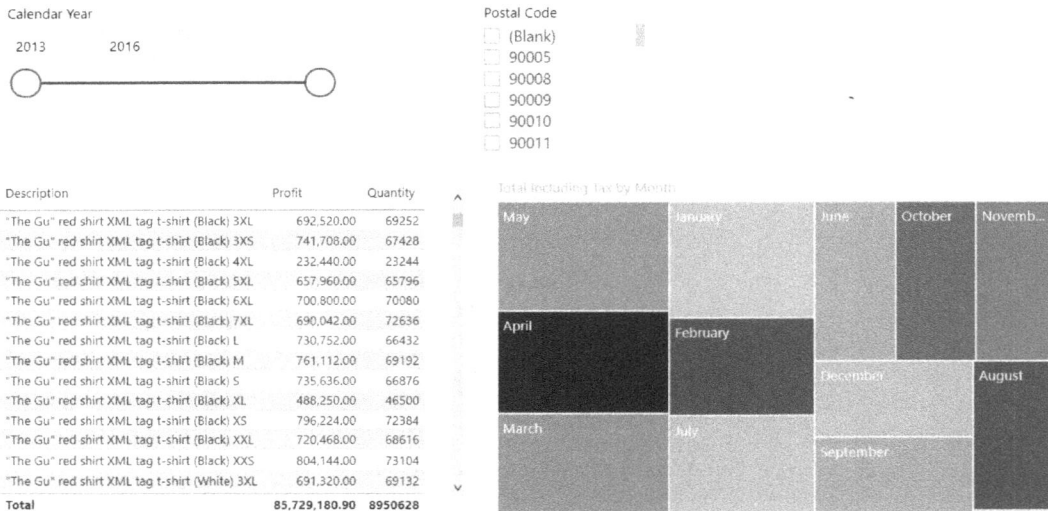

Figure 3.10 – DirectQuery report with four visuals

The performance log is generated by switching to this page from a blank page and then performing a visual refresh in the analyzer. There is a total of two user actions. The log from the user interface is shown in the following screenshot:

Name	Duration (ms) ↓
⏱ Recording started (9/2/2021 8:53:22 PM)	-
📖 Changed page	-
⊞ Slicer	2245
⊞ Slicer	1350
⊞ Total Including Tax by Month	4087
⊞ Table	5014
⟳ Refreshed visual	-
⊞ Slicer	107
⊞ Slicer	132
⊞ Table	4118
⊞ Total Including Tax by Month	3297

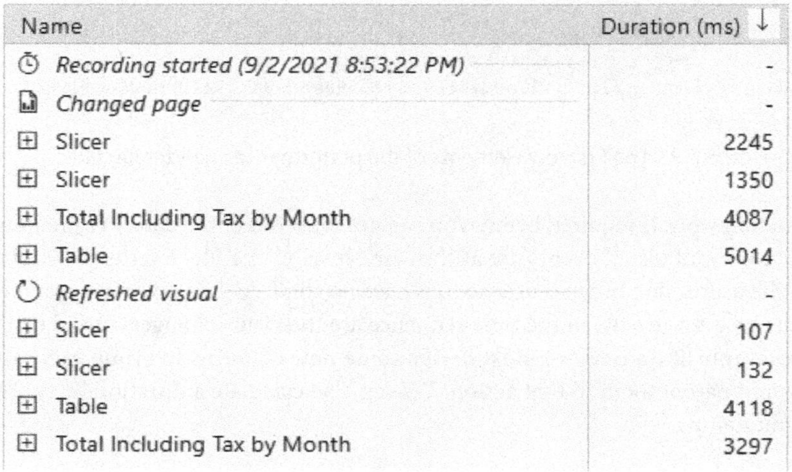

Figure 3.11 – A performance analyzer trace for the two user actions

We exported this data and then worked on it in the sample `Analyzing Desktop Performance Logs.pbix` file. The following figure shows the **Export** button.

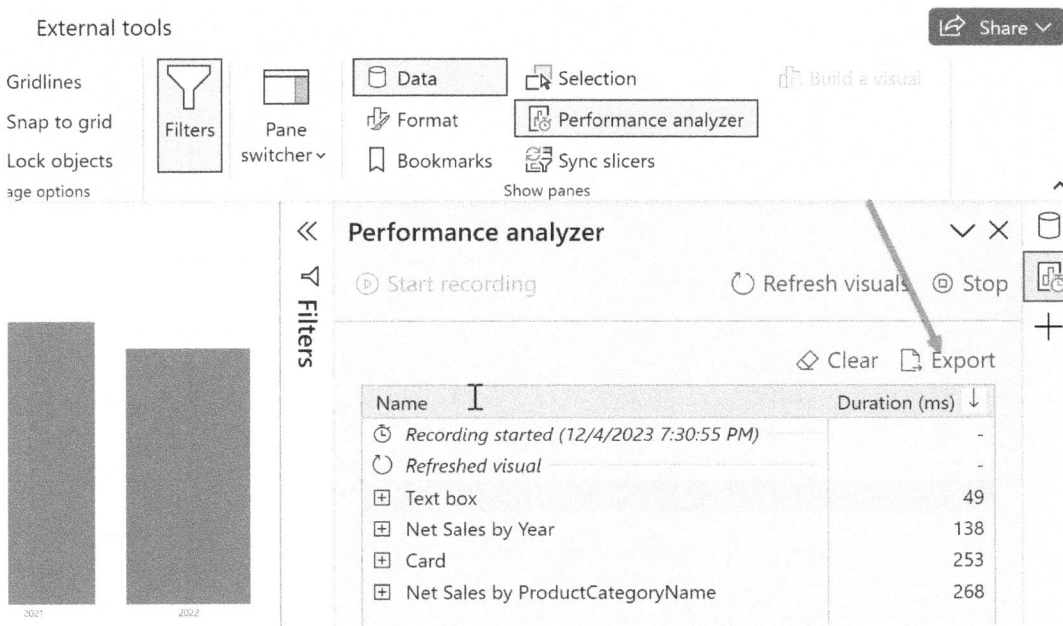

Figure 3.12 – Performance analyzer export

When the data has been shaped to our needs, we can build a simple chronological view, allowing us to filter out various event types and visuals. You can use this to investigate the sequence and duration of the events:

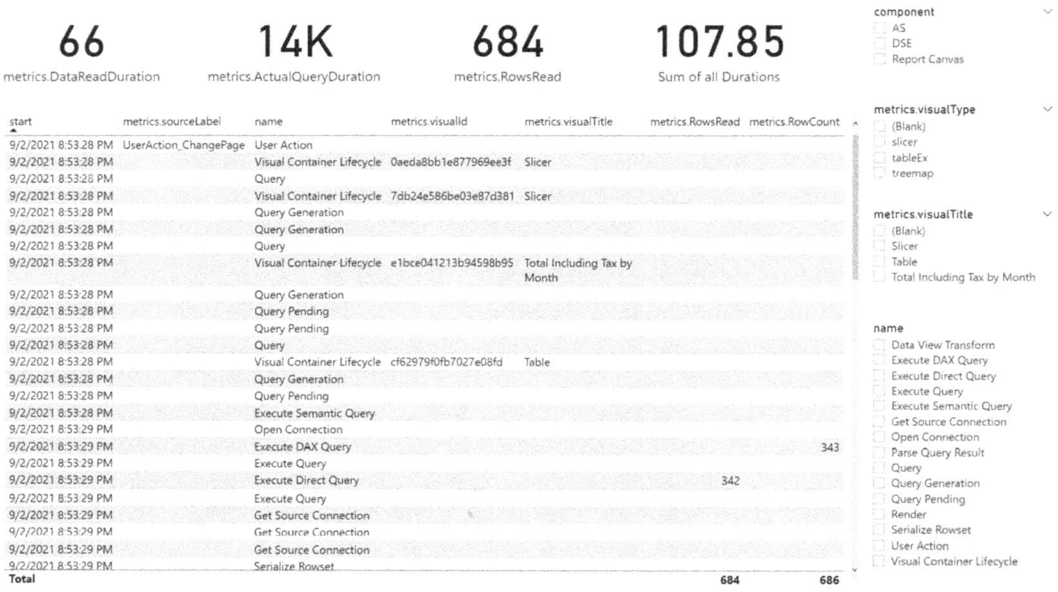
66
metrics.DataReadDuration
14K
metrics.ActualQueryDuration
684
metrics.RowsRead
107.85
Sum of all Durations
component
AS
DSE
Report Canvas
metrics.visualType
(Blank)
slicer
tableEx
treemap
metrics.visualTitle
(Blank)
Slicer
Table
Total Including Tax by Month
name
Data View Transform
Execute DAX Query
Execute Direct Query
Execute Query
Execute Semantic Query
Get Source Connection
Open Connection
Parse Query Result
Query
Query Generation
Query Pending
Render
Serialize Rowset
User Action
Visual Container Lifecycle
start
metrics.sourceLabel
name
metrics.visualId
metrics.visualTitle
metrics.RowsRead
metrics.RowCount
9/2/2021 8:53:28 PM UserAction_ChangePage User Action
9/2/2021 8:53:28 PM Visual Container Lifecycle 0aeda8bb1e877969ee3f Slicer
9/2/2021 8:53:28 PM Query
9/2/2021 8:53:28 PM Visual Container Lifecycle 7db24e586be03e87d381 Slicer
9/2/2021 8:53:28 PM Query Generation
9/2/2021 8:53:28 PM Query Generation
9/2/2021 8:53:28 PM Query
9/2/2021 8:53:28 PM Visual Container Lifecycle e1bce041213b94598b95 Total Including Tax by Month
9/2/2021 8:53:28 PM Query Generation
9/2/2021 8:53:28 PM Query Pending
9/2/2021 8:53:28 PM Query Pending
9/2/2021 8:53:28 PM Query
9/2/2021 8:53:28 PM Visual Container Lifecycle cf62979f0fb7027e08fd Table
9/2/2021 8:53:28 PM Query Generation
9/2/2021 8:53:28 PM Query Pending
9/2/2021 8:53:28 PM Execute Semantic Query
9/2/2021 8:53:29 PM Open Connection
9/2/2021 8:53:29 PM Execute DAX Query 343
9/2/2021 8:53:29 PM Execute Query
9/2/2021 8:53:29 PM Execute Direct Query 342
9/2/2021 8:53:29 PM Execute Query
9/2/2021 8:53:29 PM Get Source Connection
9/2/2021 8:53:29 PM Get Source Connection
9/2/2021 8:53:29 PM Get Source Connection
9/2/2021 8:53:29 PM Serialize Rowset
Total 684 686

Figure 3.13 – Sequence of events and performance metrics

The following screenshot shows how to build a tree view for each user action. In this example, we used the slicer to select one user action. Now, we can see its statistics and event tree:

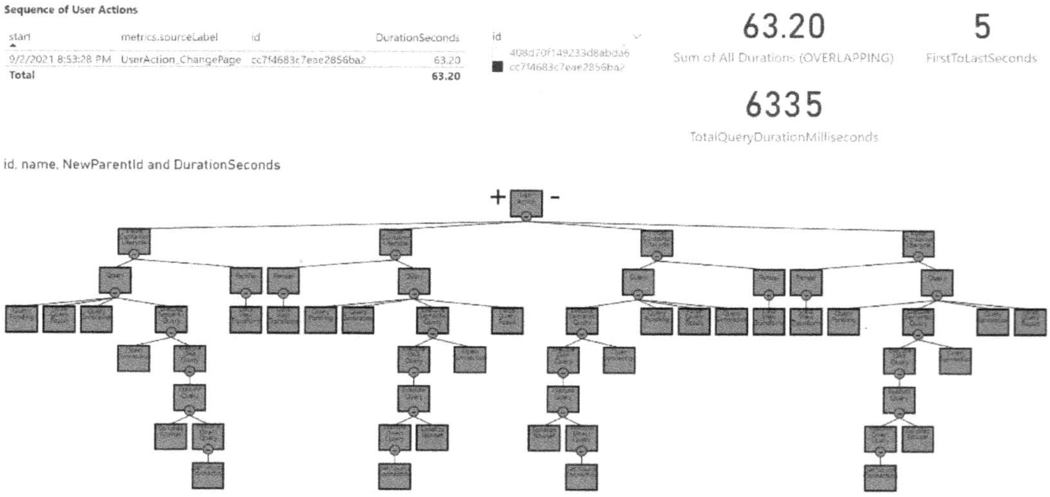
Sequence of User Actions
start
metrics.sourceLabel
id
DurationSeconds
9/2/2021 8:53:28 PM UserAction_ChangePage cc7f4683c7eae2856ba2 63.20
Total 63.20
id
63.20
Sum of All Durations (OVERLAPPING)
5
FirstToLastSeconds
6335
TotalQueryDurationMilliseconds
id, name, NewParentId and DurationSeconds
+
-

Figure 3.14 – Tree visualization of a user action

This view contains a **FirstToLastSeconds** calculation, which is from the earliest start time to the latest end time of events in scope. It tries to give you an idea of the duration of the user action itself until the last activity is completed. This addresses one gap in the desktop UI.

> **Important note**
>
> Calculating the duration of the user action using this custom method is not officially documented and should be considered approximate only. You should use it to compare the relative changes in performance from one design to another.

The transformation methods that were used in the sample file are quite basic and rely on you manually hardcoding line numbers in the file to partition user actions. This is intentional, to illustrate the structure of the JSON in a small file. You can point this sample to your log file and make changes as necessary to make it more automatic over much larger performance log files.

Now that we have finished looking at the performance analyzer, let us look at some more external tools to help performance tuning.

Using the Optimize ribbon

In the previous section, we talked about the performance analyzer in Power BI Desktop and its ability to analyze the times for visuals and queries. Now, we are going to look at some options for helping the analysis while navigating visuals and pages in a report. This is also part of Power BI Desktop. *Figure 3.15* shows the **Optimize** menu on the desktop.

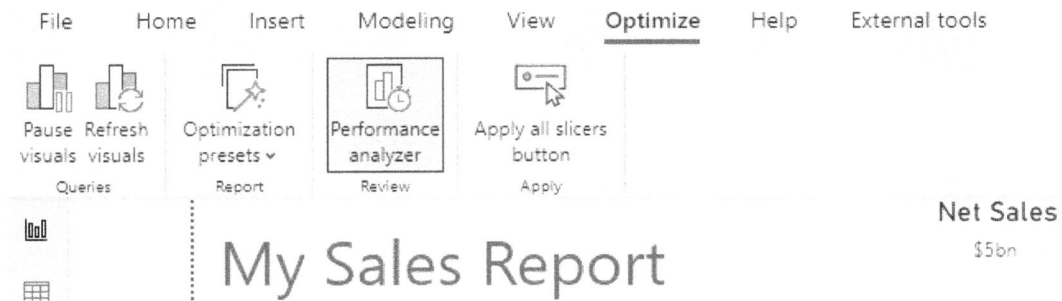

Figure 3.15 – Optimize ribbon

Pause and Refresh visuals

The first section of the **Optimize** ribbon has two buttons. The first is a way to pause visual refreshes. This stops the refreshing of slicers and visuals on a page, while we select a value in a slicer or an item in a visual. Then, the second button can refresh the visuals after the changes have been completed.

This enables the actions to not execute a refresh for every selection on a page. These options are available for all data storage modes.

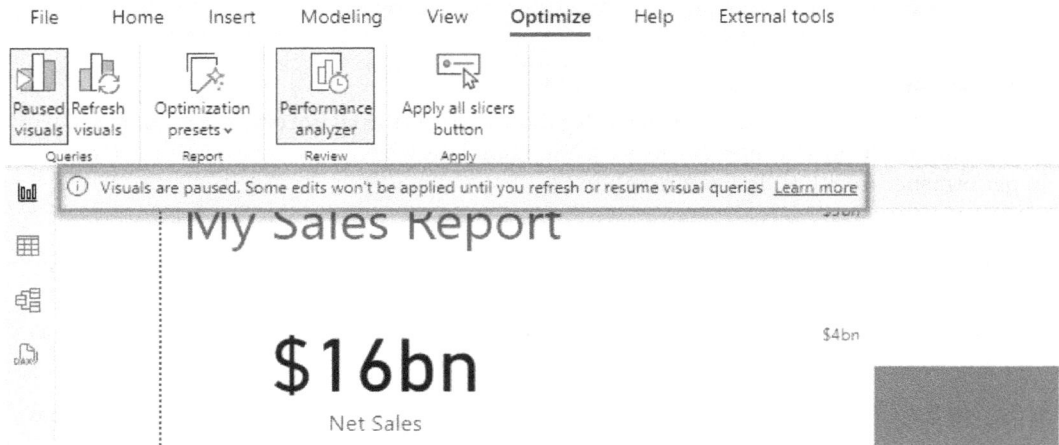

Figure 3.16 – Visuals are paused banner

Figure 3.16 shows the banner displayed for the report once the **Paused visuals** button is clicked. There is a link at the end of the banner to go to more information about this option. The banner is there to be a reminder of the state of the visuals. The following figure shows the **Refresh visuals** button that appears on visuals once a slicer or other visual has been selected.

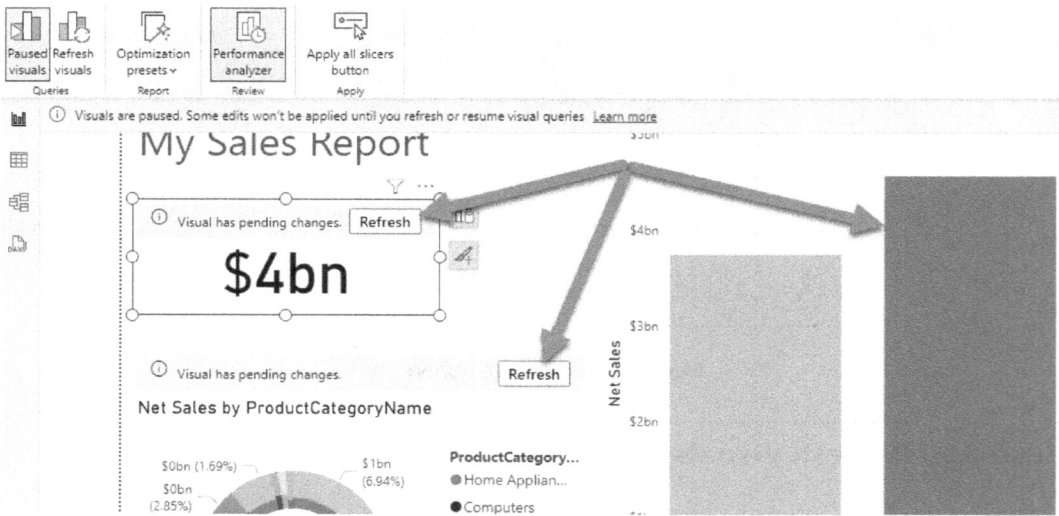

Figure 3.17 – Refresh visuals button

Optimization presets

The optimization presets are refresh scenarios that can be active on a page:

- **Query reduction**: An **Apply** button is added to the page to apply changes to visuals because cross-highlighting and cross-filtering are turned off by this option, thus reducing the number of queries

- **Interactivity**: As the default setting, all cross-filtering, cross-highlighting, and real-time changes are turned on

- **Performance analyzer**: The same option as explained previously in this chapter

- **Customize**: This option allows the user to choose which reduction settings are needed for this page

The following figure shows the **Optimization presets** menu choices:

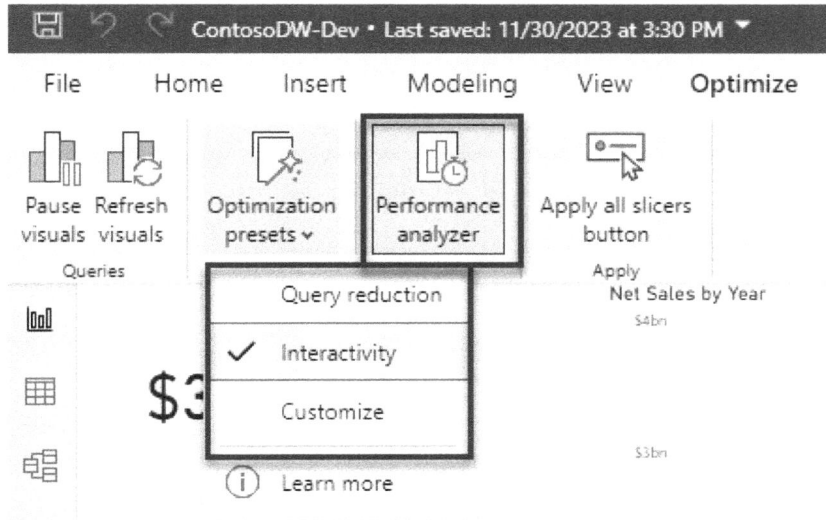

Figure 3.18 – "Optimization presets" menu choices

The Apply all slicers button

This option allows two buttons to be added to the page – one for applying all filters at once and the other to clear all slicers at once. By using these buttons, the end user of the report needs to be aware that when the slicer values are selected, the slicer values will not be filtered on the page until the **Apply all slices** button is clicked. This is another option for reducing the number of queries generated by user interaction on a page, thereby reducing queries sent to the engine(s).

Adapting external tools

The external tools mentioned here have a free version available. These are used throughout the industry to assist with performance tuning and development. Detailed examples will be shown in *Chapter 6, Third-Party Utilities*.

DAX Studio

DAX Studio is written by the folks at `https://www.sqlbi.com/`. They have combined useful tools into one application. The main query window allows connections to desktop files, deployed Power BI semantic models, as well as Analysis Services models. The query window enables users to type their own DAX queries for validation against a model. The additional options for queries can display the timings from the formula and storage engines. A DAX query plan can be extracted for advanced analysis.

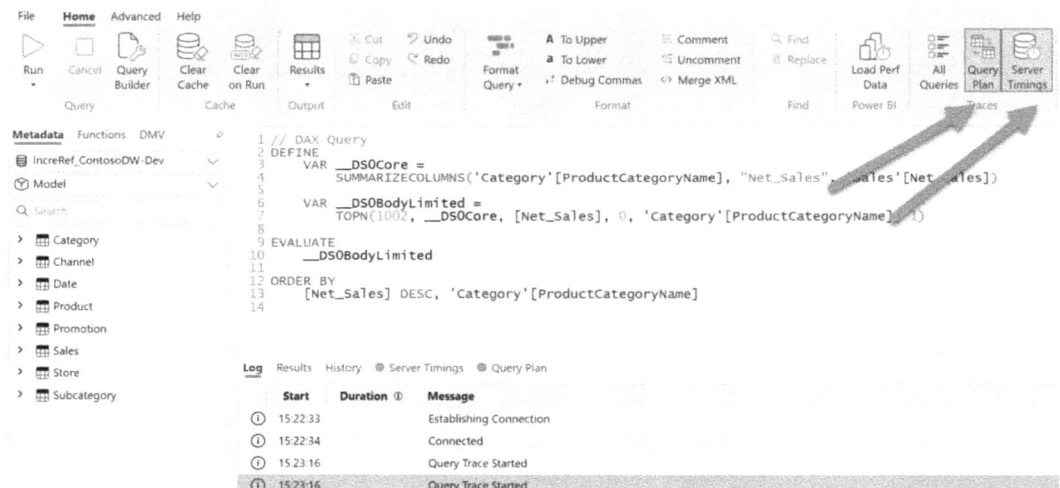

Figure 3.19 – DAX Studio

Figure 3.19 shows the query window with a queried copy from the performance analyzer for analysis. The tool also has a **View Metrics** feature in the **Advanced** ribbon for an analysis of the size and memory consumption. The whole model contains details for tables, columns, relationships, and more. This feature has a separate application called **VertiPaq Analyzer**, which can be run outside of DAX Studio. These analyses can be exported to other tools to dig further into performance. This tool is open source.

Query Diagnostics

Query Diagnostics is part of Power Query. So, this is available in Power Query online as well as in integrations with Excel and Power Pivot. *Figure 3.20* provides a view of the **Tools** ribbon in Power Query. The feature does have to be enabled in Power BI Desktop, in the**Options**/**Diagnostics** section.

Figure 3.20 – Query diagnostics

The diagnostics can be on an activity for the whole model in Power Query, or just one step – **Diagnose Step**. Starting diagnostics will start a trace of the Power Query refreshes or changes and can produce up to four queries of data that will be added to your Power Query queries pane but hidden from the model. Four diagnostic queries are displayed in the following figure.

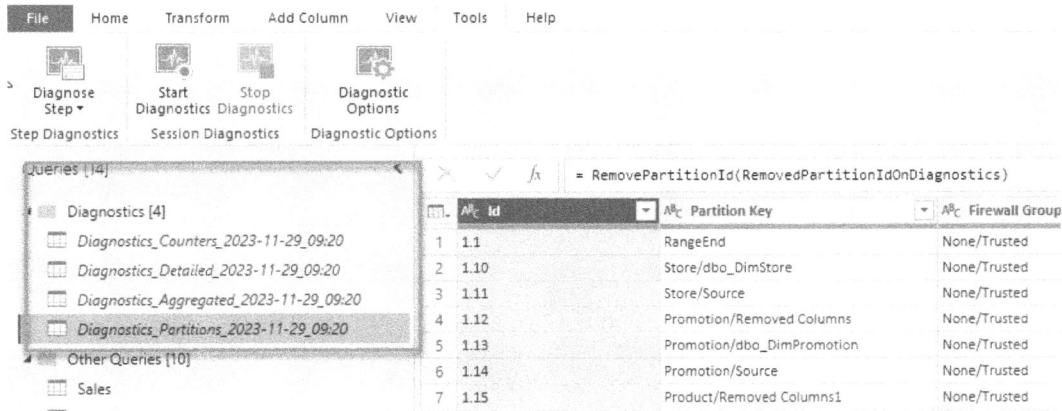

Figure 3.21 – Diagnostic queries

The key feature is finding the query folding that Power Query can do. This query folding can send a source query to the data engine for execution rather than in Power BI, thus pushing the processing to the source.

Tabular Editor

Tabular Editor (TE) is a development tool for Power BI and Analysis Services semantic models. It allows editing the metadata without having to import any data. So, if you want to change the display format of multiple columns, TE allows selecting multiple columns and applying the change at once.

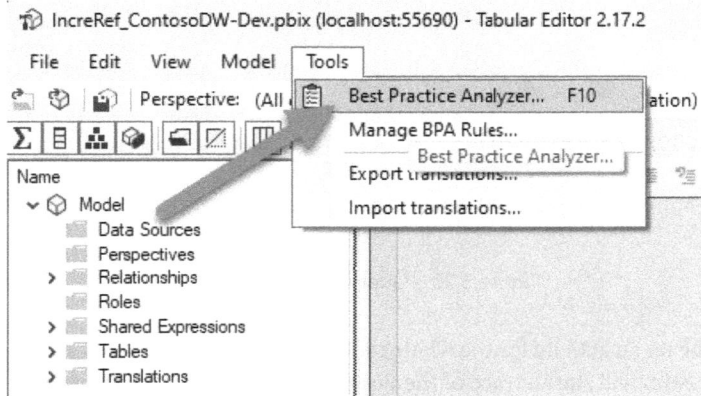

Figure 3.22 – Best Practice Analyzer

Figure 3.22 shows **Best Practice Analyzer** within TE. As far as performance tuning is concerned, the Best Practice Analyzer integrated into TE is the most helpful. Analyzing the structure of a model can be compared to a set of checks that can give useful information about the model design. Suggestions about optimization are given as well as links to the internet for more information on the optimization. The JSON file used to do the analysis can be edited manually or within TE. The rules are divided into categories such as performance, DAX expressions, error prevention, formatting, and maintenance.

Other tools

The **Profiler** from SQL Server Management Studio can be used with semantic models in Power BI and Analysis Services. This allows the capturing of events and columns during a refresh process or query from a visual.

Another option is a **Performance Metric** report, which is a **Power BI Template App** downloadable from Microsoft. It is installed in your Power BI tenant as a workspace. The report in the workspace can get statistical data for the last 30 days of activity. This data is formatted into visuals in the report. The data is scheduled to refresh regularly to update the statistical information.

Summary

In this chapter, we started with a summary of the engines in the Analysis Services process – formula and storage engines. Understanding where the processing time is taken is a good start for performance tuning a semantic model. We then introduced the performance analyzer as a built-in tool to help you assess performance for report visuals.

Breaking processing into querying, visualizing, and the other aspects helps focus performance tuning with durations and metrics. It lets you copy queries for analysis in other tools. Next, we looked at log files for durations of actions. Transforming the exported data was assisted by hierarchies as well as techniques for using it with the performance analyzer.

We concluded by looking at external tools. The first was DAX Studio, where we can see DAX queries analyzed for performance in the engines. Query diagnostics in Power Query helped analyze extraction code for timings. Tabular Editor was talked about in terms of changing metadata as well as a Best Practice Analyzer. Profiler and Performance Metric report were mentioned for additional analysis.

Part 2:
Performance Analysis, Improvement, and Management

In this part, we will identify sources of performance information in Power BI and how to access them and look at when to use DirectQuery and DirectLake for large data sources in a semantic model. You will learn which free external tools are appropriate for different layers, how to debug issues, and how to apply a structured approach to performance improvement.

This part has the following chapters:

- *Chapter 4, Analyzing Logs and Metrics*
- *Chapter 5, Optimization for Storage Modes*
- *Chapter 6, Third-Party Utilities*
- *Chapter 7, Performance Governance Framework*

4
Analyzing Logs and Metrics

In the first part of this book, we built a solid foundation for performance management in Power BI by identifying the major architectural components that can affect your experience. We learned why your choices in these areas can slow things down, and we provided recommendations and justifications in each area.

Once these theoretical concepts have been put into practice, you will need to know how to measure performance and analyze the data. This will let you make informed decisions on where to invest time to investigate further and where to make changes for performance tuning. Hence, it is time to move into the second part of this book, where we will look at the different places you can get performance-related information in Power BI and how to make sense of that data.

In this chapter, we will focus on the first part of report performance management, which is obtaining performance information. You'll learn what information is available, how to retrieve it, and what to focus on to determine the causes of bad performance.

This chapter covers the following topics:

- Power BI usage metrics
- Power BI logs and engine traces
- Monitoring Analysis Services and **Power BI Embedded** (**PBIE**)

Power BI usage metrics

In *Chapter 1*, *Setting Targets and Identifying Problem Areas*, we discussed how report loading performance is the most obvious factor regarding the speed of a **business intelligence** platform. In Power BI, a workspace administrator can get performance information using the built-in usage metrics report.

You can access usage metrics using the report drop-down menu in the content list of the Power BI workspace, as shown in *Figure 4.1*:

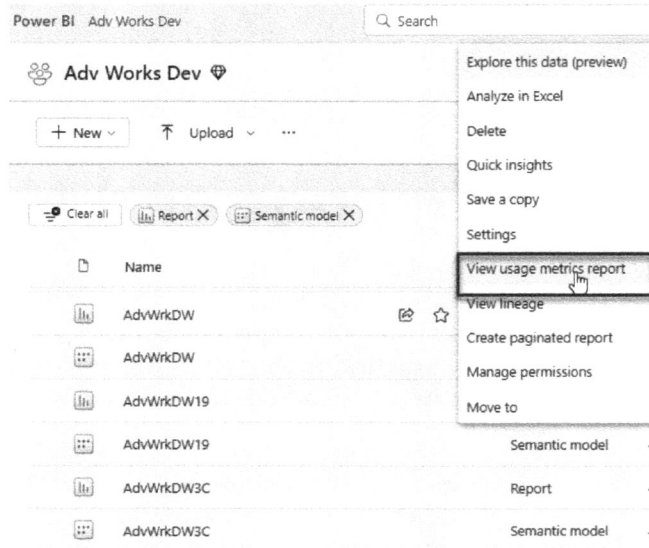

Figure 4.1 – How to view the usage metrics for a report in a workspace

You can also launch the usage metrics report from the report toolbar when viewing a report. This is shown in the following screenshot (*Figure 4.2*):

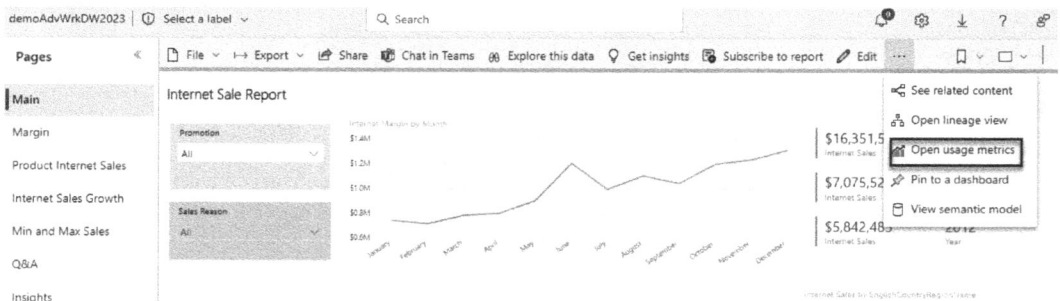

Figure 4.2 – How to view the usage metrics after opening a report

After you launch the usage metrics report, the **Report usage** page displays. This will initially show usage for the selected report. You can clear the report filter in the filter pane and see usage for all reports. The visuals show data for the last 30 days, which is the maximum number of days saved to the semantic model. You can change the date range with the date slicer in the right pane but only based on the last 30 days. This is shown in the following screenshot:

Usage Metrics: AdvWrkDW   Rank 2 across 23 reports

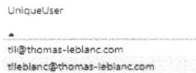

Figure 4.3 – The reported usage in the Usage Metrics report

You can look at performance-related metrics by switching to the **Report performance** tab on the left menu pane. There is a **7-day performance** tab that shows a chart smoothing the trend by a 7-day rolling aggregate. *Figure 4.4* shows the **Report performance** tab selected.

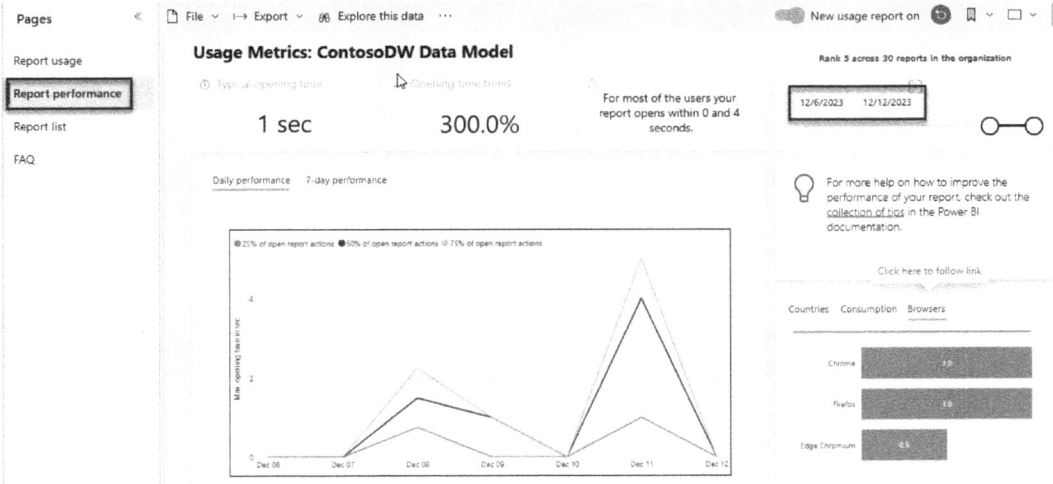

Figure 4.4 – The Report performance trend in the Usage Metrics report

> **Tip**
> Power BI currently supports two versions of usage metrics. If your usage metrics report looks different from the one shown in the preceding screenshot and does not contain any performance information, check that the **New usage report on** option is enabled in the toolbar, as shown in the preceding screenshot. You can use the toggle to switch back to the classic usage metrics if needed.

The report performance page provides a few different metrics that are worth describing:

- **Typical opening time**: This is the 50th percentile (or median) of the report load duration across the selected period in the report. It represents the middle number if you sorted all the report load durations from shortest to longest. The median can provide a better approximation of the typical duration than the average because the latter can be affected by outliers and small sample sizes.

- **Opening time trend**: This shows the percentage change in typical opening time (50th percentile), comparing the value for the first half of the reporting period to the value for the second half. In the preceding screenshot, we can see that the report has become 20% faster because the opening time has been reduced.

- **For most of the users your report opens between** [X] **and** [Y] **seconds**: This statement provides you with a range of report open durations. The lower bound (*X*) represents the 10th percentile, while the upper bound (*Y*) represents the 90th percentile. Therefore, "most" here represents 80% of the total report opens. This is a good way to think about performance since it covers a broad range and will not be heavily affected by outliers. Ideally, these two numbers will not differ by too much, though there isn't a general rule to apply here. Your goal should be to have the upper bound within your target report load duration, as discussed in *Chapter 1*, *Setting Targets and Identifying Problem Areas*.

- **25% of report open actions**: This is the 25th percentile of the report's load duration.

- **50% of report open actions**: This is the 50th percentile (median) of the report's load duration.

- **75% of report open actions**: This is the 75th percentile of the report's load duration.

Note the chart at the bottom right of the **Report performance** page. It shows the typical (50th percentile) report open duration by **Country**, **Consumption Method**, and **Browser**. We recommend monitoring performance by these categories regularly to see whether any scenarios stand out. There are additional data points available in the semantic model that power the usage metrics report, though they are not shown in the report by default. In the next section, we'll learn how to expose and use them.

Customizing the usage metrics report

The visuals in the usage metrics report provide us with an easy way to get a quick overview of the performance of a specific report. You'll likely want to build some views of this data, so next, we'll look at ways you can adjust a copy of the report or access the semantic model to build a view.

Filtering usage metrics

The usage metrics report is filtered to one report by default. You may want to look at performance for the entire workspace in aggregate or view metrics for a different report. You can achieve this by expanding the filter pane on the right, clearing any existing filters, and then selecting the report name or ID that you are interested in. The following screenshot in *Figure 4.5* shows the expanded filter pane with the default **ReportGuid is (All)** filter cleared and the list of report names expanded. Note how the metrics report title changes to **(Multiple reports selected)** to let you know that multiple reports are in scope:

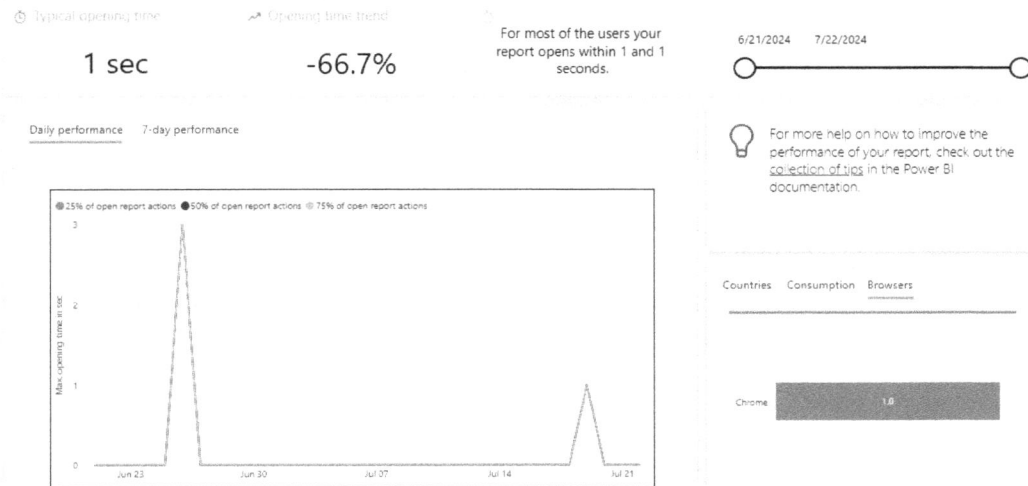

Figure 4.5 – Report load performance for the entire workspace

Now, let's learn how to open the data model behind this report and make report customizations.

Making a copy of the usage metrics report to edit

The Power BI usage metrics report is managed by the system. You are not allowed to edit it and editing options will not appear in the toolbar. However, you can work around this by creating a copy of the usage metrics report. Simply use the **File** menu and select **Save a copy**, as shown in the following screenshot:

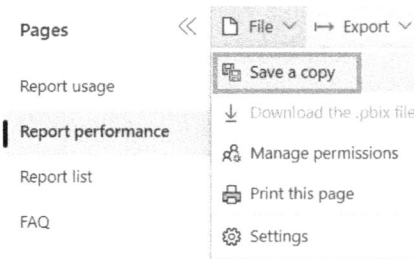

Figure 4.6 – Saving a copy of the usage metrics report

When you save a copy of the usage metrics report, it will be placed in the same workspace as the original system-managed version. You do not need to configure a refresh for this report because it uses the hidden, system-managed usage metrics semantic model as a source.

To customize the copy, you can edit the report in the portal in the same way you work with any regular Power BI report in the Power BI service. Simply navigate to it and open it, then use the **Edit** button on the toolbar and make the necessary modifications. The following figure shows the tables that are exposed when we edit the report:

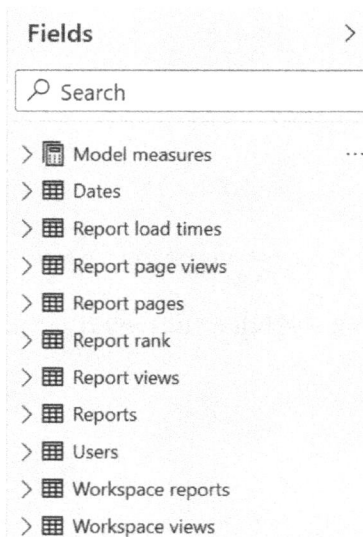

Figure 4.7 – The usage metrics semantic model is visible in a customized copy

Now, we'll briefly describe the major elements of the usage metrics semantic model to help you construct views that answer your common questions. *Figure 4.8* shows the relationships and tables with key columns in the semantic model.

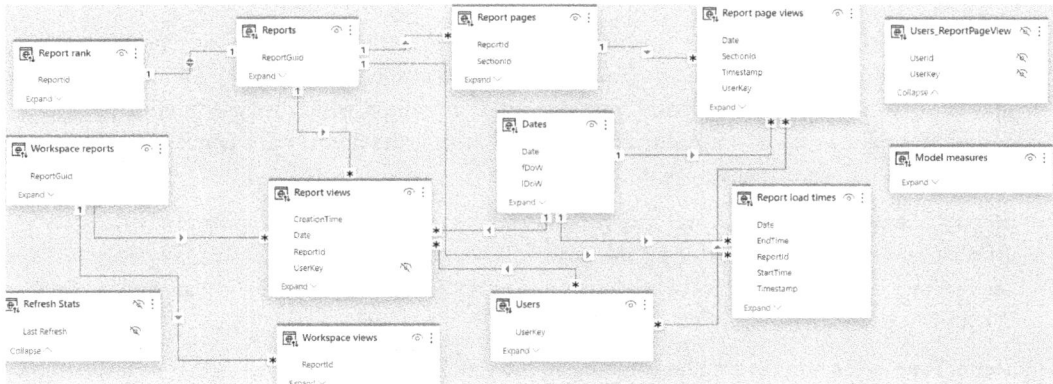

Figure 4.8 – The usage metrics semantic model tables and relationships

The measures include the following:

- **Model measures**: A logical container for the measures in the semantic model. It contains subfolders to group the measures for better manageability.

The dimensions include the following:

- **Dates**: A common date table. We recommend using this table for filtering and visualizing by date because it is connected to all the relevant log tables and will allow you to place different metrics next to each other in the same date context.

- **Reports**: A list of all reports in the workspace by name and identifier. Use the `IsUsageMetricsReport` column to exclude any system reports from your analysis – they will be set to `True`.

- **Report pages**: A list of all the report pages by name and identifier, including a mapping to the report ID that the page belongs to.

- **Users**: A list of all **user principal names** (**UPNs**) whose activity is captured in the report. The UPN is most often an email address.

The facts include the following:

- **Report page views**: A table containing an entry for each report page view, as reported by the Power BI client. Use this table to analyze views at the report page's granularity level.

- **Report load times**: This contains an entry for each report of the open activity, as reported by the Power BI client (for example, `app.powerbi.com` in a web browser or the Power BI mobile app on a phone). It contains activity start and end timestamps, which are used in the semantic model to calculate duration. A current limitation is that the report page is not identified, so the activity could be for any page of the report.

- **Report views**: This contains an entry for each report open activity, as reported by the Power BI service. This will be reported by the Power BI backend each time a report is opened. This data is not affected by client/network issues and every report open activity is expected to reach Power BI.

- **Report rank**: A static ranking table listing all the reports in the workspace and the viewership rank over the entire tenant.

- **Workspace reports**: A summary of the total days with usage and usage trends for each report. Use the `IsUsageMetricsReportWS` column to exclude any system reports from your analysis – they will be set to `True`. This data is used to populate the **Report list** page of the Power BI usage metrics report.

- **Workspace views**: A summary of the total views for each report by user, distribution method, and consumption method. This is used to power the **Report list** page of the system-generated report.

A practical way to understand how the usage metrics semantic model supports analyzing different scenarios is provided by Microsoft in the *Usage Metrics* documentation. We recommend checking out the example at the following link to see how different usage scenarios are captured and reported. This will help you interpret the usage metrics data: `https://docs.microsoft.com/power-bi/collaborate-share/service-modern-usage-metrics#worked-example-of-view-and-viewer-metrics`.

The next section will look at creating a new report with the Power BI desktop from the usage metric semantic model connection.

Accessing semantic model data with a new custom usage metrics report

You may prefer to use Power BI Desktop to author your custom performance report, or you may not want to use a copy of the system-generated usage metrics report as a base. In this case, you can create a new Power BI report in Power BI Desktop that's connected to the usage metrics semantic model in the workspace you're interested in. You will find a usage metrics semantic model in any workspace where the usage metrics have been accessed at least once.

To build reports over a usage metrics semantic model in Power BI Desktop, choose the data source called **Power BI semantic model**, then search for `usage metrics report` in the dialog box. This will list all the system-managed usage metrics semantic models and allow you to connect to the one in the workspace. *Figure 4.9* shows the result of a search where all the usage metrics semantic models are listed:

Figure 4.9 – List of usage metrics report semantic models found in Power BI Desktop

Once connected to the semantic model, the data model described in the previous section will be exposed and you can construct the desired views.

Now, we will see how to connect to the usage metric semantic model from Excel.

Model data access via Analyze in Excel over usage metrics

Another way to access the report performance and usage data is through Excel. Here, you can use the standard **Analyze in Excel** functionality once the usage metrics report has loaded. Power BI will prompt you to download an Excel file that has the necessary connection information embedded into it:

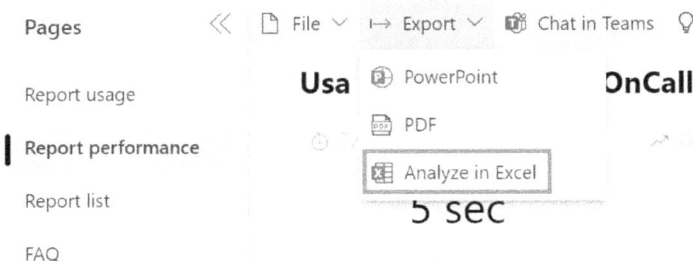

Figure 4.10 – The Analyze in Excel option for usage metrics

You can open the Excel document and construct Excel visuals over the Power BI semantic model. The same semantic model that we described earlier is exposed via the Excel pivotable interface. If you have multi-factor authentication turned on, you will be prompted to log in and authenticate to use the connection from Excel. The following figure shows a pivot table view that was created after opening the semantic model in Excel. It looks at the performance percentiles for a single report, compared by the browser:

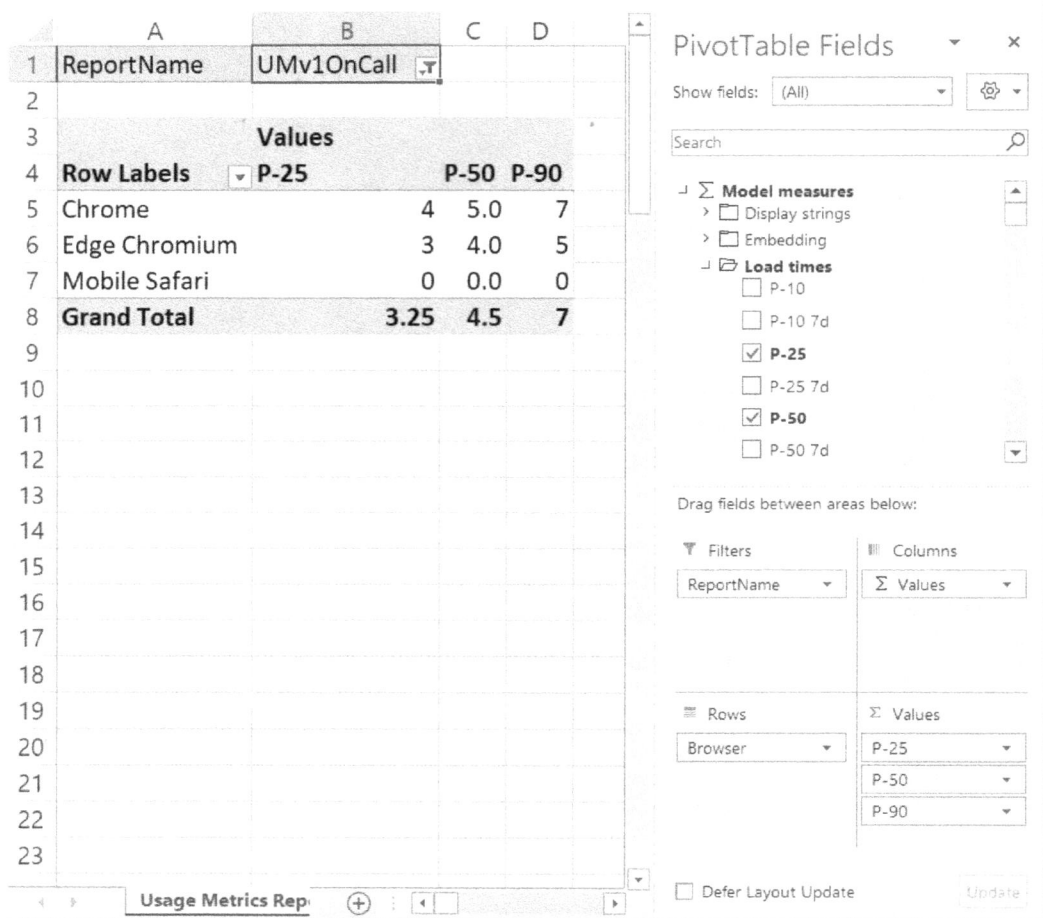

Figure 4.11 – Analyzing the usage metrics semantic model in Excel

Next, we will learn about the additional details you can get from building custom views over the usage metrics semantic model that Power BI provides.

Viewing granular performance data

Our coverage of the performance data available in usage metrics thus far has only dealt with aggregates, as provided in the default report. This is a good starting point, but aggregate data won't allow you to isolate issues and move closer to the root cause analysis. The great news is that more granular performance (and usage) data is available in the semantic model. Now that we have described the usage metrics semantic model that Power BI provides, we can construct a granular performance view using the **Report load times** table.

While we will only demonstrate one option, the same result can be achieved with any of the customization methods described earlier. *Figure 4.12* shows how a tabular and graphical view of performance can be created to analyze non-aggregated data. The goal here was to compare two reports and see how they performed over time. This can easily be extended by using the other dimensions available in the semantic model:

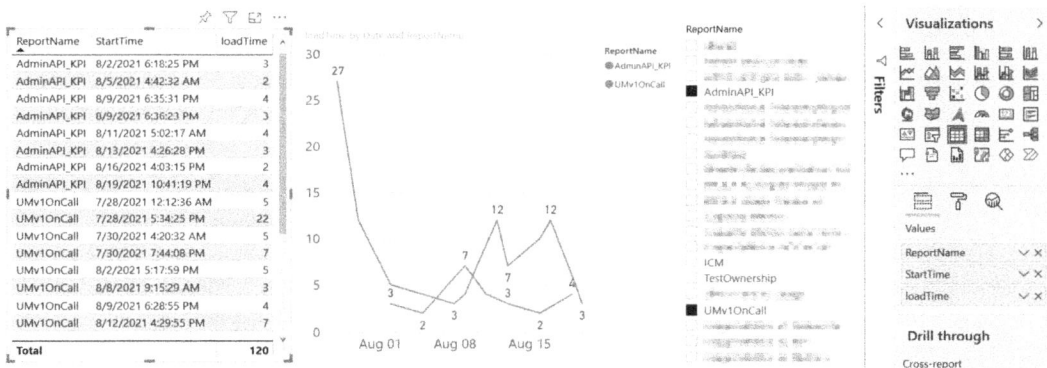

Figure 4.12 – Granular report performance view in a custom report

The loadTime (column name) data is based on a report not a page of a report, so it does not directly tie to a page. There are separate measures for reports (*report views*) and pages (*page views*) to measure specific pages in a report.

Next, let's explore what to look for in the performance data provided by Power BI, and then consider what you might do next based on your findings.

Analyzing report performance metrics

So far, we have learned about the different ways we can access and customize views for the report performance data provided by Power BI. Now, we will provide some general guidance on how to use this data to identify issues.

If you are trying to resolve a known consistent performance issue with a specific report, you must look at visuals and queries in detail. We employ a process and specific tools for this. This was covered in *Chapter 3, Learning the Tools of Performance Tuning*, and will be expanded on in *Chapter 6, Third-Party Utilities*. For now, we are going to approach report performance from a summary level, looking for trends and anomalies and learning what the next best actions are.

You don't need to customize the report performance information to get some good insights. The built-in **Performance** page can help you answer some useful questions. *Figure 4.13* serves as a guide to customizing report performance:

Question	Rationale and Next Steps
What are the slowest and fastest reports?	Identify the common characteristics of slow versus fast reports as you review them. You should focus your efforts on the slowest and most used reports. Investigate the data model, DAX, and report a visual design for problematic reports.
Is report performance consistent from day to day?	You want to determine if a report is generally slow or is being affected by user load or other system loads (more relevant for Premium). If you see that a certain period is much slower for one report, check if other reports were also affected in that period. If they were, this suggests that an external factor was the cause, not the report's design.
Is there a wide gap between lower and higher report load duration percentiles for any report?	As per the previous question, it is also useful to check if the slow runs are isolated to particular users, locations, browsers, and so on. This helps rule out report design issues.
What browsers are being used to access reports and is there a material difference in the speed?	Older browsers are officially recognized to have performance issues with Power BI. There can be a significant difference and this data can help justify decommissioning legacy browsers in large corporations that are reluctant to migrate.
Are users in certain countries or regions experiencing poor performance?	Network configuration, connection speed, and the sheer geographical distance of users from the Power BI home tenant can impact report performance. This dimension can help justify why a report can appear slow when measured in aggregate, but only because most users are far away or have poor connectivity.
Are certain platforms or distribution methods slower (for example, mobile versus the web, and embedded versus powerbi.com)?	Power BI can be deployed and consumed in various ways. Each has performance implications and may need specific optimizations. This information helps you focus your efforts on the most important scenarios for your organization.

Figure 4.13 – A guide to analyzing summary report performance data

The screenshots that follow show 1 month of real performance data of a production Power BI report that had over 60,000 views. The screenshot in *Figure 4.14* shows that the report's performance appears to be quite consistent, except for 2 days where the 75th percentile seemed to increase by 5 or more seconds than the norm. This may warrant an investigation to see whether any other reports were impacted and potentially by a more general issue. If other reports were fine, you should check whether this report experienced high usage, which suggests its design isn't scaling well. It's also possible that only users of this report were affected. Here, you can use the country and username data to visualize and isolate these reports:

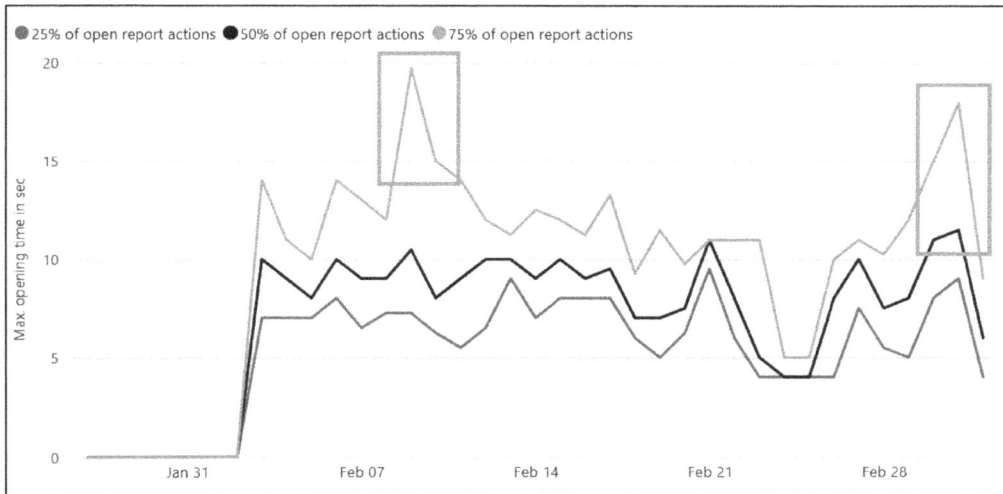

Figure 4.14 – Daily performance trend showing two abnormal spikes

Figure 4.15 shows the browser performance data for the same report, from the built-in usage metrics. Here, we can see that deprecated browsers are much slower than their modern counterparts for this report:

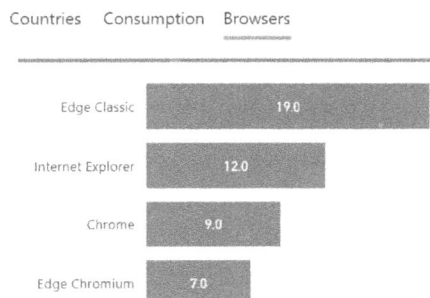

Figure 4.15 – Performance differences across browsers

Customizing the views is highly recommended. The screenshot in *Figure 4.16* shows an example of a useful custom chart you can create with the metrics data. The left box shows three reports that are much slower than the rest and have reasonable usage. The right box shows a report with very high usage. While it is nowhere near the slowest report of the entire group, it has a typical opening time of 50 seconds, which is far from ideal and should be investigated:

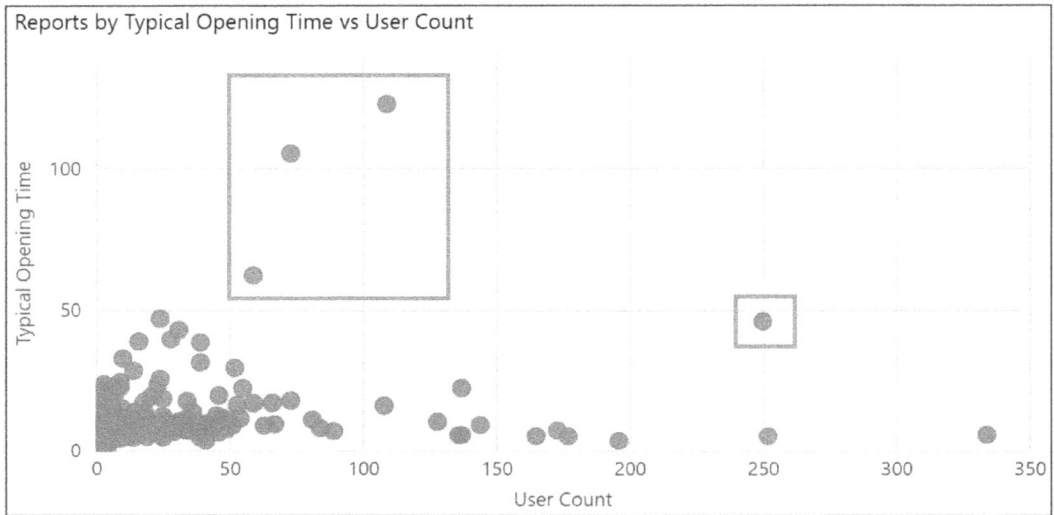

Figure 4.16 – Reports by Typical Opening Time versus User Count – this helps prioritize investigations

Now, let's learn how to collect performance metrics from multiple workspaces.

Collecting performance metrics from multiple workspaces

At the time of writing, Power BI does not provide a single place to get report performance metrics from multiple Power BI workspaces. If you need to combine usage and performance data from multiple workspaces, you will need to perform some manual steps. Here is a suggested method:

1. Use **Analyze in Excel** against the built-in usage metrics to build a flat table of the performance data you need. Pick a date range that aligns with how frequently you want to run this process and get fresh data. For example, you may choose a seven-day range if you plan to update weekly, and this is assumed for the rest of the examples.

2. Repeat *Step 1* for each Power BI workspace and save the Excel file separately.

3. Use Power BI Desktop to import and combine the Excel files. Build the query in such a way that it will load all the files in a folder. This way, each week, when you get new data, you can simply add the weekly files to the folder and refresh Power BI.

4. Each week, you can reuse the previous week's Excel files and just update the date filter.

You could design a more sophisticated solution for this, such as loading the usage data into a central database and using that as a source for any data analysis. This is more suited to administrators and those with scripting ability, and we will describe this in the next section.

Power BI logs and engine traces

The report usage and performance metrics we covered in the previous section are primarily designed for workspace administrators. For **service/tenant administrators**, Power BI has raw logs that are available, though today, they do not contain report performance metrics. However, since Microsoft has stated its intention to improve logging capabilities, it is worth briefly covering these sources as they are likely to become relevant for performance tuning in the future.

Activity logs and unified audit logs

There are two sources of administrative logs from Power BI that cover activities across the entire tenant. *Figure 4.17* describes the major similarities and differences:

Power BI Activity Log	Unified Audit Log
Accessible via the Get Activity Events REST API and Power BI Management commandlets	Accessible via the Compliance Search interface or PowerShell commandlets
Power BI or Power Platform Service Administrator privileges required	Global Office 365 Administrator or Audit privileges required
Contains only Power BI activities	Contains activity from a range of other Microsoft products besides Power BI, such as Office 365
30 days of history	90 days of history

Figure 4.17 – Comparison of activity and audit logs

Please see the *Further reading* section for more information.

You'll need to create reports to analyze activity logs, so we suggest setting up a process like the one described earlier for workspace usage metrics. The difference with audit logs is that you will not need to use Excel documents and can save **comma-separated value** (**CSV**) files instead. It is also easier to automate administrative logging due to the availability of PowerShell cmdlets and REST APIs.

The next section will cover extracting data from the Power BI activity log to import into an SQL Server table for analysis.

Import from activity logs

A JSON file can be extracted from the Power BI activity log into an SQL Server table or other data storage for analysis. To retrieve this data, the login used to run the REST API will have to be an administrator of Power BI. This section will give an example PowerShell script to retrieve the information as well as a suggested table structure for storing the data. You will want to extract this data on a frequency of daily, weekly, or monthly basis to keep a historical record of the data.

The PowerShell script will use a Power BI Management API called `Get-PowerBIActivityEvent`. The API would need to be loaded into the environment before running. You will also have to log in as a service principal or service account using `Connect-PowerBIServiceAccount` – see `https://learn.microsoft.com/en-us/powershell/module/microsoftpowerbimgmt.admin/get-powerbiactivityevent?view=powerbi-ps`. The API call will return a JSON structure you have to save to a variable and write out to a file to import into an SQL Server table.

Here is an example of calling the cmdlet to extract the activity log:

```
Get-PowerBIActivityEvent -StartDateTime 2019-08-10T14:35:20
-EndDateTime 2019-08-10T18:25:50
```

This output can be piped into a variable as follows:

```
$json = Get-PowerBIActivityEvent -StartDateTime $StartDate
-EndDateTime $EndDate | ConvertFrom-Json
```

To write to a file, try this:

```
Get-PowerBIActivityEvent -StartDateTime $StartDate -EndDateTime
$EndDate -ResultType JsonString |
    Out-File -FilePath "c:\temp\AuditLog_$(Get-Date -Date $EndDate
-Format yyyyMMdd).json"
```

The output looks like *Figure 4.18*.

```
[
  {
    "Id": "aaa-bbbb-ccc",
    "RecordType": 20,
    "CreationTime": "2023-12-08T00:04:18Z",
    "Operation": "GetSnapshots",
    "OrganizationId": "xxx-yyy-zzz",
    "UserType": 0,
    "UserKey": "100320013EB223FB",
    "Workload": "PowerBI",
    "UserId": "xyz@abc.com",
    "ClientIP": "2700:8907:1c92:b701:d501:a26c:c544:cd2e",
    "UserAgent": "Mozilla/5.0 (Windows NT 10.0; Win64; x64) AppleWebKit/537.36 (KHTML, like Gecko)
    "Activity": "GetSnapshots",
    "IsSuccess": true,
    "RequestId": "fff-ggg-hhh",
    "ActivityId": "iii-jjj-kkk",
    "ModelsSnapshots": [
      2194476
    ],
    "RefreshEnforcementPolicy": 0
  },
  {
    "Id": "aaa-bbbb-ccd",
    "RecordType": 20,
    "CreationTime": "2023-12-08T00:04:23Z",
    "Operation": "GetCloudSupportedDatasources",
    "OrganizationId": "xxx-yyy-zzz",
    "UserType": 0,
    "UserKey": "100320013EB223FB",
    "Workload": "PowerBI",
    "UserId": "xyz@abc.com",
    "ClientIP": "2700:8907:1c92:b701:d501:a26c:c544:cd2e",
    "UserAgent": "Mozilla/5.0 (Windows NT 10.0; Win64; x64) AppleWebKit/537.36 (KHTML, like Gecko)
    "Activity": "GetCloudSupportedDatasources",
    "IsSuccess": true,
    "RequestId": "fff-ggg-hhh",
    "ActivityId": "iii-jjj-kkk",
    "RefreshEnforcementPolicy": 0
  }.
```

Figure 4.18 – JSON output from an activity Log

The data from this JSON structure can be queried in SQL Server as the following figure shows. Here, we are using OPENROWSET with OPENJSON in a cross-join. The case of the column names in the WITH clause needs to match the case of the columns in the JSON structure. If it does not match, no error is thrown. The data will be null in the output, so a special inspection of the column data should be implemented before accurate results can be used in a report.

```
SELECT [Id], [CreationTime] ,[Workload] ,[UserID] ,[Activity] ,[ItemName],[WorkSpaceName], [DatasetName],
    [ReportName], [WorkspaceId], [ObjectId],[DatasetId] ,[ReportId] ,[ReportType] ,[DistributionMethod] ,
    [ConsumptionMethod], GETDATE() as [Import_Timestamp]
  FROM OPENROWSET ( BULK 'C:\Temp\AuditLog_2023.json', SINGLE_CLOB) AS jsondata
    CROSS APPLY OPENJSON( BulkColumn )
  WITH (
          [Id] varchar(50),
          [RecordType] Int,
          [CreationTime] datetime,
          [Workload] VARCHAR(50) ,
          [UserId] VARCHAR(50) ,
          [Operation] varchar(200),
          [OrganizationId] NVARCHAR(100),
          [Activity] VARCHAR(50) ,
          [ItemName] VARCHAR(255) ,
          [WorkSpaceName] VARCHAR(255) ,
          [DatasetName] VARCHAR(500) ,
          [ReportName] VARCHAR(500) ,
          [WorkspaceId] VARCHAR(50) ,
          [ObjectId] VARCHAR(500) ,
          [DatasetId] VARCHAR(50) ,
          [ReportId] VARCHAR(50) ,
          [ReportType] VARCHAR(50) ,
          [DistributionMethod] VARCHAR(50) ,
          [ConsumptionMethod] VARCHAR(50)
      ) AS Activity;
```

Figure 4.19 – Using T-SQL to query data from the JSON file

Now, we will look at using profiles to capture semantic model processing metrics.

Analysis Services server traces with the XMLA endpoint

If you are using Power BI Premium or Fabric, you will have the **XMLA endpoint** available if it has been enabled in **Tenant Settings**. This is a management endpoint that can be used to perform operations on Power BI semantic models by capturing commands directly in the Analysis Services engine. This will let you initiate a server trace from **SQL Server Profiler** on the workstation and collect detailed semantic model information in near-real time. Analysis Services data is very useful to help understand engine load, query performance, and refresh performance. We will cover engine traces in more detail in later chapters. For now, note that SQL Profiler provides a generic log capture and viewing interface, and it's not recommended. We will recommend other tools in *Chapter 6, Third-Party Utilities*. For those interested in SQL Profiler or unable to use unofficial tools, we recommend a blog post by Christopher Webb, a well-known authority on *Analysis Services*, who is the author of many books on the subject. This article can be found at the following link: https://blog.crossjoin.co.uk/2020/03/02/connecting-sql-server-profiler-to-power-bi-premium/.

The next section gives a brief description of using Log Analytics from Azure Monitoring.

Integration with Azure Log Analytics

Microsoft released a feature that allows you to connect Power BI to Azure Log Analytics workspaces. Azure Log Analytics is a platform where you can ingest logs, retain them for up to two years, perform ad hoc queries on near-real-time data, set alerts, and extract data for reporting and analytics. This feature is accompanied by sophisticated downloadable report templates. More information is available at the following link: `https://learn.microsoft.com/en-us/power-bi/transform-model/log-analytics/desktop-log-analytics-overview`.

The following section gives a brief description of some other monitoring options.

Monitoring Azure Analysis Services (AAS) and PBIE

AAS and **PBIE** are first-party Azure services. This means they are provisioned, managed, and billed via Azure. You can leverage these services in a standalone manner, directly integrating them with custom applications or using them as independent data tiers that can be scaled on-demand as needed. We will primarily use Azure tooling to look at data from these services.

Azure metrics for AAS

After you have provisioned an AAS instance, you can use built-in metrics to visualize your load and operations. Simply navigate to the AAS instance in the Azure portal and select the **metrics** link from the left navigation. You can then select various metrics to plot in the web interface, as described in the documentation (`https://docs.microsoft.com/en-us/azure/analysis-services/analysis-services-monitor`). Let's highlight some of the more important metrics and how they can help you:

- **Current User Sessions**: The number of concurrent active user sessions. Correlate this with known periods of poor performance to determine whether user load may be a contributing factor.

- **M Engine Memory**: The memory usage that's used by mashup engine processes when you're running data refreshes. Keep an eye on this to identify spikes. See whether high values coincide with reports of failures or lower-than-expected performance. You may need to reschedule refreshes, optimize content, or handle the higher load by scaling up or out.

- **M Engine QPU**: The processing power that's used by the mashup engine processes, measured in **Query Processing Units (QPUs)**. For example, if you have an S1-sized instance, then you have 100 QPUs and should ensure that there is enough headroom for queries when you hit peak QPU usage by the M engine. The exact number depends on your scenario and can be determined by load testing when there is no refresh. We will cover load testing in *Chapter 13, Optimizing Capacities in Power BI Enterprise*.

- **Memory Usage**: The total memory usage by all the server processes on the instance. If this is near the maximum that's provided on the **SKU**, query and refresh performance will likely degrade and even result in some failures.

- **QPU**: The processing power that's used across the entire instance. A well-optimized instance should operate at peak load without reaching the maximum QPU for sustained periods, though high values are not necessarily bad.

- **Query Pool Busy Threads**: The number of processor threads being used for queries. The maximum varies by SKU. If you see this reaching a maximum number and remaining flat for extended periods, this means that there are too many reports/queries being run at the same time. Some queries will have to wait before they can start executing.

Figure 4.20 shows the AAS QPU metrics displayed in the Azure portal:

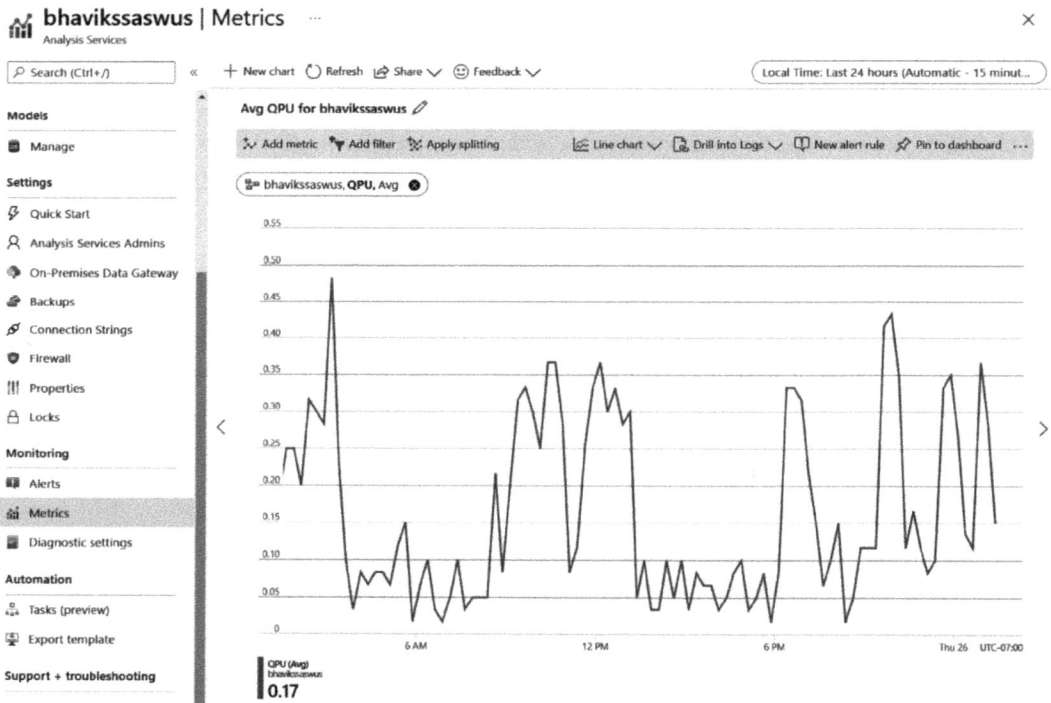

Figure 4.20 – The AAS QPU metrics trend in the Azure portal

There are also detailed server traces available for AAS. Some configuration is required to obtain these. We will explore this topic next.

Azure diagnostics for AAS

Earlier in this chapter, we described how the XMLA endpoint can be used to connect to a Premium workspace to capture engine traces. The same concept applies to AAS, though we can use Azure diagnostic logging and Azure Log Analytics to capture and analyze this information.

There are some Azure prerequisites and dependencies to satisfy before you can connect AAS to the logging service, namely provisioning a destination for the logs. This requires some administrative permissions in Azure. The setup is beyond the scope of this book, so we encourage you to read the official guidance to configure diagnostic logging, which can be found at the following link: `https://docs.microsoft.com/azure/analysis-services/analysis-services-logging`.

Azure metrics and diagnostics for PBIE

PBIE supports built-in Azure metrics that are accessed from the Azure portal in the same way we described previously for AAS. A point to note is that fewer metrics are available than with AAS. Please refer to the online documentation to get the current list. This reference also covers diagnostic logging for PBIE, which works the same way as AAS. It can be found at the following link: `https://docs.microsoft.com/power-bi/developer/embedded/monitor-power-bi-embedded-reference#metrics`.

In subsequent chapters, we will dive deeper into AS engine logs. The advice given here will apply to the AS engine within Power BI, AAS, and PBIE.

Now that we've covered the primary sources of performance information in Power BI, let's summarize what we've learned in this chapter.

Summary

Since report performance is such an important aspect of the user experience, we began by looking at Power BI's built-in workspace usage metrics, which are targeted at workspace administrators.

With the usage metrics report, we saw a report performance page to visualize report trends and break download duration. We noted that the aggregate information it provides is a good start. To reach this detailed data, we learned how to copy and customize the built-in report. All these methods allow you to access details and create more useful custom views. Finally, we looked at typical questions to ask of the performance data.

Then, we moved on to logs and traces, noting that there are tenant-wide logs available for administrators. We learned that this is an important source of data for query and refresh performance. When using Premium or Fabric semantic models, you can connect to the XMLA endpoint to start a near-real-time trace. You also have a PaaS-based option to connect Power BI to Azure Log Analytics to capture the granular data in an environment you own.

For those using AAS or PBIE, we learned that Azure metrics and diagnostic logging must be used since these are standalone Azure services. An important point is that all AS engine logs are derived from the same traces, even though they are exposed in different ways and formats.

The next part of our journey will see us diving deeper into performance analysis by using tools to analyze report and query performance data in detail, at a report page and visual level. We will begin by looking at how to use the **Power BI Desktop Performance Analyzer**. This is an important tool that will be referred to in later chapters as we look at the performance implications of various design choices.

5
Optimization for Storage Modes

With the proliferation of data lakes, more options are available for performance improvements with DirectQuery and Direct Lake. Synapse has brought **Massively Parallel Processing (MPP)** from big data to analytical databases. DirectQuery can use the column store indexes in Synapse or other cloud database systems. The use of aggregations with DirectQuery external data sources has become a common choice for large fact tables. There are optimizations that can be done in both Power BI and external sources to avoid hitting limits too quickly.

In the previous chapter, we looked at ways to get performance and usage information from the Power BI service through reports and logs. Through the usage metrics report and some template apps, Microsoft provides tools for analyzing performance data. For **Power BI reports**, we often need to know whether visuals, queries, or combinations thereof are slow. Page view granularity isn't available from the Power BI service in production at the time of writing but there are some new page view measures. However, you can get good performance information in Power BI Desktop with the built-in Performance Analyzer and analyze the queries in DAX Studio.

In *Chapter 2, Exploring Power BI Architecture and Configuration*, we looked at storage modes for Power BI semantic models and learned about **Import**, **DirectQuery**, and **Direct Lake**. In this chapter, we will look specifically at DirectQuery mode with some new information about Direct Lake in Fabric. Power BI reports issue queries in parallel by design. Each user interaction on a report can trigger multiple queries. You can have many users interacting with DirectQuery reports that use the same data source. This potentially high rate of queries to the external source must be taken into consideration when building DirectQuery models. Direct Lake will bank on the proper population of Delta tables in the pipelines, plus maintenance using an optimized function.

We will look at data modeling for DirectQuery models to reduce the chances of overwhelming the data source. You will learn how to avoid Power BI and the data source performing extra processing. You will also learn about the settings available to adjust DirectQuery parallelism. Then, ways to optimize the external data source and leverage its strengths to handle generated traffic will conclude the analysis of DirectQuery performance tuning.

This chapter is broken into the following sections:

- DirectQuery and relationships
- General DirectQuery guidance
- Direct Lake semantic models

DirectQuery and relationships

Data modeling can be thought of very simply as determining which data attributes are grouped into tables, and how those tables connect to one another. Building a DirectQuery data model in Power BI allows you to load table schema metadata and relationships from the data source. If desired, you can also define your own relationships and calculations across any compatible tables and columns.

Calculations in a DirectQuery model are translated to external queries that the data source must handle. You can check the external query that is generated in the **Power Query Editor** by right-clicking on the query step and then choosing **View Native Query**, as shown in *Figure 5.1*:

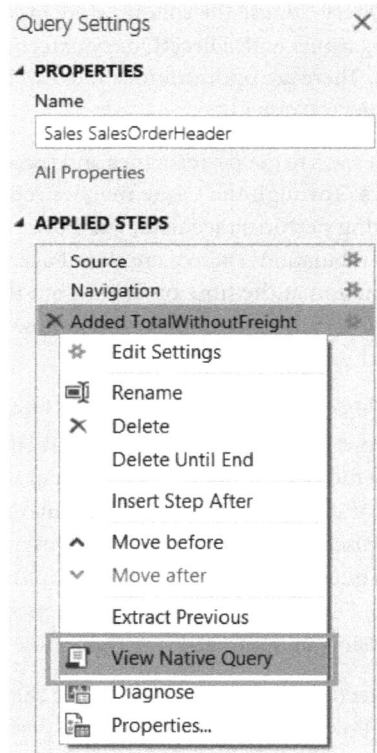

Figure 5.1 – The View Native Query option in Query Settings

You can check the native query to see how Power BI translates your calculation to the data source's native query language to assess whether it might have performance implications. The following example shows the native query for a table where a single calculation was added. The source is a **SQL Server** database and the calculation is a simple subtraction of the two numeric columns – TotalWithoutFreight:

□ ✕

Native Query

```
select [_].[SalesOrderID] as [SalesOrderID],
    [_].[RevisionNumber] as [RevisionNumber],
    [_].[OrderDate] as [OrderDate],
    [_].[DueDate] as [DueDate],
    [_].[ShipDate] as [ShipDate],
    [_].[Status] as [Status],
    [_].[OnlineOrderFlag] as [OnlineOrderFlag],
    [_].[SalesOrderNumber] as [SalesOrderNumber],
    [_].[PurchaseOrderNumber] as [PurchaseOrderNumber],
    [_].[AccountNumber] as [AccountNumber],
    [_].[CustomerID] as [CustomerID],
    [_].[SalesPersonID] as [SalesPersonID],
    [_].[TerritoryID] as [TerritoryID],
    [_].[BillToAddressID] as [BillToAddressID],
    [_].[ShipToAddressID] as [ShipToAddressID],
    [_].[ShipMethodID] as [ShipMethodID],
    [_].[CreditCardID] as [CreditCardID],
    [_].[CreditCardApprovalCode] as [CreditCardApprovalCode],
    [_].[CurrencyRateID] as [CurrencyRateID],
    [_].[SubTotal] as [SubTotal],
    [_].[TaxAmt] as [TaxAmt],
    [_].[Freight] as [Freight],
    [_].[TotalDue] as [TotalDue],
    [_].[Comment] as [Comment],
    [_].[rowguid] as [rowguid],
    [_].[ModifiedDate] as [ModifiedDate],
    [_].[TotalDue] - [_].[Freight] as [TotalWithoutFreight]
from [Sales].[SalesOrderHeader] as [_]
```

OK

Figure 5.2 – Native T-SQL query with a custom calculation

Tip

In DirectQuery mode, keep calculations simple to avoid generating complex queries for the underlying data source. For measures, initially limit them to sum, count, minimum, maximum, and average. Monitor the native queries generated and test the responsiveness before adding more complexity, especially with CALCULATE statements.

If you choose a transformation step in Power Query that is not supported by the **Naïve Query**, you will get a warning and action to convert the semantic model to Import mode – **Switch all tables to Import mode**. This is the only option to apply the added step. The conversion of the data type would need to be done on the data source side, not Power BI, or by converting to Import mode. *Figure 5.3* shows what happens if a column is converted to a different data type that is not supported.

Figure 5.3 – Data type change that is not supported by DirectQuery

Another point to keep in mind is that there does not need to be any physical relationships in the underlying data source to create virtual relationships in the semantic model. **Physical relationships** are created internally by data engineers to optimize joins between tables for common query patterns, so we want Power BI to leverage these whenever possible.

The following figure shows a simple DirectQuery model in Power BI Desktop with an arbitrary relationship created across two **Dimension** tables – **Person** and **Product**.

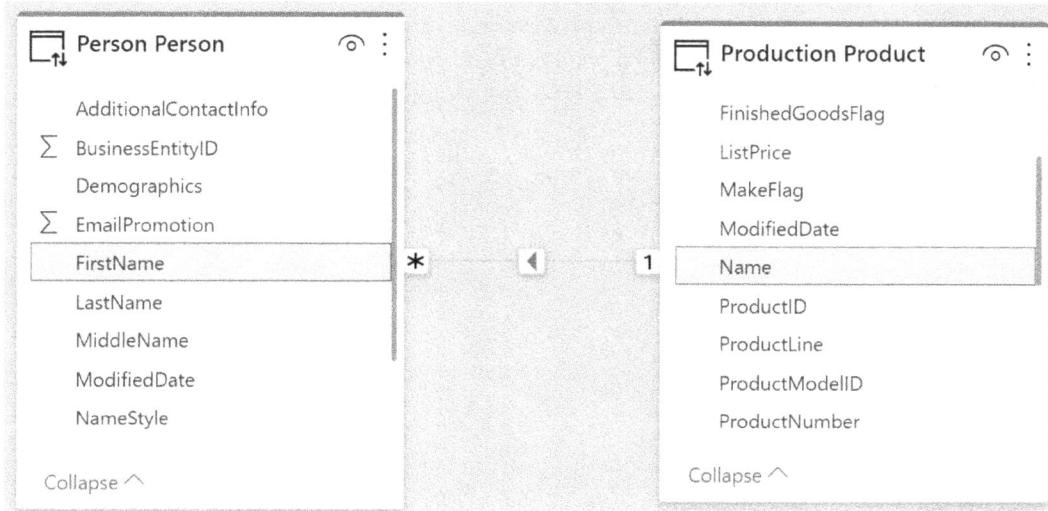

Figure 5.4 – An arbitrary relationship in DirectQuery

This trivial data model, with a single relationship, is simply for the sake of illustration. The point is that it is highly unlikely that the underlying database would have a relationship set up across these tables, and certainly not across those text columns representing the name of products and people. However, when we create such a relationship in Power BI, we are asking the data source or Power BI to perform that join on-demand. This is typically much slower as it cannot take advantage of any existing relationship optimizations at the source.

This was a good example of how the flexibility provided by Power BI can lead to unintended consequences if we do not fully understand the implications of our choices. There will be more of these as we progress through future chapters.

Optimizing DirectQuery relationships

Let's build further on **physical relationships** in the data source. There are likely to be existing **Primary Key** and **Foreign Key** columns with relationships, constraints, and indexes defined at the data source. *Figure 5.5* provides a simple example from a retail sales scenario, where the territory lookup table is related to a sales order table. The `TerritoryID` column in each table is used for the join:

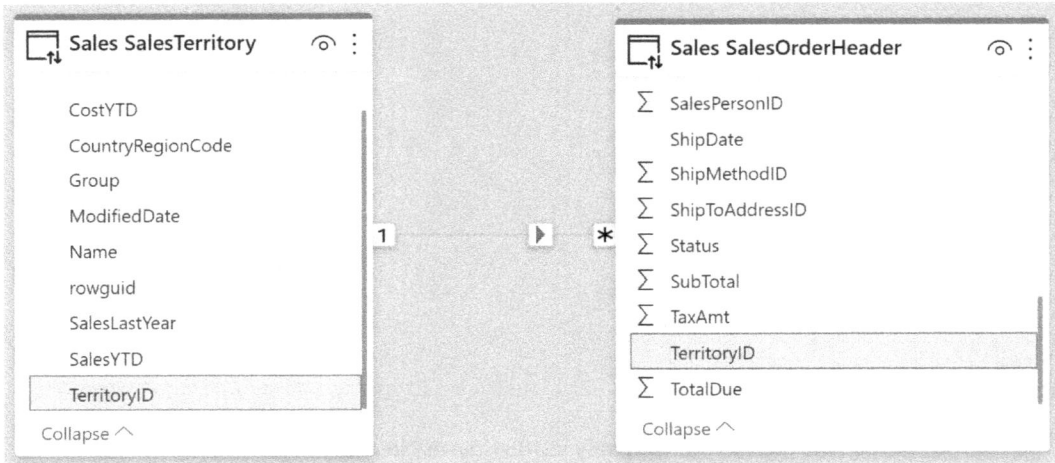

Figure 5.5 – Typical relationship to a lookup table on a numerical identifier

In cases like this, **referential integrity** may be enforced at the source. This means that the `SalesTerritory` table can be considered the master list of territories and that every entry in the `SalesOrderHeader` table must have a corresponding `TerritoryID`. This implies that there cannot be null or empty values for `TerritoryID` in either table. This is a good practice enforced in many database systems, which is important for Power BI because a DirectQuery dataset can issue more efficient queries to the remote data source if you can assume referential integrity.

In database terms, having referential integrity means Power BI can generate an `INNER JOIN` instead of an `OUTER JOIN` when pulling data across more than one table. Referential integrity means a more efficient `INNER JOIN` can be used with a safe assumption that no rows from either table will be excluded due to a failure to match keys. You need to instruct Power BI to do this in the data model for each relevant relationship. *Figure 5.6* shows where to do this in the relationship editor in Power BI Desktop for the sales example we discussed earlier:

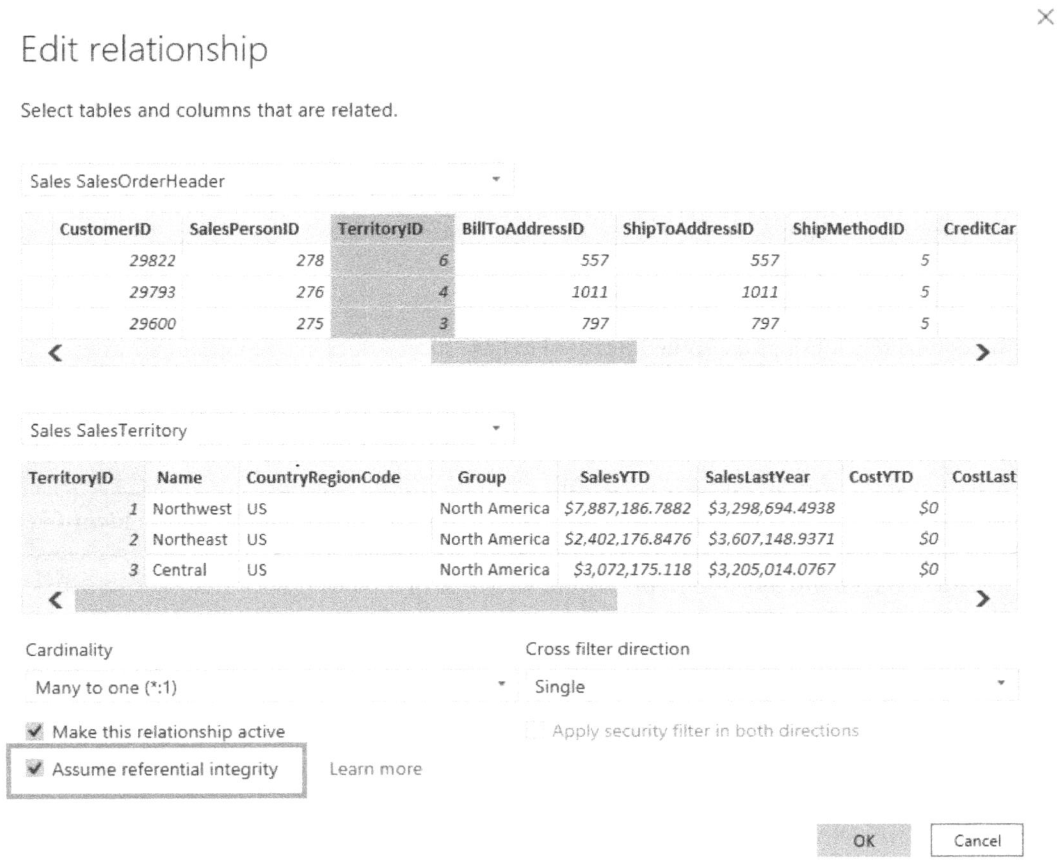

Edit relationship

Select tables and columns that are related.

Sales SalesOrderHeader

CustomerID	SalesPersonID	TerritoryID	BillToAddressID	ShipToAddressID	ShipMethodID	CreditCar
29822	278	6	557	557	5	
29793	276	4	1011	1011	5	
29600	275	3	797	797	5	

Sales SalesTerritory

TerritoryID	Name	CountryRegionCode	Group	SalesYTD	SalesLastYear	CostYTD	CostLast
1	Northwest	US	North America	$7,887,186.7882	$3,298,694.4938	$0	
2	Northeast	US	North America	$2,402,176.8476	$3,607,148.9371	$0	
3	Central	US	North America	$3,072,175.118	$3,205,014.0767	$0	

Cardinality

Many to one (*:1)

Cross filter direction

Single

☑ Make this relationship active

☐ Apply security filter in both directions

☑ Assume referential integrity   Learn more

OK   Cancel

Figure 5.6 – Setting referential integrity for a DirectQuery relationship

Another convenience provided by Power BI is the ability to define calculated columns, which also works for DirectQuery tables. Power BI supports building relationships using a single column from each table. However, occasionally, when data modeling, it may be necessary to use a combination of columns to uniquely identify some entities. A simple modeling technique to address this is to introduce a calculated column to concatenate the relevant columns into a unique key. This key column is then used to build relationships in the semantic model. Relationships across calculated columns are not as efficient as those across physical columns. This is especially true for DirectQuery.

> **Note**
>
> In DirectQuery mode, avoid creating relationships using calculated columns. This join may not be pushed down to the source and may require additional processing in Power BI. When possible, use COMBINEVALUES() to create concatenated columns because it is specifically optimized for DirectQuery relationships.

Two more aspects of relationships to consider are **Cardinality** and **Cross filter direction** (as seen in *Figure 5.6*). A cardinality setting of **Many-to-Many** will disable the referential integrity setting and might result in less efficient queries if the data does in fact support a **One-to-Many** relationship instead. Similarly, having a **Cross filter direction** set to **Both** (sometimes called a **bi-directional relationship**) could result in additional queries to the data source. This is because more tables are affected by minor report actions such as slicer changes, as the filter effect needs to be cascaded across relationships in more tables.

Tip

Bi-directional relationships are sometimes used to have slicer values in a report update as the filter state of the report changes. Consider using a measure filter on the slicer visual to achieve the same effect. Continuing with our sales scenario as an example, this technique could be used to only show values in a report slicer if the product did have some sales.

The final piece of advice on relationships in DirectQuery concerns the **Globally Unique Identifier** (**GUID**) or slightly differently defined **Universally Unique Identifier** (**UUID**). These are represented by 32 hexadecimal characters and hyphens. An example of a GUID is `123e4567-e89b-12d3-a456-426614174000`. They can be used to uniquely identify a record in a data store and are often found in Microsoft products and services.

Tip

Avoid creating relationships on GUID columns in DirectQuery. Power BI does not natively support this data type and needs to convert the data type when joining. Consider adding a materialized text column or integer surrogate key in the data store instead and use those to define a relationship.

In the next section, we will look at configuration and data source optimization that can benefit DirectQuery.

General DirectQuery guidance

There are a few settings that can be adjusted in Power BI to speed up DirectQuery semantic models. We will explore these next.

Power BI Desktop settings

In the Power BI Desktop options, there is a section called DirectQuery under the **CURRENT FILE** main menu. This option is only available if the semantic model has a DirectQuery connection. It will not appear otherwise. *Figure 5.7* shows a highlighted option for the setting that controls how many connections per data source can be made in parallel. The default is 10. This means, no matter how many visuals are in a report or how many users are accessing the report in parallel, only 10 connections at a time will be made.

If the data source can handle more parallelism, it is recommended to increase this value before publishing the semantic model to the Power BI service. However, with very busy data sources, you may find the overall performance can improve by *reducing* the value instead. This is because too many parallel queries can overwhelm the source and result in a longer total execution time. A lower value means some queries will have to wait and be issued a little later, giving the data source some breathing room.

This option to lower or raise the parallelism would need to be discussed and tested with an administrator of the source system such as a SQL Server system and the database administrator(s).

> **Important note**
>
> Power BI Desktop will allow you to enter large numbers for the **Maximum connections** setting. However, there are hard limits defined in the Power BI service that can differ depending on whether you are using a Premium capacity and what size your capacity is. These limits can change and are not publicly documented, so it is recommended to contact Microsoft Support to learn more about your scenario.

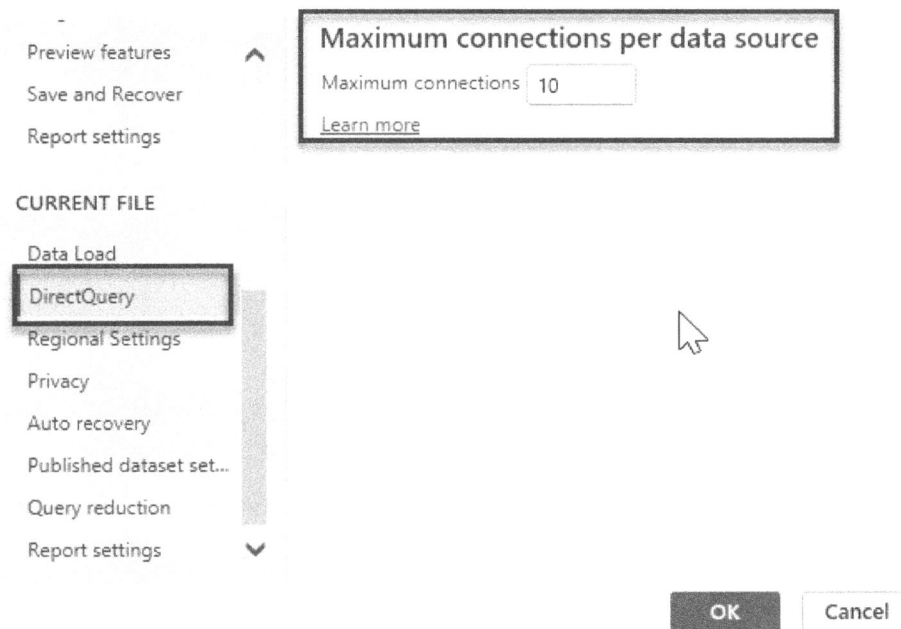

Figure 5.7 – Maximum connections per data source setting

Another useful section of Power BI Desktop options that can benefit DirectQuery is **Query reduction** (as shown in *Figure 5.8*). The figure reflects the default setting, which means that Power BI will issue queries to update visuals for every filter or slicer change a user makes in a report. This keeps the experience highly interactive but can have undesired effects with DirectQuery sources that are busy or not optimized, and with reports that have complex underlying queries. This is because the data source may not even have finished processing queries for the first filter or slicer change when the user makes further changes, which issues even more queries.

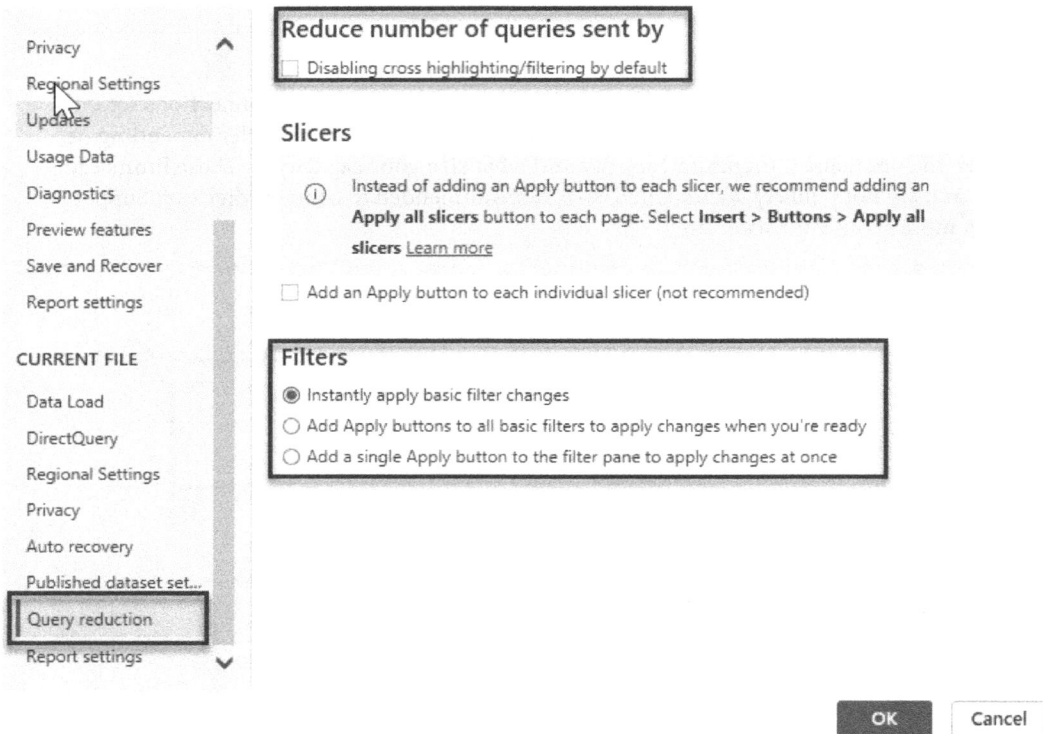

Figure 5.8 – Query reduction settings

The query reduction settings allow you to add **Apply** buttons for slicers and filters. This allows the user to make multiple selections before applying changes, so only a single set of queries will be sent. The report snippet in *Figure 5.9* shows a single slicer and the filter pane of a report after the query reduction settings have been applied:

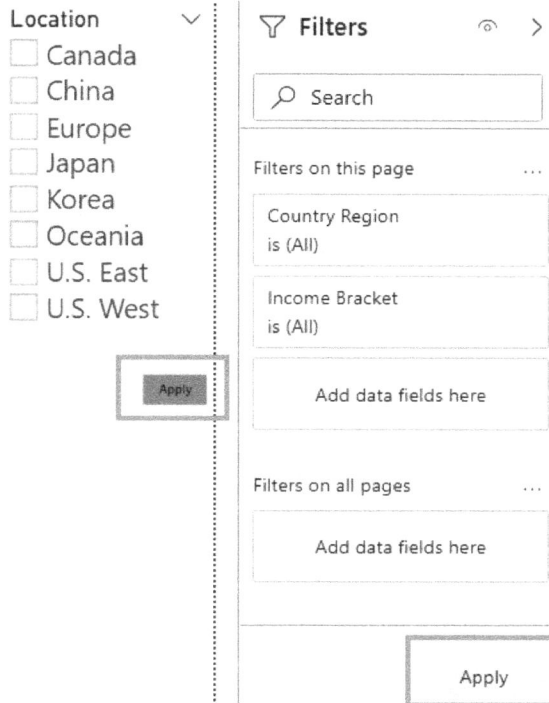

Figure 5.9 – Apply buttons added to slicers and filters

> **Note**
>
> It is no longer recommended to place a single **Apply** button on slicers. The recommended option is to add an **Apply all slicers** button on the page of a report. This option is in the **Insert** ribbon on the desktop. This suggestion is explained in the **Options** settings in *Figure 5.8*. Click the **Learn more** link for details. This is only for slicers and is not a suggestion for filters.

Next, let's look at how you can optimize the external data source to perform better in DirectQuery scenarios.

Optimizing external data sources

We have learned that DirectQuery semantic models can perform slower than import semantic models because the external source might not be designed to handle workloads from business intelligence tools.

Regardless of what technology is powering the external data source, there are some common practices that apply to many storage systems that you should consider implementing to speed up queries for Power BI. These are as follows:

- **Indexes**: An index provides a database with an easy way to find specific records for operations such as filtering and joining. Consider implementing covering indexes on columns that you use for Power BI relationships and displays or that are often used in report filters or slicers to limit data. Using the Performance Analyzer to see native queries sent to data sources can be beneficial in determining the proper index.

- **Column storage technology**: Modern data storage platforms allow you to define special indexes that use column storage instead of typical row storage principles. This can speed up aggregate queries in Power BI semantic models. Try to define indexes using columns that are often retrieved together for summaries in reports that are usually fact tables that have measures in Power BI.

- **Materialized views**: A materialized view is essentially a query whose results are pre-computed and physically stored, such as a regular table of data. SQL Server calls these views **Indexed Views**. Whenever the base data changes, the materialized view is updated to reflect the current state. You can move transformations to a materialized view in the data source instead of defining them in the Power BI semantic model. The source will have the key results ready for Power BI to consume. This works well with data that does not change very frequently. Be aware that too many materialized views can have a performance impact on the source, as it must continually keep them up to date. Over-indexing can start to reduce performance gains as well.

- **In-memory databases**: One reason import mode semantic models can perform so well is that all data is in-memory instead of slower disk storage. The DirectQuery source system may have its own in-memory capabilities that could be leveraged for Power BI.

- **Read-only replicas**: Consider creating a read-only replica of your source system dedicated to Power BI semantic models. This can be optimized for Power BI traffic independently of the original data source. It can even be synchronized periodically as a real-time replica is not necessary, which can improve performance further.

- **Scaling up/out**: You may be able to increase the power of the source system by giving it more computing and memory resources and distributing the load across multiple servers, or do so to better handle complex parallel queries. The latter is a common pattern in *Big Data* systems.

- **Maintaining database statistics**: Modern relational database systems use internal statistics to help the internal query optimizer pick the best query plan. These statistics need to be maintained regularly to ensure the optimizer is not making decisions based on incorrect cardinality and row counts. Check with the database administrator about the schedule and rules for updating statistics.

You will need to understand what queries Power BI is sending to the external data source before you can decide what optimizations will provide the best return on investment. In *Chapter 4, Analyzing Logs and Metrics*, and *Chapter 3, Learning the Tools for Performance Tuning*, you learned how to capture these queries from Power BI Desktop and the Power BI service. You also used query logging and tracing in the external source to do this, which is more typical in production scenarios where reports are published to the service.

As mentioned about scaling up/out above, the next section will look at the simplification of big data with Fabric's implementation of Delta tables, using Parquet files to help with performance in Lakehouse deployments.

Direct Lake semantic models

Microsoft Fabric introduced a new semantic model called Direct Lake. This semantic model is built in the Fabric (Power BI) service under a lakehouse or warehouse artifact. The warehouse structure is for those familiar with T-SQL and the lakehouse is for those developers using code such as Python in notebooks for ETL implementations. Both create and support what are called Delta tables. The best resource for understanding the properties of Delta tables is from Databricks: (`https://docs.databricks.com/en/delta/index.html`).

Using Delta tables in Fabric

Delta tables can be created and populated in Fabric or used in Fabric as a shortcut. Inside a warehouse or lakehouse, Delta tables can be linked to the Fabric artifact through a pointer in Fabric called a shortcut rather than to the files or table structure. *Figure 5.10* shows the Delta Table and shortcut (two types), which have different icons.

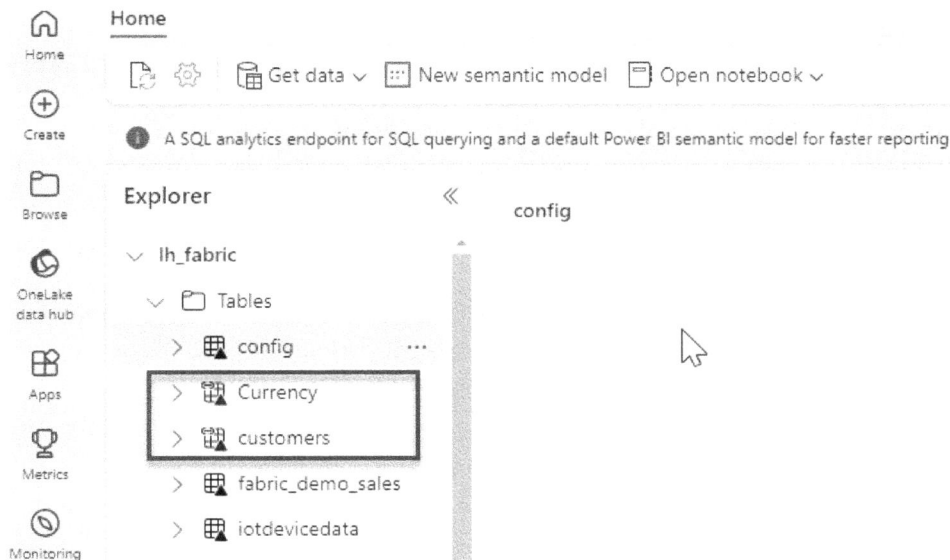

Figure 5.10 – Shortcut icon for tables

Though Delta tables are a new technology, Microsoft has taken the complexity out of using these new structures and provides methods to create and write to them as well as connect to them like you are connecting to SQL Server tables (server-less). These tables are then made into a semantic model like DirectQuery but with performance closer to Import mode.

The **Parquet** file structure is a column-store compressed format. This is like the column store compressed in the memory of an import model. The difference is Direct Lake has no import or refresh requirement, thus reducing the requirement for refreshes and making current data available for reports. The data is drawn from the Data Lake storage of the underlying files.

The following are observations for using Direct Lake:

- Used for large datasets, usually exceeding 5 GB when in the model

- ETL development to understand column store structures

- Existing Delta Tables created in other systems such as Databricks or Synapse

- Understanding and using dimensional modeling for table structures

- Allows you to take advantage of V-Order on Delta Tables: `https://learn.microsoft.com/en-us/fabric/data-engineering/delta-optimization-and-v-order?tabs=sparksql`

Dimensional modeling is discussed in *Chapter 10, Data Modeling and Row-Level Security*.

On-demand loading

On-demand loading takes only the data needed for a query and loads it in memory on demand. This in turn makes Direct Lake faster than DirectQuery. The structure of Direct Lake data is backed by a Data Lake storage system that spreads the data in a way that Big Data systems support. The data returned from the Parquet structure has the column store compressed data needed for Power BI semantic model structures.

On-demand loading was introduced back in 2012 for semantic models that get evicted from memory because of a lack of use and memory needs for other semantic models or DAX queries. This was just an Import mode feature but has been utilized for Direct Lake. To track the usage of on-demand loading, look at the `IsPageable`, `IsResident`, `Temperature`, and `Last Assessed` columns in DMV `SYSTEMRESTRICSCHEMA`. The following is a query looking at usage for a semantic model, `ContosoDW-DevOneLake`:

```
Select COLUMN_ID, SEGMENT_NUMBER, ISPAGEABLE, ISRESIDENT, TEMPERATURE,
LAST_ACCESSED
   from SYSTEMRESTRICTSCHEMA($System.DISCOVER_STORAGE_TABLE_COLUMN_
SEGMENTS, [DATABASE_NAME] = 'ContosoDW-DevOneLake')
```

On-demand loading is automatically enabled for any Premium or Fabric capacity. It requires a large model enabled on the semantic model. If you want suggestions for running a performance test on Direct Lake, please see this article: `https://blog.crossjoin.co.uk/2023/07/09/performance-testing-power-bi-direct-lake-mode-datasets-in-fabric/`.

Let's now review the key learnings for DirectQuery and Direct Lake semantic models before we move on to discuss the sources of performance metrics available in Power BI.

Summary

In this chapter, we defined basic data modeling as a process where you choose which data attributes are grouped into entities and how they are related. We learned that for DirectQuery and Direct Lake, transformations in Power Query should be kept simple to avoid generating overly complex query statements. We also learned how to use the native query viewing feature in Power Query to see the exact query used.

The chapter explained that Power BI is flexible enough to allow you to define your own relationships across DirectQuery tables, not necessarily matching those already in the data source. This must be done with care and some planning. It is better to leverage relationships and referential integrity that are already defined in the external data source where possible, as these are likely already optimized. We also explored relationship settings and their implications for DirectQuery.

We explored settings in Power BI Desktop that help control levels of parallelism. The optimization of data source systems was explained for optimization and scaling that can be used with DirectQuery semantic models. These external optimizations may require collaboration with database administrators to implement them. We concluded by introducing the latest Fabric implementation of Direct Lake in a lakehouse (or warehouse). This implementation of Delta tables with a Parquet file backend is the future for Data Lakes in Power BI.

In the next chapter, we will look at freely available third-party utilities that complement the Performance Analyzer and help you optimize your report, data model, and DAX queries.

6

Third-Party Utilities

In the previous chapters, we used tools and data provided by Microsoft to get insights into report performance. In this chapter, we will cover some popular freely available third-party utilities that complement the built-in offerings and improve productivity when investigating report performance issues.

These tools have a range of features, such as documenting our solutions, analyzing them to give recommendations, the ability to modify object properties, capturing performance traces, and running queries. It is beyond the scope of this book to cover the full functionality of these tools, so we will limit our coverage to features and techniques that help us assess and improve performance.

The utilities introduced in this chapter are largely maintained by community contributors and are often open source. All the utilities described in this chapter are widely used to the point where they are formally acknowledged by Microsoft. Power BI Desktop will recognize them if they are installed on your computer and allow you to launch them from its **External Tools** menu, sometimes even connected to the `.pbix` file you are working on. At the time of writing, these utilities are actively maintained, and the releases are generally of high quality.

However, while the development of these open-source tools is often stewarded by experts who run their own Power BI consulting and training businesses, they are not always officially supported, so you should bear this in mind. Your organization may not be able to get prompt dedicated assistance as you normally would with a support case for a paid commercial offering.

All utilities in this chapter can connect to Analysis Services semantic models running within Power BI Desktop, Azure Analysis Services, or the Power BI service. Therefore, we will simply refer to these tools connecting to Analysis Services semantic models for most of the chapter.

This chapter is broken into the following sections:

- Exploring Power BI Helper
- Working with Tabular Editor
- Tuning with DAX Studio and VertiPaq Analyzer

Technical requirements

There are samples available for some parts of this chapter. We will call out which files to refer to. Please check out the `Chapter06` folder on GitHub to get these assets: `https://github.com/PacktPublishing/Microsoft-Power-BI-Performance-Best-Practices-Second-Edition`.

Exploring Power BI Helper

Power BI Helper has a range of features that help you explore, document, and compare local Power BI Desktop files. It also lets you explore and export metadata from the Power BI service, such as lists of workspaces and semantic models plus their properties. Power BI Helper can be downloaded from the following link: `https://powerbihelper.org` and is hosted by **RADACAD**. RADACAD is a consulting company out of New Zealand that has a wealth of Power BI information online at `https://radacad.com/`.

In previous chapters, we discussed how important it is to keep Power BI semantic models smaller by removing unused tables and columns. Power BI Helper includes features to help you find these unused objects, so it could be a useful tool to incorporate into standard optimization processes before production releases.

Identifying large column dictionaries

In general, having a smaller model speeds up report loads and data refreshes, which is why it is good to be able to identify the largest items easily. For now, we simply want to introduce this capability so you are aware of this technique. We will learn about semantic model size reduction in detail in *Chapter 10, Data Modeling and Row-Level Security*. Complete the following steps to investigate the dictionary size of columns in a semantic model:

1. Open your `.pbix` file in Power BI Desktop, then connect Power BI Helper to the semantic model.
2. Navigate to the **Modeling Advise** tab.
3. Observe how Power BI Helper lists all columns sorted by their dictionary size from largest to smallest.

The **dictionary size** is how much space Power BI must reserve for unique possibilities in a column. It is not the total size a column uses but helps identify those columns that have a wide range of values referred to as **cardinality**. *Figure 6.1* shows the result of this tab:

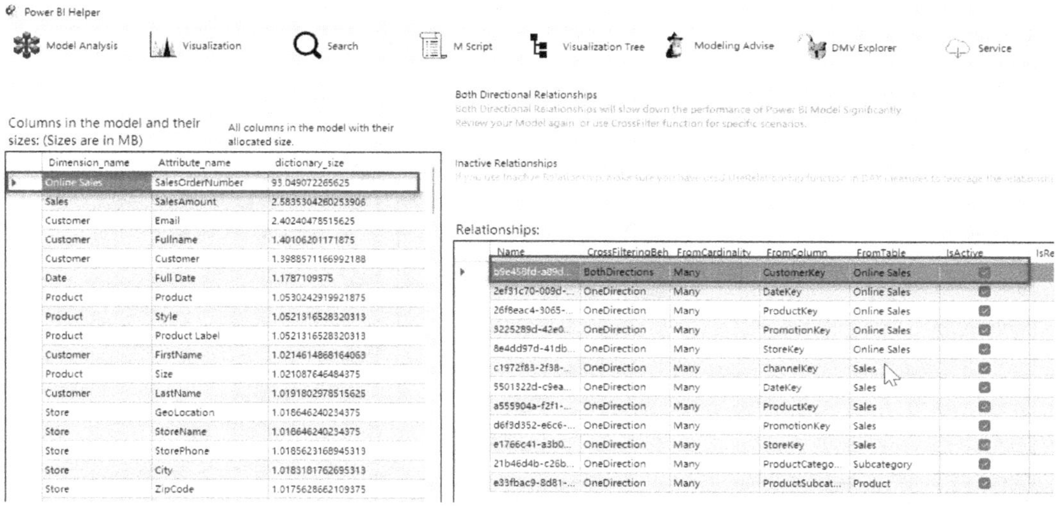

Figure 6.1 – The Modeling Advise tab showing the largest column

In this example, the `SalesOrderNumber` column (referred to as an **attribute**) takes about 93 MB. The `.pbix` file was 400+ MB. From these sizes, we can calculate that this one column's dictionary contributes to about 25% of the file size, which is significant. If this column is not being used, it can be removed. The column data type is text and since it is an identifier of the sales, there are not many duplicate values which makes Power BI use a dictionary to store the unique values. **Dictionaries** are a feature of the VertiPaq engine for storage. If you need it for reporting, relationships, or calculation purposes, try optimizing it using techniques from *Chapter 10, Data Modeling and Row-Level Security*.

> **Tip**
>
> A Power BI Desktop file in Import mode contains a complete copy of the source data. The data is contained within the `.pbix` file as an Analysis Services backup file (`.abf`). Even though the `.pbix` file size is not the same as the size of the semantic model when it is loaded into memory, it can be used for a quick approximation to judge the impact of column and table sizes on the overall size.

Identifying unused columns

Power BI Helper can identify all the unused columns in your model. You simply navigate to the **Visualization** tab and observe them in a list. You can remove them from the semantic model by right-clicking the items and selecting **Delete**. This is shown in *Figure 6.2* at the bottom right:

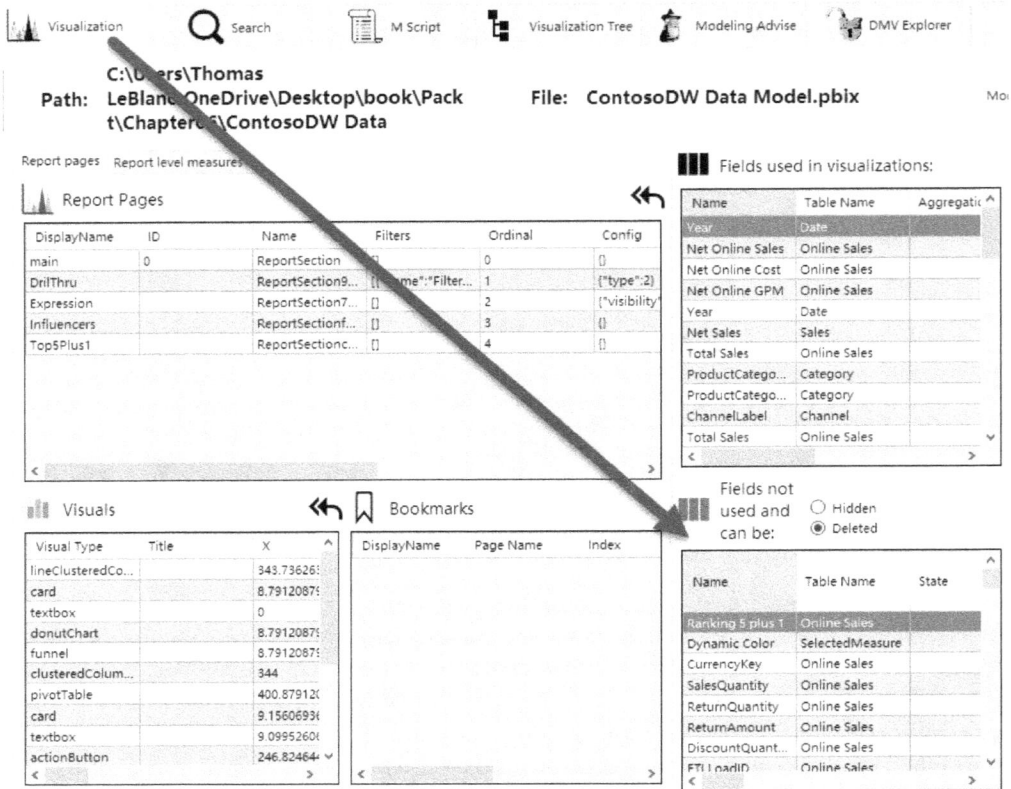

Figure 6.2 – Deleting unused columns from Power BI Helper

Note that any changes applied in Power BI Helper will be applied to the .pbix file you have open. By default, Power BI Helper will back up your original file to the location specified at the top left, as shown in the previous figure. It is recommended to use this backup feature to recover from accidental deletions.

> **Caution**
>
> This feature will only identify columns not used in the current .pbix file. If you are using the semantic model to source the data to multiple .pbix files as reports, then you should not use this feature because the columns could be used in other .pbix files or service-created reports.

Identifying bidirectional and inactive relationships

The **Modeling Advise** tab referred to in *Figure 6.1* has a relationship section on the right-hand side. You can use this to conveniently identify all bidirectional relationships in your semantic model. These can slow down queries and might have unintentional filter consequences, so it's a good idea to review each one to ensure it is really needed.

Identifying measure dependencies

Power BI Helper visualizes measure dependencies via the **Model Analysis** tab. Measures can be used within other measures, and this is the best practice for maintainability. In a chain of measure dependencies, the start of the chain is often referred to as the **base measure**. The following figure shows the measure, dependencies, and **reverse dependency tree**.

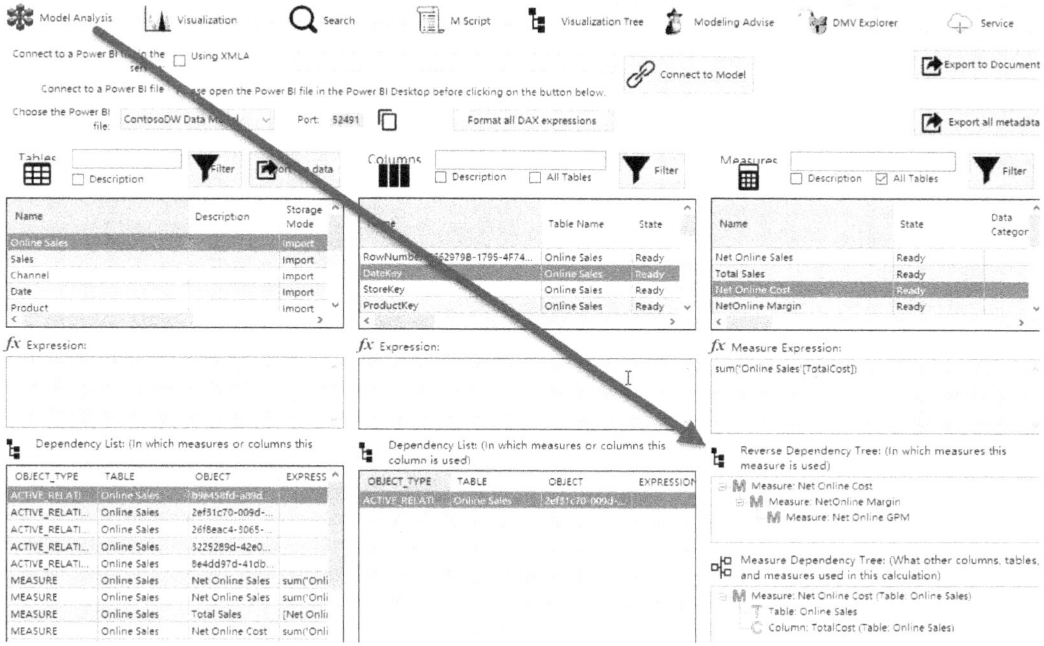

Figure 6.3 – Measure dependencies in Power BI Helper

Base measures may be used in many other measures and Power BI Helper lets you easily identify all those reserve dependencies. You can use this information to get a better return on investment when performance tuning because optimizing base measures that are used in many other measures could have a large overall impact. Conversely, you may have a complex measure that uses many other measures. In this case, Power BI Helper helps you identify all the measures it uses so you know which to consider when optimizing.

We have seen how Power BI Helper can help us identify a few common semantic model design issues. Next, we will look at Tabular Editor, another free (as well as paid version) tool that can go in more depth into semantic model design guidance.

Working with Tabular Editor

Tabular Editor is available as both a commercial offering (3.x) and an open-source version. The paid version offers some advanced development functionality and even dedicated support, which professional Power BI developers may find useful. The good news is that the free version (2.x) contains all the useful core features at the time of this writing, and it can be downloaded at the following GitHub link: `https://github.com/TabularEditor/TabularEditor`.

Tabular Editor is a productivity tool aimed at improving many aspects of the development experience offered by Power BI Desktop or Microsoft Visual Studio. These core features are beyond the scope of this book. Due to the sheer popularity of the tool with experienced business intelligence developers, you are encouraged to learn more about Tabular Editor if you expect to build and maintain complex enterprise models over many months or even years. Please follow the product documentation to become familiar with the interface and functionality of Tabular Editor. We are going to focus on a specific feature of Tabular Editor called the **Best Practice Analyzer** (**BPA**).

Using Tabular Editor's Best Practice Analyzer

Tabular Editor has a powerful extension called the **BPA**. This extension lets you define a set of modeling rules that can be saved as collections. An example of a rule is to avoid using floating-point data types for numerical columns. Once you have a set of rules defined, you can use the BPA to scan a semantic model. BPA comes with a default set of common rules. It will check all objects against applicable modeling rules and generate a report in the process.

After you have installed Tabular Editor, open the **Tools** menu. Here, you will find the option to launch the BPA and manage its rules, as shown in the following figure:

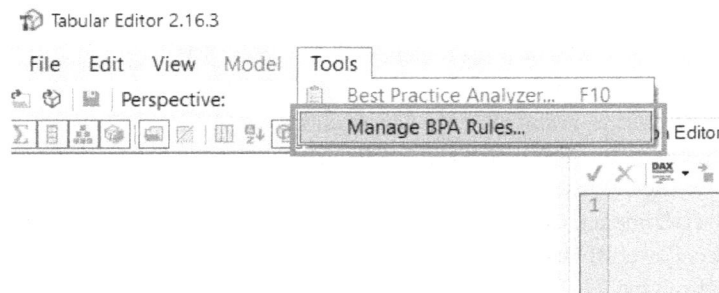

Figure 6.4 – Managing BPA rules in Tabular Editor

If this is the first time you are using Tabular Editor, you will find that there are no rules selected yet. The best way to start is to use a default set of best practices that Microsoft helped define, and you need to perform some brief manual steps to load in some default rules. For reference, you can find the rules included within the Tabular Editor project on GitHub at `https://github.com/TabularEditor/BestPracticeRules`.

To install the rules, you simply copy the `BPARules.json` file found at the previous link into the `%localappdata%\TabularEditor` folder on your computer. You can paste this exact location into Windows File Explorer to get to the appropriate place.

Once you have the rules loaded, you can view, modify, and add rules as you please. *Figure 6.5* shows what the interface looks like after the rules are imported:

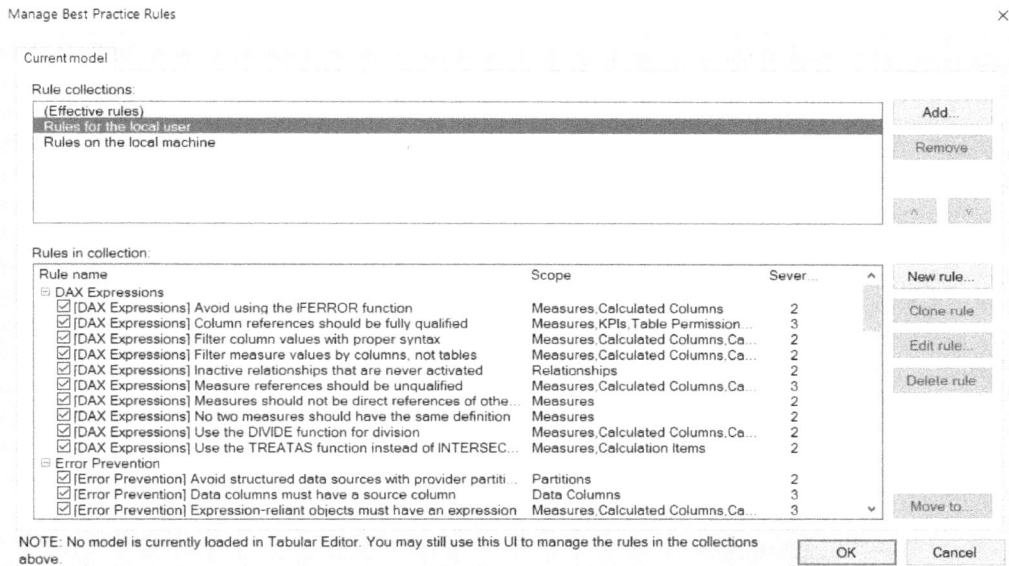

Figure 6.5 – BPA rules loaded into Tabular Editor

The following screenshot shows the rule editor, after opening an existing rule:

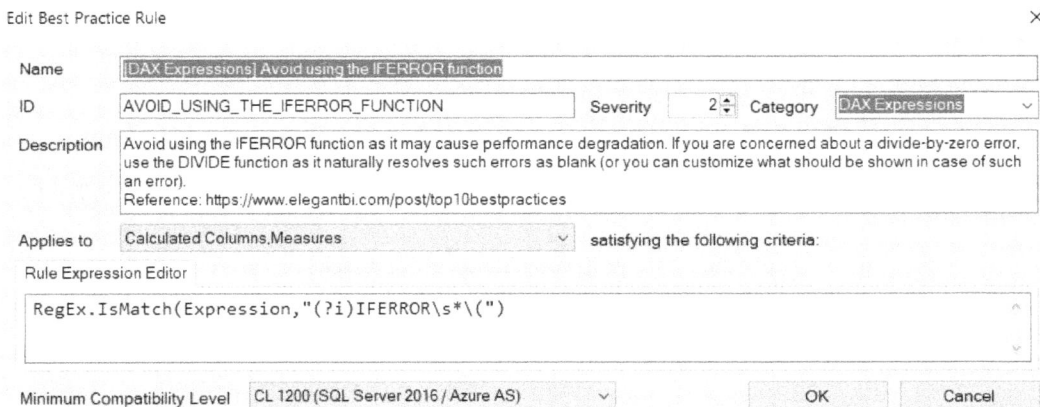

Figure 6.6 – Editing a best practice rule from BPA

When you want to run the BPA rules against your semantic model, connect to it using one of the supported methods in Tabular Editor. Once connected, run the BPA by pressing *F10* or by selecting it from the **Tools** menu, which was introduced in *Figure 6.4*.

A sample of results that can be obtained from running the BPA on a semantic model is shown in the following figure. Highlighted under the **Best Practice Analyzer** title bar are useful toolbar buttons.

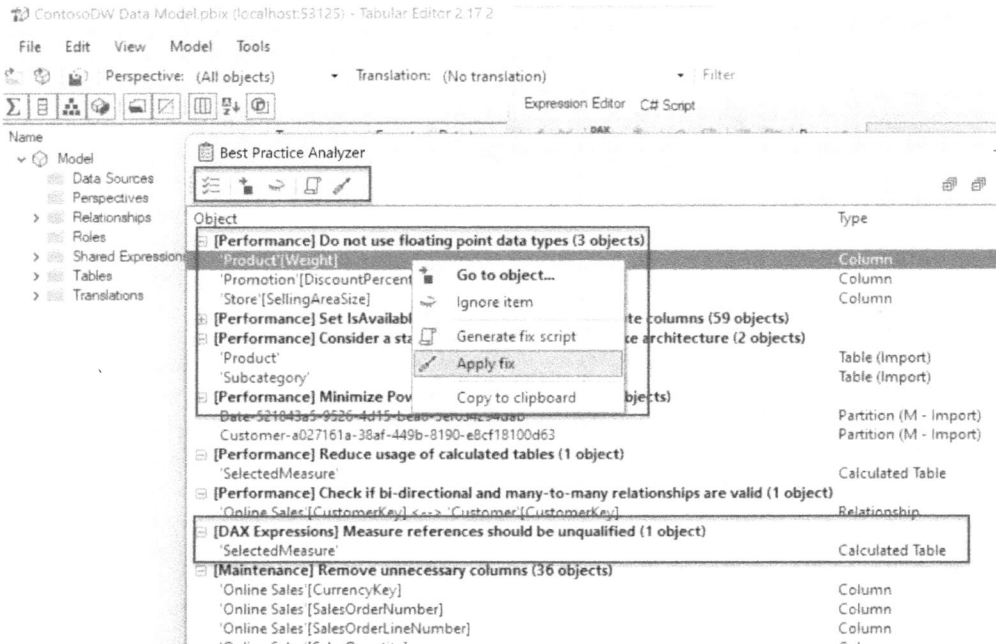

Figure 6.7 – BPA results, highlighting context-sensitive toolbar actions

Those options are as follows:

- **Go to object…**: This will open the model script at the definition of the offending object.

- **Generate fix script**: This will generate a script you can use to apply the change and copy it to the clipboard.

- **Apply fix**: This will apply the fix script to your model immediately. Be careful with this option and make sure you have a backup in place beforehand or use source control for versioning.

The other highlighted areas are as follows:

- **Performance**: Do not use floating point data types

- **DAX Expressions**: Measure references should be unqualified

Once you have the BPA results, you need to decide which changes to apply. It might seem like a great idea to simply apply all changes automatically. However, we advise a careful review of the results and applying some thought to which recommendations to apply and in what order.

> **Note**
>
> Tabular Editor can connect to a locally opened Power BI `.pbix` file as well as a semantic model deployed to the Power BI server or Analysis Services. There are also options to connect to a model `.bim` file (from developing in Visual Studio) or a folder structure with `.json` files. Please be aware of what connection was used because saving changes from the BPA will update this connection's semantic model.

The default BPA rules are grouped into six categories:

- DAX Expressions
- Error Prevention
- Formatting
- Maintenance
- Naming Conventions
- Performance

For performance optimization, we advise focusing on the **Performance** and **DAX Expressions** categories. These optimizations have a direct impact on the query and refresh performance. The other categories benefit usability and maintenance. Changes suggested by BPA will be more discussed in *Chapter 11, Improving DAX,* and *Chapter 10, Data Modeling and Row-Level Security*

> **Tip**
>
> The best way to be certain that performance optimizations have had the expected impact is to test the effect of each change in typical usage scenarios. For example, if you plan to optimize three independent DAX measures, change one at a time and check the improvement you get with each change. Then, check again with all changes applied. This will help you identify the most impactful change and not assume that every change will result in a measurable difference when stacked with others. This will also help you learn the relative impact of design patterns, so you know what to look for first next time around to get the best return on investment when optimizing designs.

Thus far, we have been introduced to some utilities that help us identify semantic model design issues.

Next, we will look at DAX Studio and VertiPaq Analyzer. These are complementary tools that give us more information and help us debug and resolve model and DAX performance issues, with the ability to customize DAX queries and measure their speed.

Tuning with DAX Studio and VertiPaq Analyser

DAX Studio, as the name implies, is a tool centered on DAX queries. It provides a simple yet intuitive interface with powerful features to browse and query Analysis Services semantic models. We will cover querying later in this section. For now, let's look deeper into semantic models.

The Analysis Services engine has supported **dynamic management views** (**DMVs**) for over a decade. These views refer to SQL-like queries that can be executed on Analysis Services to return information about semantic model objects and operations.

VertiPaq Analyzer is a utility that uses publicly documented DMVs to display essential information about which structures exist inside the semantic model and how much space they occupy. It started life as a standalone utility, published as a Power Pivot for an Excel workbook, and still exists in that form today. In this chapter, we will refer to its more recent incarnation as a built-in feature of DAX Studio 3.0.11.

It is interesting to note that VertiPaq is the original name given to the compressed column store engine within Analysis Services (**Verti** referring to columns and **Paq** referring to compression).

Analyzing model size with VertiPaq Analyzer

VertiPaq Analyzer is built into DAX Studio as the **View Metrics** features, found in the **Advanced** tab of the toolbar. You simply click the icon to have DAX Studio run the DMVs for you and display statistics in a tabular form. This is shown in the following figure:

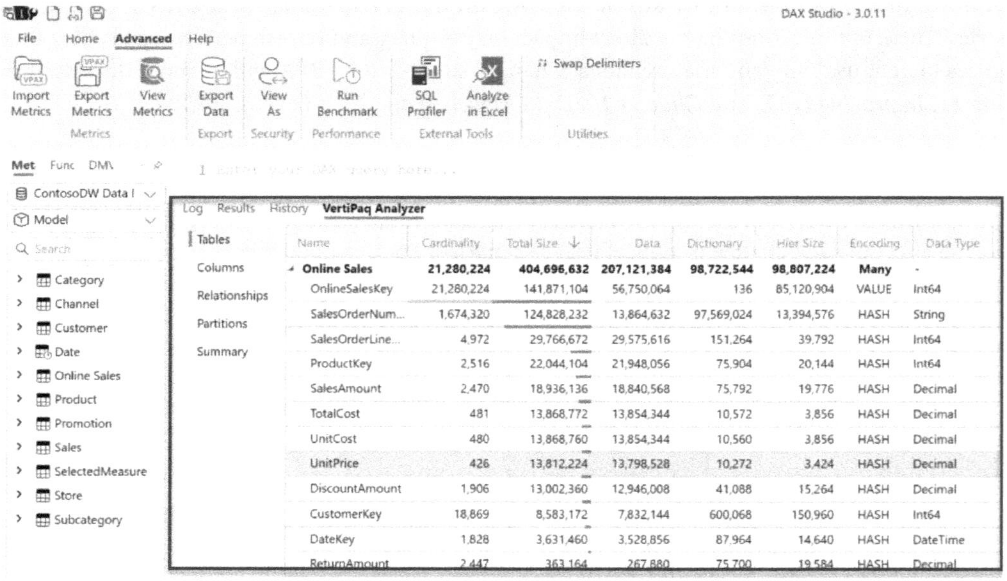

Figure 6.8 – Using View Metrics to generate VertiPaq Analyzer stats

You can switch to the **Summary** tab of the **VertiPaq Analyzer** pane to get an idea of the overall total size of the model along with other summary statistics, as shown in the following figure:

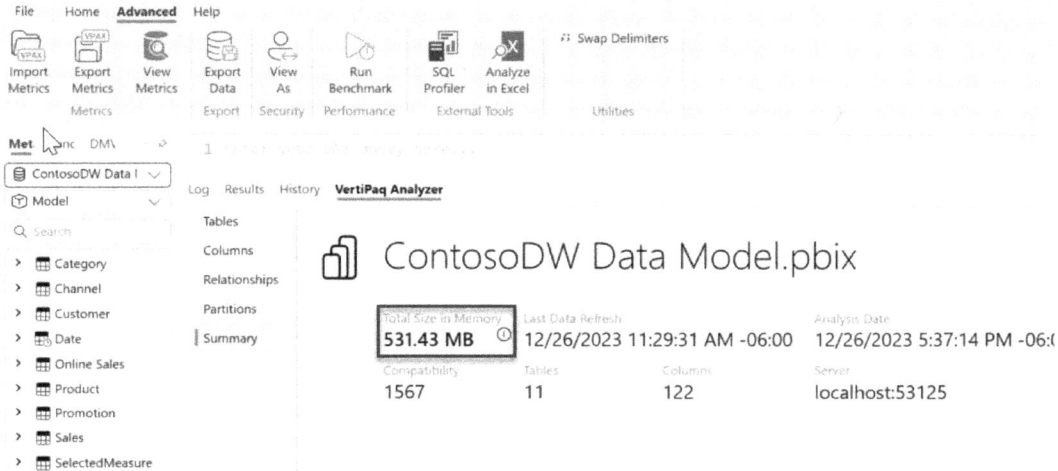

Figure 6.9 – Summary tab of VertiPaq Analyzer

The **Total Size** metric provided in the previous figure will often be larger than the size of the semantic model on disk (as a `.pbix` file or Analysis Services `.abf` backup). This is because there are additional structures required when the model is loaded into memory, which is particularly true of Import mode semantic models.

In *Chapter 2, Exploring Power BI Architecture and Configuration*, we learned about Power BI's compressed column storage engine. The DMV statistics provided by VertiPaq Analyzer let us see just how compressible columns are and how much space they are taking up. It also allows us to observe other objects, such as relationships.

The **Columns** tab is a great way to see whether you have any columns that are very large relative to others or the entire dataset. The following figure shows the columns view for the same model we saw in *Figure 6.9*. You can see how from 238 columns, a single column called `SalesOrderNumber` takes up a staggering 22.40% of the whole model size! It's interesting to see its **Cardinality** (or uniqueness) value is about twelve times lower than the next largest column (`SalesKey`):

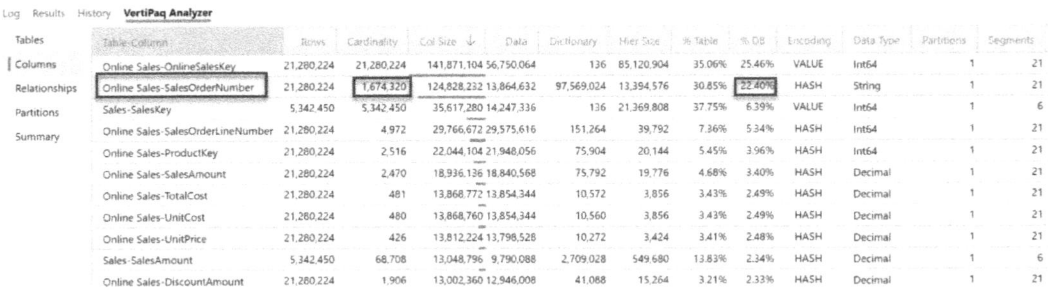

Table-Column	Rows	Cardinality	Col Size ↓	Data	Dictionary	Hier Size	% Table	% DB	Encoding	Data Type	Partitions	Segments
Online Sales-OnlineSalesKey	21,280,224	21,280,224	141,871,104	56,750,064	136	85,120,904	35.06%	25.46%	VALUE	Int64	1	21
Online Sales-SalesOrderNumber	21,280,224	1,674,320	124,828,232	13,864,632	97,569,024	13,394,576	30.85%	22.40%	HASH	String	1	21
Sales-SalesKey	5,342,450	5,342,450	35,617,280	14,247,336	136	21,369,808	37.75%	6.39%	VALUE	Int64	1	6
Online Sales-SalesOrderLineNumber	21,280,224	4,972	29,766,672	29,575,616	151,264	39,792	7.36%	5.34%	HASH	Int64	1	21
Online Sales-ProductKey	21,280,224	2,516	22,044,104	21,948,056	75,904	20,144	5.45%	3.96%	HASH	Int64	1	21
Online Sales-SalesAmount	21,280,224	2,470	18,936,136	18,840,568	75,792	19,776	4.68%	3.40%	HASH	Decimal	1	21
Online Sales-TotalCost	21,280,224	481	13,868,772	13,854,344	10,572	3,856	3.43%	2.49%	HASH	Decimal	1	21
Online Sales-UnitCost	21,280,224	480	13,868,760	13,854,344	10,560	3,856	3.43%	2.49%	HASH	Decimal	1	21
Online Sales-UnitPrice	21,280,224	426	13,812,224	13,798,528	10,272	3,424	3.41%	2.48%	HASH	Decimal	1	21
Sales-SalesAmount	5,342,450	68,708	13,048,796	9,790,088	2,709,028	549,680	13.83%	2.34%	HASH	Decimal	1	6
Online Sales-DiscountAmount	21,280,224	1,906	13,002,360	12,946,008	41,088	15,264	3.21%	2.33%	HASH	Decimal	1	21

Figure 6.10 – Two columns monopolizing the semantic model

In *Figure 6.10*, we can also see that **Data Type** is **String** for `Online Sale-SalesOrderNumber`, which was a column suggested by Tabular Editor to have a large dictionary footprint. These statistics would lead you to deduce that this column contains long, unique test values that do not compress well because there is a large cardinality. Indeed, in this case, the column contains a sales order number that is unique to each order plus is not used to group or slice analytical data in a Power BI report well.

This analysis may lead you to re-evaluate the need for this level of reporting in the analysis of sales data. You'd need to ask yourself whether the extra storage space and time taken to build compressed columns and potentially other structures is worth it for your business case. In cases of highly detailed data such as this where you do not need detail-level sales order data, consider limiting the analysis to customer-related data such as demographics or date attributes such as year and month.

Now, let's learn about how DAX Studio can help us with performance analysis and improvement.

Performance tuning the data model and DAX

The first-party option for capturing Analysis Services traces is SQL Server Profiler. When starting a trace, you must identify exactly which events to capture, which requires some knowledge of the trace events and what they contain. Even with this knowledge, working with the trace data in Profiler can be tough since the tool was designed primarily to work with SQL Server application traces. The good news is that DAX Studio can start an Analysis Services server trace and then parse and format all the data to show you relevant results in a well-presented way within its user interface. It allows us to both tune and measure queries in a single place and provides features for Analysis Services that make it a good alternative SQL Profiler for tuning semantic models.

Capturing and replaying queries

This **All Queries** command in the **Traces** section of the DAX Studio toolbar will start a trace against the semantic model you have connected to. *Figure 6.11* shows the result when a trace is successfully started:

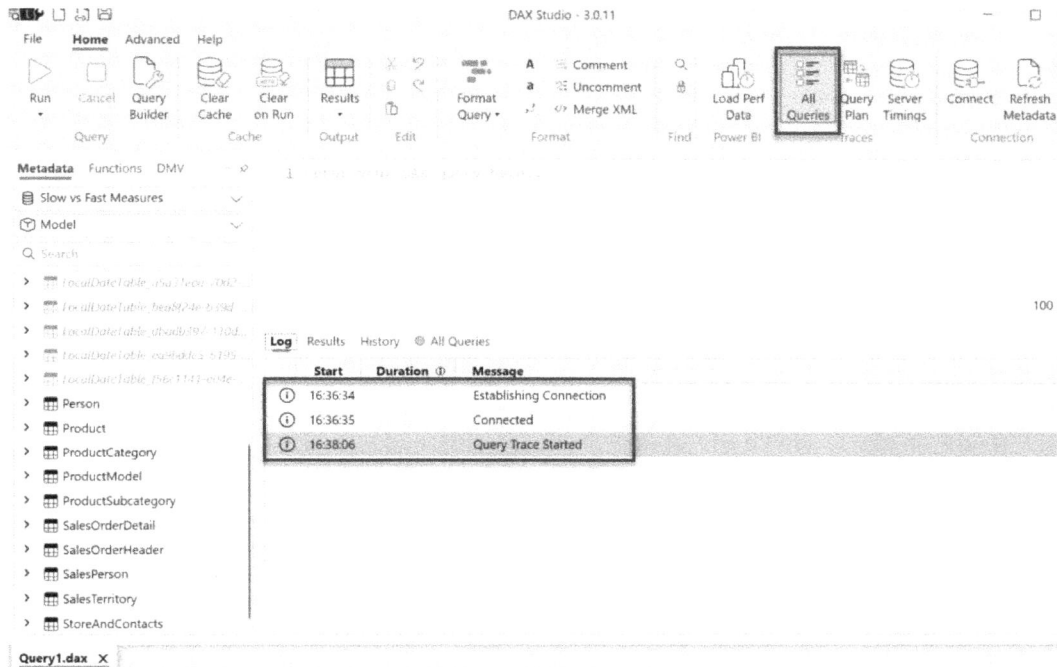

Figure 6.11 – Query trace successfully started in DAX Studio

Once your trace has started, you can interact with the semantic model outside DAX Studio, and it will capture queries for you. How you interact with the semantic model depends on where it is. For a semantic model running on your computer in Power BI Desktop, you would simply interact with the report. This would generate queries that DAX Studio will see. The **All Queries** tab at the bottom of the tool is where the captured queries are listed in time order with durations in milliseconds. The following figure shows two queries captured when opening the **Unique by Account No** page from the `Slow vs Fast Measures.pbix` sample file:

```
 1 DEFINE
 2    VAR __DS0Core =
 3        SUMMARIZECOLUMNS(
 4            ROLLUPADDISSUBTOTAL('Customer'[AccountNumber], "IsGrandTotalRowTotal"),
 5            "SumLineTotal", CALCULATE(SUM('SalesOrderDetail'[LineTotal])),
 6            "UniqueRedProducts_Slow", 'SalesOrderDetail'[UniqueRedProducts_Slow]
 7        )
 8
 9    VAR __DS0PrimaryWindowed =
10        TOPN(502, __DS0Core, [IsGrandTotalRowTotal], 0, 'Customer'[AccountNumber], 1)
11
12 EVALUATE
13    __DS0PrimaryWindowed
14
15 ORDER BY
16    [IsGrandTotalRowTotal] DESC, 'Customer'[AccountNumber]
17 |
```

100 ∨

Log   Results   History   ● **All Queries**   ⊘ ✕

○ Record   ⏸ Pause   ☐ Stop   ⟳ Clear   ⎘ Copy   ⊟ Export   ⓘ Info   ☐ Filters

StartTime	Type	Duration	User	Database	Query
04:57:29	DAX	27ms	AzureAD\...	Slow vs F...	DEFINE VAR __DS0Core = SUMMARIZECOLUMNS(ROLLUPADDISSUBTOTAL('Cust...
04:57:29	DAX	17,360ms	AzureAD\...	Slow vs F...	DEFINE VAR __DS0Core = SUMMARIZECOLUMNS(ROLLUPADDISSUBTOTAL('Cust...

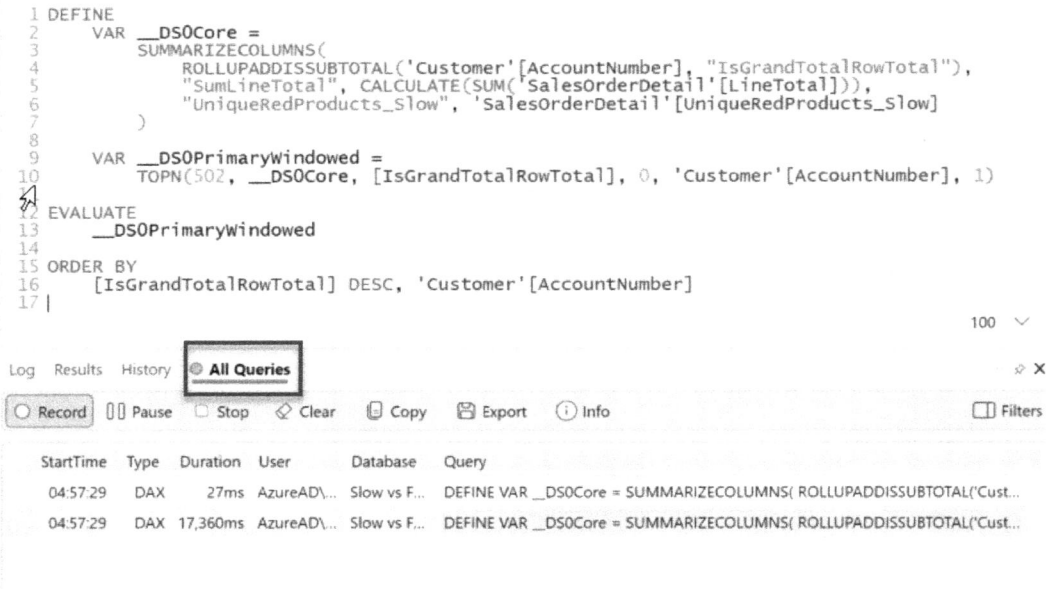

Figure 6.12 – Queries captured by DAX Studio

The preceding queries come from a screen that has the same table results in a visual, but two different DAX measures that calculate the aggregation. These measures make one table come back in less than a second while the other returns in about 17 seconds. The following figure shows the page in the report:

AccountNumber	LineTotal	UniqueRedProducts_Slow		AccountNumber	LineTotal	UniqueRedProducts_Fast
AW00011000	8,248.99	1		W00011000	8,248.99	1
AW00011001	6,383.88			AW00011001	6,383.88	
AW00011002	8,114.04			AW00011002	8,114.04	
AW00011003	8,139.29			AW00011003	8,139.29	
AW00011004	8,196.01	1		AW00011004	8,196.01	1
AW00011005	8,121.33			AW00011005	8,121.33	
AW00011006	8,119.03			AW00011006	8,119.03	
AW00011007	8,211.00	1		AW00011007	8,211.00	1
AW00011008	8,106.31	1		AW00011008	8,106.31	1
AW00011009	8,091.33			AW00011009	8,091.33	
AW00011010	8,088.04			AW00011010	8,088.04	
Total	**109,846,381.40**	**31**		**Total**	**109,846,381.40**	**31**

Figure 6.13 – Tables with the same results but from using different measures

The following screenshot shows the results of the Performance Analyzer for the tables previously. Observe how one query took over 17 seconds, whereas the other took under 1 second:

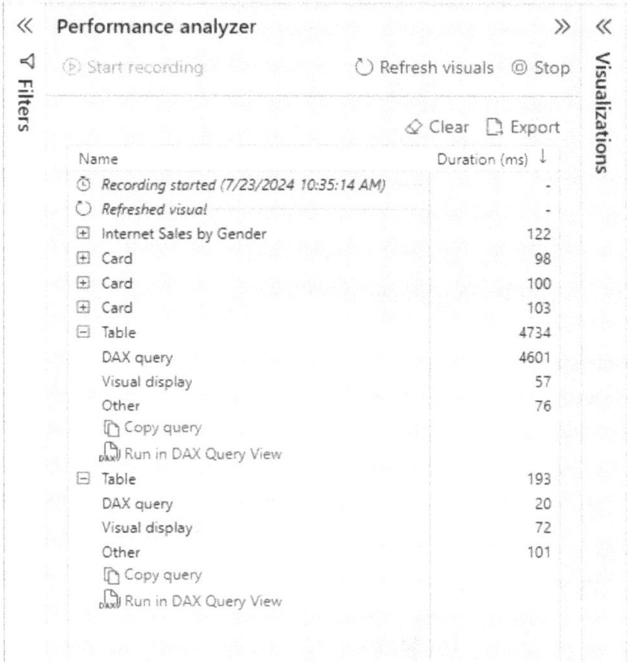

Figure 6.14 – Vastly different query durations for the same visual result

In *Figure 6.12*, the second query was double-clicked to bring the DAX text to the editor. You can modify this query in DAX Studio to test performance changes. We see here that the DAX expression for the UniqueRedProducts_Slow measure was not efficient. We'll learn a technique to optimize queries soon, but first, we need to learn about capturing query performance traces.

Obtaining query timings

To get detailed query performance information, you can use the **Server Timings** command shown in *Figure 6.11*. After starting the trace, you can run queries and then use the **Server Timings** tab to see how the engine executed the query, as shown in the following figure:

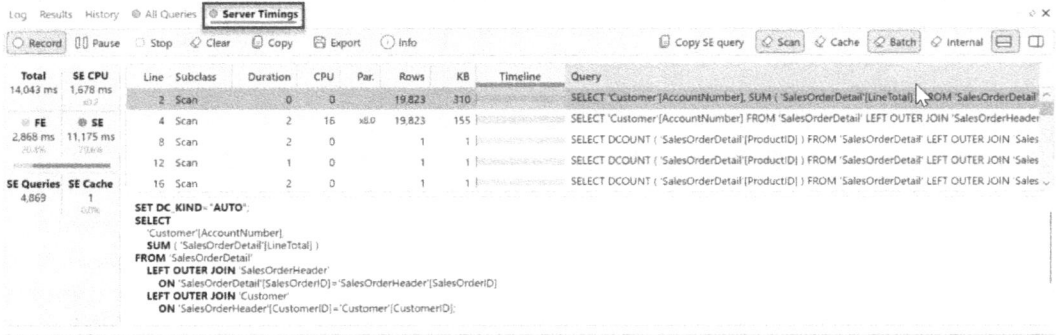

Figure 6.15 – Server Timings showing detailed query performance statistics

Figure 6.15 gives very useful information. **FE** and **SE** refer to the **formula engine** and **storage engine**. The storage engine is fast and multi-threaded, and its job is fetching data. It can apply basic logic such as filtering data to retrieve only what is needed. The formula engine is single-threaded, and it generates a query plan, which is the physical steps required to compute the result. It also performs calculations on the data such as joins, complex filters, aggregations, and lookups. We want to avoid queries that spend most of the time in the formula engine, or that execute many queries in the storage engine. The bottom-left section of *Figure 6.15* shows that we executed almost 4,900 SE queries. The list of queries to the right shows many queries returning only one result, which is suspicious.

For comparison, we look at timing for the fastest version of the query and we see the following:

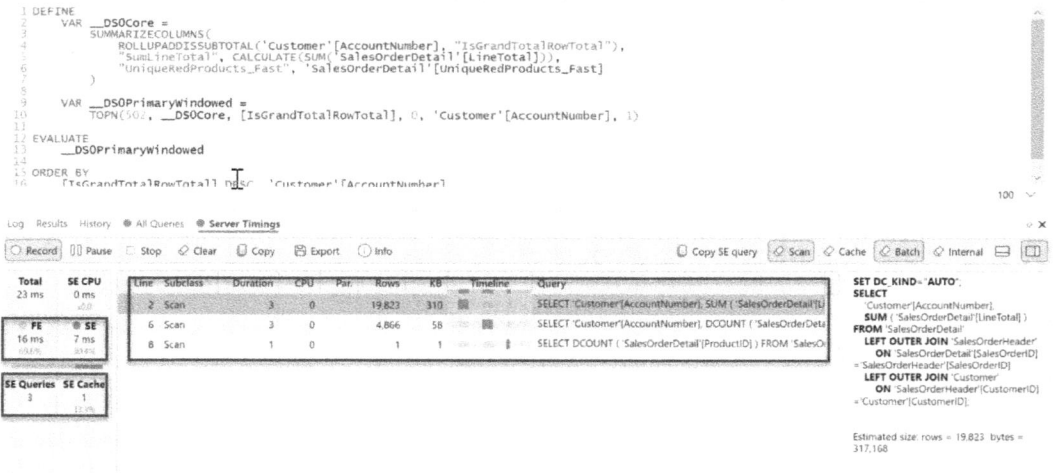

Figure 6.16 – Server Timings for a fast version of the query

In *Figure 6.16*, we can see that only three server engine queries were run this time, and the result was obtained much faster (milliseconds compared to seconds).

The faster DAX measure was as follows:

```
UniqueRedProducts_Fast =
CALCULATE (
    DISTINCTCOUNT('SalesOrderDetail'[ProductID]),
    'Product'[Color] = "Red"
)
```

The slower DAX measure was as follows:

```
UniqueRedProducts_Slow =
CALCULATE (
    DISTINCTCOUNT('SalesOrderDetail'[ProductID]),
    FILTER('SalesOrderDetail', RELATED('Product'[Color]) = "Red"))
```

> **Tip**
> The Analysis Services engine does use data caches to speed up queries. These caches contain uncompressed query results that can be reused later to save time fetching and decompressing data. You should use the **Clear Cache** button in DAX Studio to force these caches to be cleared and get a proper worst-case performance measure. This is visible in the menu bar in *Figure 6.11*.

We will build on these concepts when we look at DAX and model optimizations in later chapters. Now, let's look at how we can experiment with DAX and query changes in **DAX Studio**.

Modifying and tuning queries

Earlier in this section, we saw how we could capture a query generated by a Power BI visual and then display its text. A nice trick we can use here is to use **query-scoped measures** to override the measure definition and see how performance differs.

The following figure shows how we can search for a measure, right-click, and then pull its definition into the query editor of DAX Studio:

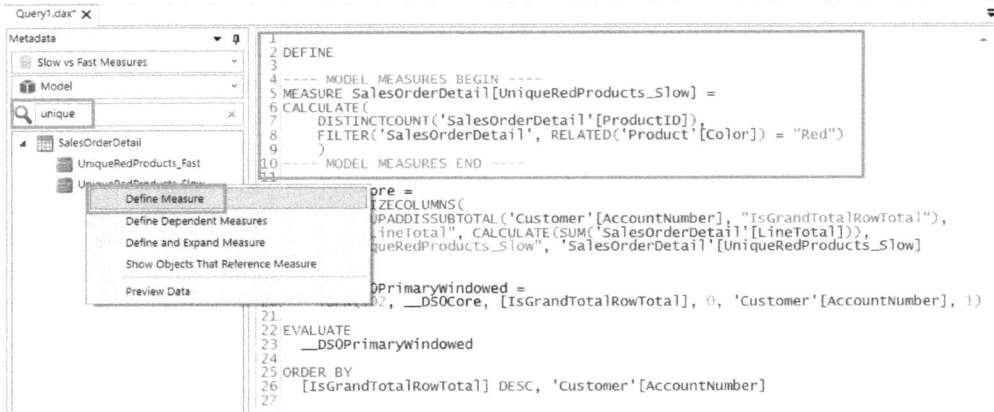

Figure 6.17 – The Define Measure option and result in the Query pane

We can now modify the measure in the query editor, and the engine will use the local definition instead of the one defined in the model! This technique gives you a fast way to prototype DAX enhancements without having to edit them in Power BI and refresh visuals over many iterations.

Remember that this technique does not apply any changes to the dataset you are connected to. You can optimize expressions in DAX Studio, then transfer the definition to Power BI Desktop/Visual Studio when ready. The following figure shows how we changed the definition of `UniqueRedProducts_Slow` in a query-scoped measure to get a huge performance boast:

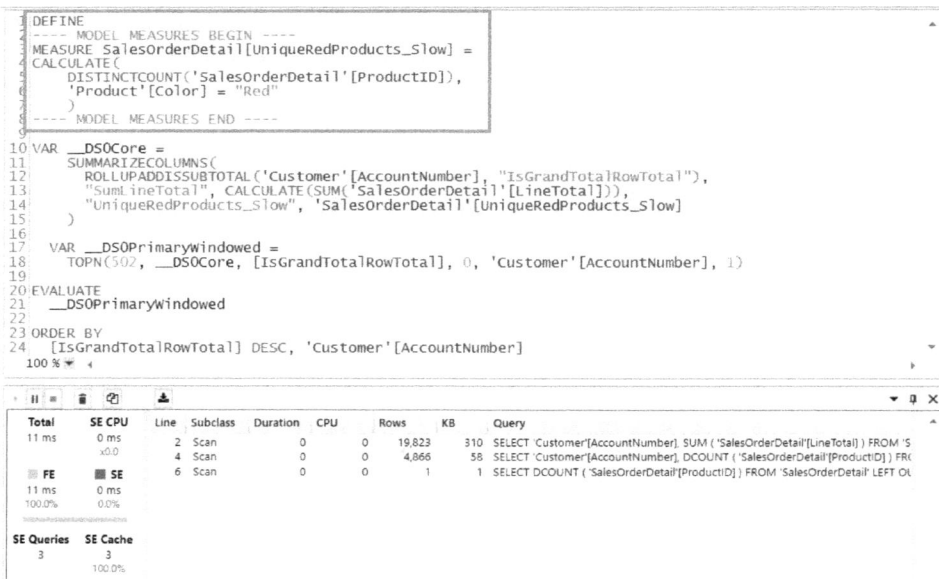

Figure 6.18 – Modified measure giving better results

The technique described here can be adapted to model changes too. For example, if you wanted to determine the impact of changing a relationship type, you could run the same queries in DAX Studio before and after the change to draw a comparison.

Here are some additional tips for working with DAX Studio:

- **Isolate measure**: When performance tuning a query generated by a report visual, comment out complex measures and then establish a baseline performance score. Then, add each measure back to the query individually and check the speed. This will help identify the slowest measures in the query and visual context.

- **Work with Desktop Performance Analyzer traces**: DAX Studio has a facility to import the trace files generated by Desktop Performance Analyzer. You can import trace files using the **Load Perf Data** button located next to **All Queries** highlighted in *Figure 6.12*. This trace can be captured by one person and then shared with a DAX/modeling expert who can use DAX Studio to analyze and replay their behavior. The following figure shows how DAX Studio formats the data to make it easy to see which visual component is taking the most time. It was generated by viewing each of the three report pages in the `Slow vs Fast Measures.pbix` sample file:

#	Visual	QueryStart	QueryEnd	Rows	Query Ms	Render Ms	Total Ms	Query
1	Table	10:35:12	10:35:12	4	44	80	124	DEFINE VAR __DS0Core = SUMMARIZECOLUMNS
2	Table	10:35:12	10:35:12	4	39	130	169	DEFINE VAR __DS0Core = SUMMARIZECOLUMNS
3	Table	10:35:18	10:35:54	502	35,527	73	35,600	DEFINE VAR __DS0Core = SUMMARIZECOLUMNS
4	Table	10:35:18	10:35:18	502	38	160	198	DEFINE VAR __DS0Core = SUMMARIZECOLUMNS
5	Filter: Sales by Date	10:35:58	10:35:58	1,124	9	2,045	2,054	DEFINE VAR __DS0Core = SUMMARIZECOLUMNS
6	Customers by Group	10:35:59	10:35:59	3	9	93	102	DEFINE VAR __DS0Core = SUMMARIZECOLUMNS
7	Card	10:35:59	10:35:59	1	13	16	29	EVALUATE ROW("SalesAmount", 'SalesOrderDeta
8	Card	10:35:59	10:35:59	1	10	30	40	EVALUATE ROW("CountSalesOrderID", CALCULA
9	Card	10:35:59	10:35:59	1	9	41	50	EVALUATE ROW("Customer_Coverage", 'Custome
10	Slicer	10:36:00	10:36:00	1	9	81	90	EVALUATE ROW("MinTotalDue", CALCULATE(MIN
11	Slicer	10:36:00	10:36:00	10	0	46	46	DEFINE VAR __DS0Core = VALUES('Product'[Colo
12	Slicer	10:36:00	10:36:00	6	0	34	34	DEFINE VAR __DS0Core = VALUES('SalesTerritory'
13	Slicer	10:36:00	10:36:00	101	15	26	41	DEFINE VAR __DS0Core = VALUES('ProductMode
14	Bonus by FirstName	10:36:01	10:36:01	17	7	116	123	DEFINE VAR __DS0Core = SUMMARIZECOLUMNS
15	SalesAmount by Product Category	10:36:01	10:36:01	21	32	50	82	DEFINE VAR __ScopedCore0 = SUMMARIZECOLU

Figure 6.19 – Performance Analyzer trace shows the slowest visual in the report

- **Export/import model metrics**: DAX Studio has a facility to export or import the VertiPaq model metadata using `.vpax` files. These files do not contain any of your data. They contain table names, column names, and measure definitions. If you are not concerned with sharing these definitions, you can provide `.vpax` files to others if you need assistance with model optimization.

Summary

In this chapter, we introduced some popular utilities that use different methods to analyze Power BI solutions and help us identify areas to improve. One caveat is that free versions of these tools are often community projects and are not officially supported. DAX Studio and Tabular Editor have been widely adopted by the Power BI community and are continuously updated as of the publication of this book.

We learned about Power BI Helper's ability to document large dictionary columns and relationships and measure dependencies. Next, we learned about Tabular Editor's BPA. This gave us an easy way to load in default rules provided by experts, and then scan a semantic model for best practices.

DAX Studio is a complete query development and tuning utility that can capture real-time query activity and timings. We learned how to generate model metrics that give us detailed information about the objects and how much space they occupy. We then moved on to query timings, so we learned about the roles of the formula and storage engine. The ability to use query-scoped measures in DAX Studio gives us a fast and powerful way to prototype DAX and model changes.

At this point in the book, we learned about optimizing largely from a high-level design perspective. We also learned about tools and utilities to help us measure performance. In the next chapter, we will propose a framework where you will combine processes and practices that use these tools to establish, monitor, and maintain good performance in Power BI.

7

Performance Governance Framework

We began this book by introducing performance management and how to set reasonable targets, borrowing from user interface research. We identified that areas of Power BI can affect report and semantic model refresh performance, and then we walked through architectural concepts and optimization choices. *Chapters 4*, *5*, and *6* focused on sources of information and tools that can help us monitor reports and query performance.

The metrics and tools in earlier chapters are essential building blocks for performance management. However, success is more likely with a structured and repeatable approach to build performance-related thinking into the entire Power BI solution life cycle. This chapter provides guidelines to set up data-driven processes to avoid sudden scaling issues with new content and prevent the degradation of existing content.

You could consider performance management as having two distinct phases. The first involves monitoring and identifying areas that are slowing you down. The second involves **root cause analysis (RCA)** and remediation. The technical topics covered prior to this chapter are sufficient to give you a great head start with Power BI performance management, mainly from a reporting perspective. Since report usage is the most common use case of a **business intelligence system (BIS)**, we'll intentionally cover the governance framework now before going deeper into detailed best practices for each product area.

We intend to give you sufficient knowledge to tackle the first phase of performance management after completing this and the previous six chapters. Once you know you have a problem and where it is, you can move on to the second phase. The tail end of this chapter gives some monitoring information for performance management. Subsequent chapters focus on the second phase and will provide specific advice on how to optimize a specific layer such as the report design, semantic model design, and M Query design.

This chapter consists of the following sections:

- Establishing a repeatable improvement process
- Knowledge sharing and awareness
- Using performance metrics reports
- Calling REST APIs for monitoring data

Establishing a repeatable improvement process

In *Chapter 1*, *Setting Targets and Identifying Problem Areas*, we learned about the potential negative impacts of poor BIS performance. It is great to have knowledge, metrics, and tools to resolve performance issues. However, a behavior that is seen too often is that these are usually leveraged reactively after an issue has had enough of an impact on the business that it is formally raised and brought to the attention of developers and administrators. This is not a good situation to be in for reasons described in the following points:

- **Production changes**: These changes are non-trivial and require careful change management. Change management involves more than just deploying new technical artifacts. One example is that users may need training and documentation may need to be updated if there are significant reports or semantic model-level changes.

- **Short deadlines**: There may be deadlines for the business to resolve performance issues, especially from leadership. RCA, evaluation enhancements, and deploying changes can be time-consuming by nature, so this time pressure can affect the quality of work and introduce other unrelated issues through human error.

- **Lack of experience and knowledge**: There may be limited expertise to resolve complex issues, due to lack of expert skills within the organization or limited availability of those staff members. This could delay a resolution indefinitely, increasing user frustration.

Now, let's cover the performance management cycle of Power BI-related projects.

The performance management cycle

It is recommended to minimize performance enhancement efforts by being pro-active about performance management. This can be achieved by thinking of performance management as a continuous cycle, shown in the following diagram:

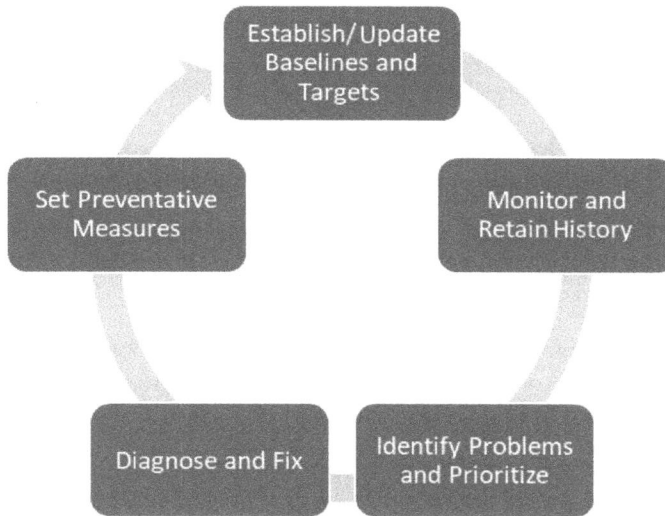

Figure 7.1 – Performance management cycle

Let's look at each of these phases in more detail to understand what they involve.

Establish/update baselines and targets

You cannot improve performance without being able to compare results from different scenarios or different system conditions. The first step is to know what a reasonable expectation is for a specific scenario, ideally under known and controlled conditions. This is what we refer to as a baseline, and it serves as the standard against which you would compare real-world measurements.

Let's put this into practical terms. Suppose we have occasional complaints about a slow report from two users. We find that the first user has a report that takes around 15 seconds, while a different user reports 45 seconds for the same report to render. If we had no other information available to us, we might spend a lot of time with both users trying to work out why the issue is occurring. While 15 seconds is not a good report load time, we don't know if that is within the expected range for that user's scenario. The same applies to the 45-second duration. Therefore, it is recommended to use baselines to help you both set expectations and understand the relative change when something slows down. Here are some guidelines to help you establish good baselines:

- A baseline metric should be an average of multiple data points for the same scenario. A minimum of three is recommended, though more is better.

- Create a baseline per semantic model and report page combination. Page granularity is important because visual designs can vary, and one page of a report can be more complex and slower than others.

- For reports, establish baselines for reports in Power BI Desktop and after publishing to the service. Comparing metrics both before and after changes can help identify architectural or configuration issues.

- Consider the effect of **row-level security (RLS)** on reports and queries. Set a baseline for the report with RLS turned off and compare it with it turned on, especially for complex security models.

- Maintain a record of when changes are deployed and what they were. This will set a clear point in your trend analysis where different results are expected. It also helps if changes need to be reassessed and compared to the original baseline.

Some of the previous guidelines apply specifically to Power BI reports. However, you can and should apply the concepts to other areas of Power BI. For example, you can establish baselines for semantic model refreshes, both in Power BI Desktop and the Power BI service.

The baseline establishment step is both the start and the end of the cycle because any performance-related work could change the overall behavior of the system for all users, not just the ones who have problems. Hence, your baseline needs to be adjusted accordingly.

Monitor and retain history

At the time of writing this book, there are 30 days of historical usage information for Power BI reports. For semantic models on capacities (Premium or Fabric), you can get the 60 most frequent refreshes for the admin portal. This may not be sufficient to build a good trending view and spot gradual performance degradation, so it is recommended to extract metrics and retain historical data to build a long-term view, as described in the last two sections of this chapter and in the *Power BI usage metrics* section of *Chapter 4, Analyzing Logs and Metrics*.

This can also help identify seasonal issues – for example, extra load caused by end-of-month processing. You should review performance against baselines and targets regularly. We recommend reviewing performance against baselines at least weekly or having alerts indicate when data is significantly longer than previous runs. You can consider plotting rolling averages to smooth out small fluctuations.

Identify problems and prioritize

This part is straightforward. Here, you will compare your actual results to baselines and targets. Those that do not meet the standard should be flagged and prioritized in terms of user impact and business impact. Try to address items that will help the most people and the most critical business process. Sometimes, this can be out of your hands and driven by executive priorities.

Diagnose and fix

The artifact with the problem must be investigated and profiled, as we described in the previous two chapters. The initial goal here is to work out which part of the process is problematic. Using a report as an example, you should work out if certain visuals are slow, if a measure is performing badly, or if a security filter expression is the issue. Detailed examples of what to look for in each area will be given in later chapters.

> **Tip**
>
> When resolving a report performance issue, it is a good idea to start with the visual layer. Even if **Data Analysis Expressions** (**DAX**) or model optimizations can help, these changes could take longer to implement safely since there could be many dependencies on the semantic model. However, the report layer can often be optimized independently and even in parallel.

Set preventative measures

An important part of being pro-active about performance management is to learn from your experiences and try not to repeat mistakes. This step is about updating standards, checklists, training, and other related material used by the development team to raise awareness.

We recommend building performance-tuning routines into your regular development cycle, at an appropriate level for the user. Enforce best practices at the initial development stage and use Power BI Desktop and third-party utilities to profile and optimize your content before deploying it to users. Also, consider scale testing before going live.

Next, we will explore ways to socialize performance practices within your organization.

Knowledge sharing and awareness

In the previous section, we talked about the importance of being pro-active about performance management. Since there are many areas to cover, some being quite technical, we need to have the right level of complexity and relevance for the audience. We will introduce these groups in general and then summarize with role-specific advice.

Helping self-service users

One of Power BI's greatest strengths is its approachability and ease of use for non-technical users or analysts who are not professional BI developers. The drawback of this is that lack of knowledge can lead to poorly optimized solutions. We recommend using the guidance in later chapters to create the following:

- **Report design guide**: This will incorporate style, theme, and design choices to avoid. These can even be supplied as a Power BI template file.

- **Data modeling and loading guide**: This will have common guidance, such as the basics of dimensional modeling, relationship pitfalls, removing unnecessary data, and Power Query tips.

- **Custom links to guides**: Guidance from other chapters in this book can be used to point developers in the right direction. For instance, the *Building efficient models* section in *Chapter 10, Data Modeling and Row-Level Security*, has a section on dimensional modeling.

Let's move on to leveraging professional developers.

Leveraging professional developers

You can establish rules about why self-service content or data subject areas need a formal performance review before going live. This can be done by embedded champions and **subject-matter experts (SMEs)** or central experts who would typically work in an enterprise BI team or **Center of Excellence (CoE)**. Microsoft has invested heavily in the CoE concept with the material at this site: `https://learn.microsoft.com/en-us/power-bi/guidance/fabric-adoption-roadmap-center-of-excellence`.

This is simply a detailed and formal performance review that covers every relevant layer of the solution – including things such as DAX tuning, which may not be left to self-service users. The point is to enforce the performance review as part of the development cycle before going live. Also, performance reviews should not be at the end of the report but iterative and frequent during development.

Approaching performance improvement collaboratively

By now, you can see that many different skillsets are required to build and optimize a large Power BI solution. Therefore, various roles must collaborate to manage performance effectively. Unfortunately, it is easy to get into a situation where one area takes all the blame. Report developers may feel pressure to fix reports without realizing measures are slow. Data engineers may feel pressure to fix slow semantic model refreshes without knowing the source system is under heavy load. These are just two examples of many similar steps in performance tuning.

It is recommended you set up a process to assist with performance tuning. Nominate champions or specialists who have specific strengths to be involved in reviews. These could be technical (for example, modeling, DAX, or report design) and business domain SMEs such as finance, inventory management, or drilling employees.

Lastly, try to stay on top of product changes through documentation updates and blogs. A good example is DAX performance. Improvements made by Microsoft are sometimes via the release of new functions with different names since the old ones are left unchanged for backward compatibility.

Now that we have understood the phases of the performance management cycle and different skill levels, we will describe different usage scenarios and the responsibilities various roles should have.

Applying steps to different usage scenarios

BI tools are used by everyone from individuals to large global corporations. Naturally, you would expect the ways in which analytics are developed and maintained to change as an organization grows. The larger the organization is, the more the need for governance and central control grows. In our opinion, even in large organizations, a healthy BI environment is one that balances the needs of individuals and small teams with centralized corporate data management practices. Individuals and small groups need to frequently perform new analyses or data mashups and prefer to have minimal technical friction and standards imposed because it slows them down.

This can clash with organizational goals of standardization, usability guides, and best practices around modeling and design, which can affect performance.

These conflicting needs are often referred to as the balance between self-service BI and corporate or IT-led BI. It is beyond the scope of this book to recommend how best to balance these needs, noting that similar-sized organizations could adopt quite different approaches with their own trade-offs. However, we will describe common scenarios in an organization, identify typical roles that work within them, and recommend their responsibilities to help apply the performance framework.

Self-service BI

This refers to a model where business users access and analyze data even if they do not have formal training in statistics or data analysis. Self-service BI is intentionally and often the fastest and least governed way to gain insights. Users can load, manipulate, mash up, and visualize data to suit their tactical needs. They may use a mixture of formal and informal sources of data, including information from external **service providers** (**SPs**) (for example, population stars or weather data). This can be thought of as primarily a "pull mode," where users find what they want and create their own reporting.

An example here is someone working for a cloud software provider who wants to test the hypothesis that demand for one of their services is higher following a public holiday. They need to quickly combine internal usage data with holiday dates from a public website. Depending on the governance model, the analysis may be shared with other individuals, teams, or even the entire organization, which has performance implications.

There is only one role here, and that is the **business user** whose performance responsibilities are the following:

- Use Performance Analyzer to help eliminate issues
- Check for acceptance performance after publishing with data

Team or domain-based BI

This refers to a model where a group with a shared function or goal is looking to perform analytics on a set of known themes or initiatives. Some examples here are a company division such as procurement wanting to analyze supplier efficiency or a virtual team for a special project such as a marketing campaign that wants to understand the **return on investment** (**ROI**) for each channel used in the campaign. There will be business SMEs in the team and potentially data SMEs who can play a role in applying best practices that help performance. As with self-service, team-based BI may employ a mix of data sources, and indeed self-service BI frequently occurs within these teams. Groups such as these usually build analytics for their own use and for management reporting.

There are three roles with performance responsibilities:

- **Business users**

  - Use Performance Analyzer to help eliminate issues

  - Check for acceptance performance after publishing with data

  - Decision makers establish performance criteria

  - Leverage guidance from SMEs and technical teams and review together before publishing

- **Business and data SMEs**

  - Maintain a central definition of common business logic such as calculations

  - Establish recommended practices for data sourcing and transformation

- **Data analyst/report developer**

  - Document common pitfalls and workarounds for loading, modeling, and visualizing

  - Leverage logs and third-party utilities to optimize artifacts

Corporate/IT-led BI

This is a model where a central team builds common artifacts for use by many different parts of the organization – dataflows, semantic models, reports, dashboards, and so on. This can be thought of as a "push model" because a central team manages distribution largely to pure consumers. There is a higher level of governance and standardization here for everything from naming conventions and data modeling standards to report design guides and corporate themes. A central BI team also often defines the infrastructure, architecture, processes, and controls that support team and self-service BI:

- **Business users**

  - As per team-based

- **Business and data SMEs**

  - As per team-based, but in collaboration with developers

- **Data analyst/report developer**

  - As per team-based, but likely more focused on visualizations

  - Review content for publication issues before broad publication

- **Data modeler**

  - Establish and document modeling standards, including domain-specific special cases that do not follow theory exactly

  - Review content for performance issues before broad publication

  - Leverage logs and third-party utilities to optimize artifacts

- **Extract, transform, load (ETL) developer**

  - Establish and document data loading and transformation standards

  - Review content for performance issues before broad publication

  - Leverage logs and third-party utilities to optimize artifacts

- **Solution architect**

  - Establish and document architectural options

  - Leverage logs and third-party utilities to inform architectural changes and future designs

  - Be aware of new product development that can improve performance (the same applies to other specialist roles)

- **BI manager/analytics lead**

  - Establish processes, roles, and responsibilities for performance management

  - Collaborate with all parties to establish realistic performance targets

  - Track solution performance over time and refine process and performance guidance assets with the team

> **Note**
>
> The previous descriptions of BI usage scenarios suggest that a common pathway for analytics in terms of solution maturity starts with self-service BI, which can evolve into corporate BI. This is true because businesses usually identify new analytical needs, but as the reach and scale of the solution grows, there is a need to apply some governance that needs guidance from IT. Therefore, we stress again the importance of applying relevant performance management for all these scenarios to reduce the overall performance remediation effort. Microsoft's guidance for different BI scenarios can be found here: `https://learn.microsoft.com/en-us/power-bi/guidance/powerbi-implementation-planning-usage-scenario-overview`.

The next section will describe two different reports provided by Microsoft to monitor activities.

Using performance metrics reports

To implement the performance management cycle, administrators will need to be able to see metrics about the service and capacities. Initially, we will want to see report performance and then proceed to background activities such as semantic model refreshes. These provide the basic monitoring functionality to start pro-actively responding to issues. It also provides a view into activities of users interacting with the system.

Let's look at the metrics for reports.

Usage metrics report

If end users are complaining about the speed of reports, the first area to examine is a usage metric report. This canned report can give insights into the performance of reports in a specific workspace. The underlying semantic model for the usage report is controlled by the Power BI service and cannot be changed by any administrator. You can, however, connect to the semantic model to build your own reports or extract information for your own reporting.

> **Note**
> There are two versions of the report using the same semantic model. The newer one will be reviewed in this chapter. The newer report expands on the metrics of the first. There is a toggle in the upper right of the report to switch between **New usage report on** or **New usage report off**.

Let's start with the menu choices. By default, the report will go to the **Report usage** page. *Figure 7.2* shows an overview of the report. Outlined are the **key performance indicators (KPIs)** most relevant for review – **Report opens**, **Report page view**, **Unique viewers**, and **Report open trend**:

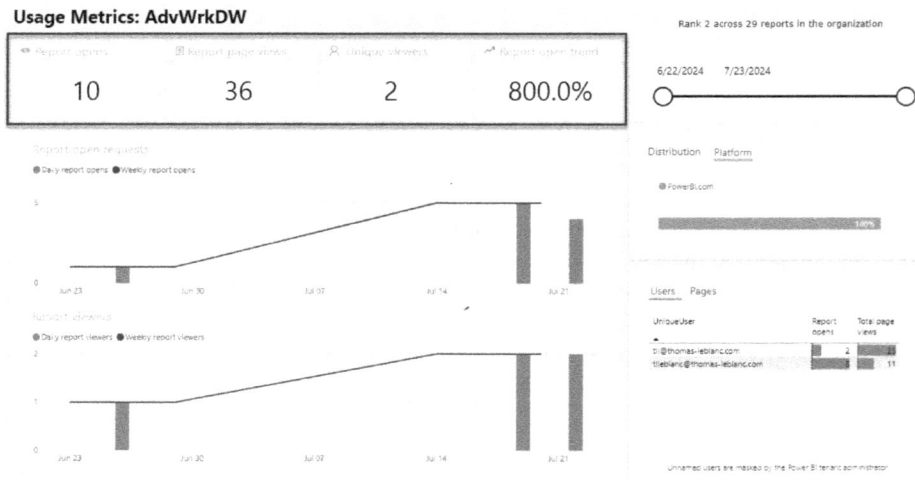

Figure 7.2 – Report usage KPIs

For performance monitoring, these are indicators of whether the report is being used and whether usage is trending up, down, or the same. From there, we can look at the **Report open requests** and **Report viewers** bar/line visual to see trends in usage on a daily or weekly basis, as shown in *Figure 7.3*:

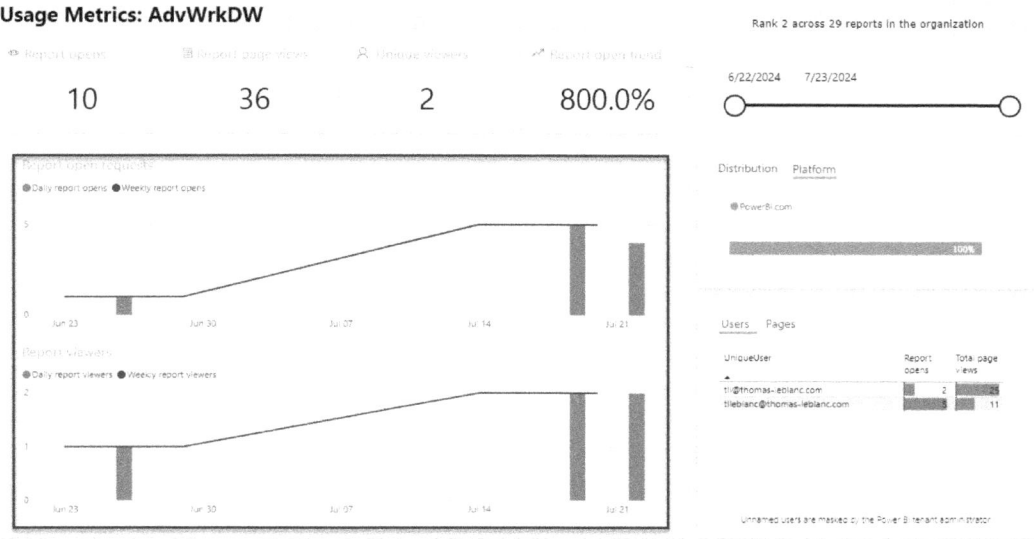

Figure 7.3 – Report open requests and Report viewers

For performance, we can see a gap in viewing the report before an increase to more recent viewing. These graphs are good indicators of usage and whether user interaction was recent or in the past. If more usage is in the past, that might be an indicator that users are decreasing the use of the report, maybe from rendering taking longer than the user tolerates.

Next, we can go to the **Report performance** menu choice on the left for more performance-related metrics. This report page indicates opening time as well as opening trends with two graphs for daily performance and 7-day performance. *Figure 7.4* shows the typical opening time for this report as 23.5 seconds. That is a problem for most users. But, if we look at the **Daily performance** graph, that issue is mainly an anomaly from late April or early May. We can change the date range in the upper right to eliminate that date and look at more recent data:

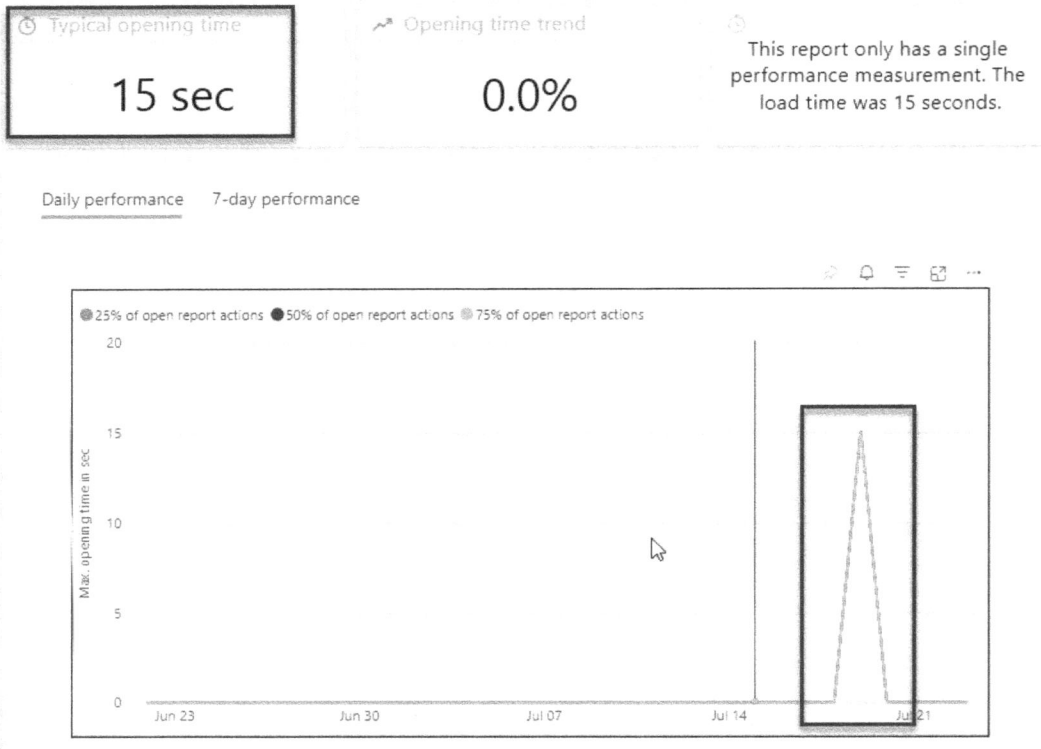

Figure 7.4 – Report performance page

The other two menu choices for this report are a listing of reports and a **frequently asked questions** (**FAQs**) page. Both are handy for understanding the reports in the workspace or understanding each metric on each page.

Let's look at the metrics for capacity.

Fabric Capacity Metrics

Fabric Capacity Metrics is a template app from Microsoft to help with an analysis of processing, interactive and background, in a capacity. The capacity can be Fabric or Premium. Pro and **Premium Per User** (**PPU**) licenses will not be able to use this template app. The template app can be installed from the **Apps** icon in the main Power BI portal, as shown in *Figure 7.5*:

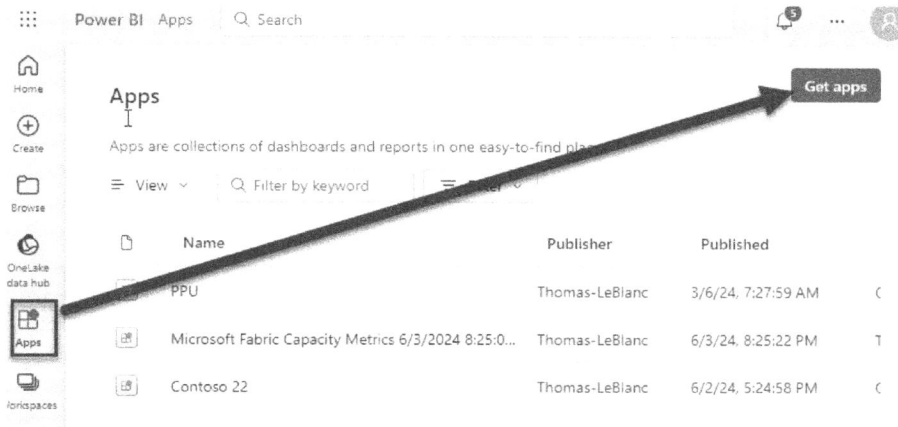

Figure 7.5 – Getting template apps

After clicking the **Get apps** button, search for `Fabric Capacity Metrics` and click **Install**. The semantic model will have to refresh before any data can be displayed. This process starts automatically for you, but the information will take 2 to 30 minutes to be available. Also, when you first come into the app, no capacity is selected. Use the **Capacity name** drop-down list (*Figure 7.6*: upper left of report) to select a capacity. The view will give you an idea of the performance of the capacity for the last 14 days. If this is on a Fabric capacity, alerts can be set up to email when visuals exceed a specific KPI measure.

The report can be viewed from the app or from the workspace, depending on the permissions of the user. We assume you are an administrator of the capacity or of Power BI. *Figure 7.6* shows a high-level view of the report with the **Capacity name** dropdown highlighted:

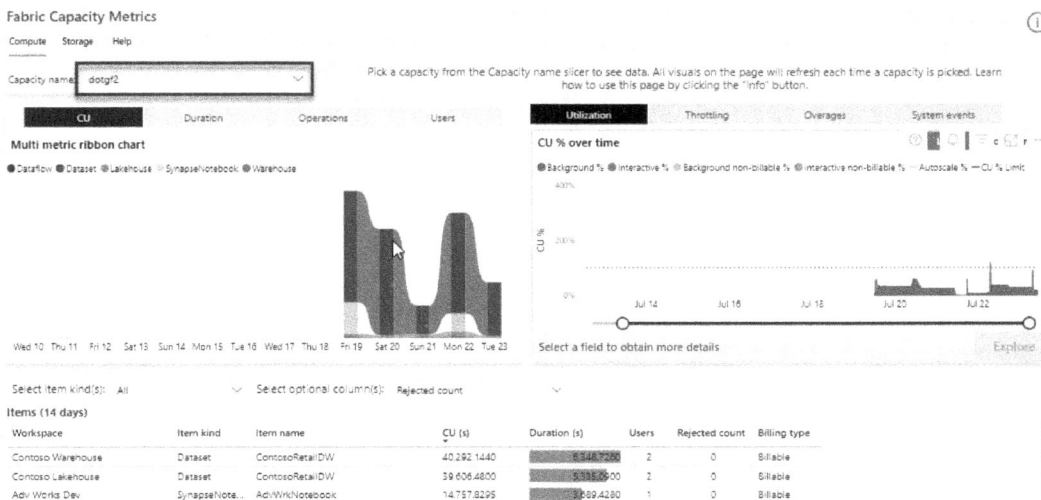

Figure 7.6 – High-level view of Fabric Capacity Metrics report

The first area of interest for performance is the bar graph visual in the upper right named **CU % over time**. This visual has four buttons to drill to various levels of monitoring performance. *Figure 7.7* zooms in on this visual:

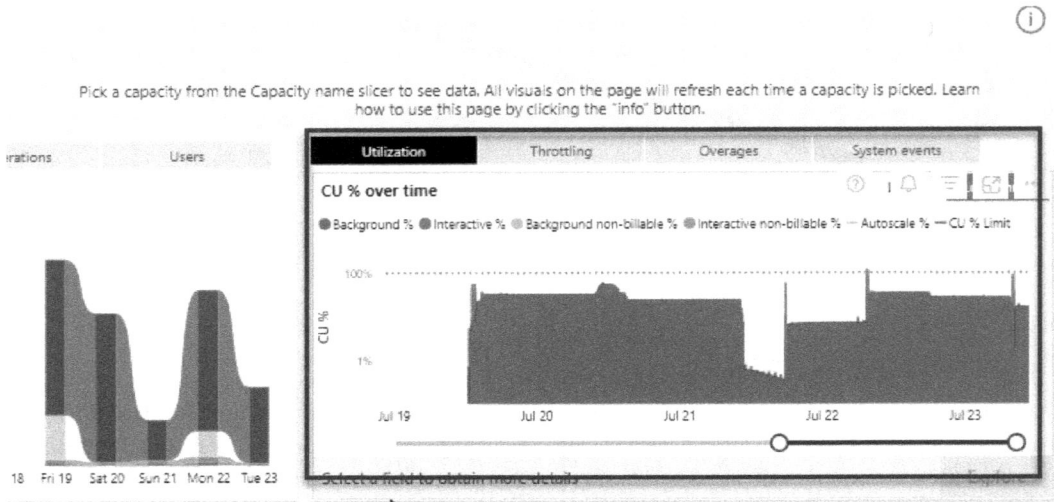

Figure 7.7 – CU % over time

This analysis shows spikes at the beginning of different days. These spikes mainly consist of semantic model refreshes along with report views. The third spike shows usage exceeding 100%. In Fabric, we can exceed the capacity, and more capacity will be added to handle the overage. You can see the smoothing (spreading) of the overage in a more detailed graph shown in *Figure 7.8*. *Chapter 13*, *Working with Capacities*, contains detailed information on smoothing **capacity units** (**CUs**) in Fabric. We can drill through to these details by right-clicking on the spike and going to the **TimePoint Detail** menu choice from the **Drill through** menu seen in *Figure 7.8*:

how to use this page by clicking the "info" button.

| Utilization | Throttling | Overages | System events |

CU % over time

● Background % ● Interactive % ● Background non-billable % ● Interactive non-billable % — Autoscale % — CU % Limit

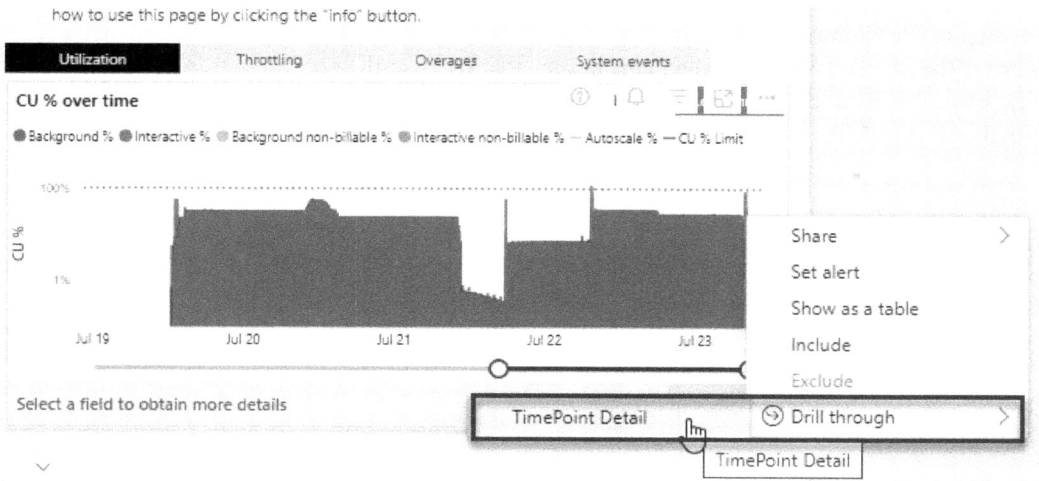

Share
Set alert
Show as a table
Include
Exclude

Select a field to obtain more details

TimePoint Detail   ⊕ Drill through

TimePoint Detail

Figure 7.8 – Drill through menu choice to TimePoint Detail page

The **TimePoint Detail** page has a visual named **Overages** in the bottom right. This shows us **Burndown** % from the previous smoothing and **Add** % because of the additional capacity required, as shown in *Figure 7.9*:

6:04:2...	Success	tlleblanc@thoma...	373	779.7440	0.2707	0	0.45%	Billable
5:56:2...	Success	tlleblanc@thoma...	106	234.0000	0.0813	0	0.14%	Billable
			7,898	25,212.89...	8.7545	0	14.59%	

Overages

| 10 mins | 60 mins | 24 hrs |

● Add % ● Burndown % ● Cumulative (Right axis) %

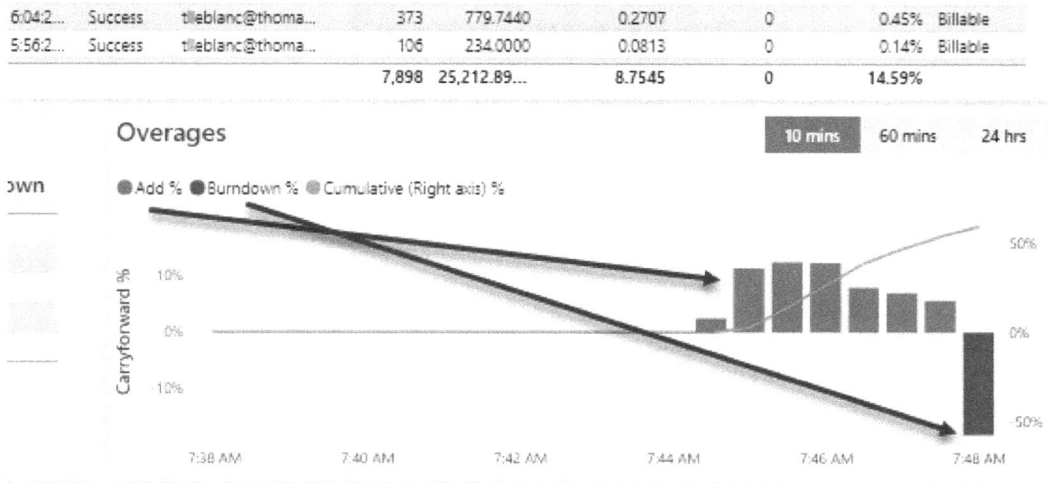

Figure 7.9 – Overages

Chapter 13, *Working with Capacities*, and *Chapter 14*, *Performance Needs for Fabric Artifacts*, provide a more detailed explanation of the usage reported here.

Returning to the **Compute** page of the report gives us some other areas of performance metrics. If you hover the mouse over one of the items in the table visual at the bottom of this report, a report tooltip gives details of the CU(s) needed for processing that event, as well as duration(s). This is featured in *Figure 7.10*:

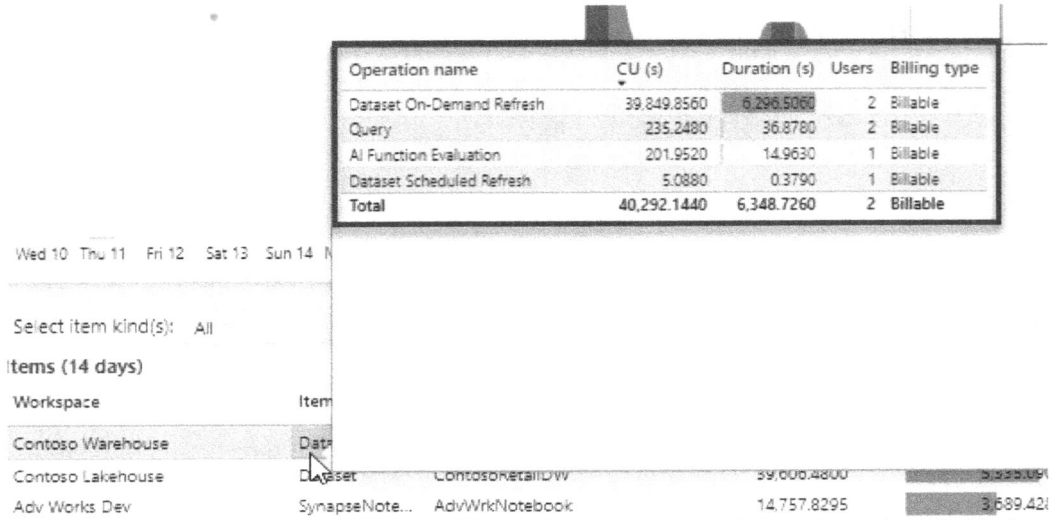

Figure 7.10 – Item processing details

This highlighted semantic model has an on-demand refresh taking over 2,200 CUs at a duration of 1,005.8 seconds. There is also CUs used for **Query** and **Dataset Scheduled Refresh**. With these numbers, we can see the refresh uses a lot more CUs than queries for reports. In this case, we would want to look at optimization techniques referenced in the following chapters to optimize this semantic model.

> **Tip**
>
> Since both reports rely on a semantic model, you can connect reporting tools such as Power BI Desktop, Power BI dataflows, and spreadsheet tools with an Analysis Services driver to view the performance information stored in the semantic model. The model's name for usage metric is **Usage Metrics Reports**, which contains all reports from one workspace. The capacity metric semantic model is named **Fabric Capacity Metrics** from the **Microsoft Fabric Capacity Metrics** workspace.

We are now going to see an example of storing monitoring data along with a custom connector to view REST API output.

Calling REST APIs for monitoring data

Performance metrics can be extracted from the Power BI service using REST API calls. These can be executed from PowerShell or an application development tool. These calls return JSON structures that can be read into a report or database. Keeping this data historically can assist with long-term planning and overall monitoring. The following is a list of common calls for monitored Power BI resources:

- **Reports**: API call to get a list of reports from a workspace or related to a semantic model:

  GET `https://api.powerbi.com/v1.0/myorg/reports`

- **Groups**: API call to get a list of workspaces in a capacity:

  GET `https://api.powerbi.com/v1.0/myorg/admin/groups`

- **Capacities**: API call to get a list of capacities the logged-in user has access to:

  GET `https://api.powerbi.com/v1.0/myorg/admin/capacities`

- **Datasets**: API call to get a list of semantic models. This call can be filtered by the workspace and other attributes:

  GET `https://api.powerbi.com/v1.0/myorg/admin/datasets?$filter={$filter}`

- **Get refresh history**: This call gets the history from the end time of the refresh. If it is blank or empty, the refresh failed or is still processing:

  GET `https://api.powerbi.com/v1.0/myorg/datasets/{datasetId}/refreshes`

These REST API calls can assist in naming assets in the service to extract relevant data for an activity. The main call for activities is `activityevents`:

GET `https://api.powerbi.com/v1.0/myorg/admin/activityevents`

This call returns a JSON structure that can be read into a database table or table structure in an application such as Power BI. Here is a list of typical activity types in the output to help with monitoring:

- `ViewReport` – A user tries to render the report in the service. There is a column in the output, `IsSuccess`, to see if the report displayed with or without an issue.

- `ViewDashboard` – Same as `ViewReport` except for a dashboard of tiles from various reports.

- `RunArtifact` – A generic activity that shows a semantic model, notebook, dataflow, and so on executing in the capacity.

- `RefreshDataset` – Activity related to the refreshing of a semantic model.

There are many more, but these are the most used for monitoring a Power BI system. You can see all calls, explanations, and examples at this site: `https://learn.microsoft.com/en-us/rest/api/power-bi/`.

> **Note**
>
> The names of some of these calls are confusing, such as *group* for workspace or *dataset* for semantic model. While Microsoft has updated its terminology for artifacts (semantic model instead of dataset), it has not updated the names of these REST APIs to match those changes. At one point in Power BI, workspaces were created by creating a group in Office 365. That is why the call to get workspaces is named *group*.

Next, we will look at a community-provided connector to help us analyze REST API calls.

Custom connectors

Custom connectors are used in Power BI Desktop like a connection to a database. The Power BI REST API Connector removes the requirement to call an API from Power Query in Power BI Desktop to retrieve results. This connector is not the answer to monitoring, but it does give an administrator a better glance at the data returned from the REST API calls without having to write code, execute it in PowerShell, and consume in a file or table. It even has a function, `GetData`, for you to pass the URL and parameters of a REST API to call an API not currently in the connector.

Figure 7.11 shows a list of the query options while using the custom connector in Power BI Desktop:

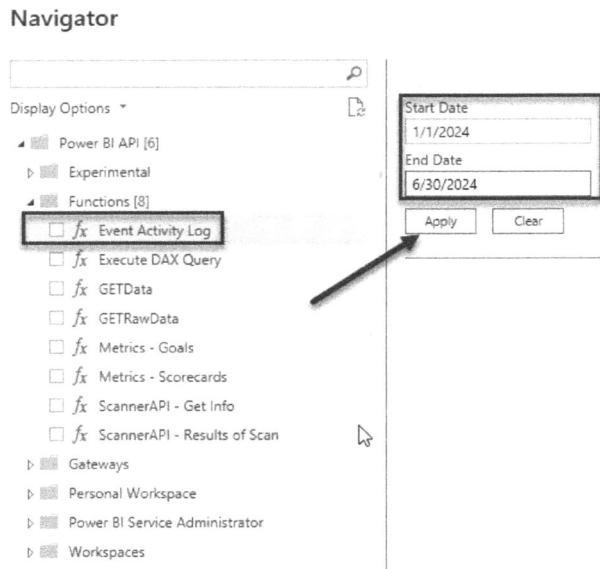

Figure 7.11 – Using a custom connector

As we see in *Figure 7.11*, there are folders for various areas of REST API calls, such as Workspaces. If we drill into the folder, we will see more items (Reports) for those areas, as seen in *Figure 7.12*:

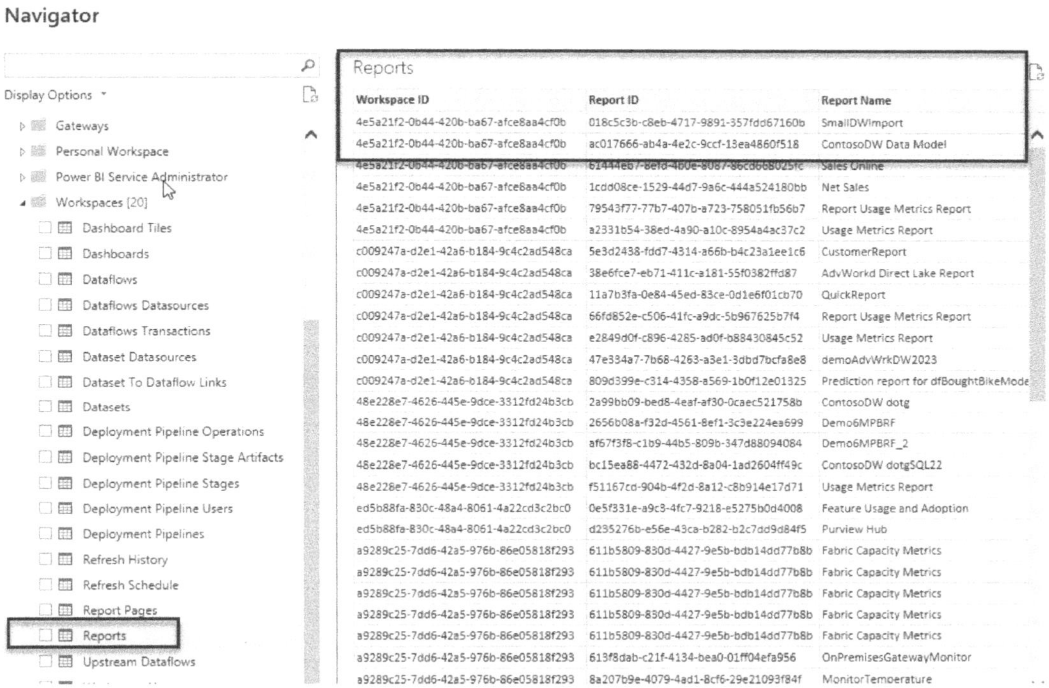

Figure 7.12 – Reports for workspaces

This custom connector is great at helping a new user understand REST API calls and the output to better prepare a custom monitoring system for their own needs. The site to get instructions on using this custom connector is https://www.thepoweruser.com/2021/02/21/power-bi-rest-api-connector/.

The last part of this section will show a table structure and REST API call in PowerShell to help store output.

Storing REST API data

Even though the custom connector is helpful with retrieving monitoring data into a Power BI report, the data is time-sensitive. You will not always have access to all this information. As of the writing of this book, activity is only available for the last 90 days. So, building a storage system to save historical data is imperative. The following is a table structure you can use to store activity data from the REST API GetActivity call:

```
CREATE TABLE [dbo].[GetActivity](
  [ActivityId] [varchar](60) NULL,
  [RecordType] [int] NULL,
  [CreationTime] [datetime] NULL,
  [UserKey] [varchar](50) NULL,
  [Workload] [varchar](50) NULL,
  [UserId] [varchar](50) NULL,
  [Activity] [varchar](50) NULL,
  [ItemName] [varchar](255) NULL,
  [WorkSpaceName] [varchar](255) NULL,
  [DatasetName] [varchar](500) NULL,
  [ReportName] [varchar](500) NULL,
  [WorkspaceId] [varchar](50) NULL,
  [ObjectId] [varchar](500) NULL,
  [DatasetId] [varchar](50) NULL,
  [RefreshType] [varchar](50) NULL,
  [LastRefreshTime] [datetime] NULL,
  [ReportId] [varchar](50) NULL,
  [ReportType] [varchar](50) NULL,
  [DistributionMethod] [varchar](50) NULL,
  [DateRan] [datetime] NOT NULL
) ON [PRIMARY]
GO
ALTER TABLE [dbo].[PowerBIActivityLog]
  ADD  DEFAULT (getdate()) FOR [DateRan]
GO
```

To populate this table from the activity REST API call, we have an example from PowerShell. The example uses a date range as well as a subset of columns to look at activity:

```
$UserName = "no-reply@thomas-leblanc.com"
$PWD = "DoNotUsePassword1"


$PWDSecure = ConvertTo-SecureString $PWD -AsPlainText -Force
$CredentialsTxt = New-Object System.Management.Automation.
PSCredential($UserName,$PWDSecure)
```

```
Connect-PowerBIServiceAccount -Credential $CredentialsTxt


$StartDate = Get-Date((get-date ).AddDays(-30))  -Format "yyyy-MM-dd"
+ 'T00:00:00'
$EndDate = Get-Date((get-date ).AddDays(-1))  -Format "yyyy-MM-
dd"$Datum + 'T23:59:59'
$json = Get-PowerBIActivityEvent -StartDateTime $StartDate
-EndDateTime $EndDate | ConvertFrom-Json
$outputjson = $json | Select Id, RecordType, CreationTime, UserKey,
Workload, UserId, Activity, ItemName, WorkSpaceName, DatasetName,
ReportName, WorkspaceId, ObjectId, DatasetId, RefreshType,
LastRefreshTime, ReportId, ReportType ,DistributionMethod


Write-SqlTableData -InputData $outputjson -ServerInstance
"MySQLServer2022" -DatabaseName "MyDatabase" -SchemaName "dbo"
-TableName "PowerBIActivityLog" -Force
```

This pattern of creating and loading historical data will allow administrators of Power BI to track activity over time. This example used a table in SQL Server, but it can be any database storage system available. The PowerShell example in this case is scheduled to run every 30 days to track the last 30 days of activity. To get related information, tables and REST API calls can be used to save workspace, semantic model, report, and other artifact information.

Other resources

Here are some additional URLs for resources created by Power BI community members for performance monitoring:

Visualise your Power BI Refresh – https://dax.tips/2021/02/15/visualise-your-power-bi-refresh/

Gateway performance monitoring – https://learn.microsoft.com/en-us/data-integration/gateway/service-gateway-performance#gateway-performance-monitoring-public-preview

Let's summarize the learnings from this chapter.

Summary

In this chapter, we introduced a repeatable process to help you manage performance pro-actively in your organization. This is important for consistency and the overall satisfaction of users. If we catch and repair issues before they become widespread, we can save time and money. We started that conversation with baselines for various artifacts and factors for baselines.

Baselines lead to maintaining performance history for trends and spotting anomalies. When problematic content is identified, the recommendation for remediation work is prioritized based on business value and use impact. That investment involves metrics and tools we described in previous chapters to profile systems and slow areas. We then learned about taking lessons from any fixes back into standards and common practices to reduce future issues.

The chapter then transitioned to ways to share knowledge and awareness of performance issues with the developer community and how to leverage guidance documentation and expert help to improve solutions. The different scenarios talked about included self-service, team-based, and IT-managed users. The roles were identified for each set of users and workflows for the performance management cycle.

We completed the chapter by looking at options for monitoring, mainly for reports and processes. The use of a custom connector helped with seeing returned data in a tool we are familiar with – Power BI. The last couple of sections showed important REST API calls for monitoring as well as a suggestion for storing historical data.

In the next chapter, we begin to dive deep into each area of a Power BI solution. Any BI solution starts with data, so we will look at how to optimize data loading and M queries in Power BI.

Part 3:
Fetching, Transforming, and Visualizing Data

In this part, you will understand how the M query engine behaves and how resources are consumed when loading, transforming, and refreshing data. We will explain how many different aspects of report design slow down performance, what to avoid, and whether there are alternatives.

This part has the following chapters:

- *Chapter 8, Loading, Transforming, and Refreshing Data*
- *Chapter 9, Report and Dashboard Design*

8

Loading, Transforming, and Refreshing Data

So far, we have focused a lot on performance monitoring and investigation. We have now reached the next phase of our journey into Power BI performance management. Here, we will begin looking at what actions we can take to remedy the performance issues we discovered while using the tools that were introduced in previous chapters. From here on, each chapter will look deeper at a specific area with solutions and guidance.

Loading new data periodically is a critical part of any analytical system and this mainly applies to Import mode for Power BI. Data refreshes and their associated transformations can be some of the most CPU and memory-intensive operations. Reports depend on current data. Failures can cause users to not trust the report data. Large semantic models that occupy a significant portion of a host's memory, and that have complex data transformations, are more prone to resource contention. Poorly designed transformations contribute to high resource usage and can result in refresh failures. They can even affect development productivity by slowing down, or in extreme cases, crashing Power BI Desktop.

In this chapter, we will learn how Power BI's **Power Query** transformation engine works and how to design queries with performance in mind. Additionally, we'll learn how to use the strengths of data sources and avoid pitfalls in query design with the aim of reducing CPU and memory use. This provides benefits when the semantic models are still in development and when they are deployed to production.

In this chapter, we will cover the following main topics:

- General data transformation guidance
- Folding and joining
- Refreshing incrementally
- Using query diagnostics
- Optimizing dataflows

Technical requirements

There are examples available for some parts of this chapter. We will call out which files to refer to. Please check out the `Chapter08` folder on GitHub to get these assets: `https://github. com/PacktPublishing/Microsoft-Power-BI-Performance-Best-Practices-Second-Edition`.

General data transformation guidance

Power Query allows users to build relatively complex data transformation pipelines through a point-and-click interface. Each step of the query is defined by a line of M script that has been autogenerated by the UI. It's quite easy to load data from multiple sources and perform a wide range of transformations in a somewhat arbitrary order. Suboptimal step ordering and configuration can use the necessary resources and slow down the data refresh.

> **Note**
>
> Using Power Query to do more than connect to a data source and add/remove column transformations should be used for small data sources. If you find yourself having to transform large tables and data sources, the data source structure should be examined with dimensional modeling techniques in mind. This will push the transformations to the ETL level instead of Power Query. Semantic models are meant for analytical reporting and adding other types of reporting to Power BI Desktop can cause lots of issues with performance.

Sometimes, the problem might not be apparent in Power BI Desktop. This is more likely when using smaller subsets of data for development, which is a common practice. Hence, it's important to apply good Power Query design practices to avoid surprises. We will begin by looking at how Power Query uses resources.

Data refresh, parallelism, and resource usage

When you perform a **full data refresh** for an Import mode semantic model in the Power BI service, the current semantic model and data stay online. It can still be queried by published reports or even from Power BI Desktop and other client tools such as Excel. This is because a second copy of the semantic model is refreshed in the background, while the original is still online and can serve users. However, this functionality comes at a price because both copies take up memory. Furthermore, transformations that are being performed on the incoming data also use memory.

> **Note**
>
> For a full refresh, you should assume that a semantic model will need at least two times its size in memory to be able to refresh successfully. Those with complex or inefficient transformations might use significantly more memory. In practical terms, this means a 2 GB dataset would need at least 4 GB of memory available to refresh.

Using an **incremental model** or customizing the partition refreshes will reduce the required memory. The amount depends on the dictionary for columns in the refreshed partition. However, it will still be significantly less than a fully refreshed partition.

The actual work of loading and transforming data in Power BI is performed by the **Power BI Query mashup engine**. The **host**, as mentioned at the beginning of the chapter, refers to the machine where this mashup engine is running. This host could be Power BI Desktop, the Power BI service, capacities, or a gateway. Each table being refreshed runs in an **evaluation container**. In Power BI Desktop, each evaluation container is allocated 432 MB of physical memory by default. If a container requires more physical memory than this, it will use virtual memory and be paged to disk, which dramatically *slows it down* or freezes up Power BI Desktop.

Additionally, the number of containers executing in parallel depends on the host. In Power BI Desktop, the number of containers running in parallel defaults to the number of logical cores available on the machine. This can be adjusted in the **Data Load** section of the Power Query settings pane. Also, you can adjust the amount of memory used by each container. These settings can be seen in *Figure 8.1*:

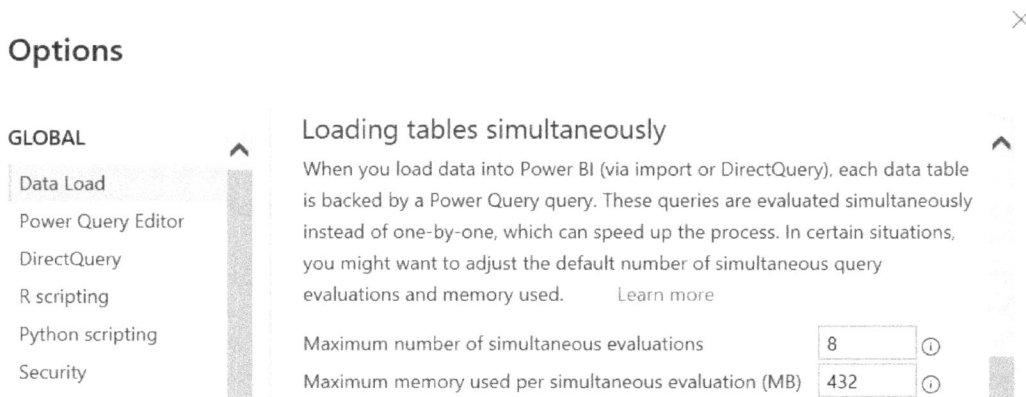

Figure 8.1 – The Power Query parallel loading settings

There are two settings:

- **Maximum number of simultaneous evaluations**: 8

- **Maximum memory used per simultaneous evaluations (MB)**: 432

Each will default to an installation value, but if you hover the mouse point over the information symbol (**i**) to the right of each value, Power BI Desktop will search your system for the best values based on the number of processors and amount of RAM in your system as shown in *Figure 8.2* and *Figure 8.3*:

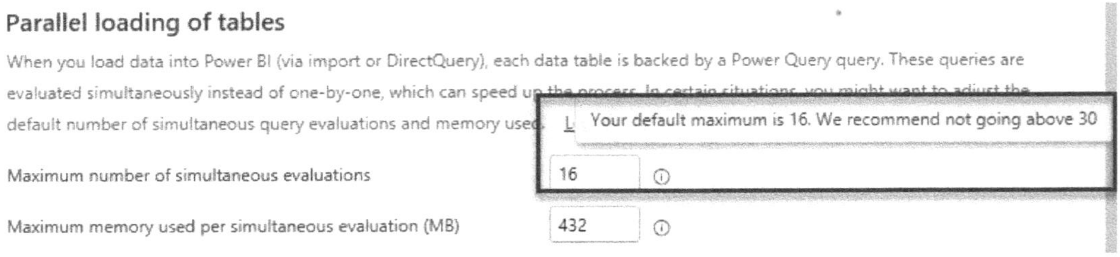

Parallel loading of tables

When you load data into Power BI (via import or DirectQuery), each data table is backed by a Power Query query. These queries are evaluated simultaneously instead of one-by-one, which can speed up the process. In certain situations, you might want to adjust the default number of simultaneous query evaluations and memory used.

Your default maximum is 16. We recommend not going above 30

Maximum number of simultaneous evaluations   16   ⓘ

Maximum memory used per simultaneous evaluation (MB)   432   ⓘ

Figure 8.2 – Maximum number of simultaneous evaluation suggestions

As you can see in *Figure 8.3*, Power BI suggests not exceeding 905 MB for optimal usage.

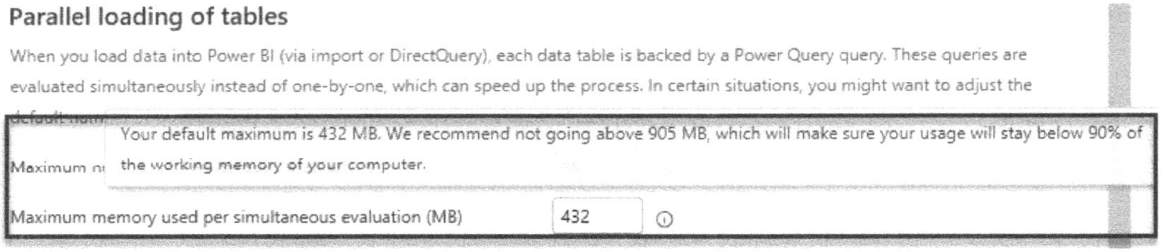

Parallel loading of tables

When you load data into Power BI (via import or DirectQuery), each data table is backed by a Power Query query. These queries are evaluated simultaneously instead of one-by-one, which can speed up the process. In certain situations, you might want to adjust the

Your default maximum is 432 MB. We recommend not going above 905 MB, which will make sure your usage will stay below 90% of the working memory of your computer.

Maximum memory used per simultaneous evaluation (MB)   432   ⓘ

Figure 8.3 – Maximum memory used per simultaneous evaluations

Increasing these settings can help with larger datasets. Some data transformations require a lot of memory for temporary data storage. If the container memory is completely used up, the operation pages to disk, which is much slower. The setting will assign one container per available logical core, and they will all run in parallel. Depending on the complexity of the transformation and what else is running on the development computer, this might have a reasonable load.

Microsoft provides a table of examples to suggest what to change with these settings based on the issue. This link provides up-to-date options and scenarios: `https://learn.microsoft.com/en-us/power-bi/create-reports/desktop-evaluation-configuration`.

For Power BI capacities, embedded, and Azure Analysis Services, you cannot modify the number of containers or memory settings through any UI. The limits depend on the SKU and are managed by Microsoft. However, using the **XMLA endpoint**, you can manually override the setting for how many tables or partitions can be processed in parallel. This is done by using the `sequence` command in a TMSL script. You can use a tool such as **SQL Server Management Studio** to connect to the semantic model and execute it. The following example uses a `sequence` command to enable 10 parallel evaluation containers:

```
{   "sequence":{
    "maxParallelism":10,
    "operations":[
      {"refresh":{
          "type":"full",
          "objects":[
            {"database":"ExampleDataset",
              "table":"ExampleLogs",
              "partition":"ExampleLogs202112" }
          // specify further tables and partitions here
  ] } } ] } }
```

Note that only one table is listed as an example. You can simply modify this script and specify more tables or partitions in the table and partition section of the script.

Now, let's see how to make working with queries faster in Power BI Desktop.

Improving the development experience

When working with significant data volumes, complex transformations, or slow data sources, Power BI Desktop development environment can occasionally slow down or become non-responsive. One reason for this is that a **local data cache** is maintained to show you data previews for each transformation step, and Power BI tries to refresh this in the background. It can also be caused if there are many dynamic queries being driven by a parameter. When properly used, **query parameters** are a good Power Query design practice. However, a single parameter change can cause many previews to be updated at once, and this can slow things down and put excess load on the data source.

If you experience such issues, you can turn off **Background Data** in the Power Query settings, as shown in *Figure 8.4*. This will cause a preview to only be generated when you select a query step. The appropriate setting is shown in the following figure:

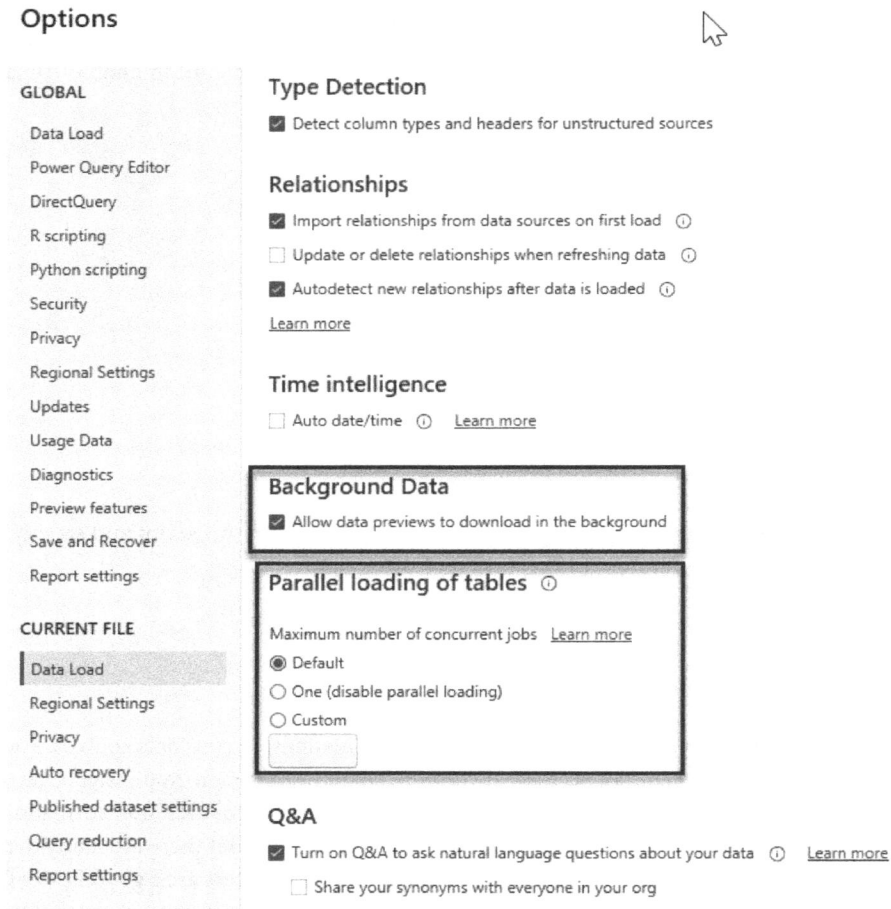

Figure 8.4 – The Data Load settings to disable complex queries

Figure 8.4 also shows a **Parallel loading of tables** setting to prevent the parallel loading of tables. This is very useful in scenarios where you are running many complex queries and know for certain that the source would handle sequential queries better. Often, this is the case when using handwritten native queries for a data source with many joins, transformations, and summarizations. The **Parallel loading of tables** setting has options for disabling (just one thread), **Default** (6 concurrent threads), and a **Custom** number (threads).

Another method for reducing the load on source data while still in development is to use a parameter. This example will use a date range to limit data in a fact table. The parameters used in *Figure 8.5* are `RangeStart` and `RangeEnd`:

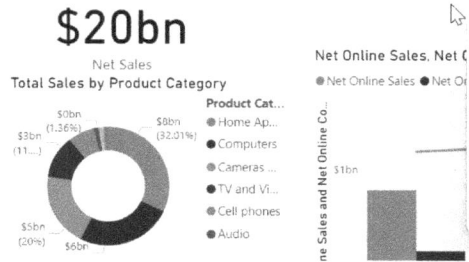

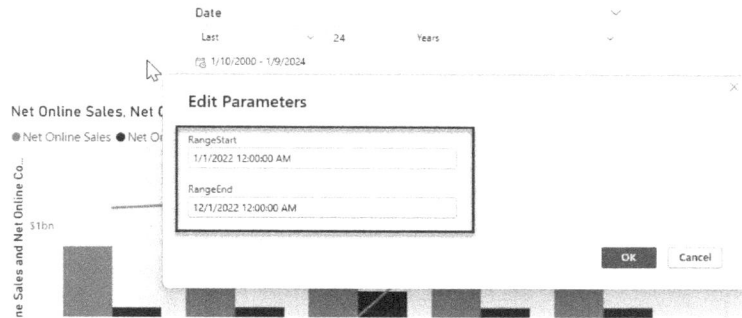

Figure 8.5 – Parameters used to filter dates

The parameters can then be used in the Power Query Editor to place a filter on the `Sales` table as in *Figure 8.6*.

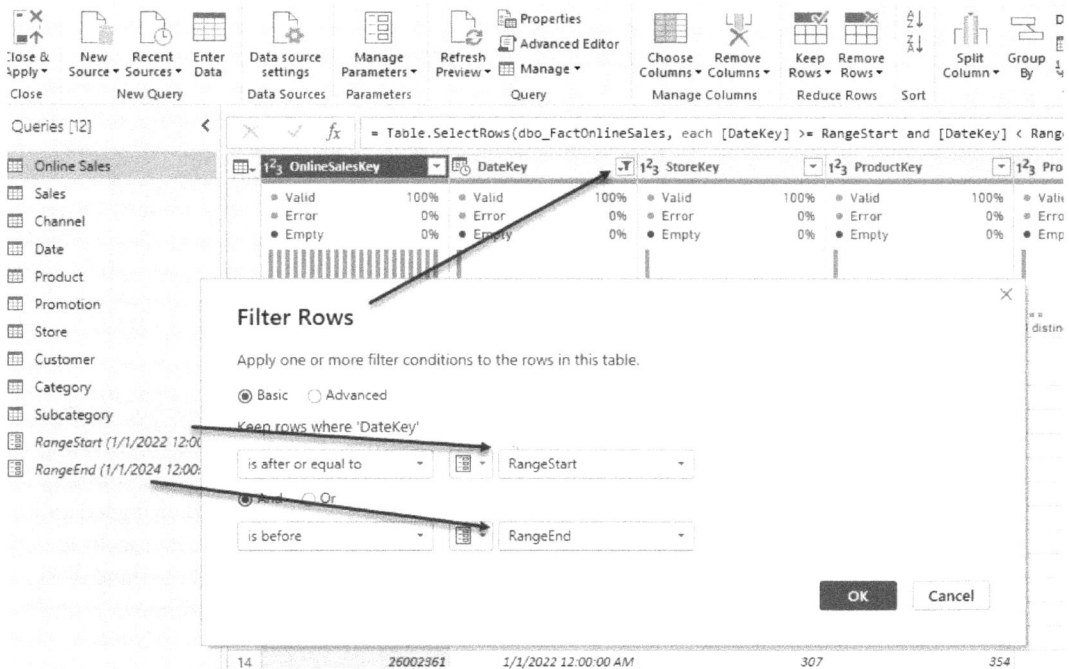

Figure 8.6 – Parameters used as filters for the Sales table

This will limit the data in Power BI Desktop to one year. Once deployed to the Power BI service, you can change the parameter values in the settings and manually trigger a refresh. *Figure 8.7* shows the deployed semantic model and its settings.

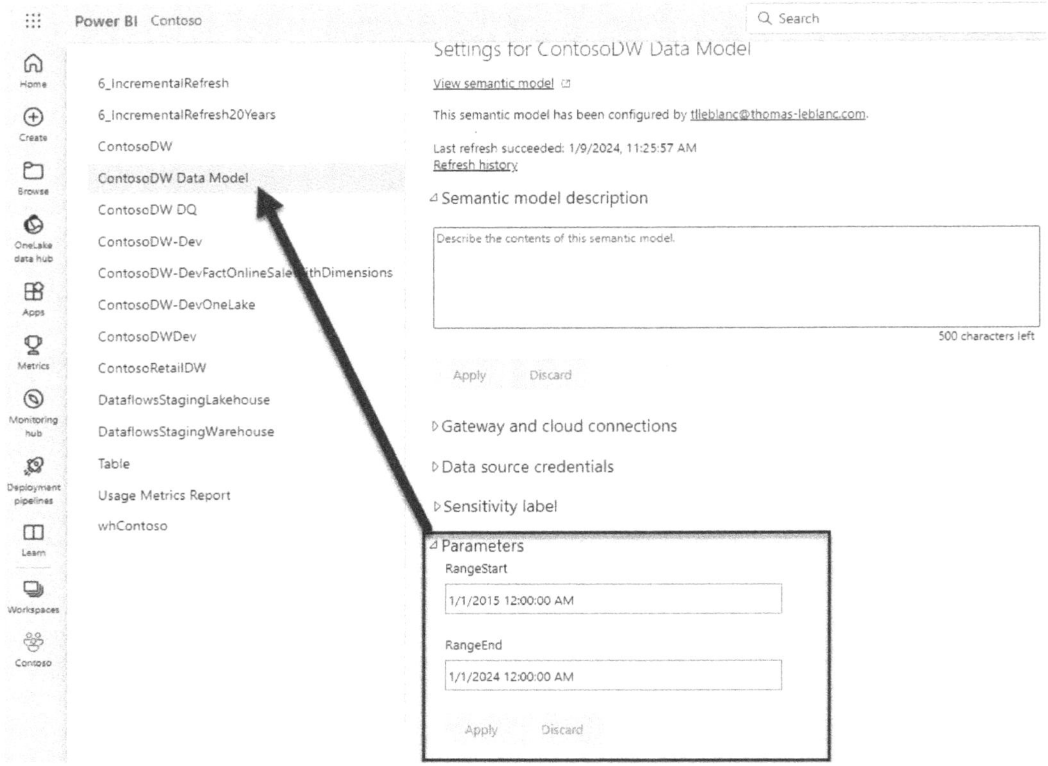

Figure 8.7 – Power BI service settings for semantic model

If you are using multiple data sources and values from one source to control the queries of another, you can experience lower performance with the default privacy settings. This is because Power Query prevents any leakage of data from one data source to another for security reasons. For example, if you use values from one database to filter data from another, the values you pass could be logged and viewed by unintended people. Power Query prevents this leakage by pulling all the data locally and then applying the filter. This takes longer because Power Query must wait to read all the data. Also, it can't take advantage of any optimizations at the source by reducing data from the source or taking advantage of indexes from a database.

If you are comfortable with the risks associated with data leakage, you can disable the **Privacy Levels** settings, as shown in *Figure 8.8*. This shows a global setting. However, note that you can also set this individually for each `.pbix` file in the **Privacy** setting for the current file (not shown in the figure).

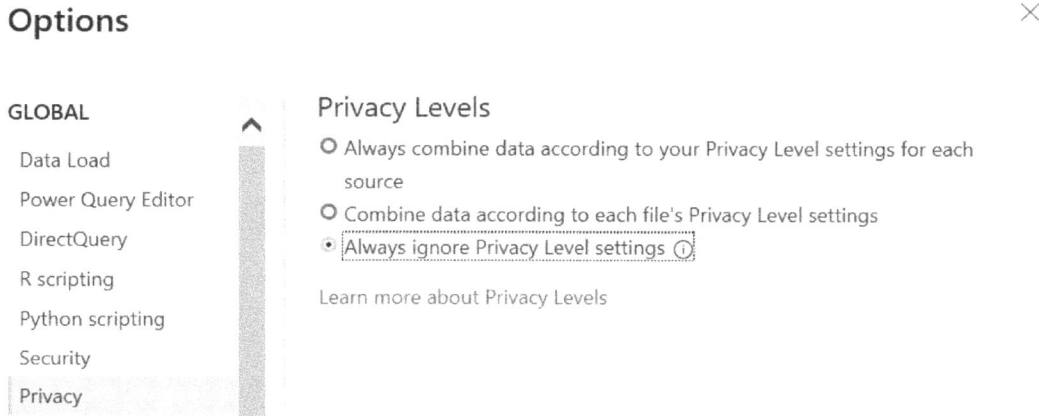

Options   ✕

GLOBAL ⌃	Privacy Levels
Data Load	○ Always combine data according to your Privacy Level settings for each source
Power Query Editor	○ Combine data according to each file's Privacy Level settings
DirectQuery	⦿ Always ignore Privacy Level settings ⓘ
R scripting	
Python scripting	Learn more about Privacy Levels
Security	
Privacy	

Figure 8.8 – Ignoring the Privacy Levels settings can improve performance

Another helpful Power Query technique is using the reference feature to use one query to start a new query. A user can right-click a query and select **Reference**. It is similar to making a copy of a query except it is a pointer to the previous query. This is useful when you need to split a data stream into multiple formats or filter and transform subsets differently.

A common mistake is to leave this reference table available in the data model even though it is never directly used in reports. Even if you hide it from users, it will still be loaded and occupy memory. In such cases, it's better to turn off the **Enable Load** option, which can be found by right-clicking on a query or table in Power Query. Disabling the load will only temporarily keep the table during refresh and reduce the semantic model's memory footprint.

In the following figure, the CSV source files contain two different groups of records, `Students` and `Scores`. Once these groups are separated into their own tables, the starting table does not need to be loaded.

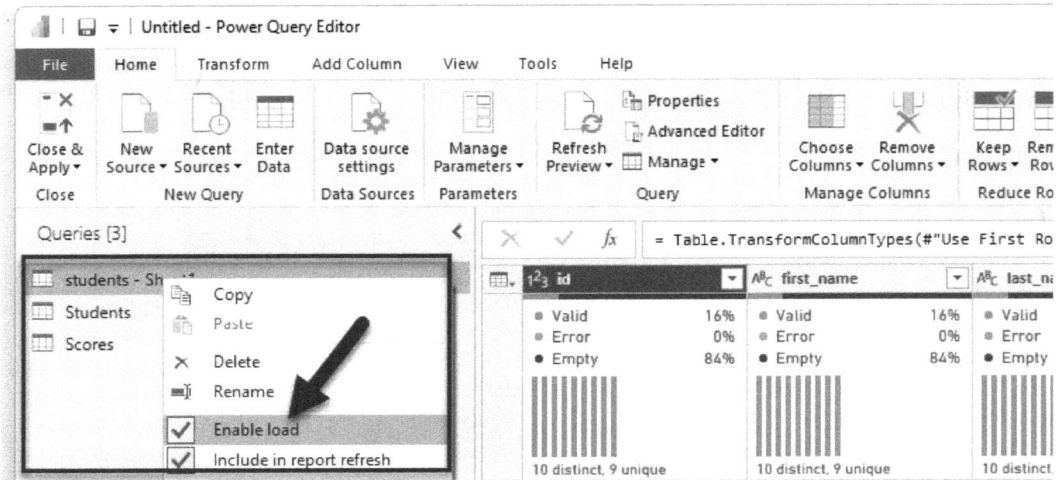

Figure 8.9 – How to turn off loading intermediate tables

A final tip is to consider whether you really need the **Auto data/time** feature in Power BI. When enabled, it will create a hidden internal date table associated with every date or date/time field found in the semantic model.

Figure 8.10 shows this auto-generated date table in DAX Studio for a `.pbix` file with this enabled.

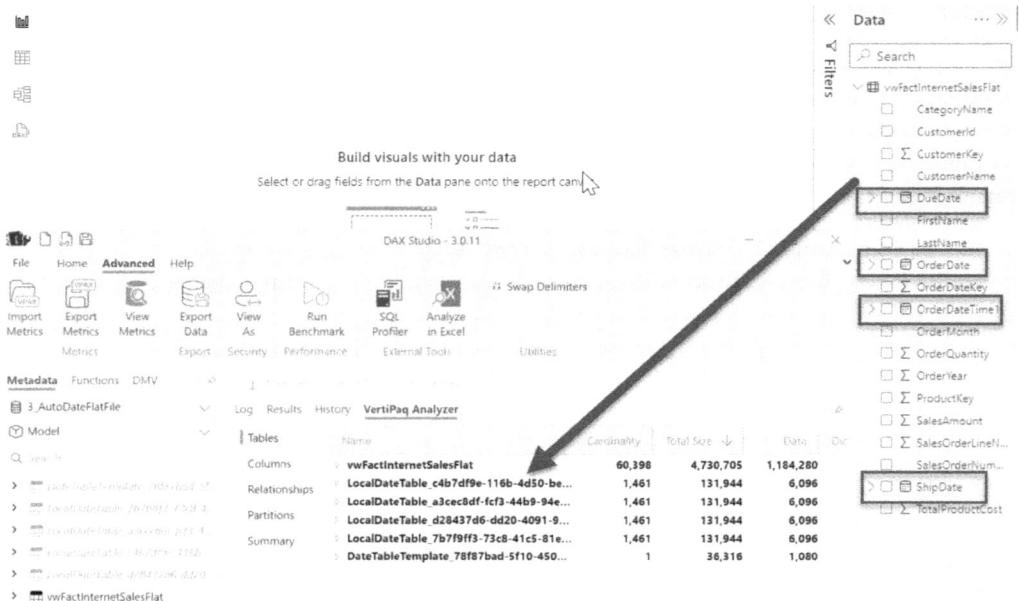

Figure 8.10 – Auto date tables in DAX Studio

This can take up significant space if you have a wide range of dates and many date fields. A better practice is to use your own date dimension table that is connected to only the meaningful dates in a fact table that need aggregations to a date attribute such as month, quarter, week, or year. The option setting for **Auto date/time** can be enabled on a `.pbix` file or set globally to any new `.pbix` file that is created. *Figure 8.11* shows the **GLOBAL** option.

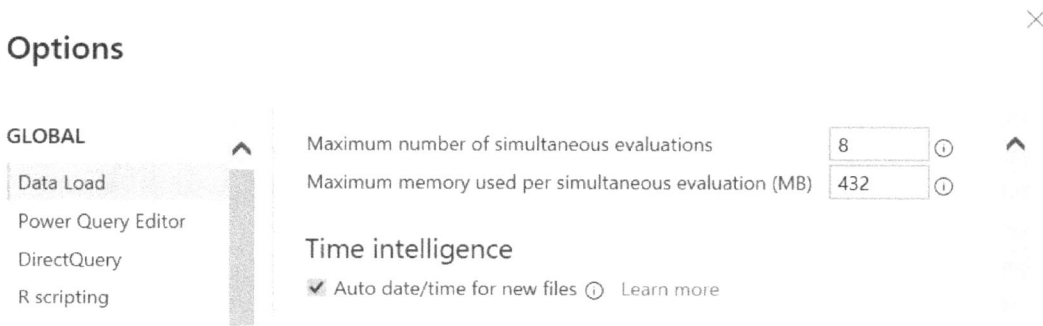

Figure 8.11 – Time intelligence in the Power Query settings

Next, we'll look at ways to leverage the strengths of large data stores for offload work from Power Query and reduce refresh times.

Folding and joining queries

Two common performance issues come with the relationship and SQL that is sent to the database relational engine. These involve joining queries by common keys and adding transformations that translate into SQL for the database engine.

Query folding

While Power Query has its own capable data shaping engine, it can push down certain transformations to data sources in their native query language. This is known as **query folding**, and formally, it means that the mashup engine can translate your transformation steps into single `SELECT` statements that are sent to the data source.

> **Tip**
> Query folding is an important concept as it can provide huge performance benefits. Folding minimizes the amount of data being returned to Power BI, and it can make a huge difference in refresh times or DirectQuery performance with large data volumes such as millions or billions of rows.

There is a bit of knowledge and trial and error required to get the best folding setup. You know a query step is folded when you can right-click on the step and see the **View Native Query** option enabled, as shown in *Figure 8.12*.

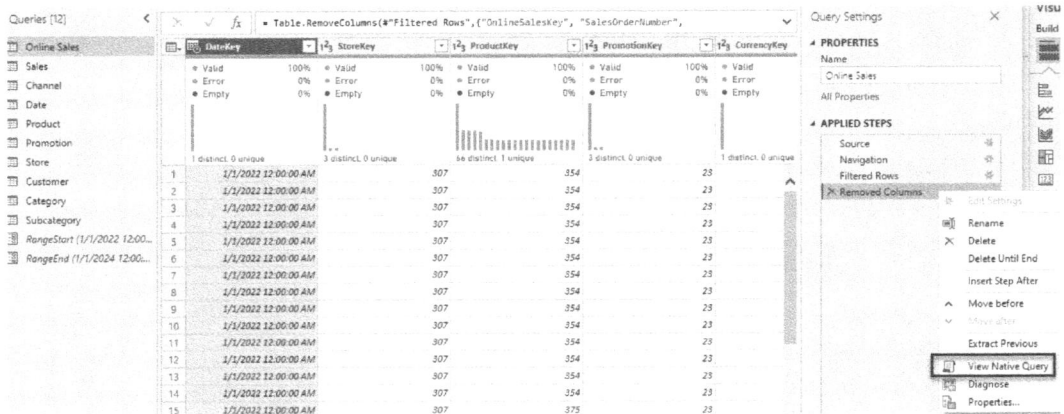

Figure 8.12 – View Native Query indicates that folding has occurred

Ideally, you will want to see the last step of your query that allows you to view the native query because this means the entire query has been folded. This seems straightforward enough, but it's important to understand which operations can be folded and which can break a chain of otherwise foldable operations. This depends on the individual data source and the documentation is not comprehensive.

> **Note**
>
> Sometimes you cannot get all the steps to fold. That is OK. Just make sure to order the steps by folding first, then end with the steps that do not fold.

Not every source supports viewing a native query: one example is **OData**, which is a standard for building and consuming **REST APIs**. You can use **Query Diagnostics** in such cases to learn more about what each step is doing. We will cover Query Diagnostics in the next section. To keep up to date on changes to query folding, use this link: `https://learn.microsoft.com/en-us/power-query/power-query-folding`.

The following list of operations is reported by Microsoft to support folding:

- **Removing columns from a query**: It is suggested to use the **Choose Column** button in the toolbar for Power Query rather than highlighting a column and deleting it. This consolidates that column removal in one step.

- **Changing the column name in the model**: This does not change the name of the data source column but does use the alias in the native query for the column.

- **Simple logic to add a new column**: These include M functions that have an equivalent function in the data source.

- **Pivot and unpivot of data**: If supported by the relational database engine.

- **Filtering rows by columns**: This will be moved to the WHERE clause of the SELECT data source.

- **Simple aggregations that are grouped**: Translate into the GROUP BY in a SELECT statement with, as an example, COUNT or SUM.

- **Merge or append queries that do not use fuzzy compares**: JOIN and UNION operations in SELECT are selected for this transformation.

The following list of operations is not foldable:

- **Column data type changes**: This has gotten better in recent releases, but it is still one to check after making a change. Relational database tables should have the proper data types, but views can help translate at the source.

- **Columns that are index types in Power Query**: These are used when no true surrogate key is available but are not used often.

- Appending and merging queries from different data sources.

- Complex logic in new columns.

> Tip
>
> If you are fluent in the native language of the data source and are comfortable writing your own query, you can use a custom query instead of letting Power Query generate one for you. This can be a last resort to ensure that everything possible has been pushed down. It is particularly useful when you know the source data characteristics such as frequency and distribution and can use source-specific capabilities such as query hints to improve speed. Complex joins and aggregations might not be completely pushed down to the source and might benefit from being implemented within a custom query.

Next, we will look at an example where the same query logic is performed in two different ways, that is, by only changing a data source. We'll show how this affects folding and how to investigate the impact on performance.

In this scenario, we have a data warehouse and want to create a wide denormalized table as a quick stopgap for an analyst. We need to take a sales fact table and enrich it with qualitative data from four dimensions, such as customer, stock, employee, and city. For the sake of this example, these tables are loaded individually into Power BI Desktop, as shown in the following figure:

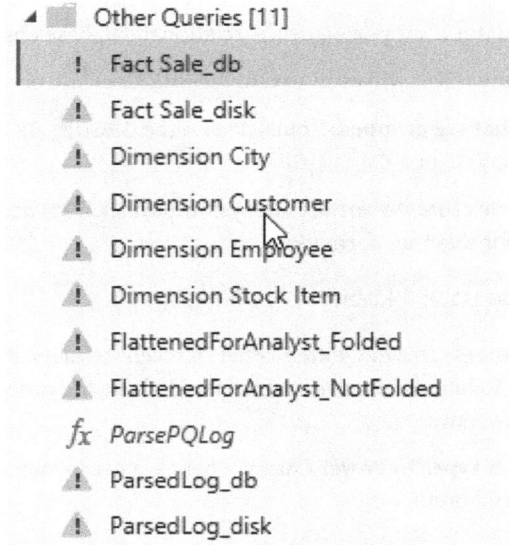

Figure 8.13 – The starting tables loaded into the semantic model

We dumped this database-hosted fact table inside a `.csv` file and named it `FactSale_disk` to provide an alternative data source to perform the comparison.

We perform a merge from the fact to the dimensions, expanding the columns we need after each merge. We expect this version to be folded. We expect the disk version to not be folded because the joins and filters are applied directly to the CSV on disk. The difference between these is shown in the comparison of query steps that follow. Note how `FlattenedForAnalyst_NotFolded` has the **View Native Query** option disabled, which confirms this difference in *Figure 8.14*.

Query Settings

⊿ **PROPERTIES**

Name

FlattenedForAnalyst_Folded

All Properties

⊿ **APPLIED STEPS**

Sales_Fact_DB ✷
Expanded Dimension Customer ✷
Merged Queries ✷
Expanded Dimension City ✷
Merged Queries1 ✷
Expanded Dimension Employee ✷
Merged Queries2 ✷
✕ Ex·

✷	Edit Settings
▣	Rename
✕	Delete
	Delete Until End
	Insert Step After
∧	Move before
∨	Move after
	Extract Previous
▣	View Native Query
▣	Diagnose
▣	Properties...

Query Settings

⊿ **PROPERTIES**

Name

FlattenedForAnalyst_NotFolded

All Properties

⊿ **APPLIED STEPS**

Sales_Fact_disk ✷
Expanded Dimension Customer ✷
Merged Queries ✷
Expanded Dimension City ✷
Merged Queries1 ✷
Expanded Dimension Employee ✷
Merged Queries2 ✷
✕ Expande

✷	Edit Settings
▣	Rename
✕	Delete
	Delete Until End
	Insert Step After
∧	Move before
∨	Move after
	Extract Previous
▣	View Native Query
▣	Diagnose
▣	Properties...

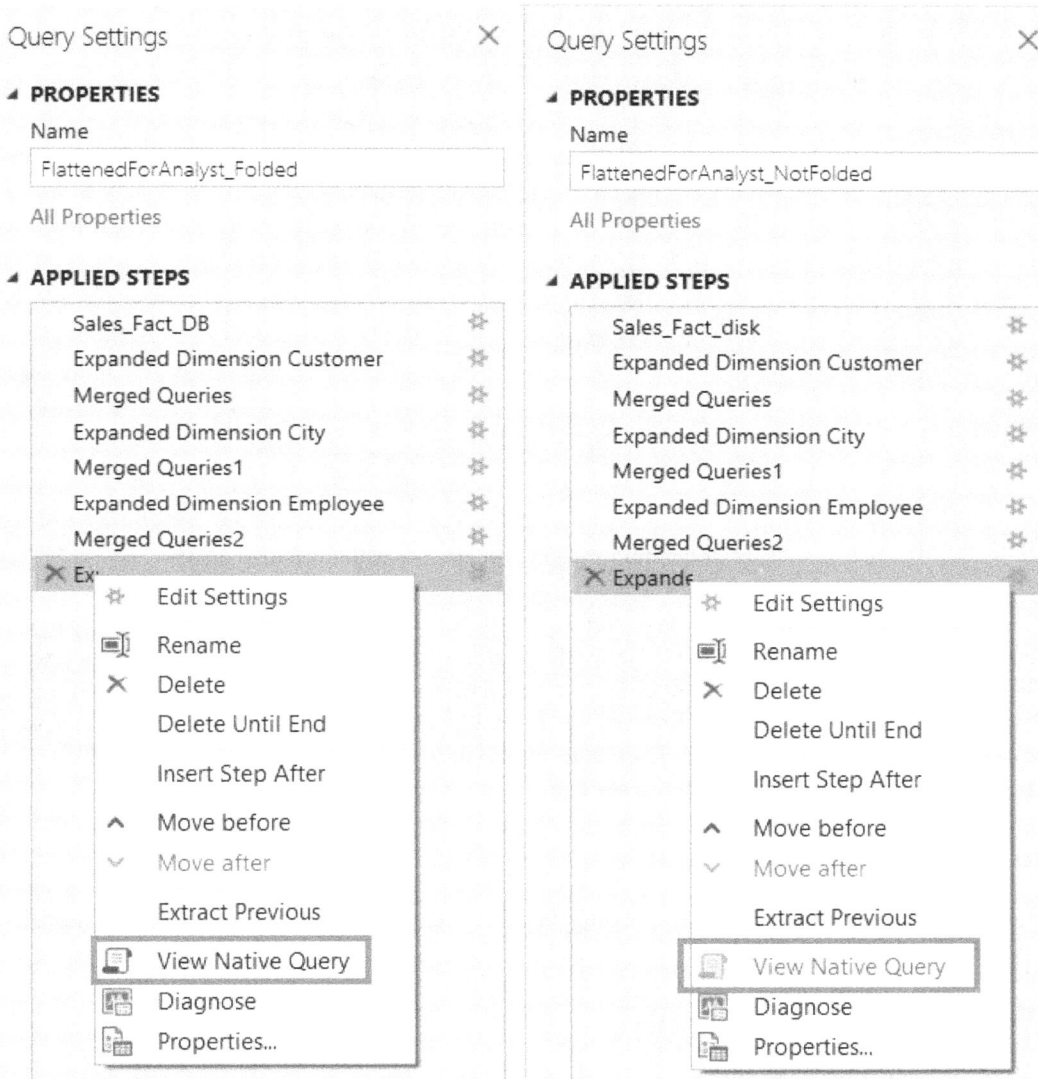

Figure 8.14 – A comparison of the same query logic using different sources

In the following figure, we compare the high-level activities and durations of these two refresh operations.

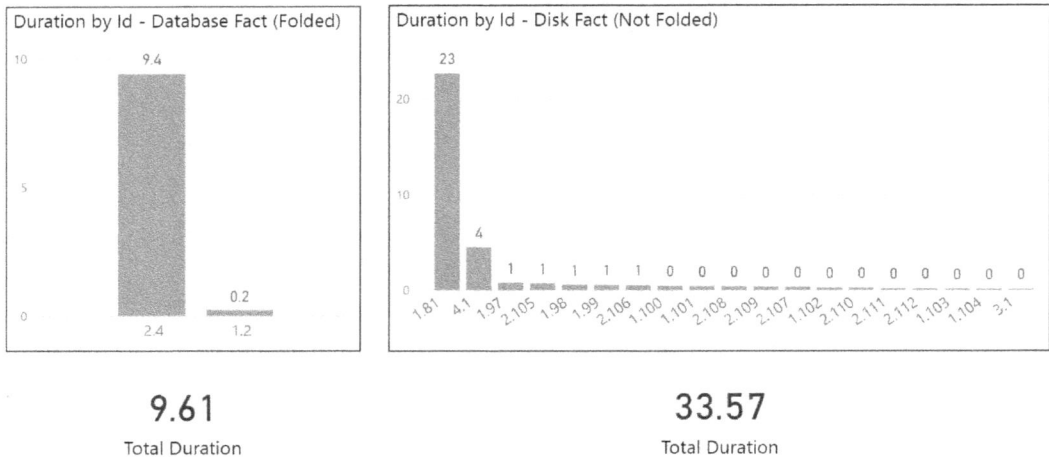

Figure 8.15 – A shorter duration and fewer operations with the folded query

We can clearly see that the pure database method was significantly faster – about 10 seconds compared to about 34 seconds for the mixed database and file method. This should not be a surprise when we think about how the mashup engine works. For the pure database method, all logic was folded and sent to the data source as a single query. However, when using the fact table from the file and dimension from the database, Power Query needs to execute queries to fetch the dimension data so that the join can perform locally. This explains why we see significantly more activities.

Joining queries

Next, we will look at how incrementally loading data can decrease refresh times for semantic model fact tables.

Refreshing incrementally

For data sources that support queries being pushed down, Power Query can use **incremental refresh**. This is used mostly on fact tables that have a column to indicate the date/time the rows were updated, and there are no changes to historical data – minimum updates to rows. This useful design pattern is considered for improving refresh speeds on large data imports. By default, Power BI requires a full load of all tables when a semantic model is using Import mode. This means all the existing data in the table is discarded before the refresh operation, and it ensures that the latest data is loaded into the semantic model.

However, this results in unchanged historical data being loaded into the semantic model each time it is refreshed. If you know that you have source data that is only ever appended and historical records are never modified, you can configure individual tables to use incremental refresh to load just the most recent data. The following steps should be followed in sequence to enable incremental refresh:

1. Before you can use the incremental fresh feature, you must add two date/time parameters, called `RangeStart` and `RangeEnd`, to control the start and end of the refresh period. The setup of the parameters is shown in the following figure:

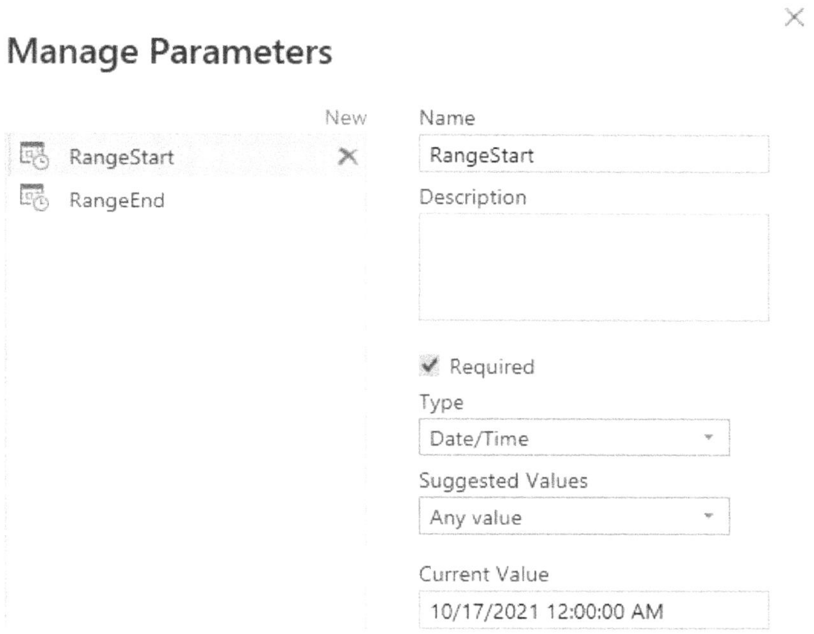

Figure 8.16 – The date/time parameters required for incremental refresh

2. Next, you must use these parameters as dynamic filters to control the amount of data returned by your query. An example of this configuration is shown in *Figure 3.17*, where the `DateKey` column is used for filtering the `Sales` table:

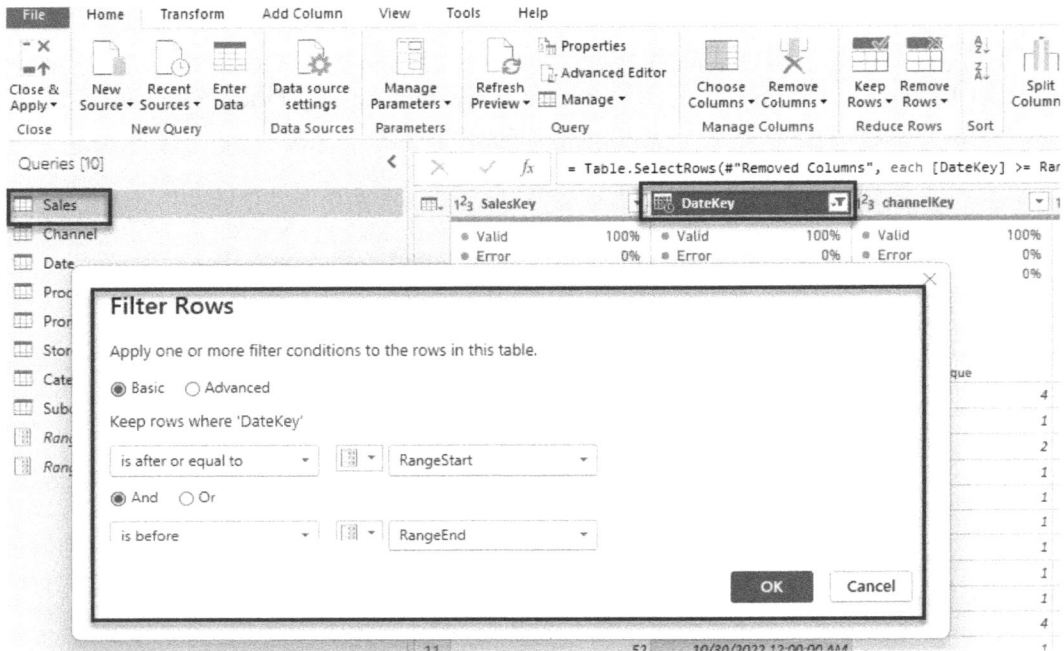

Figure 8.17 – Filter configuration to support parameterized date ranges in a query

3. Once you have a query configured to use the date range parameters, you can enable incremental refresh on this table. You simply right-click on the sales table name in the Power BI Desktop and select the **Incremental refresh** option. A column of data/time data type must exist on the table. This column needs to be the column of the filter date range used previously. *Figure 8.18* has archive data in partitions set to 10 years, while the current refresh will update the current month partition:

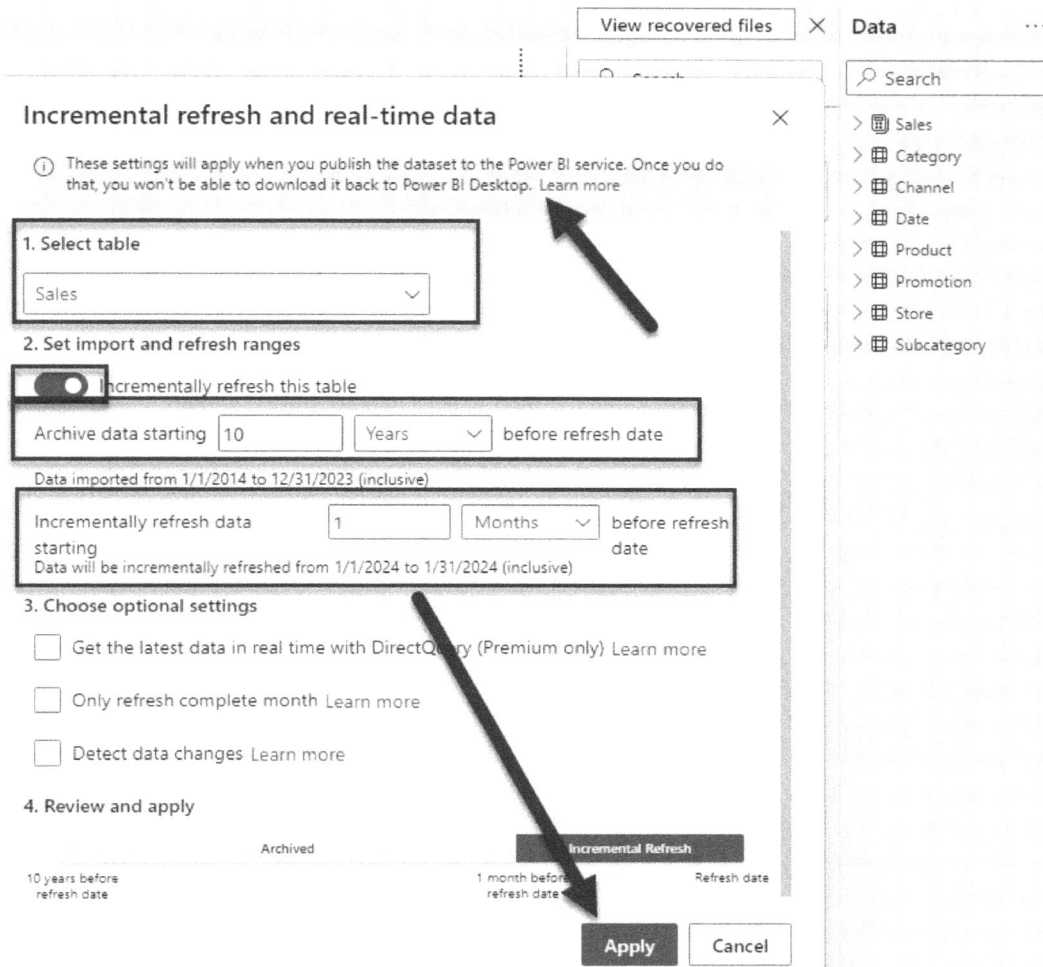

Figure 8.18 – Incremental refresh configured within a table

4. Next, the model must be deployed to the Power BI service, and a manual refresh executed. This will create the initial partitions for the archive and update partitions in the current year.

There are three other options available in the incremental refresh setup dialog that enable you to have more control:

*   **Get the latest data in real time with DirectQuery (Premium only)**: If you are using DirectQuery with incremental refresh, this is the option to refresh query data immediately or near real time.

*   **Only refresh complete month**: This will ensure that only the most recent complete month (or day or quarter, etc.) of data will be refreshed. The date option (month, day, quarter, etc.)

depends on the selection from the **Incrementally refresh data starting** setting. This is required to ensure the accuracy of some business metrics. For example, calculating the *monthly average* users for a web application would not be accurate if considering incomplete months.

- **Detect data changes**: This will allow you to choose a timestamp column in the source database that represents the last modified date of the record. If this is available in the source, it can further improve performance by allowing Power BI to only select changed rows within the refresh period.

Next, we will see how the built-in query diagnostics can help us spot and resolve performance issues.

Using Query Diagnostics

In Power BI Desktop, you can enable Query Diagnostics to get a detailed understanding of what each step of your query is doing. Even with seemingly simple queries that have few transformations, if performance is bad, you will need to know which part is slowing you down so that you can concentrate your optimization efforts. **Diagnostics** needs to be enabled in the Power Query settings, as shown in the following figure.

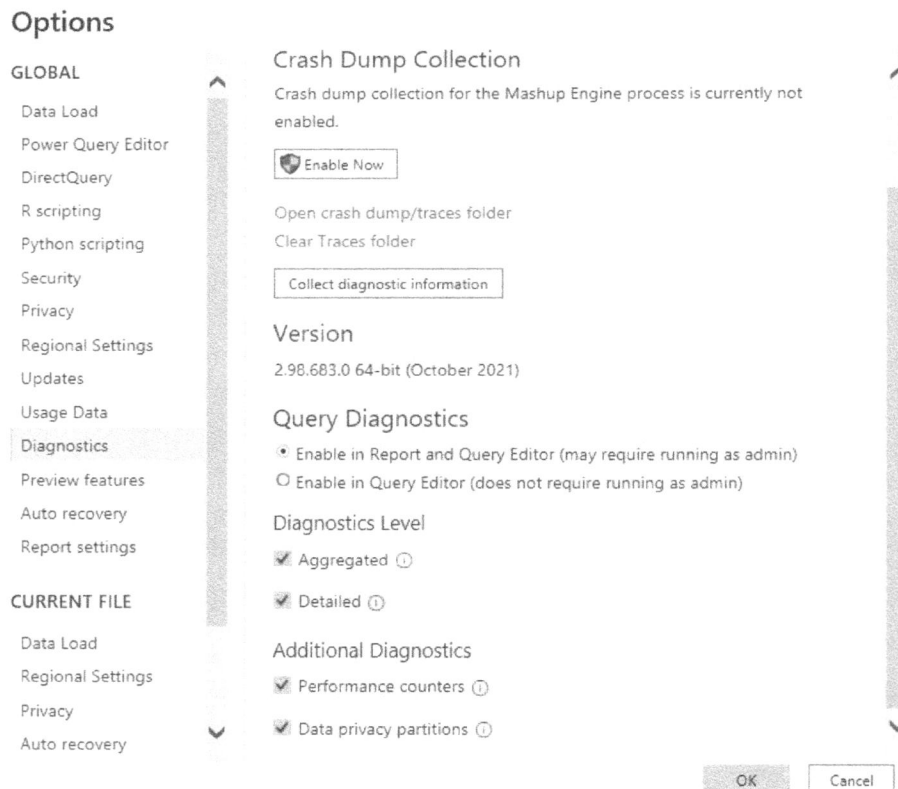

Figure 8.19 – Query Diagnostics enabled in the Power Query settings

You might not need all the traces that are shown in the previous figure. At a minimum, enable the **Aggregated** diagnostic level and **Performance counters**.

There are up to four types of logs that are available:

- **Aggregated**: This is a summary view that aggregates multiple related operations into a single log entry. The exclusive durations are summed per entry.

- **Detailed**: This is a verbose view with no aggregation. It is recommended for complex issues or where the summary log does not provide enough to determine a root cause.

- **Performance counters**: Every half second, Power Query takes a snapshot of the current memory use, CPU utilization, and throughput. This might be negligible for queries that are fast or push all the work to the data source.

- **Data privacy partitions**: This helps you identify the logical partitions that are used internally for data privacy.

Next, we will learn how to collect the traces and explore the information contained within them.

Collecting Power Query diagnostics

Diagnostic traces are not automatically collected after the settings, as shown in *Figure 8.19*, have been enabled. To save trace data to disk, you need to start diagnostics from the **Tools** menu of the **Power Query Editor** screen, as shown in *Figure 8.20*.

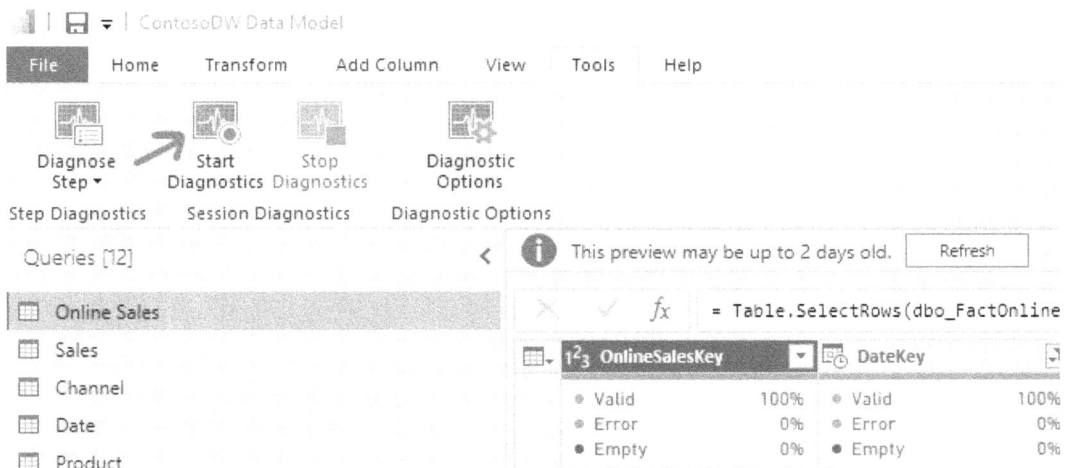

Figure 8.20 – The Power Query diagnostic controls

Select the **Start Diagnostics** button to enable data collection. From this point on, any query or refresh operations will be logged to disk. You can perform as many operations as you want, but nothing will be visible until you use the **Stop Diagnostics** button. After stopping the diagnostics, the logs are automatically added to the query editor, as shown in the following figure.

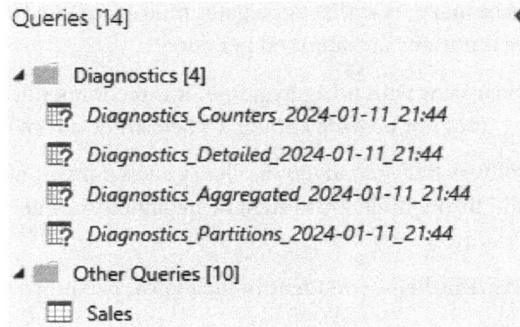

Figure 8.21 – The query logs are automatically loaded

You can only collect traces from the **Query Editor UI**. It will capture any activity, even loading previews and working in a single step. Additionally, you can capture activity from the **Report** view, which is great for tracing a full table or semantic model refresh. The choice you make will depend on the scenario you are trying to debug. You can select a single query step and use the **Diagnose Step** button to run a single step, which will create a dedicated trace file that is named after the step.

> **Tip**
> Query logs can become quite large and might become difficult to work with. The Power Query Editor UI performs background operations and caching to improve the user experience, so all the steps might not be properly represented. We recommend that you only capture diagnostics for the operations or tables you are trying to debug to simplify the analysis. Start diagnostics, perform the action you want to investigate, then stop diagnostics immediately after and analyze the files.

Analyzing the Power Query logs

The Power Query diagnostic logs have different schemas that might change over time. We recommend that you check the online documentation to understand what each field means. It can be found at https://learn.microsoft.com/en-us/power-query/query-diagnostics.

We are mostly interested in the **Exclusive Duration** field found in the aggregate and details logs. This tells you how long an operation took in seconds, and it helps us to find the slowest items. The Microsoft documentation describes how you can slice the log data by step name or ID. This is an easy way to find the slowest step, but it does not help you to understand which operation dependencies exist. The logs contain a hierarchical parent-child structure with arbitrary depth depending on your operation complexity. To make it easier to analyze this, we provide Power Query functions that can be used to flatten the logs into an explicit hierarchy that is easier to analyze using the decomposition tree visual. Please see the `ParsePQLog.txt` example file. This function is adapted from a blog post that was originally published by Chris Webb and is still relevant as of the printing of this edition: `https://blog.crossjoin.co.uk/2020/02/03/visualising-power-query-diagnostics-data-in-a-power-bi-decomposition-tree/`.

We have provided an example of how the parsed data can be visualized. The following figure is a snippet of the `Query Diagnostic.pbix` example file and shows how a decomposition tree is used to explore the most expensive operation group and its children. From the tooltip, we can see that the **Level 2** step took about 29 seconds and loaded over 220,000 rows. Additionally, we can see the exact SQL statement sent to the data source to confirm that folding occurred.

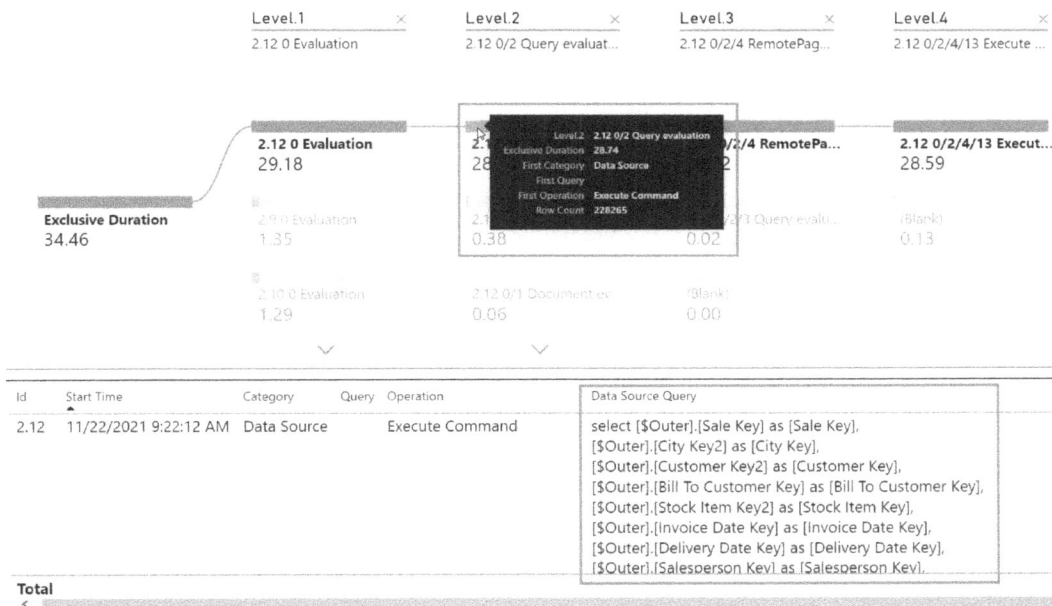

Figure 8.22 – A hierarchical view of a query log after flattening

Now, we have gained useful fundamental knowledge and analytical methods to help identify slow operations in Power Query. Next, we will explore performance tuning for dataflows.

Optimizing dataflows

A Power BI **dataflow** is a type of artifact contained within a Power BI workspace. A dataflow contains Power Query data transformation logic, which is also defined in the M query language that we introduced earlier. The **dataflow** contains the definition of one or more tables produced by those data transformations. Once it has been successfully refreshed, a Gen1 dataflow also contains a copy of the transformed data stored in **Azure Data Lake**. Gen2 adds the ability to write the output to four areas as shown in *Figure 8.23*.

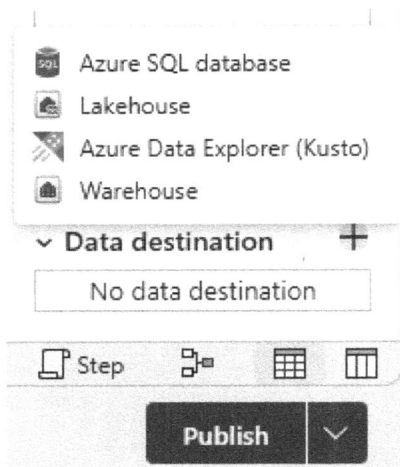

Figure 8.23 – Gen2 dataflow destination options

A dataflow might seem very similar to the query objects you define in Power BI Desktop, and this is true. However, there are some important differences, as noted in the following points:

- A data flow can only be created online through the Power BI web application via **Power Query Online**.

- A dataflow is a standalone artifact that can exist independently. It is not bundled or published with a semantic model, but semantic model items can use the dataflow as a standard data source.

- There are some UI and functionality differences between Power Query in Power BI Desktop compared to Power Query Online.

- A dataflow can be used by semantic models or even other dataflows to centralize transformation logic.

The last point in the preceding bullet list is important since it describes a key reason that dataflows exist in the first place. They are designed to promote data reuse while avoiding duplicated data transformation operations and redundant processing. Let's explore this using a practical example. This example is an organization that encourages self-serving report development so that business users can get insights quickly. They realize that many different people are trying to access a list of customers with properties from two different source systems: a finance system and a **customer relationship management** (**CRM**) system. Rather than let every person try to figure out how to transform and consolidate customer data across two systems, they could build one standard customer dataflow and have every user leverage this dataflow.

> Tip
>
> Dataflows are a great way to centralize common data transformation logic and expose the final tables to users in a consistent way. This means that the processing does not need to be duplicated for every semantic model. It reduces the total amount of data refreshes and speeds up report development by giving developers pre-transformed data. Additionally, you can update the dataflow to ensure that all downstream objects benefit from the changes without needing changes themselves (assuming that the output table structure is unchanged).

The dataflow query design benefits from all the performance optimization recommendations we provided for Power Query. You are encouraged to apply the same learnings when building dataflows. However, dataflows have some backend architectural differences that provide additional opportunities for optimization. These are detailed in the following list:

- **Separate dataflows for ingestion and transformation**: This allows you to load untransformed data into a dedicated dataflow, typically referred to as **staging**. This can speed up downstream transformations by having source data available locally, potentially reused for many independent downstream transformations for added benefits.

- **Separate dataflows for complex logic or different data sources**: For long-running or complex operations, consider putting each of them in a single **dedicated dataflow**. This allows for entity transformations to be maintained and optimized separately. This can make some entities available sooner, as they do not have to wait for the entire dataflow to be completed.

- **Separate dataflows with different refresh cadences**: You cannot select individual entities to refresh in a dataflow, so all entities will refresh when scheduled. Therefore, you should separate entities that have different refresh cadences to avoid redundant loading and processing.

- **Consider Premium or Fabric (dedicated) capacities**: Dedicated capacity has additional features that increase performance and reusability.

The following performance-enhancing features for dataflows are highly recommended. Please note that the following items are only available for dataflows running on **dedicated capacity**:

- **Incremental refresh**: This works for dataflows in the same way as described earlier for loading a table in a semantic model. Configuring this can greatly reduce dataflow refresh time after the first load.

- **Linked entities**: You can use one dataflow as a data source for a different dataflow. This allows you to break transformation logic into groups or different phases. The following figure shows how the UI uses a link icon indicator:

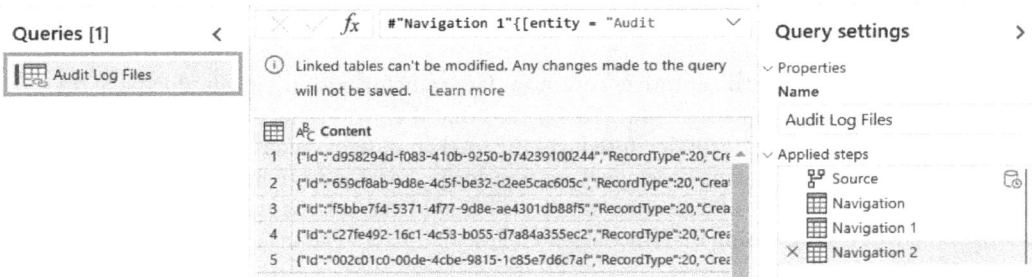

Figure 8.24 – A linked entity indicated visually

In the previous example, the `Audit Log Files` entity contains JSON log records from the activity log. The user wants to parse this log into subsets based on activity type. A linked entity is used to reuse the log data without importing it multiple times.

- **Enhanced compute and computed entities**: Dedicated capacity dataflows can take advantage of the **enhanced compute engine**, which is turned on by default for Premium capacity. This reduces refresh time for long-running transformations while using joins, distinct filters, and grouping. The engine uses an SQL-like cache that can handle query folding. The following figure shows this dataflow setting:

Figure 8.25 – Enhanced compute in the dataflow settings

The enhanced compute engine only works when using other dataflows as a source. You can tell that you have a computed entity when you see the lightning symbol on top of its icon, as shown in *Figure 8.26*. It also shows how Power BI provides a tooltip when hovering over the **Source** step, which indicates it will be evaluated externally.

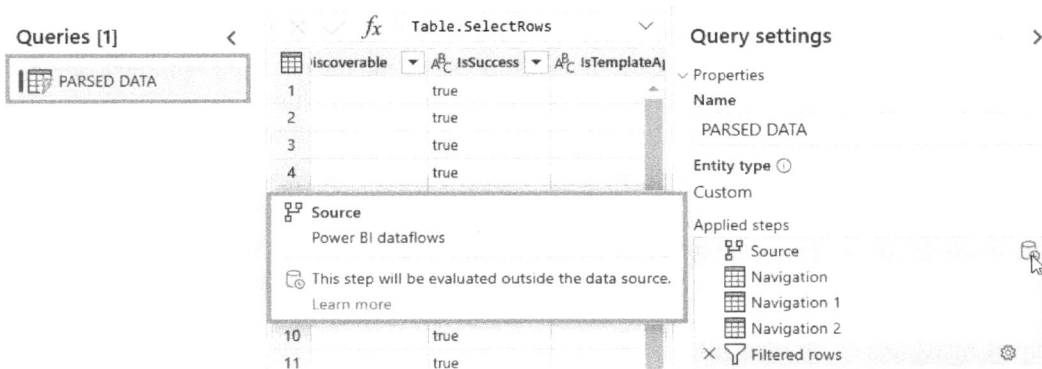

Figure 8.26 – A computed entity indicated visually

Next, we will talk about Gen2 dataflow destinations.

Gen2 destinations

The other performance area needing attention is the destination of Gen2 dataflow destinations. Gen2 dataflows do not need a destination and can be used like Gen1 dataflows. The addition of the destinations allows storage options that can be used outside of Power BI. The performance options vary based on output. See the following:

- **Azure SQL Database**: Depending on the size of the Azure resource, writing output to a table can vary because of vCPUs, memory size, and disk speed. Also, you must look at the structure of the table and what constraints, such as primary key, foreign key, and indexes, are used on the destination table.

- **Lakehouse**: Since this is a new feature of Fabric and Premium workspaces, there is not a lot of real-world experience around this option. So, performance will vary, but look for improvement as time goes by and more enterprises adopt this feature and Microsoft uses telemetry to improve the option.

- **Azure Data Explorer (Kusto)**: This is Microsoft's streaming resource for Fabric. Like Azure SQL Database, it is dependent on the resources available based on the size used when the resource is created. There is a lot of memory usage for streaming, so, the more memory, the faster it is.

- **Warehouse**: Warehouse is another structure similar to Lakehouse and the same caution is used for this option.

We now have a great understanding of how data gets transformed in Power BI and how we can minimize refresh operations and make them faster. Let's wrap up the chapter with a summary of what we've learned.

Summary

In this chapter, we began to dive deeper into specific areas of an actual Power BI solution, starting from transforming and loading data. We saw how Power Query and the mashup engine take center stage in this part of the pipeline, powered by the M query language. Additionally, we learned about parallelism and how you can change the settings to improve performance. There are settings that can be adjusted to speed up the developer experience and optimize data loading.

We moved on to transformations, focusing on operations that can slow down with large volumes of data such as filtering and joining. We introduced the mashup engine's ability to perform query folding and why we should leverage this because it pushes resource-intensive operations down to the data source. We learned how to see where folding is occurring in Power BI Desktop and examined how to configure incremental refresh to reduce the amount of data loaded.

The Power Query diagnostic logs contain information about each query step and its resource usage. We saw how these were not easy to parse, but they do offer a lot of detail that can provide valuable insights into slow query steps or data sources. We concluded the chapter by learning how dataflows can be used to reduce data loading and transformation by centralizing common logic. However, dataflows do have their own optimization tips with specific performance features such as the enhanced compute engine.

Now that we have learned how to get data into Power BI efficiently, in the next chapter, we will look at report and dashboard design tips to provide a better user experience while reducing data consumption.

Report and Dashboard Design

9

In the previous chapter, we looked at how to load data into Power BI efficiently to reduce system resource use and the amount of time taken to load data. Slow data refreshes generally do not impact a user's report performance experience directly because they usually occur in the background and are scheduled at off-peak times.

Now, we will shift our focus to the visual layer of Power BI. Here, inappropriate choices can directly affect the end user experience, from both a performance and a usability perspective. While we will continue to focus on design patterns that improve performance, we will point out when performance guidance can also improve usability.

In this chapter, we will learn how the Power BI visual framework works within reports and how these relate to queries and engine load. This will give us some fundamental knowledge of report behavior, which will help us identify what to optimize. We will then go through a range of common design pitfalls and recommend solutions that can provide better performance, covering the three options for creating visual content in Power BI.

This chapter consists of the following sections:

- Optimizing report layout
- Interaction optimization for slicing and dicing
- Optimizing dashboards and paginated reports

Technical requirements

There are samples available for some parts of this chapter. We will call out which files to refer to. Please check out the `Chapter09` folder on GitHub to get these assets: `https://github.com/PacktPublishing/Microsoft-Power-BI-Performance-Best-Practices-Second-Edition`.

Optimizing report layout

There is a direct relationship between the number of visuals and the load generated by a report. Higher loads often result in poorer performance. This load will be spread over two areas – both the client device executing visuals and the semantic model that is responding to queries. This includes queries sent to external data sources in DirectQuery mode. Therefore, you should strive to reduce the total number of visuals on a page wherever possible, especially knowing that the more you have, the more work you are asking a single CPU thread to do. You should also configure visuals in a way that avoids complex queries and try to return the least amount of data – only what is needed for the scenario.

Next, we will look at why having too many visuals causes rendering issues.

> **Note**
>
> When a report is rendered in the Power BI service, only the current page selected for the report will have queries executed. So, it is not until the end user selects a different page that the report page queries are executed against the semantic model. Some suggestions in this chapter talk about moving visuals to different pages to help performance. It is not only the filtering of the data on another page that helps with the user experience but also having multiple pages to help spread the load.

Too many elements in a report

An important point to note is the visuals are designed to execute in parallel. This has interesting implications for performance. When you open a report, all visuals execute at once. Data-driven visuals will each issue at least one query to the underlying semantic model, and the queries are sent in batches to be executed in parallel where possible. All visuals need CPU time even if they do not execute a query. Even though visuals execute in parallel, they are executed on a single CPU thread, which means time is divided between the visuals. For Power BI, it means that the more visuals you have on a page, the more time they can spend waiting for the CPU, due to the contention with all other visuals. *Figure 9.1* is going to the extreme:

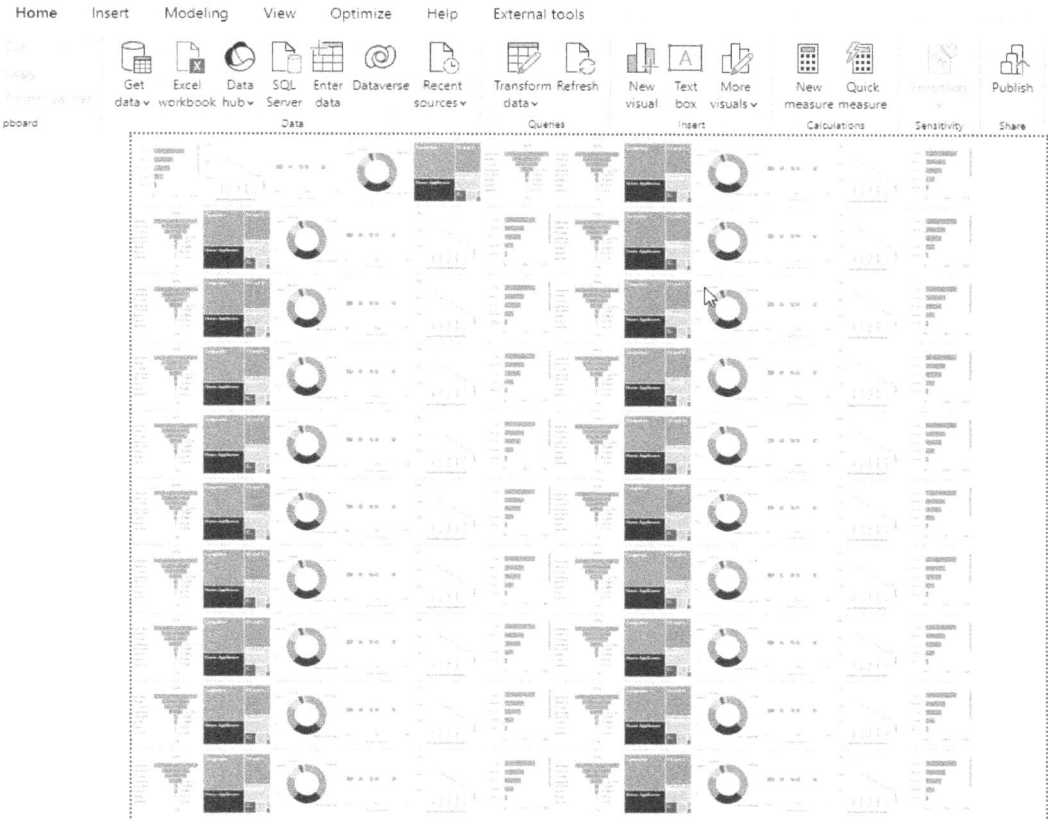

Figure 9.1 – Too many visuals

And as compared to *Figure 9.1*, the following *Figure 9.2* is a little toned down as far as number of visuals on a screen:

Contoso Sales

$20bn
Net Sales

Total Sales by Product Category

Date

Last   24   Years

7/24/2000 – 7/23/2024

Net Online Sales, Net Online Cost and Net Online GPM by Year

● Net Online Sales ● Net Online Cost ● Net Online GPM

Product Cat...
● Home Ap...
● Computers
● Cameras ...
● TV and Vi ...
● Cell phones
● Audio

$0bn
(1.37%)
$9bn
(30.8%)
$3bn
(12%)
$5bn
(20.1...)
$6bn
(25.93%)

Total Sales by Channel Label

100%

01    $16bn

02    $9bn

04    $7bn

03    $6bn

40%

Net Margin by Month

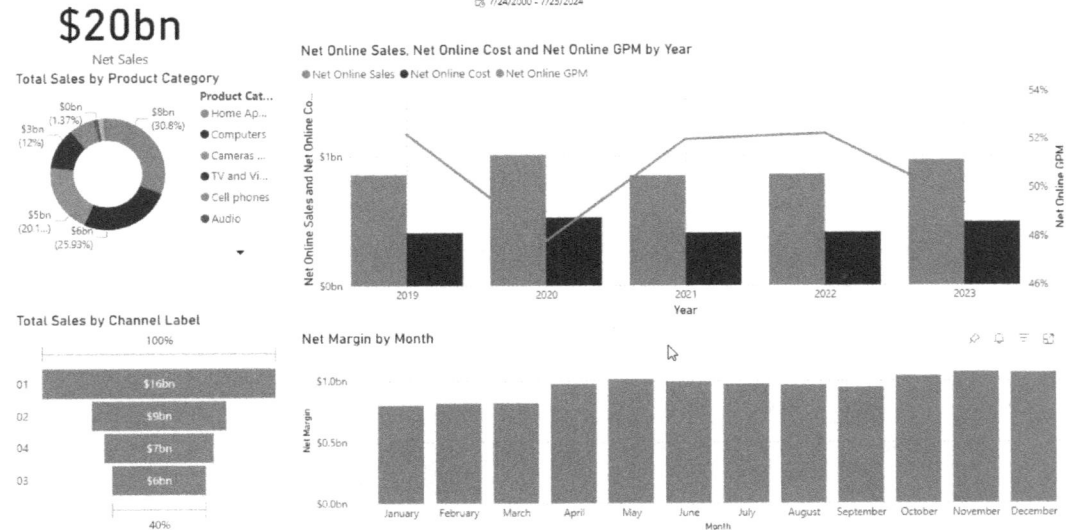

Figure 9.2 – A little toned down

There is no specific number of visuals beyond which a report will slow down. Some guidance online suggests around 20 visuals being a concern, but we do not wish to go down this path. The reason for this is that the visual type, configuration, and underlying dataset and DAX designs will have the largest effect on performance, and two reports with the same number of visuals may have vastly different performance characteristics. Instead, we recommend driving report and dataset optimization based on pre-established targets and thresholds that take user requirements and report complexity into account. This guidance was covered in *Chapter 7, Governing with a Performance Framework*, in the *Performance governance framework* section, where we talked about establishing baselines and targets.

Let's now cover a busy report table that can be used as a **Drill Through** page.

Reduce a busy report

The report in *Figure 9.3* shows a table that is refreshed with every view or selection of a visual or filter. The table does not need to be viewed until the user selects the correct filters or slicers. The end users specify, based on their requirements, that it's better to see an overview of the report before examining the table details.

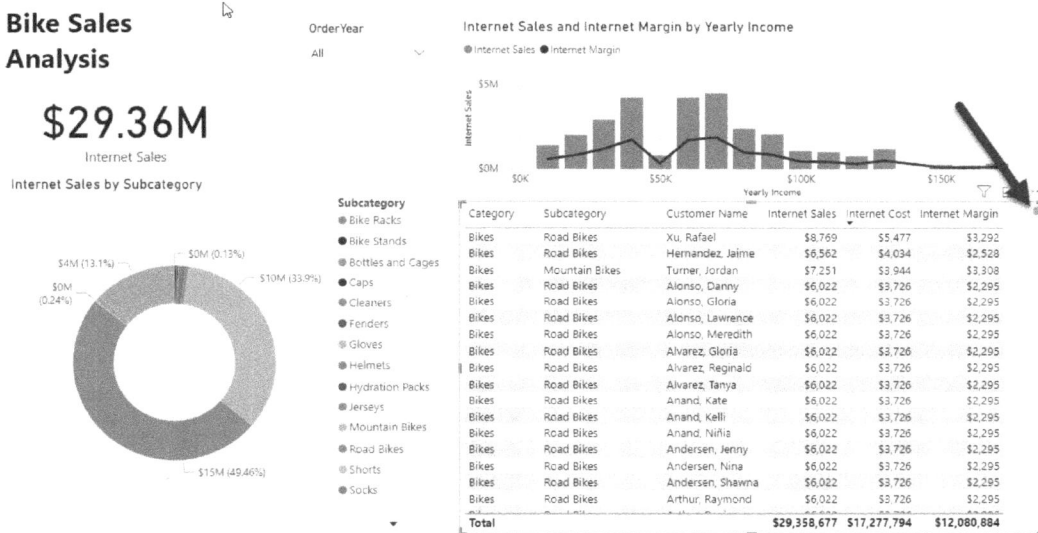

Figure 9.3 – Busy report table

The table could have millions of rows that do not look appealing to an analyst at first glance; however selecting **Subcategory** from the donut chart or a **Yearly Income** bracket from the bar/line chart would filter the table to a more reasonable size. The issue is the number of queries and amount of data returned to the table each time something triggers a refresh, especially when first entering the page without filters. *Figure 9.4* shows the right-click **Drill through** option that is available to use to go to a separate page that has the table filtered:

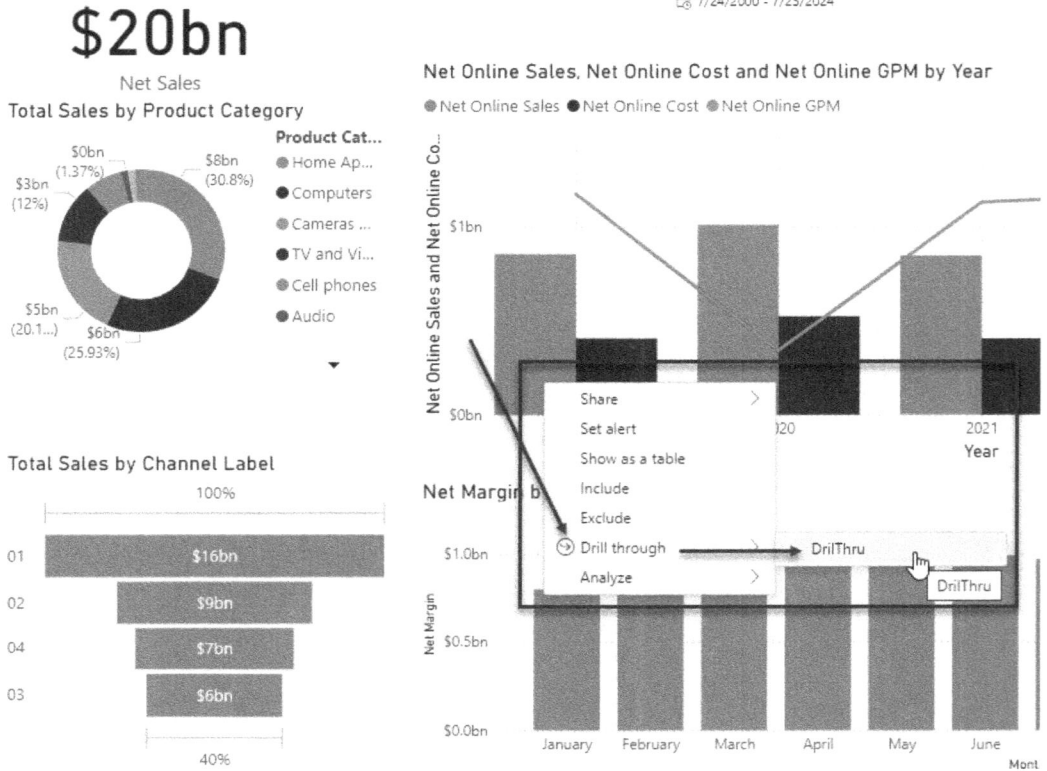

Figure 9.4 – Drill through to table report page

The resulting report page looks like *Figure 9.5*. You can see Power BI adds a back button as well as an indicator on the table being filtered:

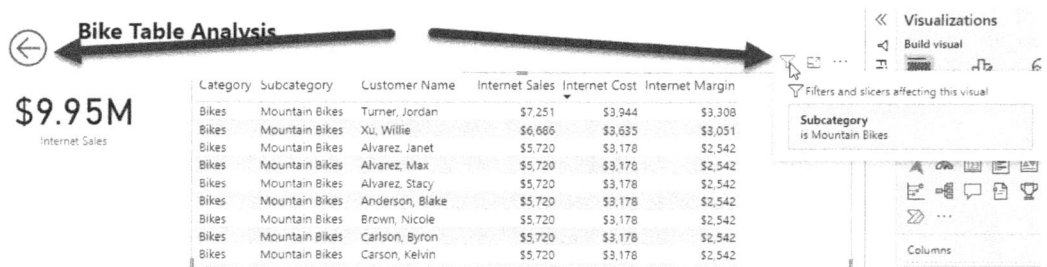

Figure 9.5 – Drill through table page

For this page to enable **Drill through**, the **Add drill through fields here** pane needs to be populated with possible filter columns from the main page:

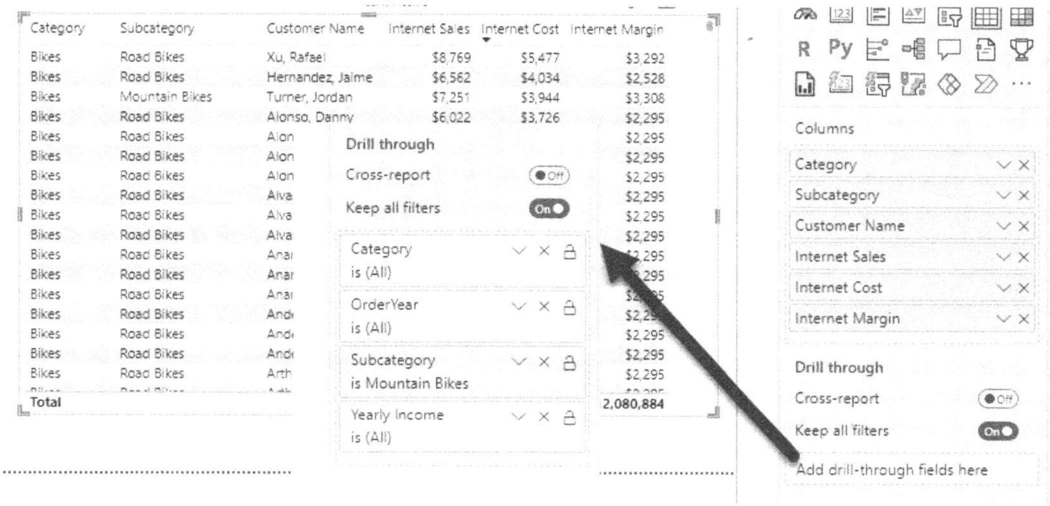

Figure 9.6 – Add Drill through fields here

One thing to keep in mind: Power BI visualizations are intended for aggregated results with visuals pointing to an analysis. Detailed reporting is available but was never intended for millions of rows in a table or matrix visual.

Next, let's look at the effect of many card visuals on one page and how to help with queries sent to the semantic model.

Reducing queries to the semantic model

You can reduce the number of queries sent to the engine by using fewer visuals. Sometimes a report developer wants to use a card visual to show amounts, percentages, or counts. Each card has a query to run to get the results. *Figure 9.7* shows the **Performance analyzer** window for each card and the query:

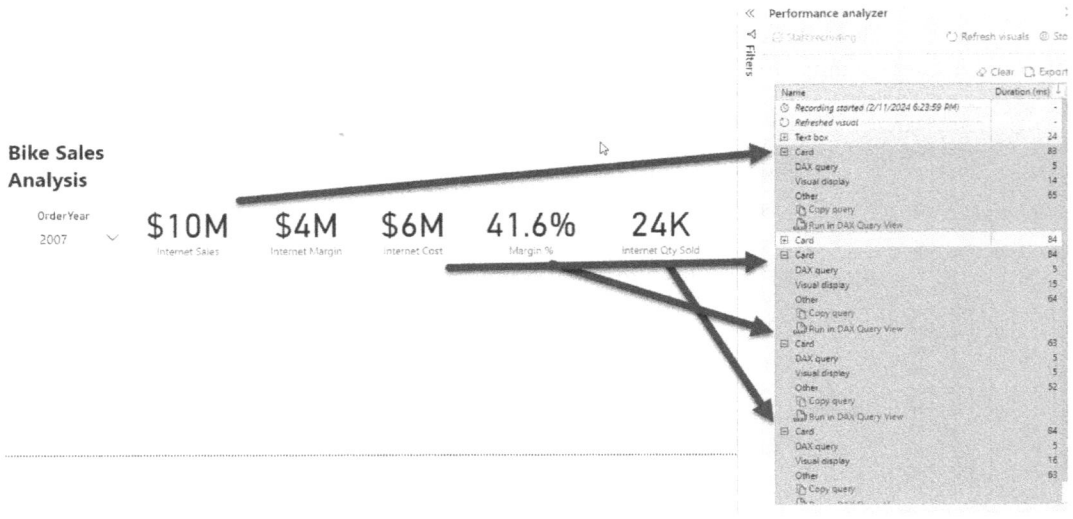

Figure 9.7 – Single card for each measure with queries

You could solve this issue with a multi-row card visual or a table as shown in *Figure 9.8*. This reduces the five queries to one for each visual instead of for the table or the multi-row card. This one change can reduce the time required for large semantic models dealing with queries issued to the engine:

Figure 9.8 – Multi-row card and table – one query each

Next, we will learn how to use small multiples for too many line chart queries.

Using the small multiples option

Small multiples is another visual that can reduce the queries to the VertiPaq engine. This is useful when a report page has line charts for different filters in the visual.

Figure 9.9 shows line charts for different categories of products and sales measures:

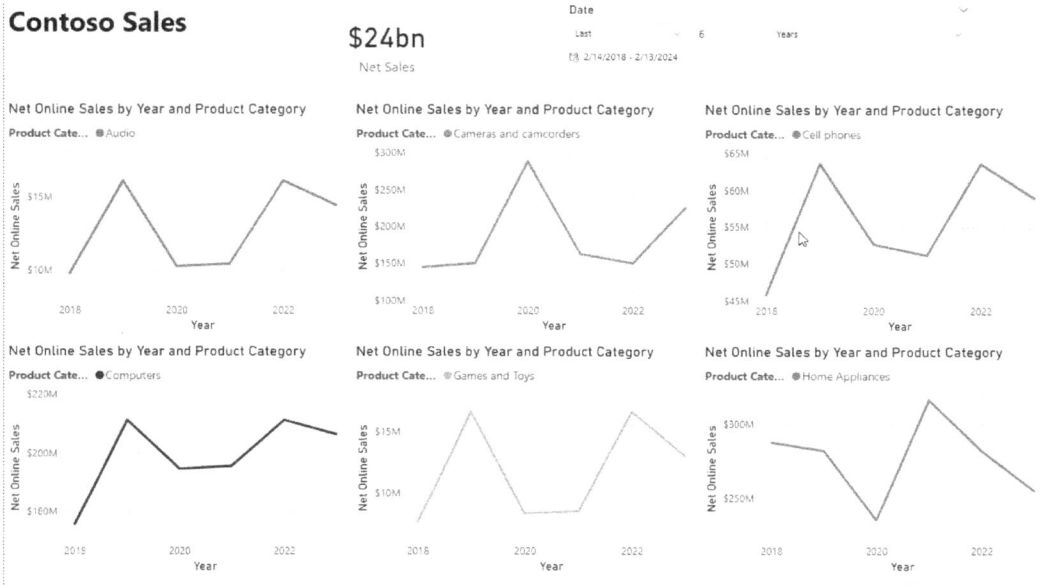

Figure 9.9 – Individual chart for each category

The filter is on each visual and produces a query for each line chart. Like the multi-card visual used in the previous example, Power BI has small multiples for line charts. *Figure 9.10* shows the small multiples for the same data as *Figure 9.9* with one filter on the categories to be reported. The change produces just one query for the line chart(s) rather than six:

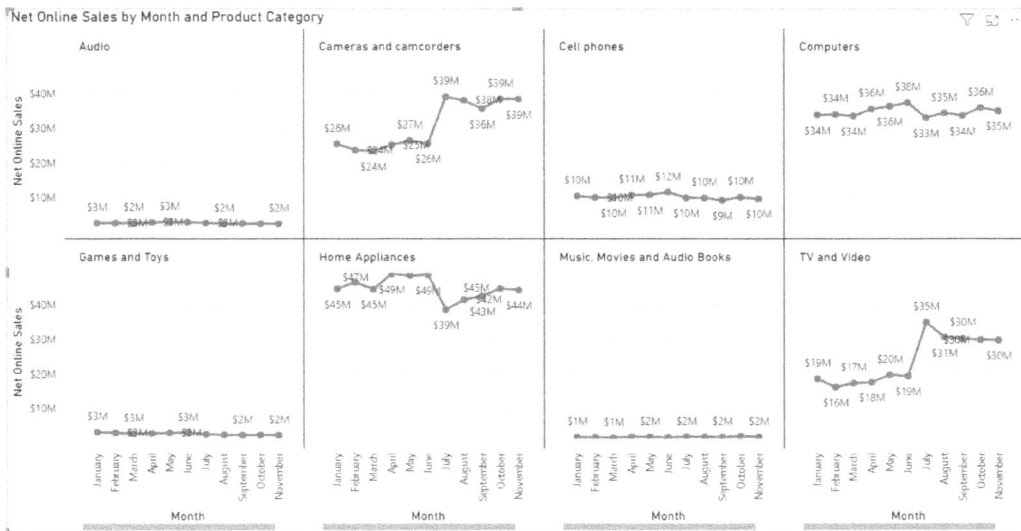

Figure 9.10 – Small multiples for line chart

The next section will look at examples of using slicers and filters for performance improvements.

Interaction optimization for slicing and dicing

When using the term **interactive**, we refer to the report page implementation experience using Power BI Desktop to create a published report to the service. These reports have dynamic visuals designed primarily for viewing on internet browsers. The visuals can resize and react to screen dimension and resolution changes. The experience is expressed as **What You See Is What You Get** (**WYSISYG**).

The term *interactive report* is unofficial and used in this book for convenience and clarity. Microsoft specifically differentiates interactive reports from paginated reports by name – only the latter is a documented term. Paginated reports were originally created by **SQL Server Report Services** (**SSRS**), but today, paginated reports can exist in the Power BI service.

The next section will talk about having a value pre-selected for a slicer.

> **Note**
>
> From here on, we will specifically refer to paginated reports. If a distinction is not made, please assume we are referring to interactive reports. Interactive reports are built by placing individual visuals along with slicers on one or more predetermined report pages. Most visuals are data-driven, which means they need to be supplied with data to render meaningful content.

Selecting a value for a slicer

If you have a very large semantic model, it can take a while to return results even after optimization. By default, Power BI will not select any values for filters and slicers. To make the initial experience faster, you can consider preselecting values for slicers or filters to limit the query space and reduce the amount of data scanned.

Figure 9.11 shows using a slicer to get a set of relative days to use on the initial display page:

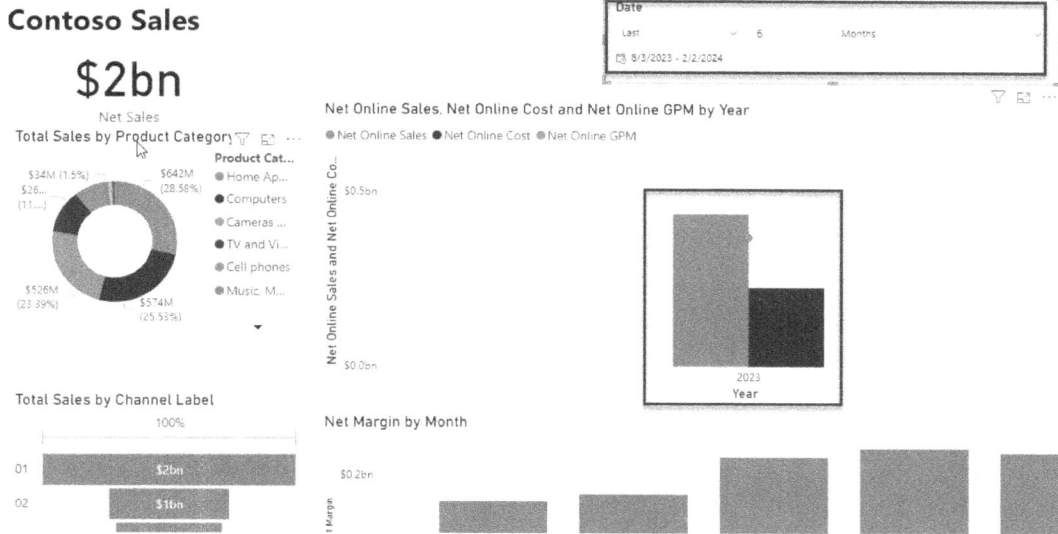

Figure 9.11 – Date slicer using relative days

This selection in the slicer will only display data for the last six months. When the page is opened, only the last six months of data based on order date will be queried. This will reduce the time for the initial page to display and the visuals populated. The query only returns a fraction of the data from the 10 years of data in the full model.

Preselect the most frequently used set of attributes to cater for the broadest set of users. Even if some users need to change the slicer selections to get the desired context, this can save them a lot of time because they avoid waiting for a very slow initial report load. To set the default filter and slicer selection, simply save the report with the filters already applied.

The next section will look at the edit interaction feature for visuals.

Disabling interaction when necessary

When you select a data point on a Power BI visual, the default behavior is to cross-filter all other visuals. Sometimes, this might not add any value to the analysis. Therefore, we recommend reviewing report interactions for every visual and removing those that are unnecessary. This will reduce the number of queries issued because a selection in one visual no longer affects every other one. This technique also applies to slicers interacting with each other. The following figure shows how this can be configured by selecting a visual and then using the **Edit interactions** option in the **Format** menu. The slicer is selected and has its interactions edited so that it no longer affects the right-hand side visual. When editing interactions, visuals indicate their behavior with small icons at the top right, as highlighted:

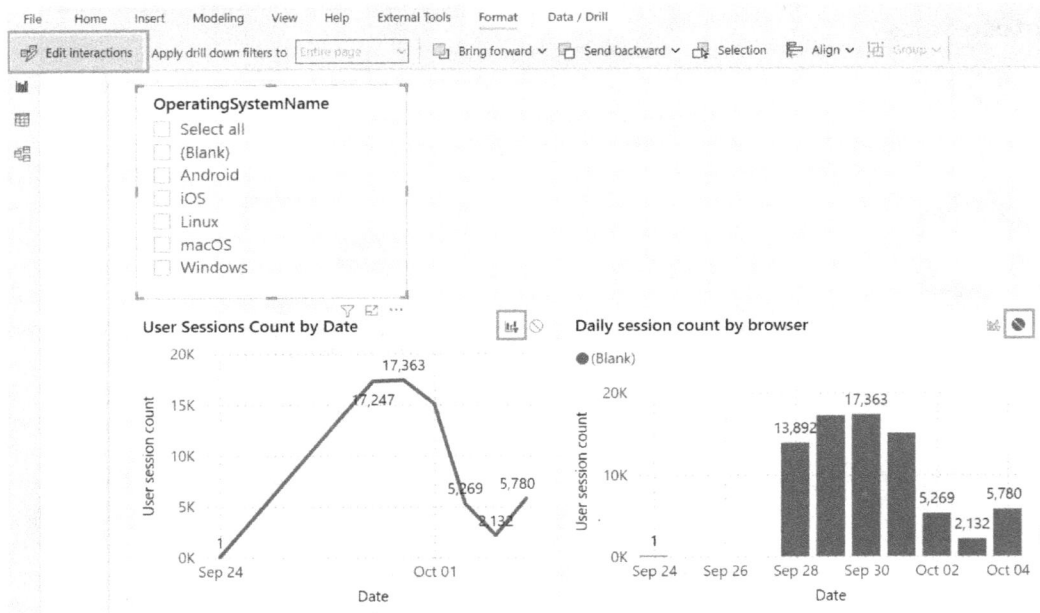

Figure 9.12 – A slicer will only affect the right-side visual, as shown by the icons

Using Top N to limit data

The example semantic model used in the previous three figures is small, so the difference to an end user is negligible. However, with larger datasets and measures of higher complexity, significant performance gains can be realized with **Top N** filtering technique.

When looking at summary information, it is good practice to highlight items with the highest or lowest values instead of listing every single one. For example, a customer-satisfaction-related visual can be limited to just the 10 customers who had the lowest satisfaction scores. This reduces the amount of data returned and can speed up the report. There are two ways you can implement **Top N** filtering: the simplest method is to use the out-of-the-box **Top N** filtering available for Power BI visuals in the **Filters** pane. This can be seen in *Figure 9.12*, where the left-side visual is in the default state, whereas the right-side visual has been configured to show the top five **Manufacturer** names ranked by **SalesAmount**:

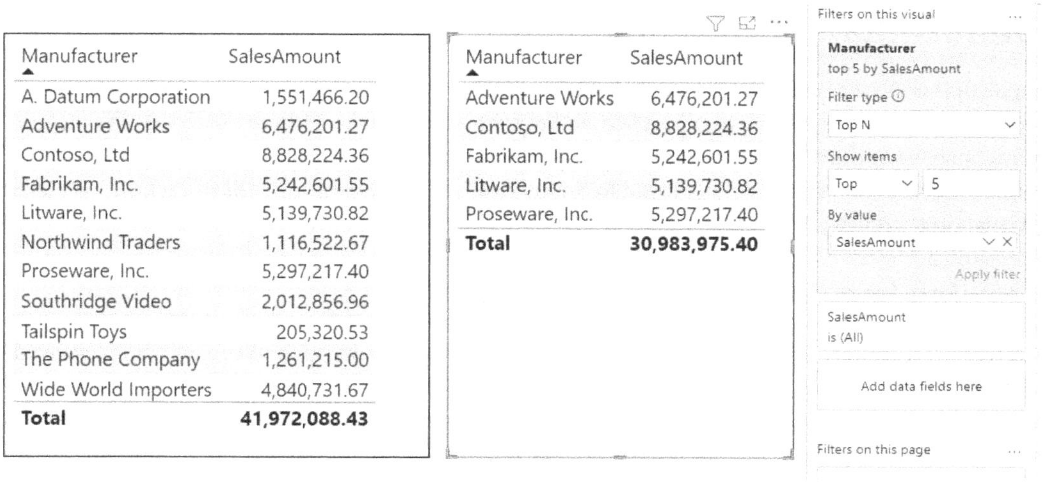

Figure 9.13 – The left is the default state and the right is configured to show the top five items

Another way to implement **Top N** is to write measures that explicitly use ranking functions. While this approach requires more effort, it allows you to perform dynamic ranking through slicer or filter values. This allows a user to choose from a list of pre-determined group sizes such as 5, 10, and 20. Whichever approach you use, we still recommend testing with and without **Top N** enabled. There can be cases where the ranking calculation itself is expensive, and this can cause the visual to be slower when limited by **Top N**.

Moving slicers to the filter pane

It is tempting to include many different slicers in a report to provide a user with a range of options to set their context when analyzing data. A slicer is a regular Power BI visual that needs to query a semantic model to populate its values. When a slicer selection is made, the default behavior in Power BI is to update all other slicers to reflect the selection made to give you a better idea of how data is distributed. The other slicers execute queries to make this update. While this functionality is useful, it can slow down reports if you have a lot of slicers with large datasets. In such cases, consider moving the least frequently used slicers to the **Filters** pane. This reduces the number of queries executed during report interaction because a filter only queries the data source to fetch values after user interaction and is not affected by slicer selections.

Next, we will progress to other report types in Power BI.

Optimization for dashboard and paginated reports

Outside of Power BI reports, workspaces allow the deployment of dashboards and paginated reports. Though different, there are still best practices to help the performance of these objects. These include making queries to the source data rather than directly from a relational database (DirectQuery) or semantic models (Import mode) deployed to the service. There are various levels of caching available for visuals and reports, such as semantic models in the service.

Following best practices for dashboards

A dashboard lets users pin visuals to one canvas that provides links back to the original deployed report. **Pinning** enables a single page to display many related visuals from various report pages. It is an easy way to create customized views of the most important elements from different and potentially unrelated reports. Dashboards were designed to be fast and behave differently than reports because, where possible, they cache the query result and visual beforehand. This greatly reduces dashboard load time because it avoids most on-demand processing. Power BI does this by executing queries and preparing dashboard tiles when the underlying data has been updated.

> **Note**
> Visuals are cached when pinned to a dashboard, but reports (called live report tiles) are not. Therefore, we recommend only pinning individual visuals to dashboards instead of report pages to take advantage of caching.

There is also the potential to add significant background load on a system when using dashboards. This is because dashboard tiles must respect security context. If you are using row-level security, there will be different roles/contexts, so Power BI will need to generate a unique tile cache for each security context. This happens automatically after a refresh for Import mode. For DirectQuery semantic models, tiles are refreshed hourly, but this can be increased to every 15 minutes. This can be changed in the settings of a semantic model, as shown in *Figure 9.13*. There is an option for a manual refresh.

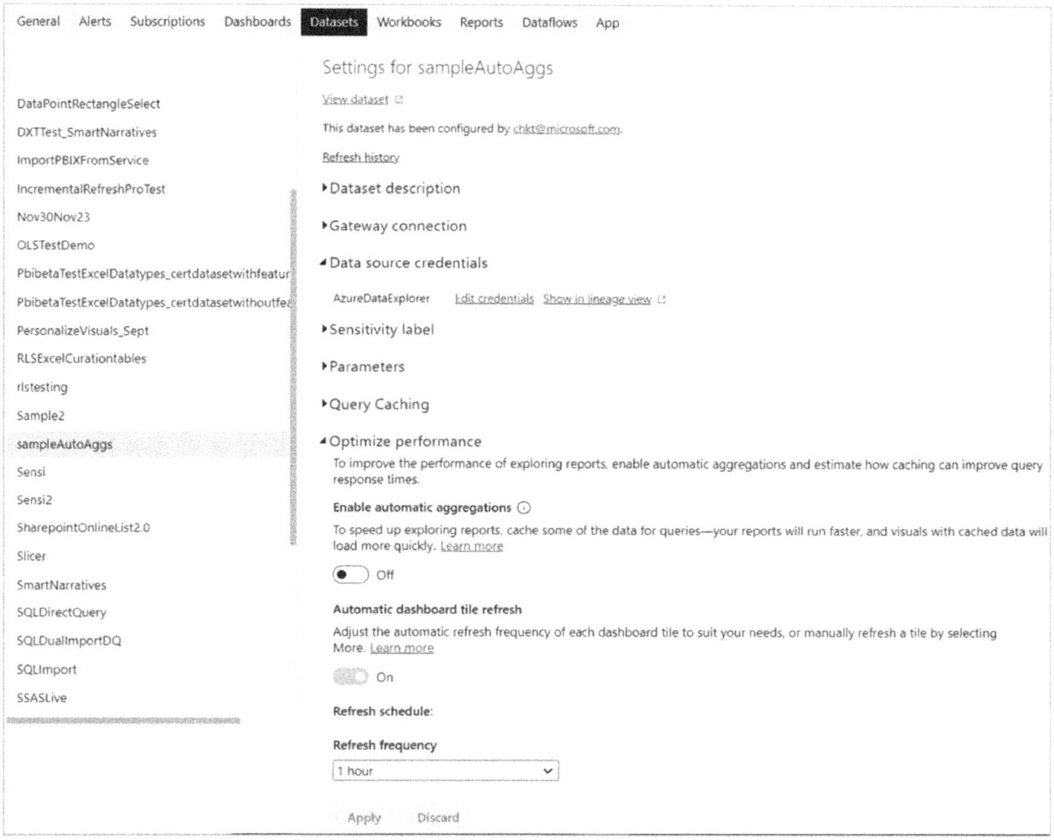

Figure 9.14 – Tile refresh in a semantic model

With large semantic models and many contexts, there is the potential to generate hundreds or thousands of background queries in a short time span. If you are not using dedicated capacities (Premium or Fabric), the most likely effect is *increased data refresh durations* because the tiles refresh is performed at the end. However, if you are using a dedicated capacity, then you have a fixed set of resources, and these background operations have a higher likelihood of impacting interactive users.

Since tile refresh is automatic and there are no settings available to configure it, we recommend testing without row-level security to determine whether tile refresh is the cause of a suspected performance issue.

Next, let's look at some best practices for paginated reports.

Optimizing paginated reports

Paginated reports use the tried-and-true **SQL Server Reporting Services** (**SSRS**) technology. This report service implements the XML-based **Report Definition Language** (**RDL**) to code reports. Often referred to as "pixel-perfect," these reports are specifically designed for printing on pages. They are designed with a pre-determined page size and borders. The report designer will lay out elements exactly where they need to appear on a page by specifying element sizes. They are very good at handling operational-style reports with many rows and pages, such as a group of sales invoices, by providing features such as page headers, footers, and margins. The designer often does not know how many pages the report will generate, as extra content simply overflows to a new page. Power BI Report Builder is the authoring tool for these types of reports.

Paginated reports can use a relational or analytical database as a data source, which can be hosted in the cloud or on-premises. The latter database type refers to dimensional model sources such as Power BI semantic models, and we will explore their optimization in detail in the next chapter. For the remainder of this chapter, we will focus on relational sources – typically, transactional database systems such as Oracle or SQL Server. Usually, line detail data is requested for these reports, and that is why a relational database is suggested rather than an analytical database. Analytical databases such as the semantic model engine are not designed to perform well with line-item detail rows. They are designed for aggregations of numeric columns while slicing by attributes.

The following points provide guidance on optimizing paginated reports:

- **Use cloud data sources**: On-premises sources are likely to be geographically distant and need to be accessed through a gateway. This can be much slower than a cloud source, especially if it is in the same region as the Power BI service.

- **Use the DAX query designer for analytical sources**: Power BI Report Builder offers an Analysis Services DAX query designer. **Data Analysis Expressions** (**DAX**) is a different query language supported by the Analysis Services engine. This designer can be used for semantic model data sources. You will get better performance using the DAX designer than by manually entering DAX queries.

- **Leverage stored procedures in the relational source**: Stored procedures encapsulate pieces of business logic. If there are performance issues, a database administrator can fine-tune the stored procedure without having to edit the Power BI semantic model. The aggregations can be included in the stored procedure if needed, which pushes the processing to the data source and is probably faster.

- **Only retrieve required data**: Everybody seems to want everything to be available. By narrowing the requirements, the performance of a report benefits from only selecting the tables and columns needed for current reporting requirements. The paginated report is used for tabular line-item results and only so many columns can fit on the report page.

- **Dataset versus parameterization**: Paginated reports can apply filters over already retrieved data (filtering) or pass a filter directly to the data source (parameterization). Suppose we have a sales report that can be filtered by country. With dataset filtering, the report will retrieve all country data upfront. When a user selects a specific country, it will perform the filtering without needing to issue new queries to the data source. With dataset parameterization, changing the country will issue a new query and retrieve only the results for the selected country.

> **Note**
> Paginated reports still use the term *dataset*. It is the query that returns results for the report. Do not confuse this term with the change in Power BI from dataset to *semantic model* mentioned in *Part 1* of this book.

    We recommend dataset filtering when you expect a different subset of the dataset rows to be reused many times – in our example, the user may switch between countries often. Here you recognize that the cost of retrieving a larger dataset can be traded off against the number of times it will be reused. However, caching large datasets on a per-user basis may negatively impact performance and capacity throughput.

- **Avoid calculated fields**: A paginated report allows you to define your own custom fields within a query result. For example, you might concatenate values or perform some arithmetic. We recommend doing this at the data source instead so that the calculation will be done beforehand and be readily available for the report. This can have a significant impact if the query returns many rows.

- **Optimize images**: Keep image file sizes as small as possible by using the lowest resolution that still gives you good quality. Compressed formats such as JPG will help reduce size, and some graphics programs let you adjust compression settings to balance size with quality.

- **Do not use embedded images**: Embedded images can bloat the report size and slow down rendering. A better alternative is to use images stored on web servers or a database, which improves maintainability through central storage. However, be aware that when using web servers, the images may load slowly if they are from an external network.

Now let's summarize the chapter.

Summary

In this chapter, we started with visualization optimization, covering into visual layouts and then slicer and interaction filtering. The busy report was mentioned, and some alternatives, such as drill-through reporting, were demonstrated. Edited interactions between visuals were used to stop some unnecessary filtering. Training was mentioned for end users selecting items in the filtering pane. A reminder was given about the potential negative impact of executing multiple queries on large semantic models.

The chapter switched to the other report types – dashboards and paginated reports. Dashboards are tiles from Power BI reports and the latter come from SSRS. Paginated reports are used for line-item types that are not good performance-wise for semantic model data. Dashboards enable visuals from different reports to be placed on one canvas.

All these types of scenarios have best practices for optimizing performance for end users. These ranged from using filters to reducing the amount of data in a report. Each scenario requires clear requirements and limits for optimal reporting to the consumer of the reports.

In the next chapter, we will get into data modeling, which is one of the most important sections of the book. A poorly performing data model can affect the reporting layer significantly and negate the guidance we covered in this chapter.

Part 4:
Data Models, Calculations, and Large Semantic Models

In this part, we will explain how to build data models that are efficient and intuitive, and how to avoid slowing down queries with sub-optimal relationships or DAX calculations. You will learn how to use aggregations and composite models for very large semantic models.

This part has the following chapters:

- *Chapter 10, Dimensional Modeling and Row-level Security*
- *Chapter 11, Improving DAX*
- *Chapter 12, High-Scale Patterns*

10

Dimensional Modeling and Row Level Security

In the previous chapter, we looked at the visual layer in Power BI, where a key point was to reduce the load on data sources by minimizing the report page complexity and number of queries sent to the Analysis Services engine. We learned that this area is usually the easiest and quickest place to apply performance-related fixes. However, experience working with a wide range of Power BI solutions has shown that issues with the underlying semantic model are very common and typically have a greater negative performance impact. Importantly, this impact can be amplified because a semantic model can be used by more than one report. Semantic model reuse is a recommended best practice to reduce data duplication and development effort.

Therefore, in this chapter, we will move one layer deeper, into Power BI semantic models with a focus on Import mode. Semantic model design is arguably the most critical piece, being at the core of a Power BI solution and heavily influencing usability and performance. Power BI's feature richness and modeling flexibility provide alternatives when you're modeling data, and some choices can make development easier at the expense of query performance and/or model size. Conversely, certain inefficient configurations can completely slow down a report, even with data volumes of far less than 1 GB.

We will discuss model design, data model size reduction, building well-thought-out relationships, and avoiding pitfalls with **row-level security** (**RLS**). We will also touch on the tools and techniques we learned about in the previous chapters to look at the impact of design decisions.

In this chapter, we will cover the following topics:

- Building efficient models
- Building a single source of truth
- Considering many-to-many relationships versus bi-directional filtering
- Avoiding pitfalls with row-level security

Technical requirements

Some samples are provided in this chapter. We will specify which files to refer to. Please check out the `Chapter10` folder in this book's GitHub repository to get these assets: `https://github. com/PacktPublishing/Microsoft-Power-BI-Performance-Best-Practices- Second-Edition`.

Building efficient models

We will begin with some theoretical concepts on how to model data for efficient storage, which leads to faster queries. These design techniques have been around the data warehouse world since the 1990s. The simplicity of dimensional modeling has always been centered around efficient structures for analytical reports. The Analysis Services engine was designed for star schemas in both the multidimensional cubes as well as tabular semantic models.

Let's review together the basics of dimensional modeling.

The Kimball dimensional model theory

Data modeling can be thought of as how to group and connect attributes in a set of data. There are competing schools of thought as to what style of data modeling is the best and they are not always mutually exclusive. Learning about dimensional modeling is the best fit for Power BI semantic models, so we will concentrate on this method.

We will be looking at **dimensional modeling**, a very popular technique that was encouraged successfully by the Kimball Group. It is considered by many to be an excellent way to present data to business users and happens to suit Power BI's Analysis Services engine like a glove. It can be a better alternative than trying to include every possible required field into a single table that's presented to the user. We recommend that you become more familiar with **Kimball techniques** as they cover the entire process of developing **business intelligence** (**BI**) solutions, starting with effective requirements gathering. Though the group is retired, the published books are still available as well as their website: `https:// www.kimballgroup.com`.

Transactional databases are optimized for efficient storage and retrieval and aim to reduce data duplication via a technique called **normalization**. This can split related data into many different tables and requires joins on common key fields to retrieve the required attributes. For example, it is common for **enterprise resource planning** (**ERP**) suites to contain thousands of individual tables with unintuitive table and column names. To deal with this problem, a central concept in the world of dimensional modeling is the **star schema**. Modeling data into a star schema involves designing data structures for faster analysis and reporting but where we don't have to store the data like normalized databases. The simplest dimensional model consists of two types of tables:

- **Dimension tables:** These tables contain attributes that slice (filter) or dice (group) measures from the related fact tables. Examples are `Employees`, `Dates`, `Products`, and so on.

- **Fact tables:** These tables contain surrogate keys that are foreign keys to dimension tables. When these surrogate keys are combined in the fact table, they define the grain of the quantitative values. Usually, these tables contain numeric facts (measures) with as few attributes (move to dimension table) as possible.

> **Note**
>
> Fact tables are defined as one of three types. The first, and most common, is a *transaction* such as sales from a company or a grade from tests or assignments. The second is a *snapshot*, which contains the data captured as its state on one day such as the end of the month. The last is *accumulative*, such as inventory processing. We mainly look at transaction data in this book. The other methods for snapshots and accumulative facts can be found on the Kimball site website: `https://www.kimballgroup.com`.

After defining the facts and dimensions in our model, we can see how the star schema gets its name. A simple star schema has a single fact table that's related to some dimension tables that surround it, like the points of a star. Multiple star schemas can have conformed dimensions between them setting up a cluster of schemas that can become a data warehouse.

Figure 10.1 shows the points of the star as dimension tables, the relationships as lines, and the middle of the star as the fact table.

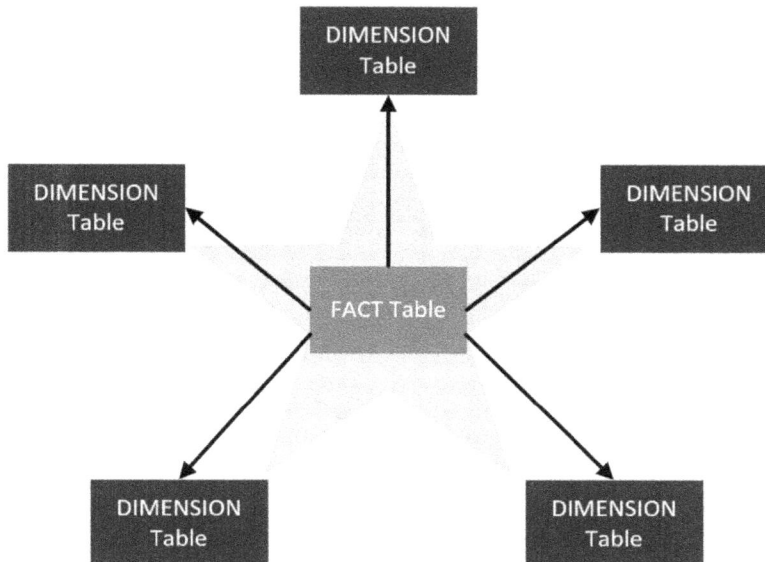

Figure 10.1 – A star schema

The diagram in *Figure 10.1* shows a five-point star simply for convenience to aid our conceptual learning. There is technically no limit to how many dimensions you can include, though there are some usability considerations when there are too many. We'll look at a practical example of a dimensional model in the next section.

Designing a basic star schema

Let's consider an example where we want to build a dimensional model to analyze employee leave bookings. We want to be able to determine the total hours they booked but also drill down to individual booking records to see how much time was booked and when the leave period starts. We need to identify the facts and dimensions and design the star schema. The Kimball Group recommends a four-step process to perform dimensional modeling. These steps are presented here, along with the results for our example scenario in parentheses:

1. Identify the business process (leave booking).

2. Declare the grain (one record per contiguous leave booking).

3. Identify the dimensions (employee and date).

4. Identify the fact (hours booked).

Now that we have completed the modeling process, let's look at a diagram of the star schema for this employee leave booking scenario. It contains the fact and dimensions we identified via the Kimball process. However, instead of two dimensions, you will see three related to the fact table. *Date* appears twice since we have two different dates to analyze – the date booked and the start date. This is known as a **role-playing dimension**, another Kimball concept, as shown in *Figure 10.2*:

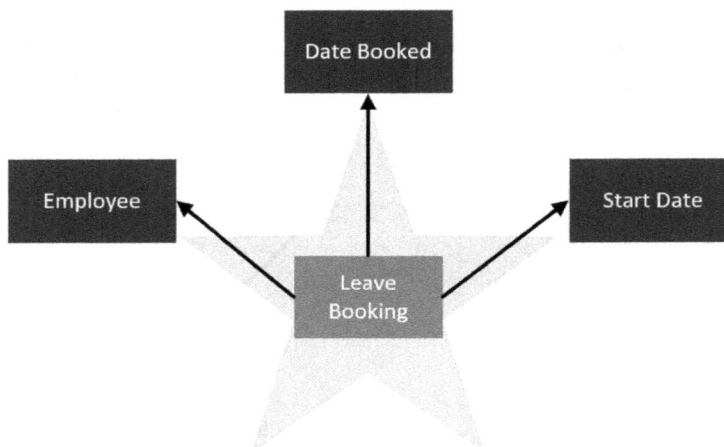

Figure 10.2 – Star schema for employee leave bookings

Steps 1 and *2* help determine our scope. The real work starts with *step 3*, where we need to define the dimensions. With star schemas, we perform **denormalization** and join some tables beforehand to bring the related attributes together into a single-dimension table where possible. Denormalized tables can have redundant, repeated values.

Grouping values for a business entity makes for easier business analysis, and repetition isn't a problem for a column-storage engine such as Analysis Services tabular models, which is built to compress repeating data.

The concept of grouping can be seen in the following diagram, which shows normalized and denormalized versions of the same employee data:

Table: Employee

EmployeeID	First Name	Last Name	Date Joined
1	Spider	Man	1-Dec-21
2	Super	Man	13-Apr-21
3	Wonder	Woman	12-Jun-21
4	Black	Panther	15-Jul-21

Table: Role

RoleID	RoleName
11	CEO
22	Manager
33	Analyst

Table: Employee_Role

ID	EmployeeID	RoleID
101	1	11
102	2	22
103	3	33
104	4	33

Dimension Table: Employee

DimEmployee_ID	EmployeeID	First Name	Last Name	Date Joined	RoleName
1001	1	Spider	Man	1-Dec-21	CEO
1002	2	Super	Man	13-Apr-21	Manager
1003	3	Wonder	Woman	12-Jun-21	Analyst
1004	4	Black	Panther	15-Jul-21	Analyst

Figure 10.3 – Denormalizing three tables into a single employee dimension

In *Figure 10.3*, we can see that the RoleName attribute has been duplicated across the last two roles since we have two employees who are in the **Analyst** role.

A **Date** dimension simply contains a list of contiguous dates (complete years), along with date parts such as day of the week, month name, quarter, year, and so on. This is typically generated using a database script, M query, or DAX formulas. How you generate the date table is up to the developer.

The final step is to model the fact table. Since we determined that we want one row per employee leave booking, we could include these attributes in the fact table in *Figure 10.4*:

Fact Table: Leave Booking

Date	DimEmployee_ID	LeaveStartDate	HoursBooked
12-Jan-22	1002	12-Jun-22	24
14-Jan-22	1003	14-Feb-22	16
11-Jan-22	1001	27-Dec-22	40
12-Feb-22	1004	3-Mar-22	8
16-Mar-22	1003	1-May-22	16
24-Mar-22	1001	1-Jul-22	28

Figure 10.4 – Leave booking fact table

We have provided a trivial example of a business problem for dimensional modeling in this book to aid learning. Note that dimensional modeling is a unique discipline, and it can be significantly more complex in some scenarios. There are different types of dimension and fact tables and even supplementary tables that can solve granularity issues. We will briefly introduce a few of these more advanced modeling topics, though we encourage you to perform deeper research to learn about these areas if needed.

Next, we look at using a single source of truth to provide a common semantic model for multiple reports.

Building a single source of truth

Once you have the concept of a star schema, it is time to move on to conformed dimensions. Additional star schemas can be linked together through a common dimension with the same surrogate keys. Using this extension to a star schema will assist the Analysis Services engine to use measures between fact tables to relate based on a dimension attribute. This process is known as a hub and spokes data warehouse. *Figure 10.5* displays conformed dimensions – **Date**, **SalesTerritory**, and **Product** – related to two different fact tables – **ResellerSales** and **InternetSales**.

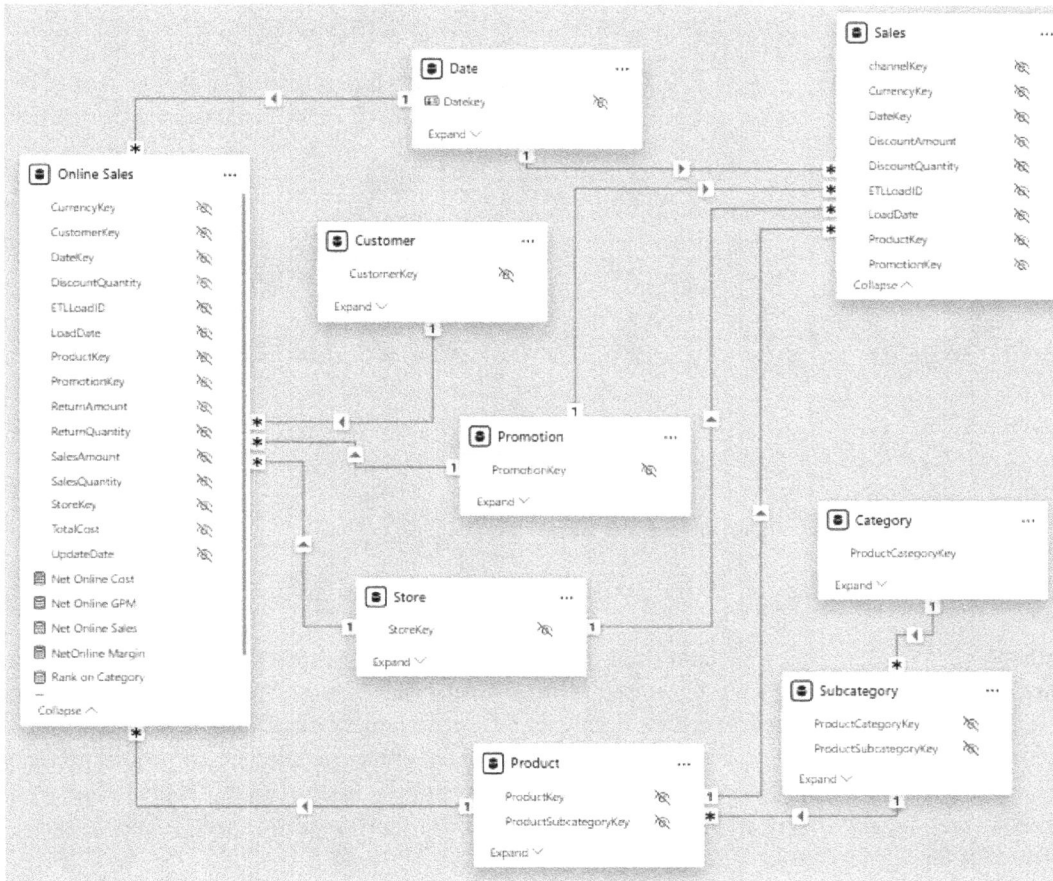

Figure 10.5 – Conformed dimensions

So, instead of creating two different semantic models, `InternetSales` versus `ResellerSales`, we can consolidate those into one semantic model called `Sales`. Conformed dimensions make this a single source of truth because the measure calculations for `ResellerSales` and `InternetSales` can be contained in one model. Now, we get an additional bonus with a single model: measures can be calculated between the conformed facts. Any attribute from **Date**, **Product**, or **SalesTerritory** can be placed in the same visual and compared. *Figure 10.6* shows the combination of `InternetSales` with `ResellerSales` sliced by **Sales Territory Country** and **Year** from the `date` dimension:

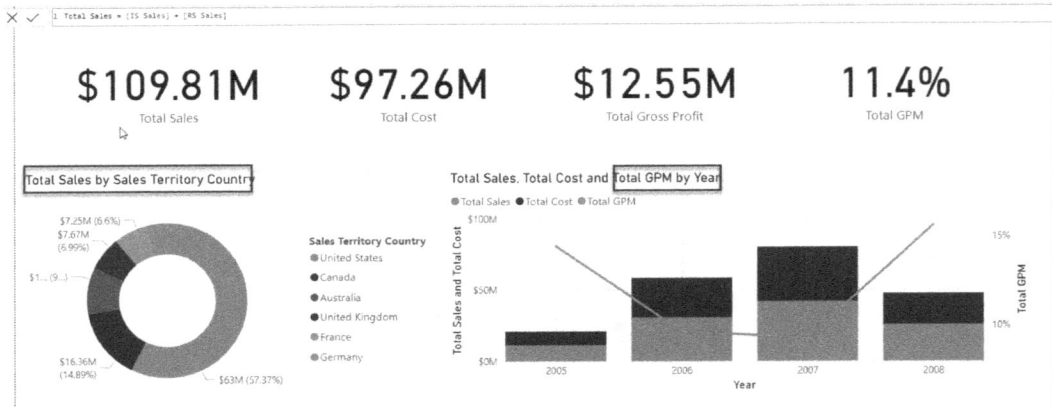

Figure 10.6 – Measures combining reseller and internet sales

Next, we will look at tasks to help with model size.

Reducing dataset size

In *Chapter 2*, *Exploring Power BI Architecture and Configuration*, we learned that the Import mode tables are stored in a proprietary compressed format by Analysis Services. We should aim to keep these tables as small as possible to reduce both data refresh and query durations. There is also the initial semantic model load to consider. Power BI does not keep every semantic model in memory all the time for practical reasons. When a semantic model has not been used recently, it must be loaded from disk into memory the next time someone needs it. This initial semantic model load duration increases as the size increases.

The benefits of smaller semantic models are beyond just speed. In general, less data to process means less CPU and memory usage, which benefits the overall environment by leaving more resources available for other processes.

The following techniques can be used to reduce semantic model size.

Removing unused tables and columns

If any table or column elements are not needed anywhere in the semantic model or downstream reports, it is a good idea to remove them. Sometimes, tables or attributes are used for calculations and not exposed to users directly, so these can't be removed easily.

Avoiding high precision and high cardinality columns

Sometimes, source data may be stored in a format that supports a much higher precision than we would ever need for our analysis. For example, a `date` column to the second is not required if we only ever analyze per day at the highest granularity. Similarly, the weight of a person to two decimal places might not be needed if we always plan to display them as a whole number. Therefore, we recommend reducing the precision in Power Query, in a pushed-down transformation, or permanently in the original data source if that's feasible and safe. Let's build on the decimal versus whole number example. Power BI stores both types as a 64-bit value that occupies 8 bytes. Initially, this won't seem like it makes a difference in terms of storage. This is true, though the semantic model size reductions will be realized because we are reducing the number of unique values with lower precision (for example, all the values between 99.0 and 99.49 collapse to 99 when we reduce the precision). Fewer unique values will reduce the size of the internal dictionary.

The same concept extends to high cardinality columns. **Cardinality** means the number of unique elements in a group. A high cardinality column will have few repeated values and will not compress well. Sometimes, you will already know that every value in a column is unique. This is typical of primary/surrogate keys such as an employee ID or employee key, which are unique by design. Be aware that you may not be able to remove unique columns because they are essential for relationships or report visuals.

Adjusting date and time settings

If you have many date columns in your semantic model, a lot of space may be taken up by the hidden date tables that Power BI automatically creates. You can disable `auto date/time` in the **Options** settings of a Power BI report. Be sure to disable this setting in Power BI Desktop, as described in *Chapter 2, Exploring Power BI Architecture and Configuration*.

If you need to perform analysis with both date and time, consider splitting the original datetime attribute into two values – that is, date only and time only. This reduces the total number of unique date elements. If we had 10 years of data to analyze and design a date table to the second granularity, we would have about 315 million unique datetime entries (10 years x 365 days x 24 hours x 60 minutes x 60 seconds). However, if we split this, we would only get 90,050 unique items – that is, a table of unique dates with 10 x 365 entries, and a table of unique times with 24 x 60 x 60 entries. This represents a raw row count reduction of over 99%.

Replacing GUIDs with surrogate keys for relationships

A **GUID** is a **Globally Unique Identifier** consisting of 32 hexadecimal characters separated by hyphens. An example of this is `123e4567-e89b-12d3-a456-426614174000`. They are stored as text in Analysis Services. Relationships across text columns are not as efficient as those across numerical columns. You can use Power Query to generate a **surrogate key** that will be substituted for the GUID in both the dimension and fact tables. This could be resource- and time-intensive for large semantic models, trading off refresh performance for query performance.

An alternative is to work with database or data warehouse professionals to have surrogate keys provided at the source if possible. This technique does cause problems if the GUID is needed. For example, someone may want to copy the ID value to look up something in an external system. You can avoid preloading the GUID in the dataset by using a composite model and a report design that provides a drilling experience to expose just one or a small set of GUIDs on-demand via DirectQuery. We will cover composite models in more detail in *Chapter 12, High-Scale Patterns*.

Composite models for very large models

When you have models that approach many tens or even hundreds of tables, you should consider creating subsets of smaller datasets for better performance. Try to include only facts that are highly correlated from a business perspective and that need to be analyzed by the same type of user in a single report visual, page, or analytical session. Avoid loading facts that have very few dimensions in common into the same dataset. For example, leave bookings and leave balances would likely belong to the same dataset, whereas leave bookings and website inquiries would likely not. You can also solve such problems using aggregations and composite models, which we will also discuss in *Chapter 12, High-Scale Patterns*. This tip also applies to slow DirectQuery models, where moving to composite models with aggregations can provide significant performance benefits.

Efficient data types

Power BI will try to choose the right data types for columns for you. If data comes from a strongly typed source such as a database, it will match the source data type as closely as possible. However, with some sources, the default that's chosen may not be the most efficient, so it's worth checking. This is especially true for flat files, where whole numbers might be loaded as text. In such cases, you should manually set the data type for these columns to integers because integers use value encoding. This method compresses more than dictionary encoding and run-length encoding, which are used for text. Integer relationships are also faster.

Offloading DAX calculated columns

Calculated columns do not compress as well as physical columns. If you have calculated columns, especially with high cardinality, consider pushing the calculation down to a lower layer. You can perform this calculation in Power Query. Aim to leverage push-down here too, using guidance from *Chapter 8, Loading, Transforming, and Refreshing Data*.

Setting the default summarization

Numeric columns in a semantic model usually default to the SUM aggregation, and occasionally to the COUNT aggregation. This property can be set in the **Data** tab of Power BI Desktop. You may have integers that do not make sense to aggregate, such as a unique identifier such as an order number. If the default summarization is set to SUM, Power BI will try to sum this attribute in visuals. This may confuse users, but for performance, we are concerned that we are doing meaningless sums. Therefore, we advise reviewing the **Summarization** settings, as shown in *Figure 10.7*:

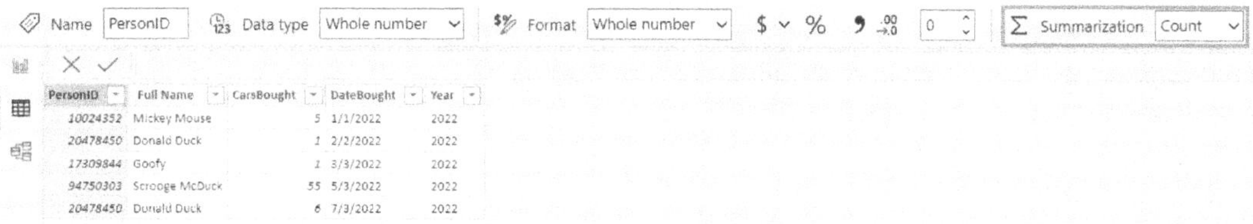

Figure 10.7 – Summarization on an identifier column set to Count instead of Sum

Next, we will look at one advanced data modeling topic that has specific relevance to Power BI.

Considering many-to-many relationships and bi-directional filtering

An important Kimball concept that has specific relevance to Power BI is **many-to-many relationships**, which we will abbreviate as **M2M**. This type of relationship is used to model a scenario where there can be duplicate values in the key columns on both sides of the relationship. For example, you may have a table of target or budget values that are set at the monthly level per department, whereas other transactions are analyzed daily. The latter requirement determines that the granularity of the date dimension should be daily. *Figure 10.8* shows some sample source data for such a scenario. It highlights the **YearMonth** field, which we need to use to join the tables at the correct granularity, and that there are duplicate values in both tables:

Calendar (filtered to first 2 days of each month)

Date	Year	MonthName	MonthNumber	YearMonth
01-Jan-22	2022	January	1	202201
02-Jan-22	2022	January	1	202201
01-Feb-22	2022	February	2	202202
02-Feb-22	2022	February	2	202202
01-Mar-22	2022	March	3	202203
02-Mar-22	2022	March	3	202203
Total	**12132**		**12**	

Budgets

YearMonth	Department	Budget
202201	Manufacturing	$520,000
202201	Research	$50,000
202201	Sales	$250,000
202202	Manufacturing	$400,000
202202	Research	$125,000
202202	Sales	$255,000
202203	Manufacturing	$450,000
202203	Research	$375,600
202203	Sales	$260,000
Total		**$2,685,600**

Figure 10.8 – Calendar and Budgets data showing duplicates in the key column

This example demonstrates a completely legitimate scenario that has different variations. When you try to build a relationship between columns with duplicates in Power BI, you will find that you can only create an M2M type, as shown in *Figure 10.9*:

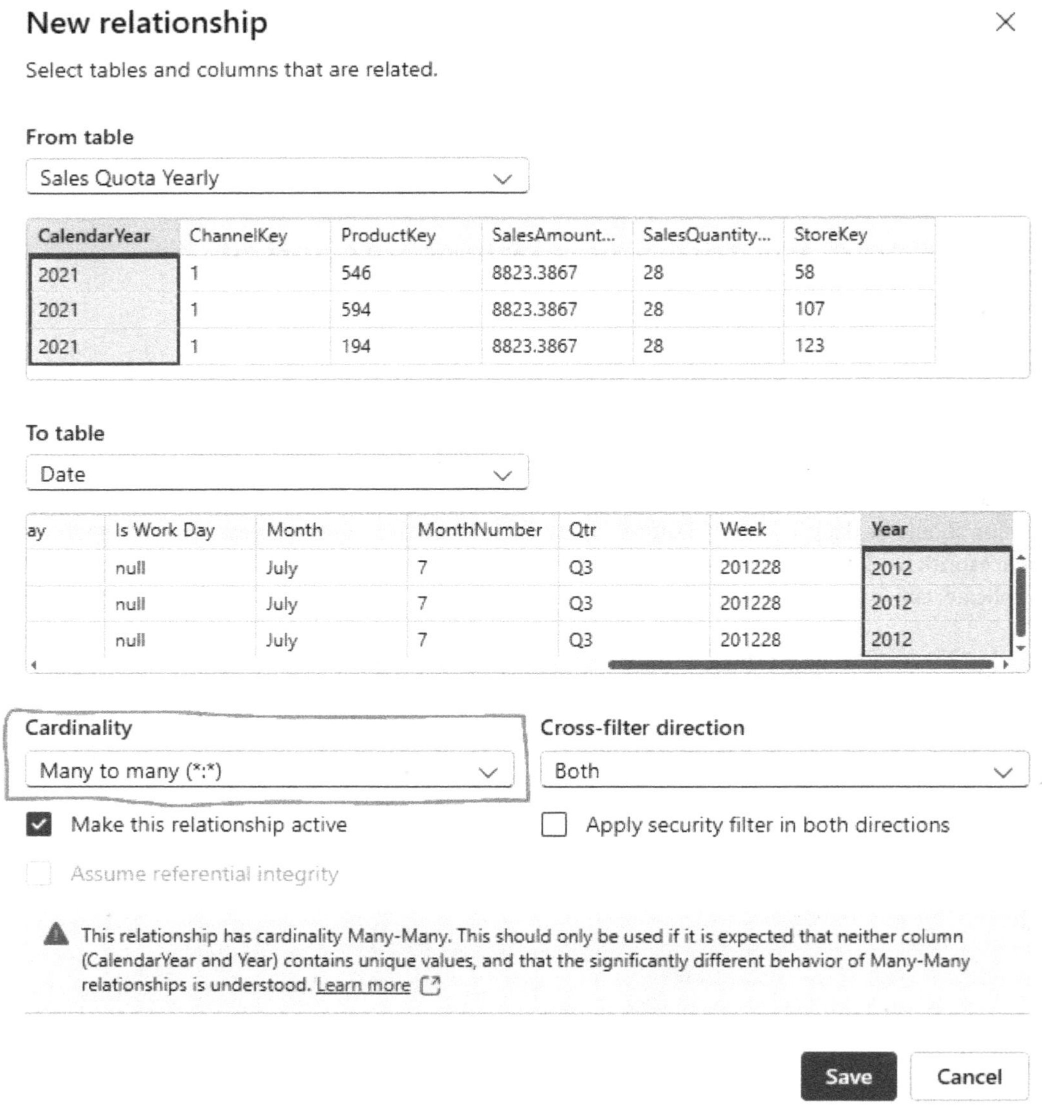

New relationship   ✕

Select tables and columns that are related.

From table

Sales Quota Yearly	∨

CalendarYear	ChannelKey	ProductKey	SalesAmount...	SalesQuantity...	StoreKey
2021	1	546	8823.3867	28	58
2021	1	594	8823.3867	28	107
2021	1	194	8823.3867	28	123

To table

Date	∨

ay	Is Work Day	Month	MonthNumber	Qtr	Week	Year
	null	July	7	Q3	201228	2012
	null	July	7	Q3	201228	2012
	null	July	7	Q3	201228	2012

Cardinality	Cross-filter direction
Many to many (*:*) ∨	Both ∨

☑ Make this relationship active   ☐ Apply security filter in both directions

☐ Assume referential integrity

⚠ This relationship has cardinality Many-Many. This should only be used if it is expected that neither column (CalendarYear and Year) contains unique values, and that the significantly different behavior of Many-Many relationships is understood. Learn more [↗]

Save   Cancel

Figure 10.9 – Many-to-many relationship configuration

Once the M2M relationship has been configured, Power BI will resolve the duplication and display the correct results in visuals. For example, if you show the total **Budget** values using the year from the **Calendar** table, the sums will be correct, as shown in *Figure 10.10*:

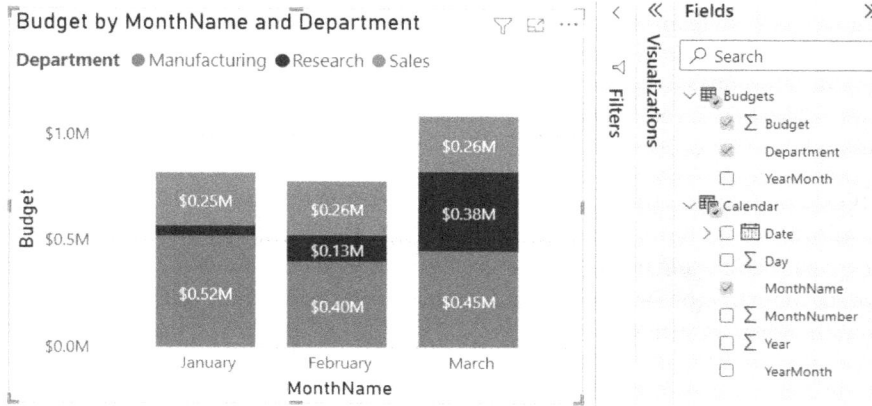

Figure 10.10 – Correct results with the M2M relationship type

Now that we have described when and how to use M2M relationships, we advise using them with care and generally with smaller semantic models.

The M2M relationship type should be avoided when you're dealing with large semantic models, especially if there are many rows on both sides of the relationship. The performance of this relationship type is slower than the most common one-to-many relationships and can degrade more as data volumes and DAX complexity increase. Instead, we recommend employing **bridge tables** to resolve the relationship into multiple one-to-many relationships. You will need to adjust the measure slightly. This approach will be described shortly.

You can avoid the performance penalty of using an M2M relationship by adding a new table to the semantic model called a bridge table. The following screenshot shows how we can introduce a bridge table between the **Calendar** and **Budgets** tables with all the relationships being one-to-many. The bridge table simply contains pairs of keys that can connect unique rows for each table. So, we need to introduce a **BudgetKey** field to the **Budgets** table to uniquely identify each row, as in *Figure 10.11*:

Figure 10.11 – A bridge table added with only one-to-many relationships

A small change is required to ensure the bridge tables work correctly with calculations. We need to wrap any measure around a CALCULATE () statement that explicitly filters over the bridge table. In our case, we can hide the **Budget** column and replace it with a calculation, as shown here:

```
BudgetMeasure = CALCULATE(SUM(Budgets[Budget]), Budget_Bridge)
```

You can see both techniques in action in the sample Many to many.pbix file that's included with this chapter. There is also an example Conformed Dimension M2M.pbix where Internet Sales have multiple Sales Reasons.

In our trivial examples with a small number of rows, creating a bridge table would seem like an unnecessary effort, and it even introduces more data into the model. The performance benefit is likely to be negligible and using the M2M relationship type would be better for easier maintenance. However, as data volumes grow, we recommend implementing bridge tables and doing performance comparisons rather than reporting scenarios.

Next, we will look at one case where bi-directional filtering is okay.

Using bi-directional relationships carefully

This type of relationship allows slicers and filter context to propagate in either direction across a relationship. If a model has many **bi-directional relationships**, applying a filter condition to a single part of the dataset could have a large downstream impact as all the relationships must be followed to apply the filter. Traversing all the relationships is extra work that could slow down queries. We recommend only turning on bi-directional relationships when the business scenario requires it. *Figure 10.12* highlights the relationship using **bi-directional filtering**:

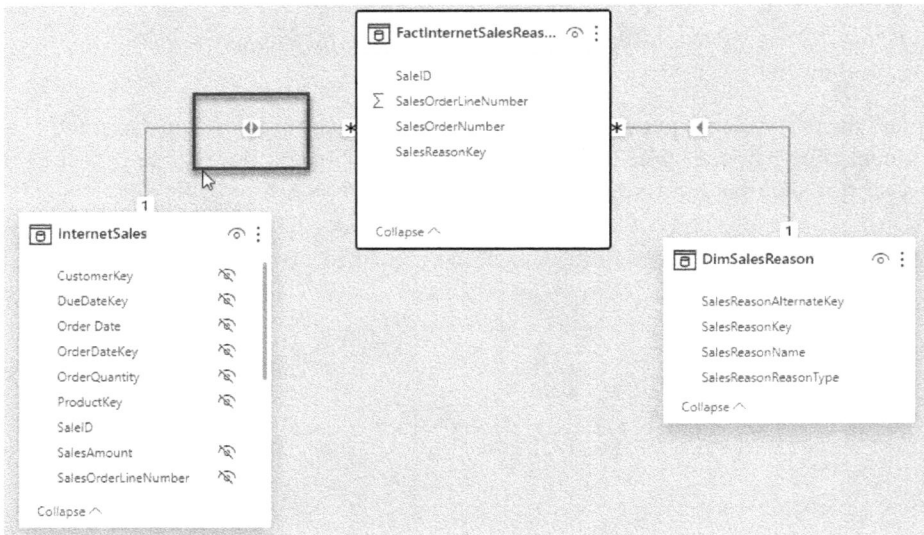

Figure 10.12 – Bi-directional filter for SalesReason

FactInternetSalesReason can have multiple SalesReasonKey values for one line item in InternetSales. FactInternetSalesReason is hidden from the report because there is nothing to report. SalesOrderNumber and SalesOrderLineNumber (SaleID) must be concatenated together to form a relationship between the two fact tables. Since this M2M is needed for reporting SalesReason for line items, the bi-directional filter applied is correct and useful to the model. Usually, requirements dictate the creation of a bi-directional filter. The improvement in performance in this example can be gained by replacing the concatenated columns with a surrogate key as an integer data type rather than the text data type of SaleID.

Next, we will look at optimizing RLS for datasets.

Avoiding pitfalls with row-level security

RLS is a core feature of Power BI. It is the mechanism that's used to prevent users from seeing certain data. It works by limiting the rows that a user can access in tables by applying DAX filter expressions.

There are two approaches to configuring RLS. The simplest configuration involves creating a role and then adding members, which can be individual users or security groups. Then, DAX table filter expressions are added to the role to limit which rows members can see. A more advanced approach (sometimes referred to as dynamic RLS) is where you can create security tables that contain user and permission information. The latter is commonly used when permissions can change often, and it allows the security tables to be maintained automatically, without the Power BI model needing to be changed.

Performance issues can arise when applying filters becomes relatively expensive compared to the same query with no RLS involved. This can happen when the filter expression is not efficient and ends up using the single-threaded formula engine, which we learned about in *Chapter 6*, *Third Party Utilities*. The filter may also be spawning a lot of storage engine queries.

General guidance for RLS configuration

It is recommended to perform RLS filtering on dimension tables rather than fact tables. Dimensions generally contain far fewer rows than facts, so applying the filter on the dimension allows the engine to take advantage of the much lower row count and then use the relationship with the fact to perform the filtering.

Operations such as conditional statements and string manipulations are formula engine-bound and can become very inefficient for large semantic models. Try to keep the DAX filter expressions simple and adjust the data model to precalculate any intermediate values that are needed for the filter expression. One example is parent-child hierarchies, where a table contains relationship information within it because each row has a parent row identifier that points to its parent in the same table. Consider the following example of a parent-child dimension for an organization structure. It has been flattened with the helper columns such as **Path** beforehand so that the DAX calculations and security can be applied to the levels. *Figure 10.12* shows a typical example in Power BI for handling a parent-child situation:

Dimension Table: Organization Structure

ID	ParentID	Path	Level Name	Level 1 Name	Level 2 Name	Level 2 ID	Level 3 Name	Level 3 ID
1		1	Whole Organization	Whole Organization				
2	1	1|2	Finance	Whole Organization	Finance	2		
3	1	1|3	Human Resources	Whole Organization	Human Resources	3		
4	2	1|2|4	Accounts Payable	Whole Organization	Finance	2	Accounts Payable	4
5	2	1|2|5	Accounts Receivable	Whole Organization	Finance	2	Accounts Receivable	5
6	2	1|2|6	Mergers & Acquisitions	Whole Organization	Finance	2	Mergers & Acquisitions	6
7	3	1|3|7	Recruitment	Whole Organization	Human Resources	3	Recruitment	7
8	3	1|3|8	Payroll	Whole Organization	Human Resources	3	Payroll	8

Figure 10.13 – A typical parent-child dimension configured for Power BI

Suppose we wanted to create a role to give people access to all of **Finance**. You might be tempted to configure a simple RLS expression, like so:

```
PATHCONTAINS('Organization Structure'[Path], 2)
```

This will work, but it does involve string manipulation because the function is searching for a character in the **Path** column. For better performance, the following longer expression is preferred because it only compares integers:

```
'Organization Structure'[Path] = 2
```

Optimize relationships

Security filters are applied from dimensions to facts by following relationships, just like any regular filter that's used in a report or query. Therefore, you should follow the relationship best practices that were mentioned in *Chapter 5, Optimization for Storage Modes*.

Power BI Desktop allows you to stimulate roles to test RLS. You should use tools such as Performance Analyzer and DAX Studio to capture durations and engine activity with and without RLS applied. Look for differences in formula engine durations and storage engine query counts to see what impact the RLS filter has on timings. It is also recommended to test a published version in the Power BI service with a realistic population data volume. This can help identify issues that may not be caught in development with smaller data volumes. Remember to establish baselines and measure the impact of individual changes, as recommended in *Chapter 7, Governing with a Performance Framework*.

Guidance that applies to dynamic RLS

Avoid unconnected security tables and LOOKUPVALUE() to not simulate relationships by using a function to search for value matches in columns across two tables. This operation involves scanning through data and is much slower than if the engine were to use a physical relationship, which we recommend instead. You may need to adjust your security table and data model to make physical relationships possible, which is worth the effort.

With dynamic RLS, the filter condition is initially applied to the security tables, which then filter subsequent tables via relationships. We should model the security tables to minimize the number of rows they contain. This minimizes the number of potential matches and reduces engine filtering work. Bear in mind that a single security table is not a Power BI requirement, so you are not forced to combine many permissions and grains into a large security table. Having a few small security tables that are more normalized can provide better performance.

Security filter operations are not cached when they use them; try to limit the security tables to less than 128,000 rows. If you have many different RLS filters from dimensions being applied to a *single fact table*, you can build a single security table using the same principles as the Kimball **junk dimension**. This can be a complete set of every possible combination of permissions (also known as a **cross-product**) or just the actual unique permission sets that are required by users. A cross-product is very easy to generate but can result in combinations that do not make sense and can never exist.

To see this technique in practice, let's consider the following setup, where one fact table is being filtered by multiple dimensions with security applied. The arrows in *Figure 10.13* represent relationships and the direction of the filter propagation:

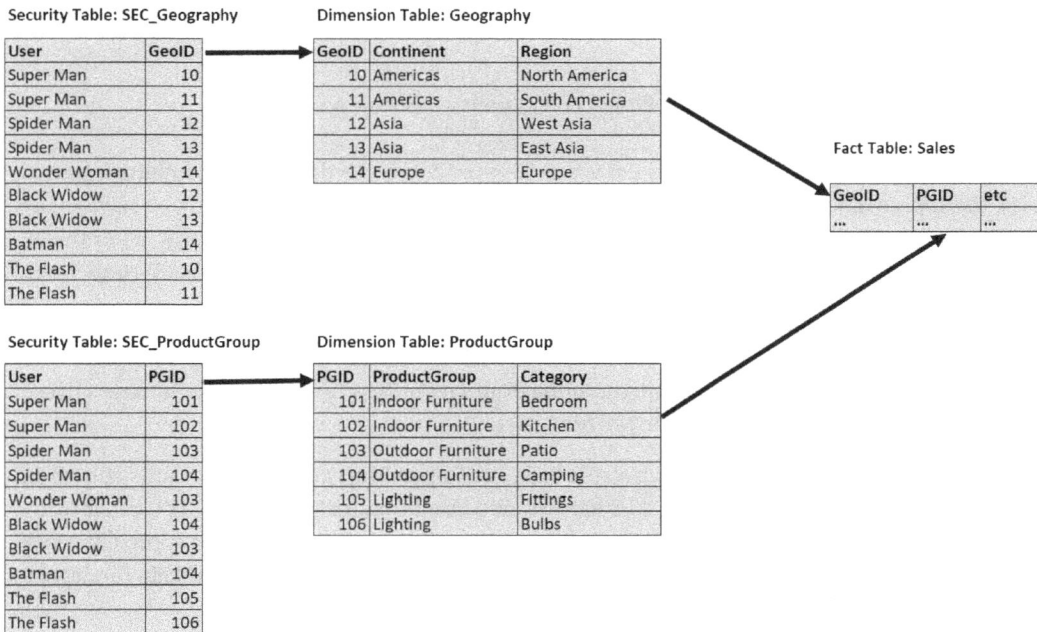

Figure 10.14 – Securing a single fact via multiple dimensions

We could reduce the amount of work that's needed to resolve security filters by combining the permissions into a single security table, as shown in *Figure 10.14*:

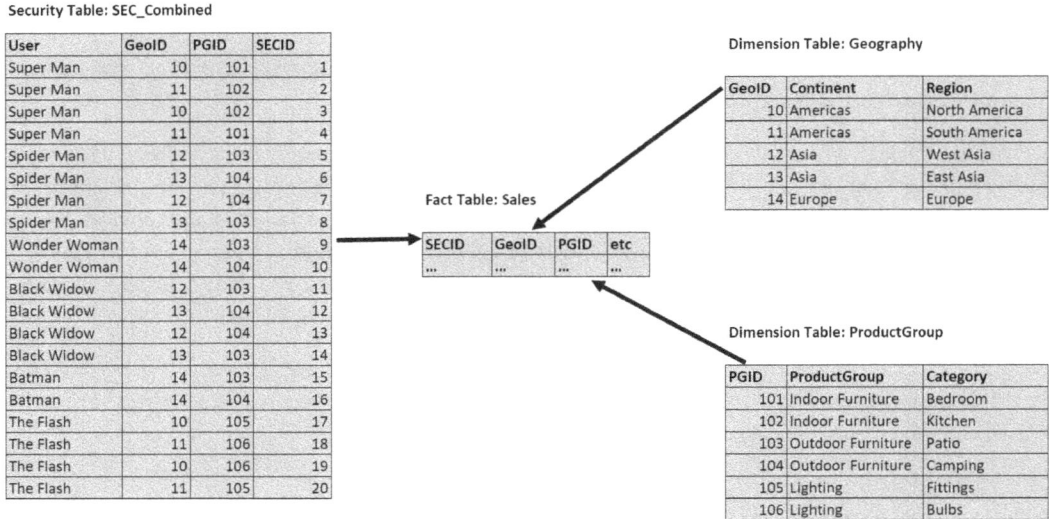

Security Table: SEC_Combined

User	GeoID	PGID	SECID
Super Man	10	101	1
Super Man	11	102	2
Super Man	10	102	3
Super Man	11	101	4
Spider Man	12	103	5
Spider Man	13	104	6
Spider Man	12	104	7
Spider Man	13	103	8
Wonder Woman	14	103	9
Wonder Woman	14	104	10
Black Widow	12	103	11
Black Widow	13	104	12
Black Widow	12	104	13
Black Widow	13	103	14
Batman	14	103	15
Batman	14	104	16
The Flash	10	105	17
The Flash	11	106	18
The Flash	10	106	19
The Flash	11	105	20

Dimension Table: Geography

GeoID	Continent	Region
10	Americas	North America
11	Americas	South America
12	Asia	West Asia
13	Asia	East Asia
14	Europe	Europe

Fact Table: Sales

SECID	GeoID	PGID	etc
...	...	...	...

Dimension Table: ProductGroup

PGID	ProductGroup	Category
101	Indoor Furniture	Bedroom
102	Indoor Furniture	Kitchen
103	Outdoor Furniture	Patio
104	Outdoor Furniture	Camping
105	Lighting	Fittings
106	Lighting	Bulbs

Figure 10.15 – More efficient configuration to secure a single fact

Note that our **SEC_Combined** table *does not* use a cross-product – it only contains combinations that exist in the source data, which will result in a smaller table. This is preferred when you have many dimensions and possible values. In our trivial example, the table contains 20 rows instead of the 30 combinations that would come from a cross-product (five **Geography** rows by six **ProductGroup** rows).

You can see the effect of this change by running some report pages or queries with and without RLS applied, as described earlier. Check out RLS.pbix and RLS Combine.pbix in the sample files to see these in action. They contain the configurations from *Figure 10.13* and *Figure 10.14*, respectively, with a single fixed role to simulate the **Super Man** user.

We ran some tests in DAX Studio using a role built for **Super Man** and got the results shown in *Figure 10.15*. Even though we only had 25,000 rows, and the durations were trivial, you can already see a 300% difference in the total duration when RLS is applied using the combined approach. With many users, dimensions, and fact rows, this difference will be significant and noticeable in the report:

Sample File	Configuration	Formula Engine (ms)	Storage Engine (ms)	Storage Engine Queries	Total (ms)
RLS.pbix	No RLS	3	1	1	4
RLS.pbix	Super Man role	4	8	16	12
RLS Combined.pbix	No RLS	2	1	1	3
RLS Combined.pbix	Super Man role	2	1	1	3

Figure 10.16 – Performance comparison of different RLS configurations

One last note about security context: the security table in this example contains multiple rows and some duplicate permission sets. For example, observe that both **Spider Man** and **Black Widow** have access to all of **Asia** and **Outdoor Furniture**. If you have many hundreds or thousands of users, security tables like this can get quite large. If users have the same permission sets, we can reduce the size significantly by performing modeling, as shown for the **Geography** dimension in *Figure 10.16*. Observe how we have much smaller security tables. Also, note the appropriate use of M2M and bi-directional filters by exception here – performance can improve massively with this setup when used correctly:

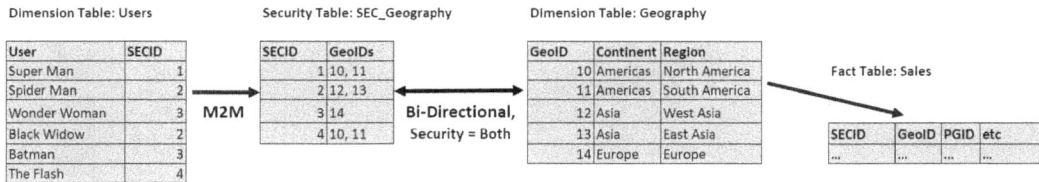

Figure 10.17 – Combining multiple users and permissions

Building specialized security tables such as the one shown can be achieved in different ways. You could build the tables externally as part of regular data warehouse loading activities, or you could leverage Power Query.

Now, let's summarize what we've learned in this chapter.

Summary

In this chapter, we learned how to speed up semantic models for Import mode. The theory from the Kimball Group was used frequently for dimensional modeling. The star schema provides an efficient use of data for semantic models. This format works well with the Analysis Services engine used in Power BI. The four-step dimensional modeling process from Kimball provides practical examples we can use for optimal performance.

Then, we focused on reducing the size of the semantic models. This is important because less data means less processing, which results in better performance and more free resources for other parallel operations. We also explored techniques to help Analysis Services compress data better, such as choosing appropriate data types, reducing cardinality for columns, and preferring numbers over text strings.

Lastly, we learned how to optimize RLS. We learned that RLS works just like regular filters and that previous guidance about fast relationships also applies to RLS. The main thing to remember with RLS is to keep DAX security filter expressions as simple as possible, especially to avoid string manipulation.

In the next chapter, we will look at DAX formulas, where we will identify common performance traps and suggest workarounds.

11

Improving DAX

In the previous chapter, we focused on the Import mode for the visual layer in Power BI, where a key point was to reduce the load on data sources by minimizing the complexity and number of queries that are issued to the semantic model.

In theory, a well-designed data model should not experience performance issues easily unless there are extremely high data volumes with tens of millions of rows or more. However, it is still possible to get poor performance with good data models due to the way DAX measures are constructed.

Learning the **Data Analysis Expressions** (**DAX**) basics may be considered easy by many people because it can be approached by people without a technical data background but who are comfortable writing formulas in a tool such as Microsoft Excel. However, mastering DAX can be challenging. This is because DAX is a rich language with multiple ways to achieve the same result. DAX code requires having knowledge of row context and filter context, which determines what data is in scope at a point in the execution.

In *Chapter 6*, *Third-Party Utilities*, we talked about the formula engine and storage engine in Analysis Services. In this chapter, we will look at examples of how DAX design patterns and being in filter context versus row context can affect how the engine behaves. We will see where time is spent in slower versus faster versions of the same calculation. We will also identify patterns that typically cause performance problems and how to rewrite them.

In this chapter, we're going to cover the following main topics:

- Understanding row and filter context
- Improving the performance of a calculated column
- Improving filter context for a measure
- DAX pitfalls and optimizations

Technical requirements

There are two files to support this chapter as examples (`DisctinctCountSaleGT500.pbix` and `DAX Optimization.pbix`) in the `Chapter11` folder in this book's GitHub repository: `https://github.com/PacktPublishing/Microsoft-Power-BI-Performance-Best-Practices-Second-Edition`.

Let's start talking about the areas where DAX is used in Power BI semantic models.

Understanding row and filter context

There is some confusion about using a calculated column versus a measure. There are no cases where one or the other can be used based on a requirement. For instance, if the requirement says give me a sum of sales, then and only then can a measure be used. On the other hand, if the requirement is to calculate the invoice line item's margin, then using a calculated column is the method to use. DAX code is used in both cases.

Next, let's look at an example of a calculated column and a measure.

Calculated column

In the realm of DAX (Data Analysis Expressions) for Power BI, grasping row and filter context is fundamental. This knowledge dictates when to employ calculated columns versus measures, ensuring accurate data computations tailored to specific needs. Let's explore these concepts through an example involving an Internet Sales Margin calculation.

```
Internet Sales Margin = InternetSales[SalesAmount] -
InternetSales[TotalProductCost]
```

Figure 11.1 displays this new column in a table:

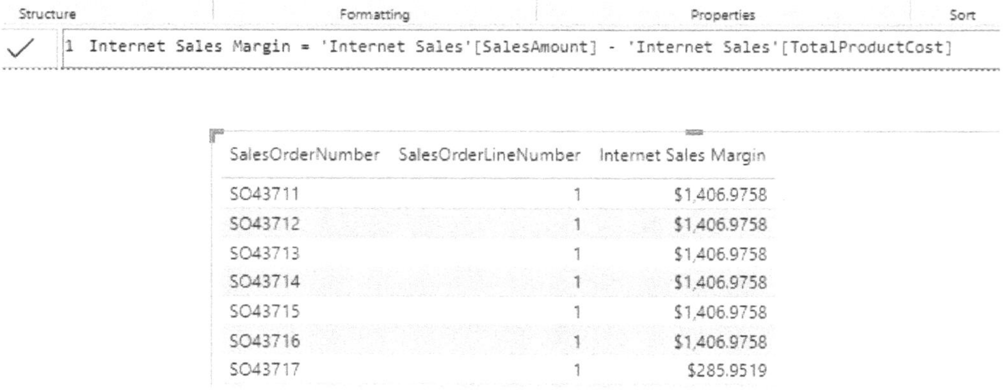

SalesOrderNumber	SalesOrderLineNumber	Internet Sales Margin
SO43711	1	$1,406.9758
SO43712	1	$1,406.9758
SO43713	1	$1,406.9758
SO43714	1	$1,406.9758
SO43715	1	$1,406.9758
SO43716	1	$1,406.9758
SO43717	1	$285.9519

Figure 11.1 – Displaying Internet Sales Margin in a table

The columns add the physical values to the table along with all imported columns for the query.

Measure

Here we introduce a measure called 'Internet Sales,' designed to calculate the total sales amount from the 'InternetSales' table. Measures like this aggregate data based on specified conditions or filters, providing insights into sales performance.

```
Internet Sales = SUM(InternetSales[SalesAmount])
```

Figure 11.2 displays the measure in a visual:

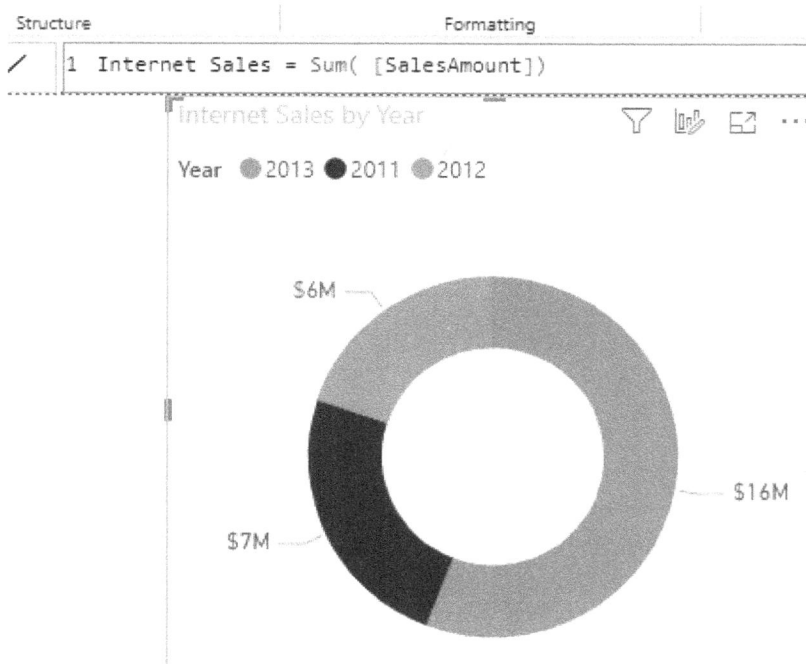

Figure 11.2 – Displaying Internet Sales in a donut chart

The calculation of the amounts for each year does not happen until the visual is rendered. It does not add space to the size of the query or the model.

Next, we will discuss row context.

Dissecting row context

Now, from the preceding calculated column example, we can see that Internet Sales Margin will be calculated row by row. Each time a row is viewed or displayed, this calculated row-level value is shown. It is also stored physically in the table with the imported columns. This is the easiest example of row context (row by row). For row 1, the value would be x and for row 2, the value is y.

Measures can also have a row context before applying a filter context. The X DAX measures do this. There is SUMX for the DAX SUM function. The same with AVERAGE (AVERAGEX), MIN (MINX), MAX (MAXX), COUNT (COUNTX), and so on. The X means that some calculation needs to be performed on each row before aggregating all the row values, as in this instance:

```
Internet Sales = SUMX( InternetSales[Qty] * InternetSales[UnitPrice])
```

In this instance of a measure, the sales amount for each row must be calculated from the Qty and UnitPrice columns before the total sum of internet sales can be shown. This use of SUMX makes the measure perform a row context (row by row) calculation before the filter context of the dataset is computed. Iterating over each row can be time-consuming and make the display of the measure take more time.

Discovering filter context

Filter context and DAX for measures go hand in hand. A measure is usually an aggregation of multiple rows to give analytical results to an end user. The result helps with business decisions or validates the options available for a path to implement. The data in a semantic model is returned from a dataset (filtered or not) to perform this aggregation. Using DAX in an efficient manner helps the determination of the aggregate during a visualization display. In *Figure 11.3*, the Internet Sales measure is aggregated as a measure for the order year and month, city of sale, and customer gender:

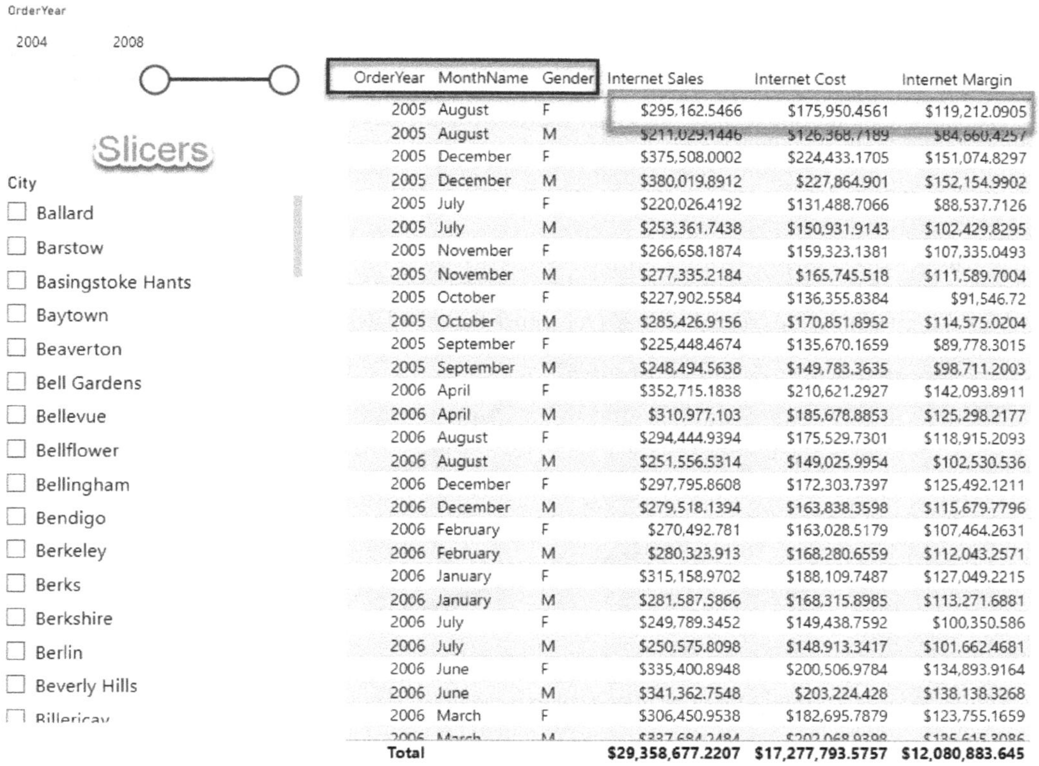

Figure 11.3 – Table used to display dimension attributes and measures

The current filter context for the table of data is the intersection of the year, month, city, and gender. The SUM DAX measure for Internet Sales is coded here:

```
Internet Sales = Sum( [SalesAmount])
```

This is a simple measure and DAX formula and an easy way to see data. If the slicer for Year is used to show only 2012, the filter context of the table would change (filter) to only show the rows for 2012. Also, if the City slicer selects Berlin or multiple cities, the filter context of the table would change to the cities selected plus the year selected.

> **Note**
>
> To learn more about using DAX, there are many helpful resources available. A good suggestion to browse DAX functions is https://dax.guide.

Next, we will see how to move a calculated column to the Power Query step to reduce the size of a model.

Improving the performance of a calculated column

This example uses the customer name from the customer dimension. The table has the first name and last name, but the requirements indicate to use customer name by concatenating the last name with the first name with a comma and space between them. The **calculated column** would be like this:

```
Customer Name = Customer[LastName] & ", " & Customer[FirstName]
```

This is a valid DAX code. This creates a new column in the customer entity and leaves `FirstName` and `LastName` in the table. `FirstName` and `LastName` must exist in the table in the semantic model for this column to be created. *Figure 11.4* shows the calculated column:

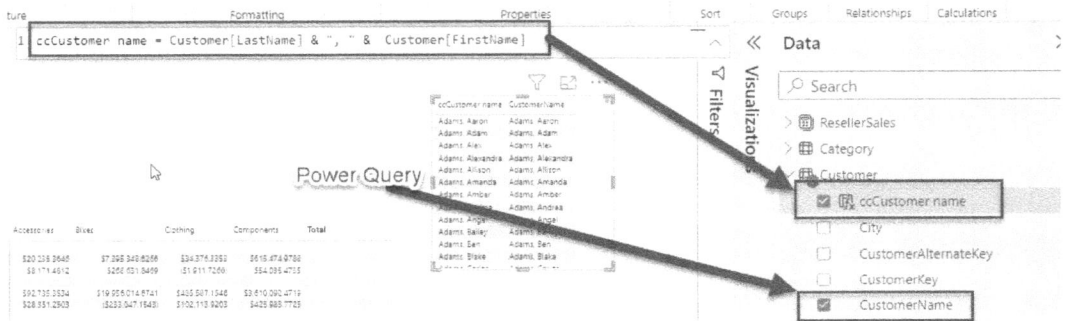

Figure 11.4 – Calculated column called ccCustomer name

Figure 11.4 also displays the `CustomerName` column created in Power Query. Both columns, `ccCustomerName` and `CustomerName`, contain the same data. *Figure 11.5* shows the difference in size from the DAX Studio metrics viewer:

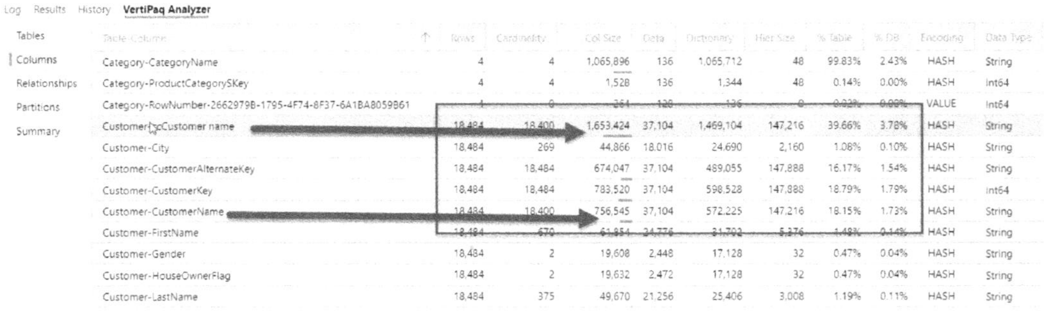

Figure 11.5 – Size for calculated column versus Power Query in DAX Studio view metrics

The **Power Query** column is smaller in this case. Also, `FirstName` and `LastName` do not need to exist in the final table or query because the concatenation happens in the T-SQL being sent to the data source. That is another by-product of creating this column in Power Query. The processing is in the native query on the data source, thus saving CPU resources when refreshing the semantic model.

Next, we will see an example of a DAX measure that performs poorly but is changed to improve performance.

Improving filter context for a measure

In this example, the measure will invoke a row-by-row comparison rather than a table filter before counting distinct orders. *Figure 11.6* shows the report page with two different count measures that look for large customer sales:

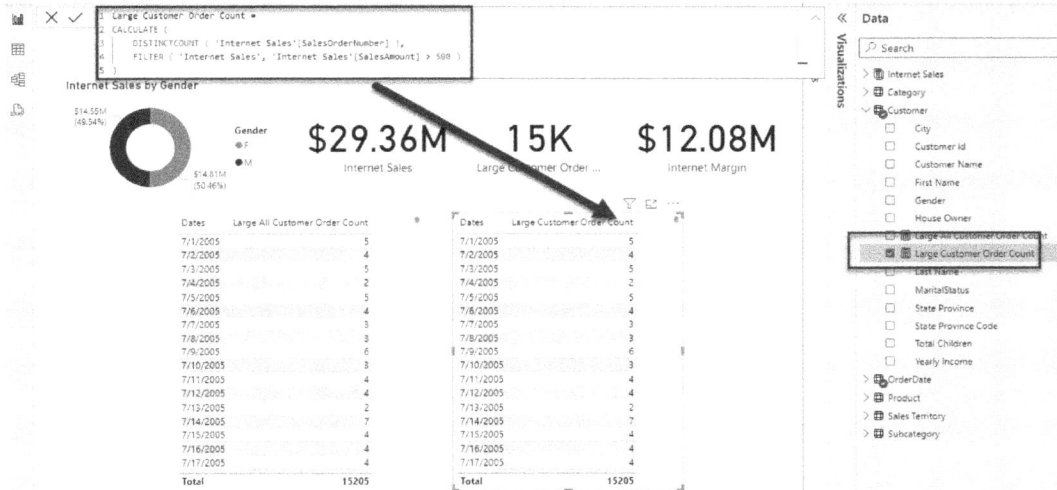

Figure 11.6 – Large customer distinct count measure

This is the code for the measure:

```
Large Customer Order Count =
CALCULATE (
    DISTINCTCOUNT ( 'Internet Sales'[SalesOrderNumber] ),
    FILTER ( 'Internet Sales', 'Internet Sales'[SalesAmount] > 500 )
)
```

The distinct count on the sales is filtered by a sales amount of over 500. The issue with this calculation is that the distinct count will be performed first, and then a filter applied to each row of the distinct count to see whether the sales amount of the order is above 500. This will iterate row by row until the comparison is complete. *Figure 11.7* shows the query in DAX Studio and the number of query executions for each comparison:

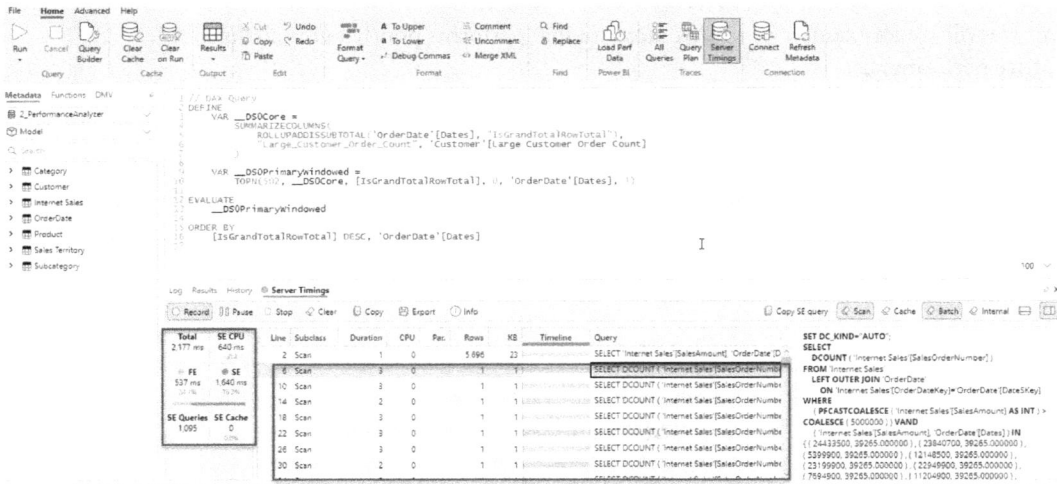

Figure 11.7 – Query server timings from DAX Studio

This method of analysis is explained in the *Performance tuning the data model* section of *Chapter 3, Learning the Tools of Performance Tuning*.

The issue with the measure in *Figure 11.7* shows that 1,000+ queries are executed in the storage engine for filtering on the sales amount greater than 500. A simple change to this measure will improve the performance with fewer queries. Here, we add the ALL function to the FILTER of the measure:

```
Large All Customer Order Count =
CALCULATE (
    DISTINCTCOUNT ( 'Internet Sales'[SalesOrderNumber] ),
    FILTER ( all( 'Internet Sales'[SalesAmount]), 'Internet
Sales'[SalesAmount] > 500 )
)
```

This will change the filter context of the measure to look at all the rows in the Internet Sales table first and filter the row set to only sales above 500. Then, the filter context of the visual and slicers/filters will be applied after the distinct count of sales is returned from the whole query. *Figure 11.8* shows the DAX Studio server timings with the different measures.

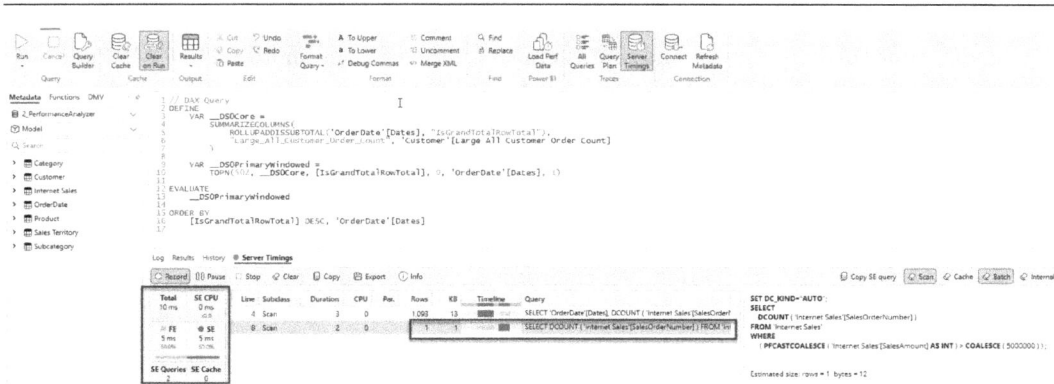

Figure 11.8 – Query server timings from DAX Studio using the ALL DAX function

Next, we will cover the pitfalls along with optimizations you can use as best practices for improved performance of DAX expressions.

Understanding DAX pitfalls and optimizations

Before we dive into specific DAX improvements, we will briefly review the following suggested process to tune your DAX formulas, as shown earlier.

Tuning DAX

In *Chapter 3*, *Learning the Tools for Performance Tuning*, and *Chapter 6*, *Third-Party Utilities*, we provided detailed information and examples of how to use various tools to measure performance. We'll take this opportunity to remind you of which tools can help with DAX tuning and how they can be used. A recommended method to tune DAX is as follows:

1. Review DAX expressions in the semantic model. Ideally, use the **Best Practice Analyzer** (**BPA**) to identify potential improvements. The BPA does cover some of the guidance provided in the next section, but it's a good idea to check all the rules manually.

2. Rank the suggestion in terms of estimated effort, from lowest to highest. Consider moving some calculations or even intermediate results to Power Query. This is usually a better place to perform row-by-row calculations.

3. In a development version of the semantic model, implement trivial fixes right away, but always check your measures to make sure they are still providing the same results.

4. Using the **Power BI Desktop Performance Analyzer**, check the performance of the report pages and visuals. Copy the queries that have been captured by the Analyzer into DAX Studio. Then, use the server timing feature in DAX Studio to analyze the load on the formula engine versus the storage engine.

5. Modify your DAX expressions and confirm that performance has improved in DAX Studio – remember that DAX Studio allows you to safely overwrite measures locally without changing the actual semantic model.

6. Make DAX changes in the semantic model and check the report again with Performance Analyzer in Power BI Desktop to ensure that there are no unexpected performance degradations and that the results are still correct.

7. Test the changes in a production-like environment using realistic user scenarios and data volumes. If successful, deploy to the production environment; otherwise, repeat the process to iron out any remaining issues.

Next, let's review some DAX guidance.

DAX guidance

We will continue with the theme of having the Analysis Services engine do as little work as possible, with as little data as possible. Even with optimized datasets that follow good modeling practices, inefficient DAX can make the engine unnecessarily scan rows or perform slow logic in the formula engine. Therefore, our goals for tuning DAX are as follows:

*   Reduce code that executes on the single-threaded formula engine

*   Reduce the total number of internal queries that are generated by a DAX query

*   Avoid scanning large tables

> **Note**
>
> In this section, we will only show the performance results for the first few tips. Please be aware that you can use DAX Studio, Desktop Performance Analyzer, and other tools to measure performance and tune DAX for all cases mentioned here.

The following list represents some common design choices that lead to lower performance. We will explain why each one can be problematic and what you can do instead:

*   **Use variable instead of repeating measure definitions**: Sometimes, when we are creating a measure, we need to reuse a calculation multiple times to get the result. We will use an example where we have some sales figures and need to calculate the variance percentage compared to the same period in the previous year. One way to write this calculation is as follows:

    ```
    YoY% =
    (
    SUM('Fact Sale'[Total Sales])
    - CALCULATE(SUM('Fact Sale'[Total Sales]), DATEADD('Dimension
    Date'[Date], -1, YEAR))
    ```

```
)
/
CALCULATE(SUM('Fact Sale'[Total Sales]), DATEADD('Dimension
Date'[Date], -1, YEAR)
```

Observe that we are referencing the prior year's sales value twice – once to calculate the numerator and again to calculate the denominator. The Analysis Service engine will have to run this code twice. It is better to let the engine use caching with a variable. Notice the variable and the use of DIVIDE to handle division errors:

```
YoY% VAR =
VAR _PY_Sales =
CALCULATE (
SUM('Fact Sale'[Total Sales]),
DATEADD('Dimension Date'[Date], -1, YEAR))
RETURN  DIVIDE (
    SUM('Fact Sale'[Total Sales]) - _PY_Sales),
    _PY_Sales
)
```

The difference here is that we have introduced the VAR statement to define a variable called _PY_Sales, which will hold the value of the previous year's sales. This value can be reused anywhere in the formula simply by name, without incurring recalculation.

You can see this in action in the sample file, which contains both versions of the measure. The *Without Variable* and *With Variable* report pages contain a table visual, as in *Figure 11.9*:

| Calendar Year | 2014 | | 2015 | | 2016 | |
Month	Total Sales	YoY%	Total Sales	YoY%	Total Sales	YoY%
January						
1	239,249	Infinity	200,959	-16.0%	232,040	15.5%
2	230,158	602.9%	260,229	13.1%	106,474	-59.1%
3	129,815	-29.6%	150,456	15.9%	174,732	16.1%
4	219,301	40.6%	51,394	-76.6%		-100.0%
5	78,483	-36.7%		-100.0%	266,416	Infinity
6		-100.0%	273,002	Infinity	264,426	-3.1%
7	192,654	Infinity	164,946	-14.4%	310,255	88.1%
8	171,123	-40.9%	142,349	-16.8%	289,464	103.3%
9	123,393	23.2%	200,223	62.3%	227,649	13.7%
10	84,998	-47.7%	160,666	89.0%	148,332	-7.7%
11	260,385	33.4%	59,860	-77.0%		-100.0%

Figure 11.9 – Table visual showing a year-on-year % growth measure

We captured the query trace information in DAX Studio to see how these perform. The results can be seen in *Figure 11.10*:

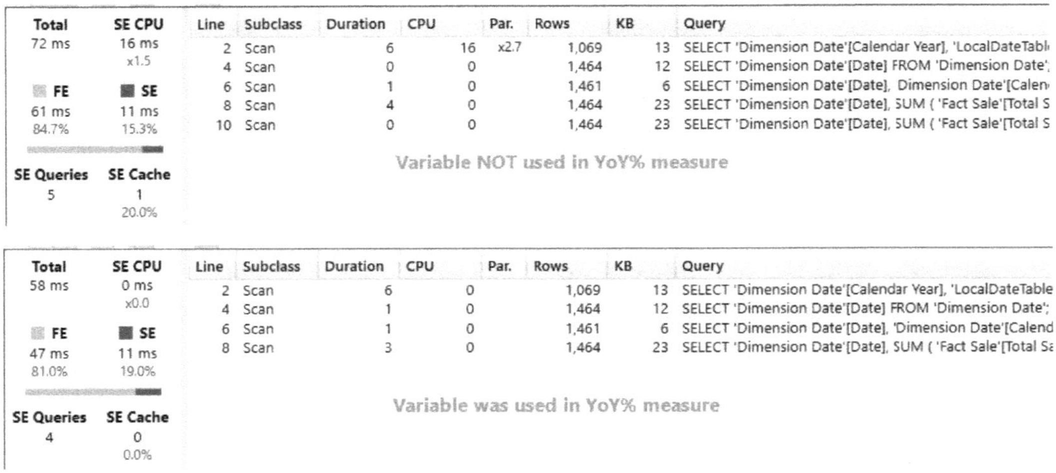

Total	SE CPU	Line	Subclass	Duration	CPU	Par.	Rows	KB	Query
72 ms	16 ms	2	Scan	6	16	x2.7	1,069	13	SELECT 'Dimension Date'[Calendar Year], 'LocalDateTabl
	x1.5	4	Scan	0	0		1,464	12	SELECT 'Dimension Date'[Date] FROM 'Dimension Date';
▦ FE	▪ SE	6	Scan	1	0		1,461	6	SELECT 'Dimension Date'[Date], Dimension Date'[Calen·
61 ms	11 ms	8	Scan	4	0		1,464	23	SELECT 'Dimension Date'[Date], SUM ('Fact Sale'[Total S
84.7%	15.3%	10	Scan	0	0		1,464	23	SELECT 'Dimension Date'[Date], SUM ('Fact Sale'[Total S

SE Queries	SE Cache
5	1
	20.0%

Variable NOT used in YoY% measure

Total	SE CPU	Line	Subclass	Duration	CPU	Par.	Rows	KB	Query
58 ms	0 ms	2	Scan	6	0		1,069	13	SELECT 'Dimension Date'[Calendar Year], 'LocalDateTable
	x0.0	4	Scan	1	0		1,464	12	SELECT 'Dimension Date'[Date] FROM 'Dimension Date';
▦ FE	▪ SE	6	Scan	1	0		1,461	6	SELECT 'Dimension Date'[Date], 'Dimension Date'[Calend
47 ms	11 ms	8	Scan	3	0		1,464	23	SELECT 'Dimension Date'[Date], SUM ('Fact Sale'[Total Sa
81.0%	19.0%								

SE Queries	SE Cache
4	0
	0.0%

Variable was used in YoY% measure

Figure 11.10 – DAX Studio showing less work and duration with a variable

In *Figure 11.10*, the first query without the variable was a bit slower. We can see it executed one extra storage engine query, which does appear to have hit a cache in our simple example. We can also see more time being spent in the formula engine than with the version with a variable. In our example, where the fact table contains about 220,000 rows, this difference would be unnoticeable. This can become significant with higher volumes and more sophisticated calculations, especially if a base measure is used in other measures that are all displayed at the same time.

> **Note**
>
> Using variables is probably the single most important tip for DAX performance. There are so many examples of calculations that need to use calculated values multiple times to achieve the desired result. You will also find that Power BI automatically uses this and other recommended best practices in areas where it generates code for you, such as **Quick Measures**.

- **Use DIVIDE instead of the division operator**: When we divide numbers, we sometimes need to avoid errors by checking for blank or zero values in the denominator. This results in conditional logic statements that add extra work for the formula engine. Let's continue with the example from *Figure 11.10*. Instead of year-over-year growth, we now want to calculate a profit margin. We want to avoid report errors by handling blank and zero values:

```
Profit IF =
IF(
```

```
        OR(
            ISBLANK( [Sales]), [Sales] == 0
            ),
        BLANK(),
        [Profit]/[Sales}
    )
```

An improved version would use the `DIVIDE` function as follows:

```
    Profit DIVIDE = DIVIDE( [Profit], [Sales])
```

This function has several advantages. It automatically handles zeros and blank values at the storage engine layer, which is parallel and faster. It has an optional third parameter that allows you to specify an alternative value to use if the denominator is zero or blank. It is also a much shorter measure that is easier to understand and maintain.

When we look at the performance numbers in DAX Studio, we can see stark differences. The first version is nearly three times slower than the optimized version, as shown in *Figure 11.11*:

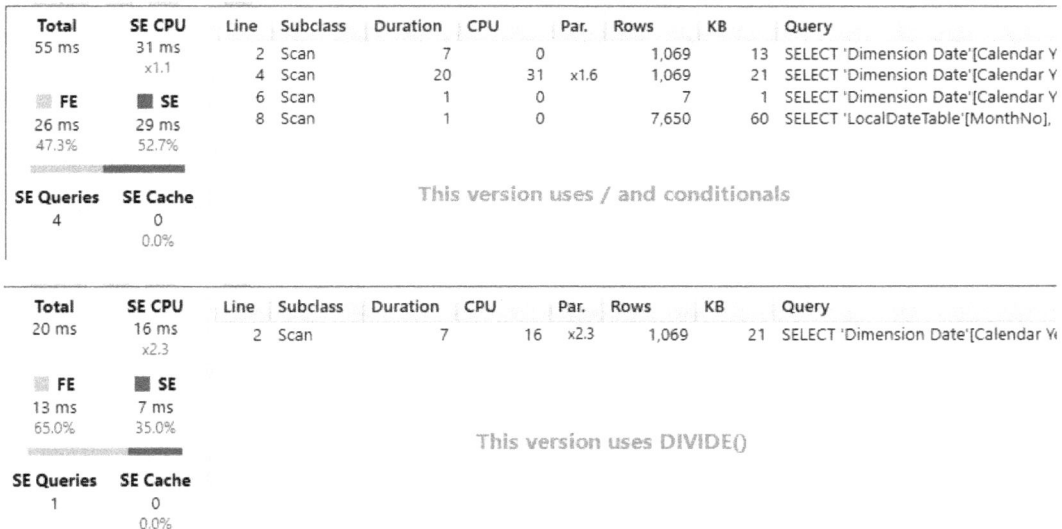

Total	SE CPU	Line	Subclass	Duration	CPU	Par.	Rows	KB	Query
55 ms	31 ms	2	Scan	7	0		1,069	13	SELECT 'Dimension Date'[Calendar Y
	x1.1	4	Scan	20	31	x1.6	1,069	21	SELECT 'Dimension Date'[Calendar Y
FE	SE	6	Scan	1	0		7	1	SELECT 'Dimension Date'[Calendar Y
26 ms	29 ms	8	Scan	1	0		7,650	60	SELECT 'LocalDateTable'[MonthNo],
47.3%	52.7%								

SE Queries	SE Cache		This version uses / and conditionals
4	0		
	0.0%		

Total	SE CPU	Line	Subclass	Duration	CPU	Par.	Rows	KB	Query
20 ms	16 ms	2	Scan	7	16	x2.3	1,069	21	SELECT 'Dimension Date'[Calendar Y
	x2.3								
FE	SE								
13 ms	7 ms								
65.0%	35.0%		This version uses DIVIDE()						

SE Queries	SE Cache
1	0
	0.0%

Figure 11.11 – DAX Studio showing less work done by DIVIDE

Figure 11.11 also shows us that the slower version issued more internal queries and spent about four times longer in the storage engine. It also spent about twice as much time in the formula engine. Once again, this is just a single query for one visual. The difference can be compounded for a typical report page that runs many queries. You can experiment with this using the `Profit IF` and `Profit Divide` pages in the sample file.

- **For measures, avoid converting blank results into zero or some text value**: Sometimes, for usability reasons, people write measures with conditional statements to check for a blank result and replace it with zero. This is more common in financial reporting, where people need to see every dimensional attribute value (for example, `Cost Code` or `SKU`), regardless of whether any activity occurred. Let's look at an example. We have a simple measure called `Sales` in our sample file that sums the `'Fact Sale'[Total Including Tax]` column. We have adjusted it to return zero instead of blanks, as follows:

```
SalesNoBlank =
    VAR _SumSales = SUM( 'Fact Sale'[Total Including Tax])
RETURN
    IF( ISBLANK( _SumSales ), 0, _SumSales )
```

Then, we constructed a matrix visual that shows sales by product barcode for both versions of the measure. The results are shown in *Figure 11.12*. At the top, we can see the values for 2016, which implies there are no sales for the product barcodes in other years. At the bottom, we can see 2013 onward, which we can scroll through:

STANDARD SUM MEASURE:

Year	8302039293647	8302039293929	8792838293234	8792838293236	8792838293289	8792838293728	8792838293820	8792838293987	Total
2016	143,550.00	161,164.08	148,975.20	170,418.60	147,620.88	144,686.52	190,056.24	140,172.12	1,246,643.64
January	22,968.00	32,503.68	22,120.56	40,178.16	31,149.36	32,729.40	33,632.28	24,829.20	240,110.64
February	20,288.40	24,829.20	25,957.80	28,892.16	26,183.52	15,574.68	38,372.40	22,572.00	202,670.16
March	36,748.80	41,306.76	30,246.48	34,760.88	32,052.24	29,343.60	32,729.40	31,375.08	268,563.24
April	29,475.60	36,340.92	28,215.00	34,760.88	27,989.28	41,758.20	34,760.88	31,826.52	265,127.28
May	34,069.20	26,183.52	42,435.36	31,826.52	30,246.48	25,280.64	50,561.28	29,569.32	270,172.32
Total	143,550.00	161,164.08	148,975.20	170,418.60	147,620.88	144,686.52	190,056.24	140,172.12	1,246,643.64

MODIFIED MEASURE TO REPLACE BLANKS WITH ZERO:

Year	8302039293647	8302039293929	8792838293234	8792838293236	8792838293289	8792838293728	8792838293820	8792838293987	Total
2013	0.00	0.00	0.00	0.00	0.00	0.00	0.00	0.00	0.00
January	0.00	0.00	0.00	0.00	0.00	0.00	0.00	0.00	0.00
February	0.00	0.00	0.00	0.00	0.00	0.00	0.00	0.00	0.00
March	0.00	0.00	0.00	0.00	0.00	0.00	0.00	0.00	0.00
April	0.00	0.00	0.00	0.00	0.00	0.00	0.00	0.00	0.00
May	0.00	0.00	0.00	0.00	0.00	0.00	0.00	0.00	0.00
June	0.00	0.00	0.00	0.00	0.00	0.00	0.00	0.00	0.00
July	0.00	0.00	0.00	0.00	0.00	0.00	0.00	0.00	0.00
August	0.00	0.00	0.00	0.00	0.00	0.00	0.00	0.00	0.00
Total	143,550.00	161,164.08	148,975.20	170,418.60	147,620.88	144,686.52	190,056.24	140,172.12	1,246,643.64

Figure 11.12 – The same totals but many more rows when replacing blanks

Both results shown in *Figure 11.12* are technically correct. However, there is a performance penalty for replacing blanks. If we think about a dimensional model, in theory, we could record a fact for every possible combination of dimensions. In practical terms, for our `Sales` example, in theory, we could sell things every single day, for every product, for every employee, in every location, and so on. However, there will nearly always be some combinations that are not realistic or simply don't have activities against them. Analysis Services is highly optimized to take advantage of empty dimension intersections and doesn't return rows for combinations where all the measures are blank. We measured the query that was produced by the visuals in the proceeding screenshot. You can see the performance difference in *Figure 11.13*:

Total	SE CPU	Line	Subclass	Duration	CPU	Par.	Rows	KB	Query
20 ms	0 ms x0.0	2	Scan	5	0		18,900	296	SELECT 'Dimension

FE	SE
15 ms	5 ms
75.0%	25.0%

STANDARD SALES MEASURE

SE Queries	SE Cache
1	0
	0.0%

Total	SE CPU	Line	Subclass	Duration	CPU	Par.	Rows	KB	Query
27 ms	16 ms x2.0	2	Scan	1	16	x16.0	12	1	SELECT 'Dimension Stock
		4	Scan	1	0		1,575	13	SELECT 'LocalDateTable'[Y
		6	Scan	5	0		18,900	296	SELECT 'Dimension Stock
		8	Scan	1	0		7	1	SELECT 'LocalDateTable'[Y

FE	SE
19 ms	8 ms
70.4%	29.6%

SALES MEASURE REPLACING BLANK WITH ZERO

SE Queries	SE Cache
4	0
	0.0%

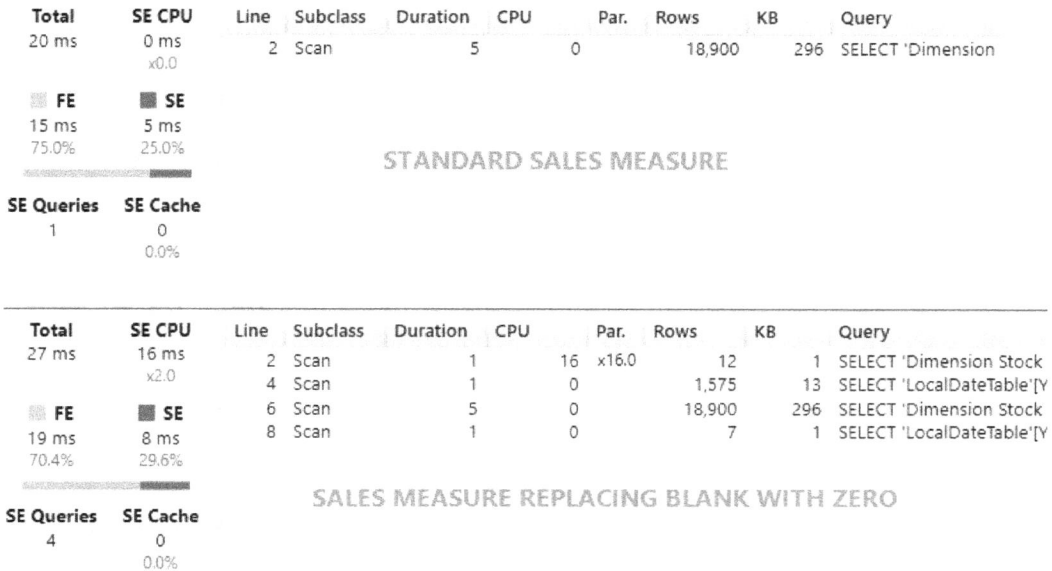

Figure 11.13 – Slower performance when replacing blanks

Figure 11.13 shows a longer total duration, more queries executed, and significantly more time spent in the formula engine. You can see these on the `MeasureWithBlank` and `MeasureNoBlank` report pages in the sample file.

Consider not replacing blanks in your measure but solving this problem on a per-visual basis. You can do this by selecting a visual and using the **Fields** pane in Power BI Desktop to enable **Show items with no data** for specific attributes of a dimension, as shown in *Figure 11.14*. This change with still produce a less optimal query, but not one that's quite as slow as using a measure:

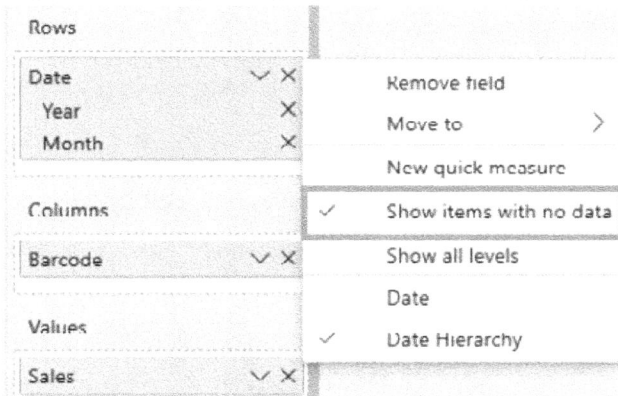

Figure 11.14 – Show items with no data

Another advantage of the visual-based approach is that you are not forced to take a performance hit everywhere the measure is used. You can balance performance selectively.

If you still need to implement blank handling centrally, you could consider making the measures more complex to only substitute a blank for the correct scope of data. We recommended checking out the detailed article from SQLBI on this topic, which shows a combination of DAX and data modeling techniques to use, depending on your scenario: `https://www.sqlbi.com/articles/introducing-summarizecolumns`.

A final point here is to avoid replacing blanks in numerical data with text values such as `No Data`. While this can be helpful for users, it can be even slower than substituting a zero because we are forcing the measures to become a string. This can also create problems downstream if the measure is used in other calculations.

- **Use SELECTEDVALUE instead of VALUES**: Sometimes, a calculation is only relevant when a single item from a dimension is in scope. For example, you might use a slicer as a parameter table to allow users to dynamically change measures such as scaling by some factor. One pattern to access the single value in scope is to use `HASONEVALUE` to check for only one value, and then use the `VALUES` DAX function. If we had a parameter table called `Scale`, our measure would look like this:

```
Sales by Scale =
DIVIDE (
    [Sales Amount],
    IF( HASONEVALUE ( Scale[Scale] ), VALUES ( Scale[Scale] ), 1
)
)
```

Instead, we suggest that you use `SELECTEDVALUE`, which performs both steps internally. It returns blank if there are no items or multiple items in scope and allows you to specify an alternative value if there are zero or multiple items in scope. A better version is as follows:

```
Sales by Scale =
DIVIDE (
    [Sales],
    SELECTEDVALUE ( 'Scale'[Scale], 1 )
)
```

You can see this technique in use in the sample file on the `SELECTEDVALUE` report page.

- **Use IFERROR and ISERROR appropriately**: These are helpful functions that a data modeler can use to catch calculation errors. They can be wrapped around a measure to provide alternatives if there are calculation errors. However, they should be used with care because they increase the number of storage engine scans required and can force row-by-row operations in the engine. We recommend dealing with data errors at the source or in the ETL stages to avoid performing error checking in DAX.

This may not always be feasible, so depending on the situation, you should try to use other techniques, such as the following:

- The FIND or SEARCH functions to search for and substitute values for failed matches

- The DIVIDE or SELECTEDVALUE functions to handle zeros and blanks

- **Use SUMMARIZE only for text columns**: This is the original function that's included in DAX to perform grouping. While it allows any column type, we advise not using numerical columns for performance reasons. Instead, use SUMMARIZECOLUMNS, which is newer and more optimized. There are many examples and use cases here, so we recommend checking out the following article by SQLBI, which provides much deeper coverage: https://www.sqlbi.com/articles/introducing-summarizecolumns.

- **Avoid FILTER in functions that accept filter conditions**: Functions such as CALCULATE and CALCULATETABLE accept a filter parameter that is used to adjust the context of the calculation. The FILTER function returns a table, which is not efficient when it's used as a filter condition in other table functions. Instead, try to convert the FILTER statement into a Boolean expression:

```
Wingtip Sales FILTER =
CALCULATE(
    [Sales],
    FILTER('Dimension Customer', 'Dimension Customer'[Buying
Group] == "Wingtip Toys")
)
```

It is better to replace the table expression with a Boolean expression, as follows:

```
Wingtip Sales =
CALCULATE(
    [Sales],
    'Dimension Customer'[Buying Group] == "Wingtip Toys")
)
```

The FILTER function can force row-by-row operations in the engine, whereas the improved Boolean version will use more efficient filtering on the column stores.

- **Use COUNTROWS instead of COUNT**: We often write measures to count the number of rows in a table without context. Two choices will provide the same result, but only if there are no blank values. The COUNT function accepts a column reference, whereas the COUNTROWS function accepts a table reference. When you need to count rows and do not care about blanks, the latter will perform better.

- **Use ISBLANK() instead of = BLANK() to check for empty values**: They achieve the same result, but ISBLANK() is faster.

- **Optimize virtual relationships with TREATAS**: There are times when we need to filter a table based on column values from another table but cannot create a physical relationship in the semantic mode. It may be that multiple columns are needed to form a unique key, or that the relationship is many-to-many. You can solve this using FILTER and CONTAINS, or INTERSECT. However, TREATAS will perform better and is recommended.

Look at the TREATAS report page in our sample file. *Figure 11.15* shows an example where we added a new table to hold rewards groupings for customers based on their buying group and postal code. We want to filter sales using the new Reward Group column. We will not be able to build a single relationship with more than one key field:

Reward Group	Buying Group	Postal Code
Wingtip Premium	Wingtip Toys	90031
Wingtip Select	Wingtip Toys	90005
Tailspin Premium	Tailspin Toys	90031
Tailspin Select	Tailspin Toys	90011
Wingtip Premium	Wingtip Toys	90041
Wingtip Select	Wingtip Toys	90043
Tailspin Premium	Tailspin Toys	90041
Tailspin Select	Tailspin Toys	90045

Customer Key	WWI Customer ID	Customer	Bill To Customer	Category	Buying Group	Primary Contact	Postal Code
162	162	Tailspin Toys (Glen Park, NY)	Tailspin Toys (Head Office)	Novelty Shop	Tailspin Toys	Nu Bach	90026
170	170	Tailspin Toys (Eastchester, NY)	Tailspin Toys (Head Office)	Novelty Shop	Tailspin Toys	Daniella Barbosa	90031
341	540	Wingtip Toys (Weld, ME)	Wingtip Toys (Head Office)	Novelty Shop	Wingtip Toys	Ăšani Nair	90031
300	499	Wingtip Toys (East Fultonham, OH)	Wingtip Toys (Head Office)	Novelty Shop	Wingtip Toys	Masa Buecek	90032
311	510	Wingtip Toys (Grabill, IN)	Wingtip Toys (Head Office)	Novelty Shop	Wingtip Toys	Manish Ghosh	90032
247	446	Wingtip Toys (Saint Landry, LA)	Wingtip Toys (Head Office)	Novelty Shop	Wingtip Toys	Chetana Kamath	90033

Figure 11.15 – The new Reward Group table cannot be connected to the Customer table

We can write a measure to handle that using CONTAINS, as follows:

```
RG Sales CONTAINS =
CALCULATE ( [Sales],
    FILTER (
        ALL('Dimension Customer'[Buying Group]),
        CONTAINS (
            VALUES(RewardsGroup[Buying Group]),
            RewardsGroup[Buying Group],
            'Dimension Customer'[Buying Group]
        ) ),
    FILTER (
        ALL('Dimension Customer'[Postal Code]),
        CONTAINS (
            VALUES(RewardsGroup[Postal Code]),
            RewardsGroup[Postal Code],
            'Dimension Customer'[Postal Code]
        ) ) )
```

This is quite long for a simple piece of logic, and it does not perform that well. A better version that uses TREATAS would look like this:

```
RG Sales TREATAS =
CALCULATE( [Sales],
    TREATAS(
SUMMARIZE(RewardsGroup, RewardsGroup[Buying Group],
RewardsGroup[Postal Code]),
'Dimension Customer'[Buying Group],
'Dimension Customer'[Postal Code]
)
)
```

We have not shown the INTERSECT version here, but note that this will be a little easier to write and can provide better performance. However, the TREATAS version is much shorter and easier to read and maintain. It will also perform better. Here, we visualized a simple table, as shown in *Figure 11.16*, and managed to get nearly a 25% speed improvement with TREATAS. We also reduced the number of storage engine queries from 11 to 8:

Reward Group	First Characters	RG Sales CONTAINS	⌃
Tailspin Premium	"The Gu" red sh	90,417.60	
Tailspin Premium	10 mm Anti stat	28,922.50	
Tailspin Premium	10 mm Double si	49,162.50	
Tailspin Premium	20 mm Anti stat	61,548.00	

Figure 11.16 – The visual that was used to test CONTAINS versus TREATAS performance

Now that we have learned about DAX optimization and row versus filter context, let's summarize what we've learned in this chapter.

Summary

In this chapter, we started with row and filter context and progressed to learning about optimization techniques for DAX functions that perform the same calculations. This is because the DAX pattern directly influences how Analysis Services retrieves data and calculates query results.

Using calculated columns can cause unneeded processing at the engine level instead of the import step. Using Power Query for additional columns helps with performance and optimization. DAX tuning tools are the go-to for examining the functions and their individual performance in the storage and formula engine. We recommended starting the Performance Analyzer to capture the queries to test in DAX Studio for server timings. It is important to look at the total duration, number of internal queries, and time spent in the engines.

Next, we looked at a range of common DAX pitfalls and alternative designs that can improve performance. We learned that, in general, we are trying to avoid formula engine work and wish to reduce the number of queries. Explanations of the performance penalties as well as examples of alternatives rounded out the chapter.

Considering what we've learned so far, there may be still issues where the sheer volume of data can cause problems where additional modeling and architecture approaches need to be used to provide acceptable performance. Therefore, in the next chapter, we will look at techniques that can help us manage big data that reaches the terabyte scale.

12
High Scale Patterns

In the previous chapter, we learned how to optimize DAX expressions. So far, we have covered all the advice on optimizing different layers of a Power BI solution, from the semantic model layer to report design. In this chapter, we will take a step back and revisit architectural concepts and related features that help deal with very high data volumes.

The amount of data that organizations collect and need to analyze is increasing all the time. With the progression of streaming data such as the **Internet of Things (IoT)** and predictive analytics, certain industries, such as energy and resources, are collecting more data than ever before. It is common for a modern mine or gas plant to have tens of thousands of sensors, each generating many data points at a granularity much higher than a second.

Even with Power BI's data compression technology, it isn't always possible to load and store massive amounts of data in an Import mode model in a reasonable amount of time. The problem is worse when you must support hundreds or thousands of users in parallel. This chapter will cover the options you have to deal with such issues by leveraging composite models and aggregations, **Premium** or **Fabric** capacities, and Azure technologies. The concepts in this chapter are complementary and can be combined in the same solution as required.

In this chapter, we will cover the following topics:

- Scaling with capacities and **Azure Analysis Services (AAS)**
- Scaling with aggregations and composite models
- Using Azure Synapse and Fabric for data source improvements

Technical requirements

There is a combined sample file available for this chapter. All the sample references can be found in the `Composite and Aggs.pbix` file, in the `Chapter12` folder in this book's GitHub repository: `https://github.com/PacktPublishing/Microsoft-Power-BI-Performance-Best-Practices-Second-Edition`. Since this example uses DirectQuery to access a SQL server database, the Adventure Works database(s) can be downloaded from GitHub; we have included the `AdvWrk17.bak` SQL backup. Restore that database to a SQL server and update the connection in Power BI Desktop to run the sample successfully.

Scaling with capacities and Azure Analysis Services

Power BI users can use a Pro or **Premium Per User** (**PPU**) desktop license to develop reports that can be published to the service for others to view. The default area is called **Shared capacity**. To provide a consistent and fair experience for everyone, there are certain limits in Shared capacity. One that affects data volumes is the 1 GB size limit of a compressed semantic model. Once a company reaches enterprise levels of data, a larger, dedicated capacity will be required to avoid the "noisy neighbors" in a shared service. With a dedicated capacity that is not shared with any other company, models and reports can be monitored within the company's service.

Leveraging Fabric for data scale

Microsoft first introduced Premium capacities to handle this volume size. It came in five different SKUs. Recently, in October 2023, Microsoft released Fabric capacities to **General Availability** (**GA**). Microsoft announced in March of 2024 that renewals for Premium capacities will be guided to Fabric capacity. *Figure 12.1* shows a comparison of capacities. The third column shows **P** for **Premium**, **E** for **Embed**, abd **A** for **Azure**, while **Fabric** (**F**) is in the first column:

SKU Fabric	Capacity Unit (CU)	SKU (P for Premium, E for Embedded, or A for Azure)	v-cores	RAM limit model load size	Automatic query memory limit	Maximum memory in GB
F2	2	-	0.25	1 GB	1 GB	3
F4	4	-	0.5	2 GB	1 GB	3
F8	8	EM/A1	1	3 GB	1 GB	3
F16	16	EM2/A2	2	5 GB	2 GB	5
F32	32	EM3/A3	4	6 GB	5 GB	10
F64	64	P1/A4	8	10 GB	10 GB	25
F128	128	P2/A5	16	10 GB	10 GB	50
F256	256	P3/A6	32	10 GB	10 GB	100

SKU Fabric	Capacity Unit (CU)	SKU (P for Premium, E for Embedded, or A for Azure)	v-cores	RAM limit model load size	Automatic query memory limit	Maximum memory in GB
F512	512	P4/A7	64	10 GB	20 GB	200
F1024	1024	P5/A8	128	10 GB	40 GB	400
F2048	2048	-	256	10 GB	40 GB	400

Figure 12.1 – Mapping Fabric to other capacities and limits

Customers can purchase these capacities, as shown in *Figure 12.1*. The purchased model can be fixed cost per month or **pay-as-you-go**. The **EM** and **A SKU** capacities were mainly for embedded users of reports shared on websites. SKUs were also used to extend Premium SKUs with AutoScale. These services are created in the Azure portal and managed differently than Premium. Premium is licensed, purchased, and billed differently than Azure resources. Fabric capacities are created in Azure and fold back into your company's Azure portfolio. Going forward, Microsoft will only sell new licenses for Fabric and not Premium. Renewals for Premium can be obtained if on an Enterprise agreement, but only until January 2025.

> **Note**
>
> The main issues with Premium capacities that were preventing important features from being used with Power BI include security with VNet and private endpoints, as well as the ability to turn on or off (pause/resume) the capacity. These also include integration with Synapse-type features that are now in Fabric, including streaming services.

Figure 12.2 shows the **Large semantic model storage format** setting on a published semantic model. It is part of the **Semantic model** page and can be accessed from a Power BI workspace. You can enable this to remove the model's size limit:

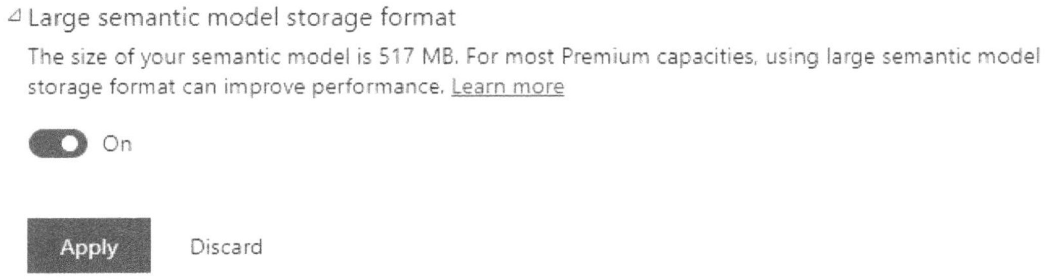

◿ Large semantic model storage format

The size of your semantic model is 517 MB. For most Premium capacities, using large semantic model storage format can improve performance. Learn more

🔘 On

Apply   Discard

Figure 12.2 – Large semantic model storage format option in Dataset settings

> **Tip**
>
> If your semantic model will grow beyond 1 GB in size, you should consider using a Fabric capacity. This capacity will allow you to upload a semantic model to a size between 1 and 10 GB, depending on the capacity. (See *Figure 12.1* for a reminder of the limits.) The semantic model can then be refreshed with more data to grow beyond the load limit. However, if you choose the large semantic model format, the model will have no size limits. The available capacity memory is the only limiting factor. You can even provision capacities of different sizes and spread load accordingly. Always plan to have free memory on the capacity to handle temporary storage for queries, which can include uncompressed data. Lastly, the large model format can also speed up write operations performed via the XMLA endpoint.

Be aware that you can set the large model format to be the default on a Fabric capacity. Administrators can set a limit on the maximum semantic model size to prevent users from consuming significant amounts of a capacity.

Next, we will see a feature presented in Fabric capacities to help with overages.

Throttling and smoothing in Fabric capacity

From time to time, a refresh or report query can result in usage over the SKU capacity. Fabric offers a throttling and smoothing process that initially lets the capacity usage exceed its limits and tries to smooth the usage for billing purposes over a 24-hour period. The throttling will limit new queries or processes until the CPU and/or memory free up in the capacity. Microsoft has multiple ways to notify administrators when the capacity is beyond normal parameters:

- **Alerts**: Once CU usage exceeds a threshold, email alerts can be sent to certain email addresses or security groups

- **Monitoring**: Microsoft provides a thorough app to monitor capacity: `https://learn.microsoft.com/en-us/fabric/enterprise/metrics-app`

If throttling consistently happens, an administrator will need to investigate a larger capacity.

Next, we will see how AAS can be used for semantic models and a better scaling out of resources for large models.

Leveraging AAS for data and user scale

AAS is a **Platform-as-a-Service** (**PaaS**) offering. The engine from AAS is the same engine used in Power BI semantic models. A corporation can choose not to build semantic models in Power BI and instead use AAS as the analytical database engine. The advantage of using AAS is seamless migration from an on-premises analysis service to Azure. Another advantage is that you can use the Visual Studio developer environment like an on-premises development and not lose any functionality.

AAS is part of a broader suite of data services offered by Microsoft in the Azure cloud. A range of SKUs are available, with processing power stated in **Query Processing Units** (**QPU**). AAS can be considered as the cloud alternative to **SQL Server Analysis Services** (**SSAS**), which is used with on-premises servers or VMs. For organizations that already use SSAS and want to migrate to the cloud. AAS provides a seamless transition.

> **Note**
>
> At the time of writing, third-party applications such as AML Toolkit and Tabular Editor can provide ways to migrate on-premises SSAS to Power BI semantic models. Just be aware that there are limitations to the editing of the models once one of these tools is used to migrate, such as not being able to modify the model without Tabular Editor after it is deployed to a workspace. Also, the connections to on-premises data sources will have to go through a data gateway, unless there is a direct link between the Power BI service and the on-premises network.

AAS is billed on a *pay-as-you-go* basis. Fabric capacity can also be *pay-as-you-go* as well as a fixed monthly cost. This means that the service can be paused and scaled on-demand while it offers comprehensive support for Power BI Pro developer tools, such as Microsoft Visual Studio with version control. This option helps with using DevOps and **Continuous Integration/Continuous Development** (**CI/CD**). Like SSAS, AAS is a data engine only, so it only supports hosting semantic models and the mashup engine. You would still need to use a client tool, such as Power BI Desktop, or a portal, such as `app.powerbi.com`, to host reports that read from AAS. AAS can be considered a subset of Premium or Fabric features. This is because there are differences, such as dynamic memory management, which is only offered in Premium or Fabric, and **Query Scale Out** (**QSO**), which is only available in AAS (the standard tier). QSO is a great way of handling high user concurrency with minimal maintenance.

Using QSO to achieve higher user concurrency

Power BI Premium, Fabric, and AAS have the same data size limits, so you can host the same data volumes on any of them. However, QSO offers certain advantages. Let's see what they are.

The unique performance enhancements of QSO

QSO is a unique capability of AAS that allows it to handle many more concurrent users by spreading the query read load across multiple redundant copies of data. You simply configure the service to create additional read replicas (up to a maximum of seven replicas). When client connections are made, they are load-balanced across query replicas. Note that not every region and SKU supports seven replicas, so consult the documentation for information on availability by region at `https://docs.microsoft.com/azure/analysis-services/analysis-services-overview`. Also, note that replicas do incur costs, so you should consider this aspect when you review your performance gains.

Another useful performance-related feature of AAS is its ability to separate the query and processing servers when we use QSO. This maximizes the performance of both processing and query operations. This separation means that at refresh time, one of the replicas will be dedicated to the refresh, and no new client connections will be assigned to it. New connections will be assigned to query replicas only so that they can handle reads, while the processing replica can handle writes.

Configuring replicas can be done via the Azure portal or scripted via PowerShell. *Figure 12.3* shows an example where we are allowed to create one additional replica:

Figure 12.3 – An AAS server with one replica highlighting the query pool separation setting

Note that creating replicas does not allow you to host larger semantic models than if you were not using QSO. It simply creates additional identical copies with the same server SKU.

Now, let's talk about how to determine the right time to scale out.

Knowing when to scale out with QSO

You can observe AAS metrics in the Azure portal to look at QPU over time. If you find that you regularly reach the maximum QPU of your service and that those time frames are correlated with performance issues, it is time to consider QSO. *Figure 12.4* shows the QPU metric for an S0-sized AAS server that has a QPU limit of 40. S0 is the lowest source size for AAS, and represents the standard edition. There are other tiers, such as B for basic and D for Developer. S0 has 20 **Query Processor Units** (**QPUs**) and a maximum size of 3 GB of memory. The largest can be 1,280 QOUs and 400 GB of memory.

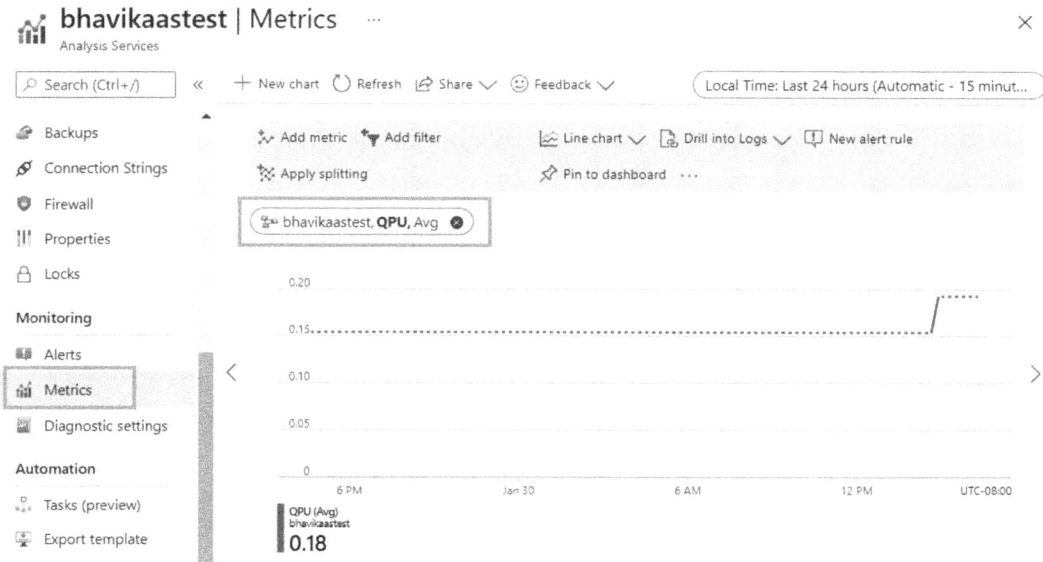

Figure 12.4 – Metrics in the Azure portal showing QPU over time

In the preceding figure, we can see that we are not hitting that limit right now.

Synchronization modes for query replicas in QSO

The final performance-related point concerns **synchronization mode** for query replicas. When semantic models are updated, the replicas that are used for QSO also need to be updated to give all users the latest data. By default, these replicas are rehydrated in full (not incrementally) and in stages. Assuming there are at least three replicas, they are detached and attached two at a time, which can disconnect some clients. This behavior is determined by a server property called **ReplicaSyncMode**. It is an advanced property that you can set using SQL Server Management Studio, as shown in *Figure 12.5*. This setting can be changed to make synchronization occur in parallel. Parallel synchronization updates in-memory caches incrementally and can significantly reduce synchronization time. It also provides the benefit of not dropping any connection because replicas are always kept online:

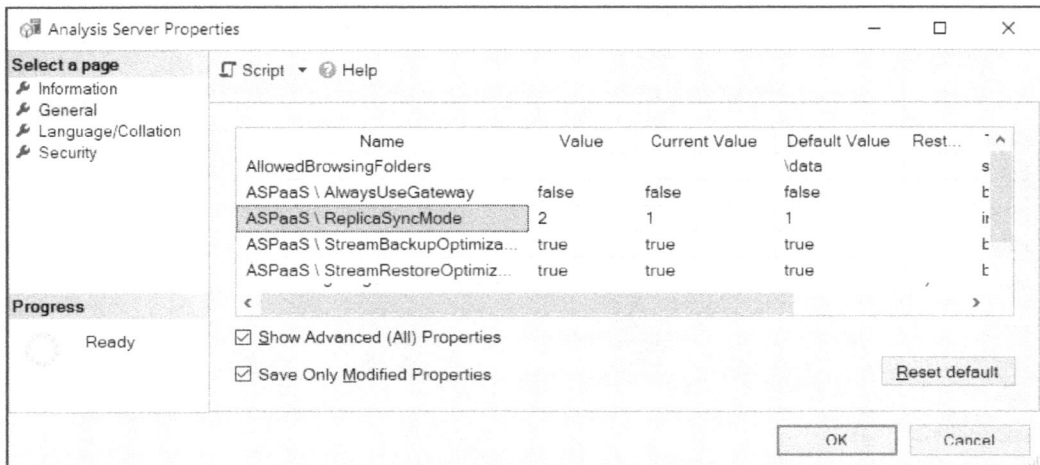

Figure 12.5 – Analysis Server Properties, showing that ReplicaSyncMode has been updated

The following settings for **ReplicaSyncMode** are allowed:

- **1**: Full rehydration performed in stages. This is the default.
- **2**: Parallel synchronization.

Next, we'll learn how partitions can improve refresh performance.

Using partitions in the fact table

Support for partition tables is available for the Premium, Fabric, and AAS semantic models. Partitions simply divide a table into smaller parts that can be managed independently. Typically, partitioning is done by date and is applied to fact tables. For example, you could have 5 years of data split into 60 monthly partitions. In this case, you can process individual partitions separately and even perform entirely different operations on them, such as clearing data from one while loading data into another.

From a performance perspective, partitions can speed up data refresh operations in two ways:

- Firstly, you can only process new and updated data by leaving historical partitions untouched and avoiding a full refresh.
- Secondly, you can get better refresh performance, since partitions can be processed in parallel.

Maximum parallelism can be used to process multiple streams of data imported into a model, and its use assumes that there are sufficient compute and memory resources available, and that the data source can support the load. The AAS engine automatically utilizes parallel processing for two or more partitions, and there are no associated configuration settings for it.

> **Note**
>
> The large semantic model storage format uses a segment size of 8 million rows. Segments are the internal structures that are used to split columns into manageable chunks, and compression is applied at the segment level. Therefore, we recommend employing a strategy where partitions have at least 8 million rows when fully populated. This will help the engine get the best compression and avoid the need for extra maintenance work on many small partitions. Over-partitioning can slow down a semantic model refresh and result in slightly larger models.

Tables defined in a semantic model have a single partition by default. You cannot directly control partitioning in Power BI Desktop, but you can define them in third-party tools. Also, when you implement incremental refreshes, partitions are automatically created and managed, based on the time granularity and data refresh settings.

So, when we use AAS or a capacity, we need to define partitions manually using other tools. Partitions can be defined at design time in Visual Studio using the **Partition Manager** screen for AAS models. Power BI semantic models would need to use a tool such as Tabular Editor to create the partitions. Post-deployment, they can be managed using SQL Server Management Studio by running the **Tabular Model Scripting Language** (**TMSL**). You can also manage them programmatically via the **Tabular Object Model** (**TOM**). You can control parallelism at refresh time by using the TMSL parameter, called `MaxParallelism`, which limits the total number of parallel operations, regardless of the data source. Some sample code for this was provided in the first section of *Chapter 8*, *Loading, Transforming, and Refreshing Data*.

A simple approach would use monthly partitions. A more advanced approach could be to have yearly or monthly historical partitions with daily active partitions. This provides you with a lot more flexibility to update recent facts and minimize re-processing if refresh failures occur, since you can re-process at the single-day granularity. However, this advanced strategy requires extra maintenance, since partitions would need to be merged. For example, at the end of each month, you can merge all the daily partitions into a monthly one, but performing this type of maintenance manually can become tedious. Therefore, it is recommended that you automate this process with the help of some tracking table to manage date ranges and partitions. A detailed automated partition management sample has been published by Microsoft that we recommend looking at; the `Automated Partition Management for Analysis Services Tabular Models.pdf` file is located on GitHub at `https://github.com/microsoft/Analysis-Services/tree/master/AsPartitionProcessing`.

In the next section, we'll learn how to take advantage of composite models to address large data volumes and slow DirectQuery issues.

Scaling with aggregations and composite models

So far, we have discussed how Import mode offers the best possible speed for semantic as **Direct Lake** from Fabric capacity is catching up. However, sometimes, high data volumes and their associated refresh limitations may lead you to select DirectQuery mode instead, especially for large detail data in a fact table. We may, at this point, return to *Chapter 5, Optimization for Storage Modes*, to understand the storage options for Power BI semantic models.

We also discussed how the AAS engine is designed to aggregate data efficiently because **Business Intelligence (BI)** solutions typically aggregate data most of the time. When we use DirectQuery, we want to push these aggregations down to the source where possible to avoid Power BI having to bring all the data over to compute them. With very large tables containing tens of millions or billions of rows, these aggregations can be costly and time-consuming, even when the source has been optimized. This is where the composite models and aggregation features become relevant.

Let's dig deeper into composite models in the next section.

Leveraging composite models

So far, we have discussed the Import and DirectQuery modes separately. This may have implied that you must choose only one mode, but this is not the case. A composite model (also known as Mixed mode) is a feature of Analysis Services that lets you combine DirectQuery and Import mode in the same semantic model. This opens interesting possibilities. You could enhance a DirectQuery source with infrequently changing import data that is held elsewhere. You could even combine different DirectQuery sources. For more information on DirectQuery, *Chapter 5, Optimization for Storage Modes*, explains the use of the DirectQuery, Import, and Direct Lake modes.

Regardless of the requirement, you are advised to follow all the latest recommended guidelines provided in this book for Import and DirectQuery. There are some additional performance concepts and considerations for composite models that we will introduce later in this chapter.

AAS maintains storage mode at the table level. This allows us to mix storage modes with a semantic model. The bottom-right corner of Power BI Desktop gives us an indication of the type of model. An Import mode model will not show any status, but DirectQuery and Composite will show some text, as shown in *Figure 12.6*:

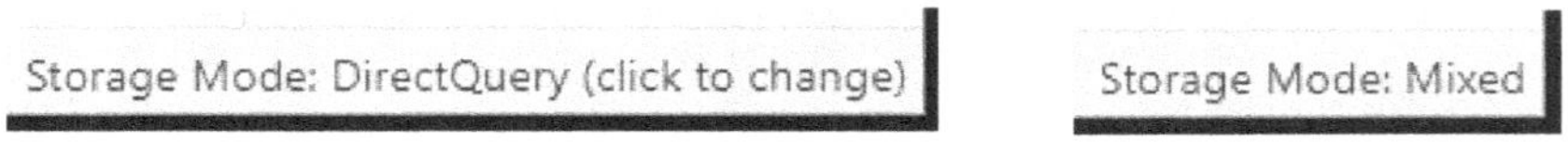

Figure 12.6 – Power BI Desktop, indicating the DirectQuery or Mixed (composite) storage mode

There are different ways to achieve a Mixed model in Power BI Desktop. You could add a new table in the Import model to an existing DirectQuery model, or vice versa. Another way is to directly change the storage model in the Model view of Power BI Desktop, as shown in *Figure 12.7*:

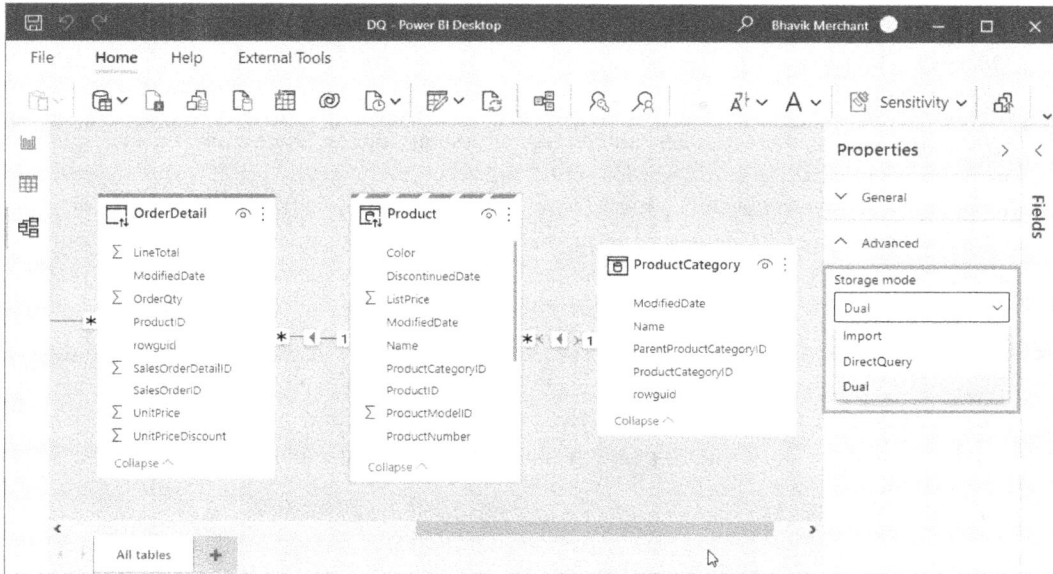

Figure 12.7 – The Storage mode setting in the Model view

The are interesting things to note in the proceeding figure. The Storage mode dropdown offers **Import**, **DirectQuery**, and **Dual** storage modes. In the model diagram view, the table header's colors and icons indicate what type of storage model is used. With Dual mode, depending on the query's scope and grain, AAS will decide whether to use the in-memory cache or the latest data from the data source. Let's look at the storage modes and learn how to use them:

- **DirectQuery**: This is the blue header bar with the DirectQuery icon (for example, **OrderDetail**). Choose this mode for tables that contain very large data volumes, or where you need to fetch the latest results all the time (**near-real-time analytics**). Power BI will never import this data during a refresh. Typically, these would be fact tables or transaction data.

- **Import**: This is the plain white header bar with the Import icon (for example, **ProductCategory**). Choose this mode for smaller or very compressible tables that need to be fast and don't change as frequently as the DirectQuery source.

- **Dual**: This is the branded blue and white header bar with the DirectQuery icon (for example, **Product**). Choose this mode for tables that act as dimensions that are used to filter or group data in the fact table – that is, DirectQuery. This means there are scenarios where the table will be queried together with fact tables as the source.

Now, let's explore how these storage modes are used by the engine in different scenarios. This will help you design and define the storage modes appropriately. This is important because it determines the type of relationship that's used, which directly impacts performance. The following are some possible query scenarios:

- **Query uses Import or Dual table(s) only**: This populates slicers or filters, typically on dimension tables. Such queries achieve the best performance by using the local in-memory cache.

- **Query uses Dual or DirectQuery table(s) from the same source**: This occurs when the query needs to relate Dual model dimension tables to DirectQuery fact tables. It will issue one or more native queries to the DirectQuery source and can achieve relatively good performance if the source is optimized. One-to-one or one-to-many relationships within the same data source are evaluated as regular relationships that perform better. A regular relationship is where the column on the "one" side contains unique values.

- **Any other query**: Any query that needs to resolve relationships across different data sources falls into this category. This happens when a Dual or Import mode table from source A needs to join a DirectQuery table from source B. Here, the engine uses limited relationships, which are slower. Many-to-many relationships and relationships across different data sources are limited.

Next, we will introduce aggregations and how they relate to composite models.

Leveraging aggregations

Most analytical scenarios involve aggregating data in some way. It is common to look at historical trends, exceptions, and outliers at a summary level, and then drill down to more detail as required. Let's look at an example of a logistics company tracking thousands of daily shipments to watch for delays. They are unlikely to start this analysis at the individual package level. They will, more likely, have some performance indicators grouped by transportation type or region. If they see unsatisfactory numbers at the summary level, they may drill down to more and more detail to narrow down the root cause. In *Chapter 9, Report and Dashboard Design*, we recommended designing report experiences like this to provide better performance and usability.

You can follow the recommended design principles and still have performance issues with very large DirectQuery semantic models. Even with great optimizations, there is still a physical limit as to how fast you can process data with fixed computing resources. An aggregation table is a summary of another fact table but one that's always stored in Import mode in memory. As such, aggregation tables must be reloaded during data refresh.

We will build on the example shown in *Figure 12.7* to illustrate this. We want to add aggregations to the `OrderDetail` table to avoid generating an external DirectQuery. Our requirements have determined that many reports aggregate total sales at the product level. We can achieve better performance by adding an aggregation table. We will add a table to the Import model, called `Agg_SalesByProduct`, that's defined by the following SQL expression:

```
SELECT
ProductID,
sum(sod.LineTotal) as TotalSales,
sum(sod.OrderQty) as TotalQuantity
FROM
[SalesLT].[SalesOrderDetail] sod
GROUP BY ProductID
```

Once the aggregation table exists, we need to tell Power BI how to use it. Right-click the `OrderDetail` table in the model view, select the **Manage aggregations** option, and configure the aggregations, as shown in *Figure 12.8*:

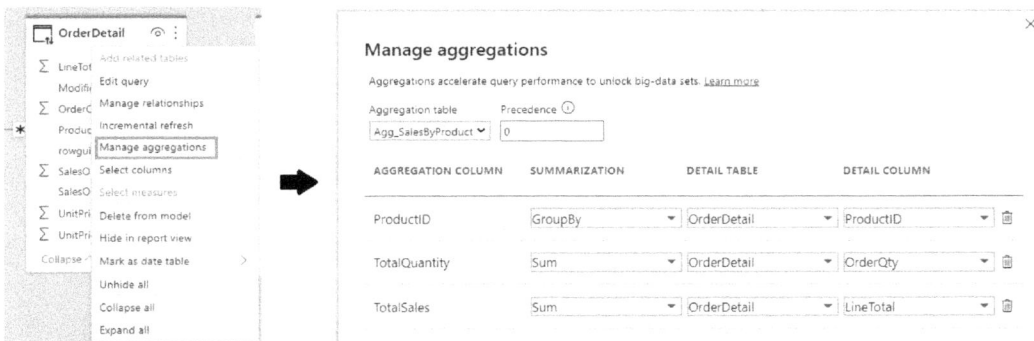

Figure 12.8 – Configuring the aggregations for OrderDetail

There are a few things to note in the previous statement. First, we had to tell Power BI which table we wanted to use as an aggregate for `OrderDetail`. We also had to map the columns and identify what type of summarization was used. There is also the option to select a **Precedence** value because you can have multiple aggregation tables at different granularities. **Precedence** will determine which table is used first when the result can be served by more than one aggregation table. Once the aggregations have been configured, the final step is to create the relationship between the aggregation table and the **Product** dimension, as shown in *Figure 12.9*:

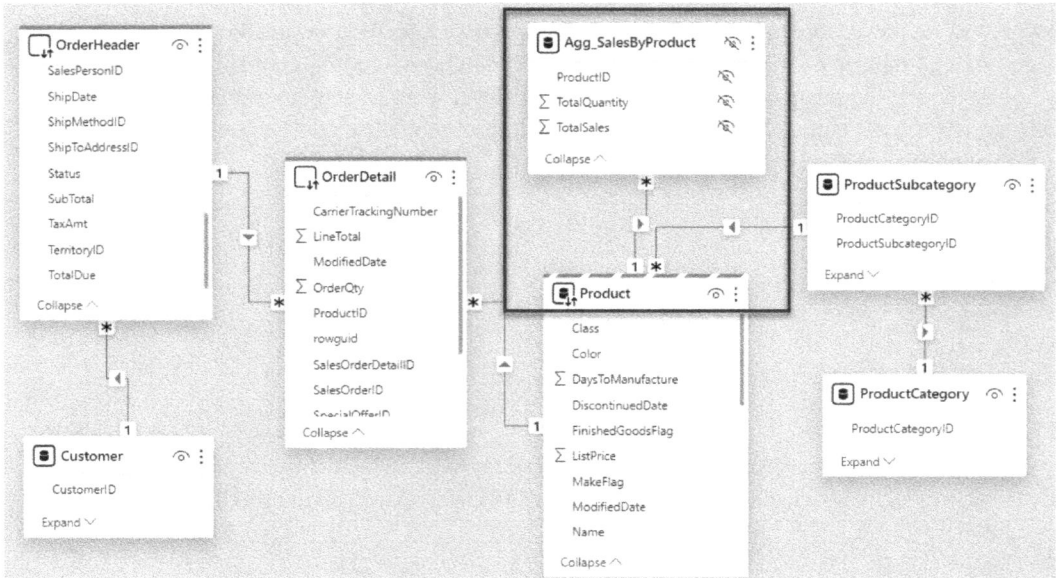

Figure 12.9 – The Agg_SalesByProduct table related to the Dual-mode Product table

In *Figure 12.9*, note that the aggregation table and its columns are all hidden in the Power BI semantic model. Power BI will do this by default, since we do not want to confuse users. We can hide aggregation tables and rely on the engine to pick the correct tables internally.

> **Note**
>
> The example shown in the preceding figures demonstrates aggregations based on relationships. We rely on a relationship so that the values from the `Product` table can filter `OrderDetails`. We added the aggregation table, as we needed to create this relationship. In typical big data systems such as Hadoop, data is often stored in wide denormalized tables to avoid expensive joins at query time. The aggregation function of AAS still works in these scenarios.

Next, we'll learn how to identify when and which aggregations are used with **DAX Studio**. We will begin by constructing three table visuals, showing different sales groupings. You can see these in the sample file on the `Agg Comparison` report page:

Color	LineTotal	OrderQty
	1,099,318.91	48289
Black	38,247,018.63	81937
Blue	9,602,850.96	23659
Multi	649,849.16	25073
Red	21,623,269.54	29229
Silver	19,777,339.95	25023
Silver/Black	147,483.91	3931
White	29,745.13	5217
Yellow	18,669,505.22	32556
Total	**109,846,381.40**	**274914**

Name	LineTotal	OrderQty
Accessories	1,272,072.88	61932
Bikes	94,651,172.70	90268
Clothing	2,120,542.52	73670
Components	11,802,593.29	49044
Total	**109,846,381.40**	**274914**

Name	AccountNumber	LineTotal	OrderQty
Accessories	AW00011000	90.95	4
Accessories	AW00011001	85.93	6
Accessories	AW00011002	34.99	1
Accessories	AW00011003	51.25	5
Accessories	AW00011004	91.96	3
Accessories	AW00011005	42.28	3
Accessories	AW00011006	14.98	2
Accessories	AW00011007	131.95	5
Accessories	AW00011008	52.26	4
Accessories	AW00011009	37.28	2
Accessories	AW00011012	81.26	5
Accessories	AW00011013	113.96	5
Total		**109,846,381.40**	**274914**

Figure 12.10 – Different sales groupings to test aggregations

The visual titles in *Figure 12.10* refer to tables in the sample report, which are shown in *Figure 12.9*. We constructed the visuals at different granularities, using different grouping tables, to see how the queries behave. We used DAX Studio to capture the output and discovered the following:

- **Grouping by the Product table**: The query was completely satisfied through the Import tables. Only one storage engine query was needed. Note how DAX Studio provides information on the `RewriteAttempted` event subclass, which means the engine recognized that aggregations were present and tried to use them. You can click on the event to get the detail on the right-hand side, confirming which aggregation table was used, as shown in *Figure 12.11*:

Figure 12.11 – Query performance information for table visual for Color

- **Grouping by the ProductCategory table**: Again, the query was completely satisfied through the Import tables. What is great here is that even though `ProductCategory` is not directly related to the aggregation table, the engine does use it, leveraging the `Product` and `ProductSubcategory` tables as a snowflake dimension relationship. This has allowed us to avoid an external query for a scenario that we did not originally plan for, as shown in *Figure 12.12*:

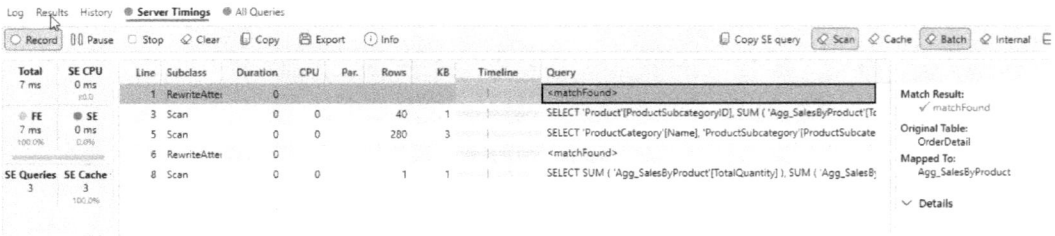

Figure 12.12 – Query performance information for table visual for Category

- **Grouping by the Product and Customer table**: This time, the query tried to use aggregation for a customer but was unable to, since we did not define our aggregation at the customer granularity level. The engine did use an external query, which is proven by the SQL event subclass. However, it was still able to use the aggregation table later, as shown in *Figure 12.13*:

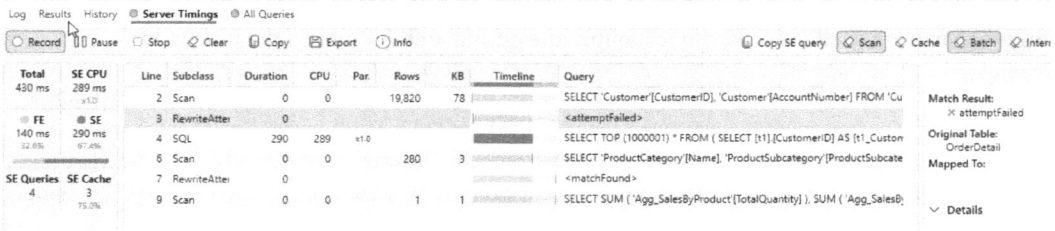

Figure 12.13 – Query performance information for the table visual with AccountNumber

The previous examples demonstrate how aggregations are used, but we have not compared the same query with and without aggregations yet. To test this, we can simply delete the aggregation table and profile the same visuals in DAX Studio, with the query durations shown in *Figure 12.14*:

	No Aggregations	With Aggregations	Comments
Visual A	80 ms	3 ms	Aggregations much faster.
Visual B	155 ms	5 ms	Aggregations much faster.
Visual C	340 ms	500 ms	Aggregations were a bit slower due to multiple source overhead with small data volumes.

Figure 12.14 – A performance comparison of different visual groupings with aggregations

In our example, designing and managing aggregations would be simple. In the real world, it can be difficult to predict the complexity, volume, and frequency of the queries that will be generated. This makes it hard to design aggregations beforehand. Microsoft has considered this problem and has released automatic aggregations as an enhancement to user-defined aggregations.

With automatic aggregations, the system uses machine learning to maintain aggregations automatically, based on user behavior. This can greatly simplify aggregation management if you use it.

> **Note**
>
> Automatic aggregations are currently available for the Premium, PPU, Embedded, and Fabric capacities. The feature is well-documented in the following website from Microsoft: `https://docs.microsoft.com/power-bi/admin/aggregations-auto`.

Finally, let's look at Azure Synapse and Fabric using a data lake. These are first-party technologies from Microsoft, which you may wish to consider for external data storage in big data scenarios that need DirectQuery or Direct Lake.

Improving performance with Synapse and Fabric

Many data analytics platforms are based on a **symmetric multi-processing** (**SMP**) design. This involves a single computer system with one instance of an operating system that has multiple processors, working with shared memory and shared disk arrays. An alternative example is a **massively parallel processing** (**MPP**) system. This involves a grid or cluster of computers, each with processors, an operating system, memory, and a disk array. Each server is referred to as a node.

In practical terms, consider computing a sum across 100 billion rows of data. With SMP, a single computer would need to do all the work. With MPP, you could logically allocate the sum of its group in parallel, and then add up the sums. If we wanted the results faster, we could spread the load further with more parallelism, such as by having 50 machines processing about 2 billion rows each. Even with communications and synchronization overhead, the latter approach will be much faster.

Big data systems such as Hadoop, Apache Spark, and Azure Synapse use the MPP architecture because parallel operations can process data much faster. MPP also gives us the ability to both scale up (bigger machines) and scale out (more machines). With SMP, only the former is possible until you reach a physical limit regarding how large a machine you can provision.

The increased rate of ingestion from modern global applications, such as IoT systems, creates an upstream problem when we consider data analysis. BI applications typically use cleaned and modeled data, which requires modeling and transformations beforehand. This works fine for typical business applications. However, with big data, such as a stream of sensor data or web app user tracking, it is impractical to store raw data in a traditional database, due to the sheer volume. Hence, many big data systems use files (specially optimized, such as Parquet) that store denormalized tables. They perform **Extract-Load-Transform** (**ELT**) operations, instead of the typical **Extract-Transform-Load** (**ETL**) operations that we can do in Power Query. With ELT, raw data is shaped on the fly in parallel.

Now, let's relate these concepts to the modern data warehouse architecture and the Azure offerings.

The modern data warehouse architecture (Synapse)

We can combine traditional ETL-style analytics with ELT and big data analytics using a hybrid data warehouse architecture, based on a data lake. A data lake could be described as a landing area for raw data. Data in the lake is not typically accessed directly by business users.

Once data is in the lake, it can be used in different ways, depending on the purpose. For example, data scientists may want to analyze raw data and create subsets for machine learning models. Conversely, business analytics team members might regularly transform and load some data into structured storage systems, such as SQL Server. *Figure 12.15* shows a highly simplified view of Azure components that could make up a modern data warehouse:

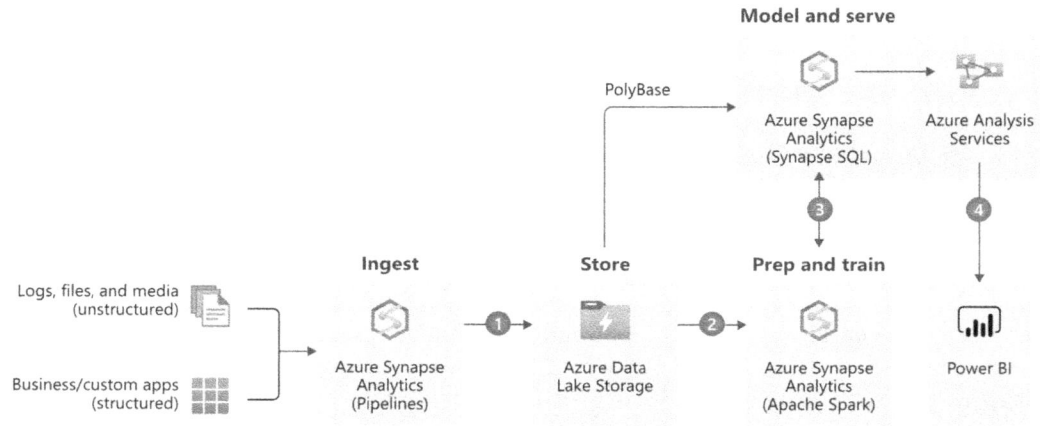

Figure 12.15 – A Synapse modern data warehouse architecture (image credit: Microsoft)

The numbered steps in the preceding diagram indicate typical activities:

1. Store all types of raw data in **Azure Data Lake Storage Gen2** (**ADLS**) using pipelines.
2. Leverage Synapse Analytics to clean up data.
3. Store clean, structured data in Synapse tables.
4. Model data in AAS or Power BI semantic models.
5. Build reports in Power BI.

> **Note**
>
> These steps are ordered, and the diagram shows connections between components. This represents production-style data paths and is only to aid learning. In a modern enterprise, it is realistic to skip some steps or connect different technologies, depending on the scenario and a user's skill level. For example, a data engineer may connect Power BI directly to ADLS to explore data format and quality.

Now, let's look closer at some technologies that help with data scaling.

ADLS

ADLS is a modern data store from Microsoft that's designed for all data scenarios. It provides limitless storage and is compatible with non-proprietary technologies, such as **Hadoop Distributed File System (HDFS)**, which is a core requirement for many Hadoop-based systems. Note that the current version is referred to by Microsoft as ADLS Gen2, indicating that we are in the second generation offering. Gen2 is the only ADLS available for new work from Microsoft. Synapse and Fabric services are optimized to work with data in parallel in ADLS Gen2. The Parquet file format is the suggested structure, with first-level ingestion to **Delta Tables**.

Azure Synapse Analytics and Fabric

Azure Synapse and Fabric capacities are analytics platforms that contain different services that address the special needs of different data stages. Synapse was previously called SQL Server Data Warehouse, and at the time, the focus was to provide a distributed version of SQL Server to handle multi-TB and larger data volumes. Fabric is a new capacity from Microsoft that integrates Synapse pipelines and Azure Data Factory services with ADLS Gen2 storage, providing a one-stop shop for analytics, including streaming. Both provide similar options.

Synapse Analytics

Synapse Analytics offers the following options:

- **Synapse Studio**: This is a web-based environment that serves multiple personas. People can ingest, transform, explore, and visualize data here.

- **Power BI integration**: You can link Power BI workspaces to your Synapse workspace in Synapse Studio. Then, you can analyze data hosted in Synapse services using Power BI.

- **Notebook integration**: Synapse Studio supports Python notebooks for interactive data exploration and documentation. These notebooks can switch between languages such as PySpark, Scala, SparkSQL, and C#.

- **Serverless and dedicated SQL pools**: These offer structured SQL Server storage in the cloud. A serverless pool needs little configuration and management – you do not need to provision a server, the service auto-scales, and you pay per query. A dedicated pool must be configured beforehand and is billed constantly over time. Dedicated pools can be paused and scaled up and down. These options provide a balance between costs and management overhead.

- **Serverless and dedicated Spark pools**: Apache Spark is a very popular open source big data platform. It is an in-memory technology and offers a SQL interface over data. It also offers integrated data science capabilities. Synapse integrates with Spark pools directly, allowing analysts to run Spark Jobs from the workspace.

- **Dataflows**: This is a PowerQuery interface that provides visually designed data transformations to cleanse and shape data, using a Spark engine.

- **Data pipelines**: This allows users to orchestrate and monitor data transformation jobs.

The Fabric capacity

The Fabric upgrade to the Power BI service includes the following:

- **A web-based interface**: End users can create a lakehouse or warehouse to ingest, transform, explore, and visualize data.

- **Power BI integration**: All artifacts are within a Power BI workspace.

- **Notebook integration**: Notebooks can be created to utilize various languages such as PySpark, Scala, and SparkSQL. The experience is interactive for data exploration and documentation.

- **Dataflows**: Allows analytic engineers to use a graphical interface for data ingestion and transformations.

- **Pipelines**: Orchestration can be performed to chain artifacts together for workflows.

- **Power BI administration and monitoring**: All the features of a Premium tenant are available in Fabric capacities.

There are many options and variations within the modern data warehouse architecture. Unfortunately, it is beyond the scope of this book to cover these in detail. Microsoft offers multiple reference guides as well as learning paths for all the aforementioned services.

Now that we have introduced the Azure technologies we can use to deal with data at a high scale, let's summarize what we've learned in this chapter.

Summary

In this chapter, we looked at large data volumes. We reviewed the limitations of desktop licenses as well as the capacities available to handle large loads. Technically, we can use all the available memory on the capacity, which is 400 GB on the largest Fabric or Premium capacity. We also provided suggestions for addressing CPU and memory issues with capacities and AAS.

After that, we looked at improving DirectQuery performance with composite models, a feature that lets you combine Import mode and DirectQuery data sources. The Dual model demonstrated examples that included monitoring in DAX Studio. Aggregations were reviewed to improve composite models, particularly when dealing with large fact tables where queries are frequently aggregated by dimensional attributes. DirectQuery was then used for reporting involving more rows, which can go to DirectQuery for results and result in longer query times. These situations are not frequently encountered by users, and it is understood that reporting will take more time.

Finally, we looked at other technologies in the Azure space that can deal with large data volumes requiring a modern data warehouse. Ingesting and transforming would be better at the storage level than PowerQuery in Power BI. The systems use multiple processing and storage distributions that can take advantage of big data technology. This also included introductions to Azure Data Lake Storage Gen2 with Azure Synapse Analytics and Fabric capacities.

In the next chapter, we will focus on optimizing the capacity that Microsoft provides for enterprise-level companies.

Further reading

Note that, just like Power BI, every area of Synapse benefits from specific performance-tuning guidance. The following are some references to the relevant performance guidance materials:

- *Serverless SQL pool best practices*: `https://docs.microsoft.com/azure/synapse-analytics/sql/best-practices-serverless-sql-pool`

- *Optimizing Synapse query performance tutorial*: `https://docs.microsoft.com/learn/modules/optimize-data-warehouse-query-performance-azure-synapse-analytics`

- *Fabric optimizations*: `https://learn.microsoft.com/en-us/fabric/data-warehouse/guidelines-warehouse-performance`

Part 5:
Optimizing Capacities in
Power BI Enterprises

This part will help you become familiar with various capacities available today such as Premium, Fabric, Azure, and Embedded. These all have settings and resource limits to be aware of. You will gain a deep understanding of workload prioritization and memory management in capacities, learn how to size and load test capacities, and see capacity limits side by side for different SKUs.

This part has the following chapters:

- *Chapter 13, Working with Capacities*
- *Chapter 14, Performance Needs for Fabric Artifacts*
- *Chapter 15, Embedding in Web Apps*

13

Working with Capacities

In the previous chapter, we looked at ways to deal with high data and user scales. The first option we provided was to leverage Power BI Premium and Fabric capacities because they have higher data size limits than shared capacity.

In this chapter, we will take a much closer look at the Fabric and Premium capacities. Even though they are purchased and billed separately, they offer similar options, with Fabric slated to replace Premium in 2025. When talking about performance optimization on a capacity in general, the type of capacity will not be mentioned if they are the same. Specific text will point out when it relates to Premium only or when it relates to Fabric only.

We will learn that there are more than just increased resources and semantic model sizes with a capacity. Capacities offer unique services that are not available in shared capacities. This is because the capacity is dedicated to your company. The caveat is that these extra capabilities come with additional management from capacity administrators. We will review those options for capacity settings as well as workload areas to watch.

Then, we will learn how to determine adequate capacity size and plan for future growth. One important technique is load testing to help determine the limits and bottlenecks of your data and usage patterns. We will also learn how to use the Fabric Capacity Metrics app to identify areas of concern, perform root cause analysis, and determine the best corrective actions.

In this chapter, we will cover the following topics:

- How a noisy neighbor impacts shared capacity
- Controlling capacity settings in the admin portal
- Capacity planning, monitoring, and optimization

First, we will look at how shared capacity can have a noisy neighbor that affects the performance of deployed semantic models and report queries.

How a noisy neighbor impacts shared capacity

Shared capacity is used for deployed semantic models and reports when not using a dedicated capacity. Dedicated capacities are Premium, Embedded, or Fabric licenses. If you are using a Power BI Pro or Premium Per User license for the desktop and have not purchased a dedicated capacity, you are deploying to the service that is considered shared. A shared capacity is based on the idea of a multitenant system that uses pooled resources among users.

The term *noisy neighbor* is used for services that share tenant resources where one tenant uses a disproportionate amount of those resources. This noisy neighbor degrades the performance of other tenants using the same pool of resources. Power BI allows this for companies that do not purchase or use capacities, which in turn saves money. Even if a company has a capacity, the workspace must be assigned to that capacity; otherwise, it uses a shared capacity. *Figure 13.1* shows the license mode for assigning a workspace to a license mode:

{% raw %}General

| License info

Azure connections

System storage

Git integration

OneLake

Workspace identity

Network security

Power BI   ∨

Data   ∨
Engineering/Science

Data Factory   ∨

○ **Premium capacity**
   Select premium capacity if the workspace will be hosted in a premium capacity. When you
   share, collaborate on, and distribute Power BI and Microsoft Fabric content, users in the
   viewer role can access this content without needing a Pro or Premium per-user license.
   Learn more ⌐⌐

○ Embedded ○
   Select embedded if the workspace will be hosted in an Azure embedded capacity. ISVs
   and developers use Power BI Embedded to embed visuals and analytics in their
   applications. Learn more ⌐⌐

◉ **Fabric capacity**
   Select Fabric capacity if the workspace will be hosted in a Microsoft Fabric capacity. With
   Fabric capacities, users can create Microsoft Fabric items and collaborate with others
   using Fabric features and experiences. Explore new capabilities in Power BI, Data Factory,
   Data Engineering, and Real-Time Intelligence, among others. Learn more ⌐⌐

○ Trial
   Select the trial per-user license to try all the new features and experiences in
   Microsoft Fabric for 60 days. A Microsoft Fabric trial license allows users to create
   Microsoft Fabric items and collaborate with others in a Microsoft Fabric trial capacity.
   Explore new capabilities in Power BI, Data Factory, Data Engineering, and Real-Time
   Intelligence, among others. Learn more ⌐⌐

License capacity

Please specify the remote computing resources your items will use with this workspace.

| dotgf2 - North Central US   ∨ |

Workspace settings

General

| License info

Azure connections

System storage

Git integration

OneLake

Workspace identity

Network security

Power BI   ∨

Data   ∨
Engineering/Science

Data Factory   ∨

License info

Choose a license for this workspace.

⊕ License Configuration

License mode

Select a license to determine the capabilities of this workspace.

○ Pro
   Select Pro to use basic Power BI features and collaborate on reports, dashboards, and
   scorecards. To access a Pro workspace, users need Pro per-user licenses. Learn more ⌐⌐

○ Premium per-user
   Select Premium per-user to collaborate using Power BI Premium features, including
   paginated reports, dataflows, and datamarts. To collaborate and share content in a
   Premium per-user workspace, users need Premium per-user licenses. Learn more ⌐⌐

○ Premium capacity
   Select premium capacity if the workspace will be hosted in a premium capacity. When you
   share, collaborate on, and distribute Power BI and Microsoft Fabric content, users in the
   viewer role can access this content without needing a Pro or Premium per-user license.
   Learn more ⌐⌐

○ Embedded ○
   Select embedded if the workspace will be hosted in an Azure embedded capacity. ISVs{% endraw %}

Figure 13.1 – Assigning a license mode to a new workspace

In *Figure 13.1*, the Premium and Fabric capacities are the only available selections to create a workspace on a dedicated capacity. The other two available options, Pro and Premium Per User, are shared capacity.

> **Note**
>
> The only way to determine whether a noisy neighbor is an issue is to get a support ticket with Microsoft to investigate. You would need to save any statistical information about the issues to send to the support team. The difficulty is that the issue often occurs at some point, but then the problem seems to go away on its own. You will also want to have proof that your model is optimized and following the best practices for design and implementation before creating a support call because that is the first type of question that is usually asked by Microsoft support. Many chapters in this book are about applying best practices to the model.

The noisy neighbor issue comes from sharing a capacity in the service when another company's artifacts are using most of the resources available. An example is when you are refreshing a semantic model and it takes hours rather than the usual minutes, and the refresh happens at the same time of day as previous days. The other issue could be that a report that normally renders in seconds now takes minutes to render, especially when selecting slicer or filter values that did not have an impact on performance before today.

With the addition of Fabric capacities that are smaller than the default Premium P1, the cost of having a dedicated capacity is now lower than ever. Not only is it dedicated, but you also have tools to monitor the performance that a Pro or PPU license does not offer. Fabric capacities can be paused to help save even more money when the resources are not in use and restarted when reports or processing need to happen.

Now, let's explore how capacity workloads are categorized and which load settings can be controlled through the admin portal.

Controlling capacity workloads and settings

Premium and Fabric capacities provide reserved resources for your organization. This isolates you from noisy neighbors that you may experience in the shared capacity. Let's start by briefly reviewing the capabilities of the capacity resources that differentiate them by providing greater performance and scale:

- **Ability to Autoscale**: Premium allows for additional Azure capacity to be created for Autoscale. With Fabric, the Autoscale is automatic with additional resources and smoothing over time for overages.

- **Higher storage and semantic model size limits**: The resources have 100 TB of total storage and a semantic model size of 400 GB (100 GB in PPU).

- **More frequent semantic model refreshes**: The refreshes happen 48 times per day via the UI and potentially more often via scripts through the XMLA endpoint.

- **Greater refresh parallelism**: You can have more refreshes at the same time, ranging from 1 to 1280 depending on the capacity.

- **Advanced dataflow features**: Capacity dataflows have a performance enhancement, such as the enhanced compute engine.

On-demand load with large semantic model storage formats: Capacities do not always keep every semantic model in memory. Semantic models that are unused for a period are evicted to free up memory. Using the large semantic model format will speed up the initial load of data. The on-demand process will only load the data needed to satisfy a query rather than loading the whole model in memory. The whole model will be needed in memory if a large semantic model storage format is *not* used.

Other capabilities in capacities are not directly related to performance. We'll list them here for awareness. Note that the final three items are not available for PPU:

- **Availability of paginated reports**: Highly formatted reports based on SQL Server Reporting Services that are optimized for printing and broad distribution

- **XMLA endpoint**: API access to allow automation and custom deployment and refresh configurations

- **Application Life Cycle Management** (**ALM**): You can use deployment pipelines, manage development, and evaluate app versions

- **Multi-region deployments**: You can deploy Premium capacities in different regions to help with data sovereignty requirements

- **Bring Your Own Key** (**BYOK**): You can apply your encryption key to secure data

Next, we will examine the settings that can be adjusted for workloads on capacities.

Capacity settings

The scale and performance of workloads can be controlled in a capacity by adjusting some admin settings. The **Power BI workloads** settings are under **Capacity settings,** as shown in *Figure 13.2.* These are accessed in the Power BI Admin Portal. The user will have to be a capacity admin or Power BI admin to access these settings:

Admin portal

Tenant settings `New`

Usage metrics

Users

Premium Per User

Audit logs

Domains `New`

Capacity settings

    Refresh summary

Embed Codes

Organizational visuals

Azure connections

Workspaces

Custom branding

Protection metrics

Featured content

Help + support

◿ Power BI workloads

AI

Allow usage from Power BI Desktop
🔵 On

PAGINATED REPORTS

Block Outbound Connectivity
⚪ Off

SEMANTIC MODELS

Observe XMLA-based workspace settings (which may override capacity settings)
🔵 On

Enable parallel queries for DirectQuery
🔵 On

Query Memory Limit (%)
`0`

Query Timeout (seconds)
`3600`

Max Intermediate Row Count
`10000`

Max Result Row Count
`21474`

Max Offline Dataset Size (GB)
`0`

Automatic page refresh
🔵 On

Minimum refresh interval
`5` `Minutes ⌄`

Change detection measure
🔵 On

Minimum execution interval
`30` `Seconds ⌄`

XMLA Endpoint
`Read Write ⌄`

Apply   Discard

Figure 13.2 – The capacity settings that are relevant to performance tuning

This list can help safeguard against issues in semantic models or from ad hoc reports that generate complex, expensive queries.

AI

Next are the safeguards for AI functions.

Allow usage from Power BI Desktop: For Power BI Desktop to use some AI function in Power Query, a user must be logged into a tenant with the setting enabled and access to a workspace with a capacity assigned. Disabling this item can prevent capacity (resources) from being used, which can be significant for some AI functions. This is not something to give everyone access to.

Paginated reports

Next are the safeguards for paginated reports:

- **Block outbound connectivity**: If this is disabled, paginated reports in Power BI capacity can fetch external files such as images, execute Azure functions, or call external APIs. If it is enabled, those options are not available and can save memory and CPU cycles.

Semantic models

Next are safeguards for semantic models:

- **Observe XMLA-based workspace settings (which may override capacity settings)**: This lets you enable control over XMLA activities at the workspace level. XMLA calls affect resources and performance.

- **Enable parallel queries for DirectQuery**: This option allows Power BI to send multiple queries to the data source and parallel process the returned data for reporting. This will improve the refresh of visuals in a report using DirectQuery.

- **Query memory limit (%)**: This is the maximum percentage of memory that a single executed query can use. The default value, 0, means no limit.

- **Query timeout (seconds)**: This refers to the number of seconds a query is allowed to execute before being considered for a timeout. The default value (3600) represents one hour. The 0 value disables the timeout.

- **Max intermediate row count**: For DirectQuery, this limits the number of rows that are returned by a query, which can help reduce the load on source systems.

- **Max result row count**: This refers to the maximum number of rows that can be returned by a DAX query. DAX and Power BI are not structured for long lists of rows to be reported. They rely on designs to report analytical results such as sum and average aggregations.

- **Max offline dataset size (GB)**: This determines how large an offline semantic model can be, which translates to the size on the disk. A limit can be placed here for an administrator to limit the size of models that developers can deploy.

- **Automatic page refresh**: This enables a report page that is connected to a DirectQuery model to refresh on an interval, which is the minimum refresh interval setting.

- **Minimum refresh interval**: This is the interval in selected time periods when a report connected to a DirectQuery model will refresh automatically. This can override any developer-set time of refresh in a report.

- **Minimum execution interval (for change detection measures)**: This is like the previous point but applies to the frequency of checking the change detection measure.

Next, we will learn how capacities evaluate load and what happens when the capacity gets busy.

How capacities manage resources

Capacities evaluate load every 30 seconds, with each bucket referred to as an evaluation cycle. We will use practical examples to explain how the load calculations work in each cycle and what happens when the capacity threshold is reached.

Power BI evaluates capacity utilization using **Capacity Unit** (CU) time, which is measured in eight CUs per one vCPU when compared to previous Premium-only capacities. If a single vCPU is completely utilized for one second, this is eight CUs. However, this is different from the actual duration when it's measured from start to finish. Taking our example one step further, if we know that an operation took eight CU seconds, that does not necessary mean that the start-to-finish duration was one second. It could mean that a single vCPU core was 100% utilized for one second or that the operation used less than 100% of the vCPU for more than one second.

> **Note**
>
> **P** capacities refer to Premium, while **F** capacities refer to Fabric. There is a comparison of the two main capacity types in the *Determining the initial capacity size* section later in this chapter.

We will use a **P1** (F64) capacity for our examples. The capacity comes with four backend cores and four frontend cores. The backend cores are used for core Power BI functions such as query processing, semantic model refresh, and R/Python server processing, while the frontend cores are responsible for user experience aspects such as web service, content management, permission management, and scheduling. Capacity load is evaluated against the backend cores only.

Knowing that Power BI evaluates the total load every 30 seconds, we can work out the maximum CU time that's available to us over this time during the evaluation cycle of a P1 (F64). This is 30 seconds multiplied by 4 cores to get a result of 120 vCPU seconds, but 960 CU seconds. So, for a P1 (F64) capacity, every 30 seconds, the system will determine whether workloads are consuming more or less than 960 CU seconds. As a reminder, with a capacity, it is designed to temporarily consume more than 960 CU seconds since spare capacity is available. For a premium capacity, the next situation depends on whether you have Autoscale turned on. With Fabric, the over-usage can be spread over a 24-hour period by default with spare capacity.

Before we describe this in more detail, it is useful to know how CU load is aggregated, since interactive and background operations are counted within the evaluation cycle in which they ran. CU usage for background operations is smoothed in both Premium and Fabric capacities over a rolling 24 hour period, which is evaluated regularly in the same 30-second buckets. The system smooths the background operations by spreading the last 24 rolling hours of background CU time evenly over all the evaluation cycles. There are 2,880 evaluation cycles in 24 hours.

Let's illustrate this with a simple but realistic example. Suppose we have a P1 capacity that has just been provisioned. Two scheduled refreshes named A and B have been configured and will complete by 1 AM and 4 AM respectively. Suppose that the former refresh will take 14,400 CPU seconds (5 per evaluation cycle), while the latter will take 5,760 CPU seconds (2 per evaluation cycle). Finally, suppose that users start running reports hosted on the capacity at around 9 AM and do not hit the capacity threshold. The following diagram shows how load evaluation works for this scenario and how the available capacity changes over time. We have marked four different evaluation cycles to explain how the operations contribute to the load score. The example scenario we've described covers a period similar to a 24-hour period. Let's visualize this behavior and load like in *Figure 13.3*:

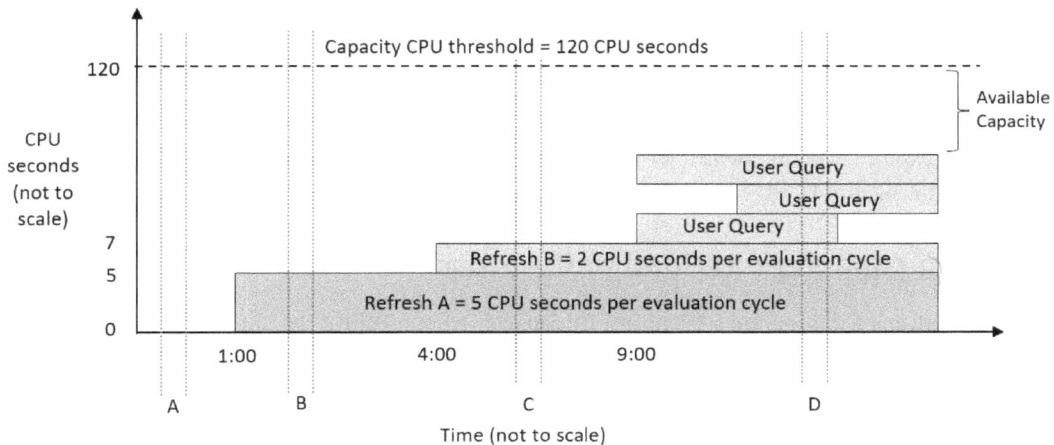

Figure 13.3 – Load evaluation for a P1 capacity at different times (A to D)

> **Note**
>
> In *Figures 13.3* and *13.4*, since the background refresh activity is spread out over 2,880 evaluation cycles, it is correct to show the load that's been incurred by those operations as being constant over time once they have been completed. For the interactive operations shown in green, the CPU load will vary over time for each operation. However, for simplicity, we have illustrated interactive operations as if they generate a constant load.

Let's walk through the four evaluation cycles to understand how the capacity load is calculated at each of these points:

1. **Evaluation cycle A**: At this point, the capacity is brand new and completely unused. There is no prior background activity to consider in this evaluation cycle.

2. **Evaluation cycle B**: This occurs after refresh A has completed but before refresh B starts. The background load for refresh A is 14,400 CPU seconds divided into 30-second buckets, which gives 5 CPU seconds per evaluation cycle. Since there are no other activities, the total load during this cycle is 5 CPU seconds.

3. **Evaluation cycle C**: This occurs after refresh B has been completed. The background load for refresh B is 5,750 CPU seconds, which smooths to 2 CPU seconds per evaluation cycle. This time, the background activities from refreshes A and B are both considered because they are both within 24 hours of the current evaluation cycle. Even though both refreshes are already complete at this point, their smoothed activity carries forward, so the total load on capacity is 7 CPU seconds.

4. **Evaluation cycle D**: Now, we have both the background activity and interactive activity occurring at the same time. The total load on the capacity is the background contribution of 7 seconds, plus the actual work that's been done by the queries in that cycle. The number is not important for this example. The main point is that the total activity in the evaluation cycle is less than 120 CPU seconds.

Next, we will explore what happens if we reach an overload situation. This term is used to describe a capacity that needs more CPU resources than have been allocated.

Managing capacity overload and Autoscale

The next situations will separate a Premium P1 capacity from a Fabric capacity as far as overage is concerned. As of the printing of this book, Microsoft is going to sunset Premium capacities unless the **Enterprise Agreement** (**EA**) with a company does not expire before January 1, 2025. Otherwise, only Fabric capacities will be created with or without an EA. After January 1, 2025, companies are encouraged to work with Microsoft to start planning moves from Premium capacities to Fabric capacities. *Chapter 12, High Scale Patterns*, has a chart comparing Premium and Fabric capacities with some resource limits in the *Leveraging Fabric for data scale* section.

Premium capacity overage

For a P1 capacity, overload means that the total load (including smoothed background activity) exceeds 120 CPU seconds (960 CU seconds) during an evaluation cycle. When this state is reached, the system starts to perform throttling, also called **interactive request delay mode**, unless Autoscale is enabled. The system will remain in delay mode while each new evaluation cycle exceeds the available capacity. In delay mode, the system will artificially delay interactive requests such as reports. The amount of delay is dynamic and increases as a function of the capacity load.

The delay mode does not completely shut down access to the capacity. This feature was added in Gen2 of Premium and improved with Fabric capacities. Delaying new interactive requests when overloaded may seem like it would make the problem worse, but this is not the case. For users who experience delayed requests, the experience will be slower than if the capacity was not overloaded. However, they are still much more likely to have their requests completed successfully. This is because delaying operations gives the capacity time to finish ones that are already in progress, preventing them from being overloaded to the point where new interactive actions fail. *Figure 13.4* illustrates how request delays work. Observe that in cycle A, we needed more capacity than was allocated. This is indicated by the queries stacking up higher than the 120-second capacity, which protects the capacity and reduces the degradation of the user experience:

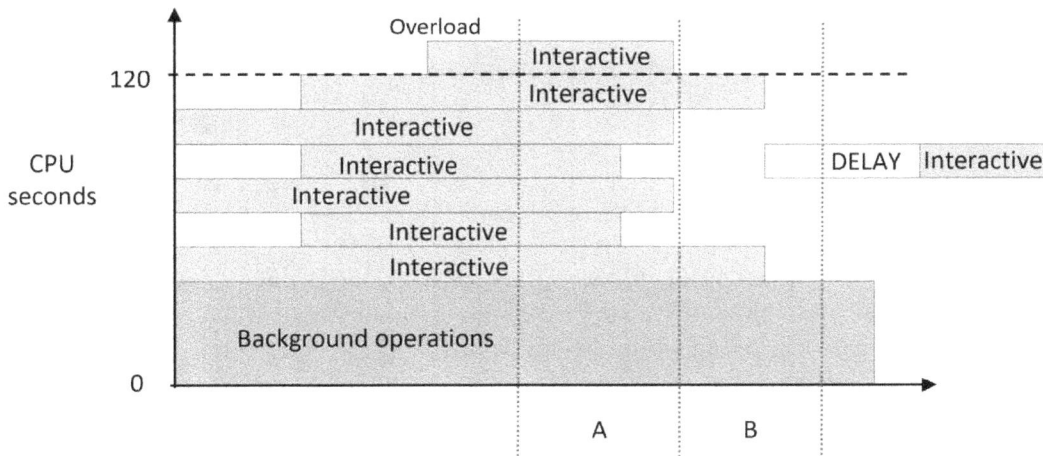

Figure 13.4 – Interactive operations are delayed due to the overload in cycle A

If you often experience overload, you should consider scaling up to a larger capacity. However, a larger capacity represents a significant cost increase, which may be hard to justify when the scale issues are transient and unpredictable. You could also manually scale out by spreading workspaces around multiple capacities so that a single capacity does not experience a disproportionately high load. If you only have one capacity available to you, distributing the load in this way is not an option.

Fabric capacity overage

For Fabric capacities in the same scenario, Autoscale is not needed. Instead, Fabric uses additional capacity behind the scenes and uses a burndown method to have the overage spread over an evaluation period. If the overage is more than the evaluation period can absorb, additional costs could be added to the Azure bill. If this happens frequently, a higher Fabric capacity should be purchased if there is no other option to move the processing to a different resource period. *Figure 13.5.* shows the overage burndown (the blue lines) for the evaluation period:

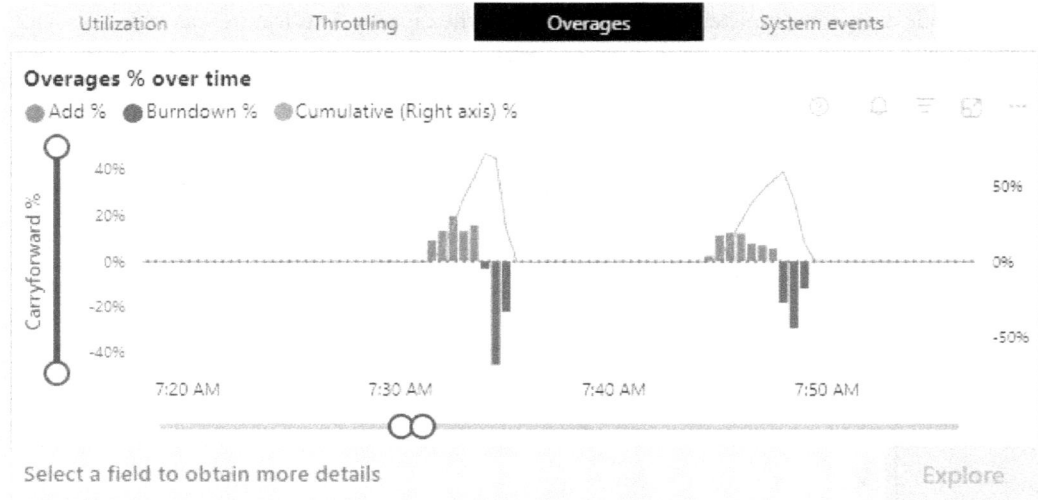

Figure 13.5 – Fabric overage burndown over time

This overage is for CU usage (vCPUs in Premium). For three of the cycles, the green lines indicate that **Add %** was over 100%. The blue lines show the burndown of this overage over time until the additional CU used over the capacity side is smoothed out.

This still does not stop other types of errors if, say, the process uses more memory than is allowed for the capacity. This error message is shown in *Figure 13.6:*

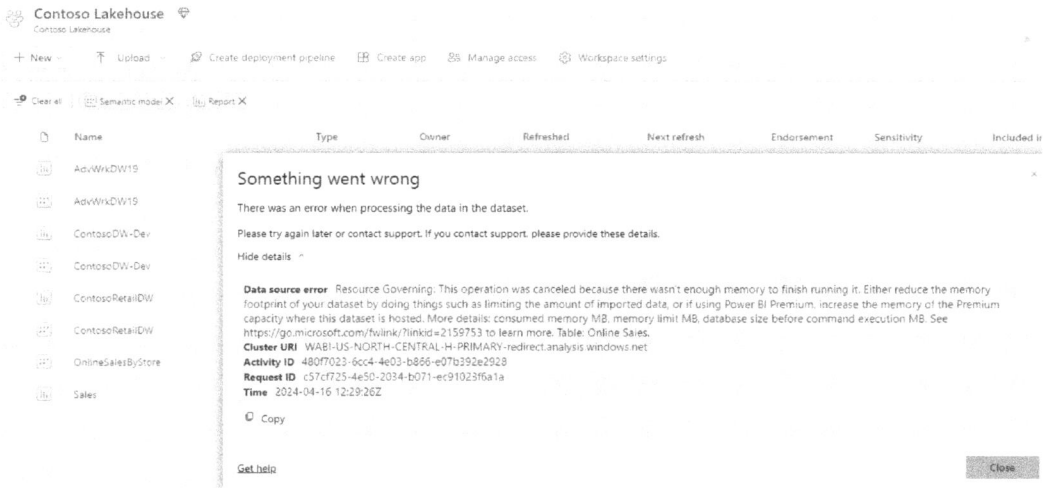

Figure 13.6 – An out-of-memory error for a semantic model refresh

In this case, the size of the semantic model would need to be reduced or the capacity would need to be increased. To reduce the size of a model, you can use this article from Microsoft to help:

`https://learn.microsoft.com/en-us/power-bi/guidance/import-modeling-data-reduction`

Figure 13.9 provides the memory limitations for Premium, Embedded, Azure, and Fabric capacities.

First, let's look at another way to mitigate peak load.

Handling peak loads in Premium capacity with Autoscale

An efficient way to manage excessive load in premium capacities without incurring upfront costs is to use the Autoscale capability.

> **Note**
>
> Autoscale is not needed for Fabric because capacities in Fabric already have an auto scaling capability. Autoscale is not available for Embedded (EM and A **Stock Keeping Unit** (**SKU**)) capacities in the same way it is for Premium. For Embedded, you must use a combination of metrics and APIs, or PowerShell, to manually check resource metrics and issue the appropriate scale-up or scale-down commands. This requires the skills of an Azure infrastructure person.

Autoscale in Premium works by linking an Azure subscription to a Premium capacity and allowing it to use extra v-cores when an overload occurs. Fabric does this automatically for you without provisioning an A SKU in Azure. Power BI will assign one v-core at a time to the maximum allowed, as configured by the administrator. V-cores are assigned for 24 hours at a time and are only charged when they're assigned during these 24-hour overload periods. *Figure 13.7* shows the **Autoscale settings** pane, which can be found in the **Capacity settings** area of the admin portal:

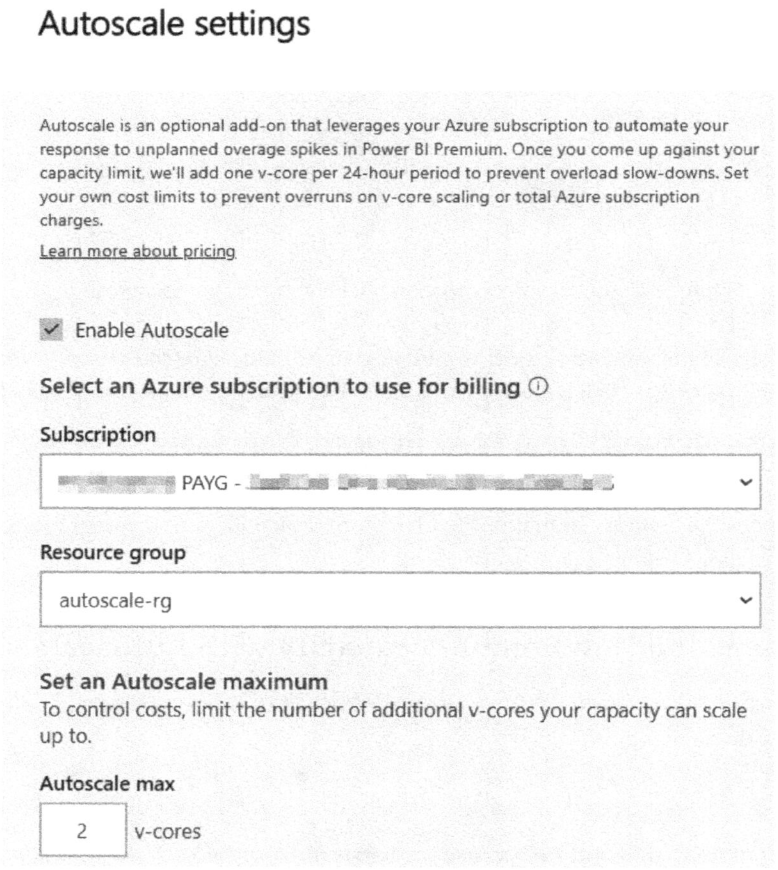

Autoscale settings

Autoscale is an optional add-on that leverages your Azure subscription to automate your response to unplanned overage spikes in Power BI Premium. Once you come up against your capacity limit, we'll add one v-core per 24-hour period to prevent overload slow-downs. Set your own cost limits to prevent overruns on v-core scaling or total Azure subscription charges.

Learn more about pricing

☑ Enable Autoscale

Select an Azure subscription to use for billing ⓘ

Subscription

| PAYG - ▓▓▓▓▓▓▓▓▓▓▓▓▓▓ | ⌄ |

Resource group

| autoscale-rg | ⌄ |

Set an Autoscale maximum
To control costs, limit the number of additional v-cores your capacity can scale up to.

Autoscale max

| 2 | v-cores |

Figure 13.7 – The Autoscale settings to link an Azure subscription and assign v-cores

Figure 13.8 shows how the overload scenario that we described in *Figure 13.4* would change if Autoscale was enabled. We can see that a v-core was assigned in the next evaluation after an overload occurred, which increased the capacity threshold. It is also important to note that the interactive operation that occurred after the overload is now not delayed:

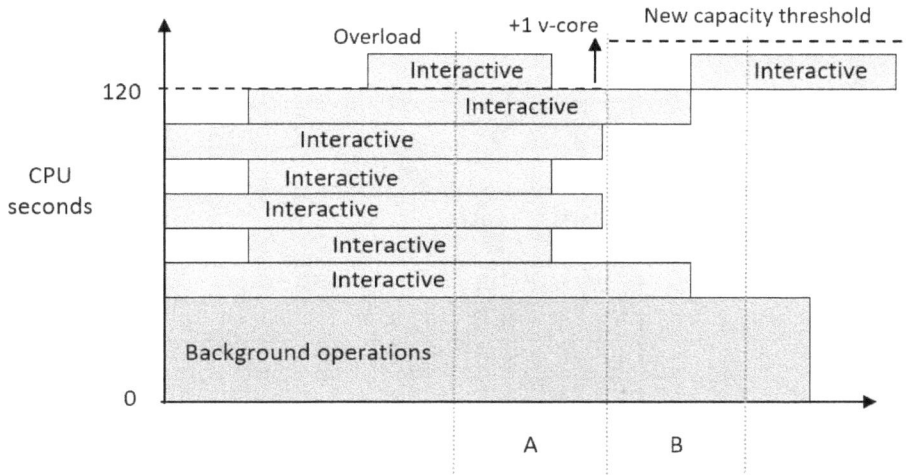

Figure 13.8 – Autoscale assigns an additional core and avoids delays

Now that we have learned how capacities evaluate load and can be scaled, let's learn how to plan for the right capacity size and keep it running efficiently.

Capacity planning, monitoring, and optimization

A natural question that occurs when organizations consider purchasing Premium, Embedded, or Fabric capacity is what size to provision. We know that there are different services available in capacities and we can safely assume that workload intensity and distribution vary between organizations. This can make it difficult to predict the correct size based on simple metrics such as total users. Capacity usage naturally increases over time too, so even if you have the right size to begin with, there may come a point where you need to scale. Therefore, in the next few sections, you will learn about the initial sizing and then how to monitor and scale.

Determining the initial capacity size

Earlier in this chapter, we mentioned that Power BI capacities are available in varied sizes through different licensing models. We will assume that you will choose the appropriate SKU based on your organizational needs. We would like to provide a reminder here that feature-based dependencies may force you to use a certain minimum size if you considering the A or F series of SKUs from Azure, or the P and EM series that are available via Office. For example, paginated reports are not available on the A1-S3 or EM1-EM3 capacities, and AI is not available on A1, EM1, or F2-F32.

It is useful to have these capacities in mind when you start planning. At the time of writing this, these capacities and limits are shown in *Figure 13.9*:

SKU Fabric	CU	SKU (P-Premium, EM-Embedded, or A-Azure)	v-cores	RAM limit model load size	Automatic Query Memory Limit	Maximum memory in GB	DirectQuery or Live connections per second
F2	2	-	0.25	1GB	1GB	3	1
F4	4	-	0.5	2GB	1GB	3	<2
F8	8	EM/A1	1	3GB	1GB	3	3.75
F16	16	EM2/A2	2	5GB	2GB	5	7.5
F32	32	EM3/A3	4	6GB	5GB	10	15
F64	64	P1/A4	8	10GB	10GB	25	30
F128	128	P2/A5	16	10GB	10GB	50	60
F256	256	P3/A6	32	10GB	10GB	100	120
F512	512	P4/A7	64	10GB	20GB	200	240
F1024	1024	P5/A8	128	10GB	40GB	400	480
F2048	2048	-	256	10GB	40GB	400	960

Figure 13.9 – The available SKUs and their limits

Now, let's look at what to consider when sizing a capacity. We will consider all of these in the next section on load testing:

- **Size of individual semantic model**: Focus on larger, more complex semantic models that will have heavier usage. You can prototype semantic models in Power BI Desktop and use DAX Studio and VertiPaq Analyzer to estimate the compressibility of data to predict the semantic model's size. Ensure that the capacity you choose has enough room to host the largest semantic model. The VertiPaq Analyzer is part of DAX Studio and is used to analyze the storage structure of a semantic model. This is the best tool to use to view table and column sizes in a semantic model and helps determine the type of storage used by Analysis Services engine used in Power BI.

- **Number and complexity of queries**: Think about how many users might be viewing different reports at the same time. Consider centralized organizational reports, and then consider adding this percentage from how broadly the organization wishes to support self-service content. You can determine the number and complexity of queries from typical report actions using Desktop Performance Analyzer and DAX Studio.

- **Number and complexity of data refreshes**: Estimate the maximum number of semantic models you may need to refresh at the same time at various stages of your initiative. Choose a capacity that has an appropriate refresh parallelism limit.

Also, bear in mind that a semantic model's total memory footprint is the sum of what's used by its tables and data structures, execution of queries, and background data refreshes. If this exceeds the capacity limit, the refresh will fail.

- **Load from order services**: Remember that other artifacts can be created in the capacity such as dataflows, AI functions, paginated reports, and now Fabric data resources such as a Lakehouse or Warehouse, as well as pipelines and notebooks. These require a Spark engine. If some of these Fabric items are not to be used, disable them in the admin portal.

- **Periodic distribution of load**: Capacity load will vary at different times of the day in line with work hours. There may also be predictable times of extra activity, such as month-ends or holiday sales. We suggest that you compare regular peak activity to these unique events. If the unique events need far more resources compared to normal peak times, it would be better to rely on Autoscale for Premium capacities. See the note that follows for Fabric scaling.

> **Note**
> Fabric capacities can be scaled up and down in Azure. This does not require a new purchasing agreement with Microsoft like EM and Premium SKUs would. Once the large load is finished, the capacity can be scaled back down. As of the printing of this book, automation of the scale-up and scale-down is in public preview.

Validating capacity size with load testing

Once you have a proposed capacity size, you should perform testing to gauge how the capacity responds to different situations. Microsoft has provided two sets of PowerShell scripts to help simulate load in different scenarios. These tools take advantage of REST APIs that are only available in the Premium or Fabric capacities. You can configure the tool to execute reports that are hosted in a reserved capacity under certain conditions. You should try to host semantic models and reports that represent realistic use cases so that the tool can generate actionable data. This activity will be captured by the system and will be visible in the **Fabric Capacity Metric** app, which we will describe later in this section. We will use this app to investigate resource usage, overload, and smoothing.

First, let's review the testing provided by Microsoft. Both suites are available in subfolders at the same location on GitHub:

```
https://github.com/microsoft/PowerBI-Tools-For-Capacities
```

These are described as follows:

- **LoadTestingPowerShellTool**: This tool is simple. It aims to simulate a lot of users opening the same reports at the same time. This represents a worst-case scenario that is unlikely to occur, but it provides value by showing just how much load the capacity can manage for a given report in a short amount of time. The script will prompt you to specify the number of reports you want to run, authenticate with the user you wish to test each report, and define which filter values to cycle through. When the configuration is complete, it will open a new browser window for each report and continuously execute it, looping over the filter values you supply.

- **RealisticLoadTestTool**: This is a more sophisticated script that requires additional setup. It is designed to simulate a realistic set of user actions, such as changing slicers and filters. It also allows time to be taken between actions to simulate users interpreting information before interacting with the report again. This script will also begin to ask you how many reports you want to test and which users to use. At this point, it will simply generate a configuration file called PBIReport.json in a new subfolder named with the current date and time. Then you need to edit that file to customize the configuration. This time, you can load specific pages or bookmarks, control how many times the session restarts, specify filter or slicer combinations with multiple selections, and add "think time" in seconds between the actions. The following sample file is a modified version of one that's been included with the tool and clearly illustrates these configurations:

```
reportParameters={
"reportUrl":"https://app.powerbi.com/
reportEmbed?reportId=36621bde-4614-40df-8e08-79481d767bcb",
"pageName": "ReportSectiond1b63329887eb2e20791",
"bookmarkList": [""],
"sessionRestart":100,
"filters": [
{
"filterTable":"DimSalesTerritory",
"filterColumn":"SalesTerritoryCountry",
"isSlicer":true,
"filtersList":[
"United States",
["France","Germany"]
]
},
{
"filterTable":"DimDate",
"filterColumn":"Quarter",
"isSlicer":false,
"filtersList":["Q1","Q2","Q3","Q4"]
}
],
&"thinkTimeSeconds":1
};
```

Note that the scripts have prerequisites:

- PowerShell must be executed with elevated privileges (**Run as Administrator**).

- You need to set your execution policy to allow the unsigned testing scripts to run `Set-ExecutionPolicy Unrestricted`.

- The Power BI `commandlet` modules must be installed by running `Install-Module MicrosoftPowerBIMgmt`.

More information is available at `https://docs.microsoft.com/en-us/azure/load-testing/overview-what-is-azure-load-testing`.

Next, we will examine settings within the capacity for alerts when limits are reached for certain resources.

Alert notifications

Power BI allows a capacity administrator to configure customized notifications for each capacity. They are available in the capacity settings and allow you to set thresholds that will trigger email alerts. We recommend configuring the items shown in *Figure 13.10* so you can be proactively notified when problematic conditions are met:

Admin portal

Tenant settings (New)	▷ Disaster Recovery
Usage metrics	
Users	▷ Capacity usage report
Premium Per User	
Audit logs	◿ Notifications
Domains (New)	Get notified when you're close to exceeding your available capacity (which includes base and Autoscale v-cores).
Capacity settings	
Refresh summary	**Send notifications when**
Embed Codes	☑ You're using [85] % of your available capacity
Organizational visuals	☑ You've exceeded your available capacity and might experience slowdowns
Azure connections	☑ An Autoscale v-core has been added
Workspaces	☑ You've reached your Autoscale maximum
Custom branding	
Protection metrics	**Send notifications to**
Featured content	☑ Capacity admins
Help + support	☑ These contacts:
	(T) Thomas-LeBlanc × Enter email addresses
	Apply Discard
	▷ Contributor permissions
	Enabled for the entire organization

Figure 13.10 – The capacity notification settings

We suggest configuring the first notification so that it's around 85%. This will help you identify peaks before they become a problem. This gives you time to plan for an increased capacity scale or identify content that could be optimized to reduce load. The rest of the checkboxes depicted in *Figure 13.10* are self-explanatory. The Autoscale options are specific to Premium capacities.

All your planning is not worth much if you cannot examine the effects that organic growth, design choice, and user behavior have on the capacity. You will need a way to determine load issues at a high level, then investigate deeper at varying levels of granularity. Microsoft provides a template app called the Microsoft Fabric Capacity Metrics app that can help with this. It is not built into the service and must be manually installed from the AppSource portal. You can access it directly here, though note that you must be a capacity admin to install it:

```
https://learn.microsoft.com/en-us/fabric/enterprise/metrics-app-
install?tabs=1st
```

Currently, the app contains 14 days of near-real-time data and allows you to drill down to the artifact and operations levels. An obvious example of an artifact is a semantic model, and the operations that are performed on it could be data refreshes or queries from reports.

The official documentation describes each page and visual of the report sequentially and in detail. We will not repeat this, but we will illustrate how to use the report to investigate a few scenarios. We performed our testing on an F2 and F4 Fabric capacity for most figures. There are some processes and reports using a P1 Premium capacity; they are noted where different. F2 and F4 were selected because they were small enough to be overloaded.

Next, we will introduce the monitoring app and learn how to use it to identify and diagnose capacity load issues.

Monitoring capacities

The easiest way to monitor a dedicated capacity is to use the template app provided by Microsoft. You can install it by following the instructions at `https://learn.microsoft.com/en-us/fabric/enterprise/metrics-app-install?tabs=1st`. The documentation suggests that you install to a new workspace in a Pro license and not a dedicated capacity workspace. This separates the app from the production system running models and reports in a capacity.

> **Note**
> Many large companies write their own monitoring tools. Most consist of calling Power BI REST APIs to gather data and save, historically in a database or data storage area. This enables more control over the overall monitoring but requires maintenance and code to achieve good results. The template app only shows the last 14 days of data.

Next, let's break down the different areas for the monitoring app.

Understanding the compute report page

The main page of the app has three sections. *Figure 13.11* shows these areas with a boundary around each:

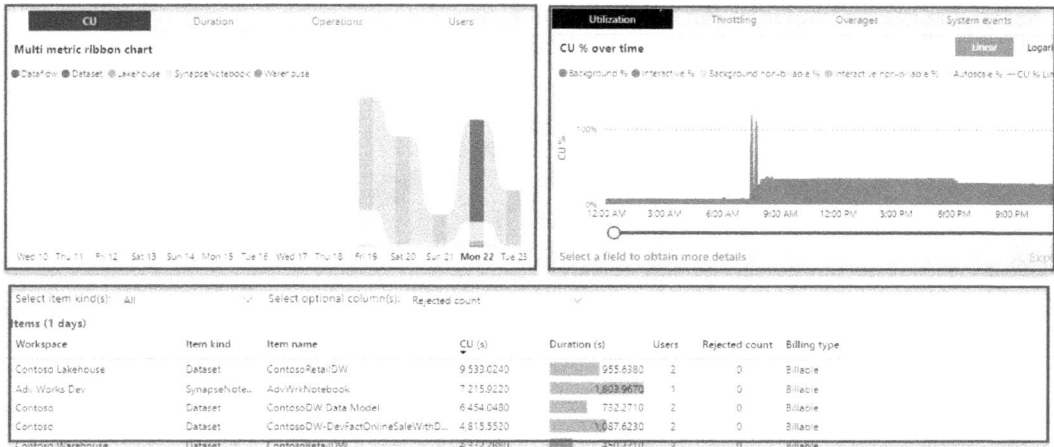

Figure 13.11 – The Fabric capacity metrics

The top two visuals on the report are to monitor a capacity. These visuals can only show results if a capacity is selected, which is available in the upper left of *Figure 13.12*:

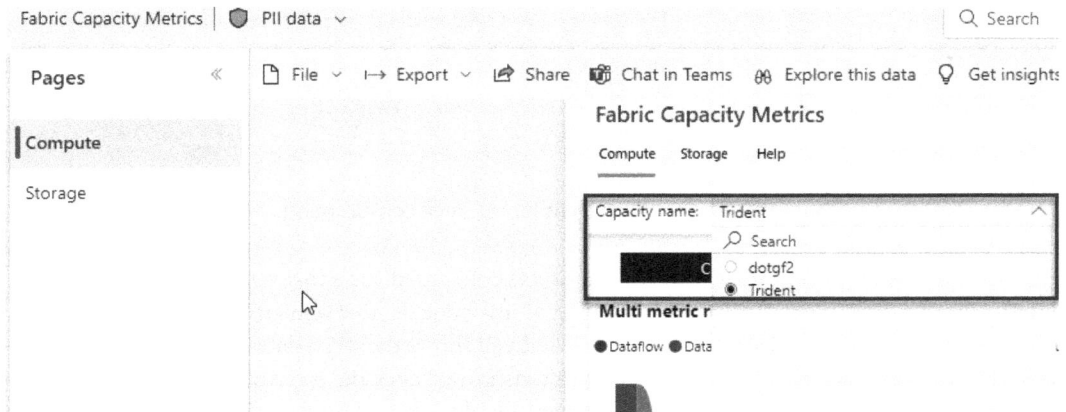

Figure 13.12 – Selecting a capacity for a Fabric Capacity Metrics report

The ribbon chart depicted in the upper left in *Figure 13.11*, **Multi metric ribbon chart**, will look at the last 14 days and determine which artifacts used resources in that period. The top part of the chart has buttons to switch between Compute Usage, Duration, Operations, and Users. The flow of a period shows the changes in resources sliced by time like in *Figure 13.13*:

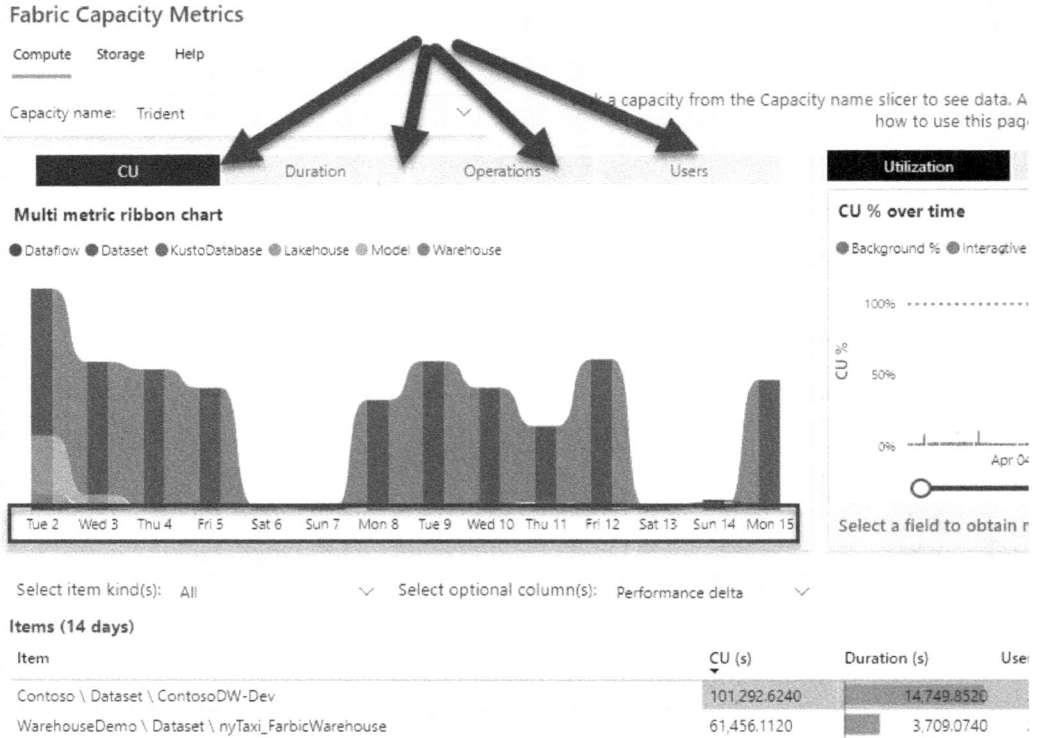

Figure 13.13 – A ribbon chart for resource consumption

Figure 13.13 shows that **semantic models** (datasets) consumed the most resources over time. A dataset's new name, as referenced at the beginning of this book, is now semantic model, though this report has not been updated with the new syntax and still shows the word dataset. If you ever have a question about what each resource means, select the visual and click the exclamation point in a circle (information object) in the upper right like in *Figure 13.14*:

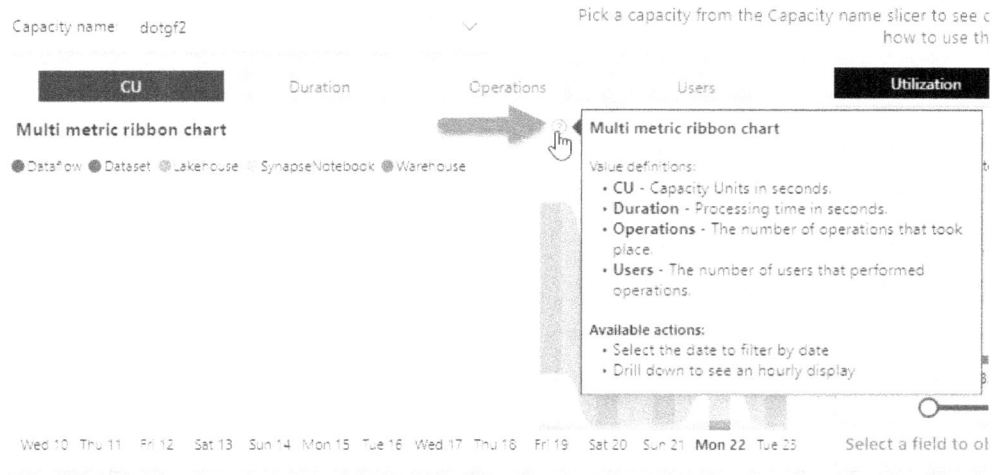

Figure 13.14 – The information object from a visual

The visual in the upper right, **CU % over time**, shows a time series bar chart with a time slider and multiple legends. The title and displayed measures are based on the selected type of resource used in the previous chart, **Multi metric ribbon chart**. So, if we had selected Duration instead of CU, the title and charted measure would change. *Figure 13.5* shows the CU percentage over time:

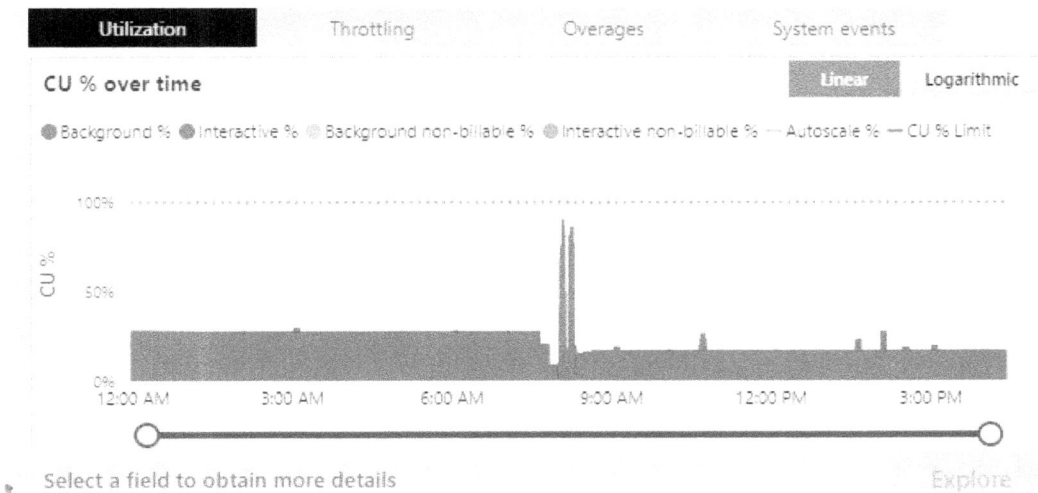

Figure 13.15 – The CU percentage over time

The larger matrix visual in the lower part of the page, **Items (x days)**, lists the artifacts from the capacity and sorts the listing by CU(s) used. The values displayed, as well as the days of data, are based on the selected visual in the **Multi metric ribbon chart**. If no days are selected, all 14 days are summarized like in *Figure 13.6*:

Select item kind(s): All		Select optional column(s): Rejected count					
Items (14 days)							
Workspace	Item kind	Item name	CU (s)	Duration (s)	Users	Rejected count	Billing type
Contoso Warehouse	Dataset	ContosoRetailDW	40,292.1440	6,348.7260	2	0	Billable
Contoso Lakehouse	Dataset	ContosoRetailDW	39,606.4800	5,335.0900	2	0	Billable
Adv Works Dev	SynapseNote...	AdvWrkNotebook	14,757.8295	3,689.4280	1	0	Billable
Contoso 22	Dataset	ContosoDW Data Model 2222	12,710.6880	2,770.7100	2	0	Billable
Contoso 22	Dataset	ContosoDW dotgSQL22	12,501.7920	2,728.3230	2	0	Billable
Contoso 22	Dataset	ContosoDW-Dev2222	10,516.4640	2,448.6810	2	0	Billable
Contoso	Dataset	ContosoDW Data Model	6,454.0480	732.2710	2	0	Billable
DataWarehouses	Dataset	ContosoDW Data Model	5,787.1040	1,878.7720	2	0	Billable
Contoso Lakehouse	SynapseNote...	Delta Analyzer	4,976.6025	1,244.1400	1	0	Billable

Figure 13.16 – An items (14 days) visual

The next section has specific data from certain days to show how to monitor the performance of a system and explain some of the processes.

Utilization overage

In this example, a Fabric F2 capacity had an overage for the day. You can see this issue in the **Utilization** section for the **CU % over time** visual in *Figure 13.17*:

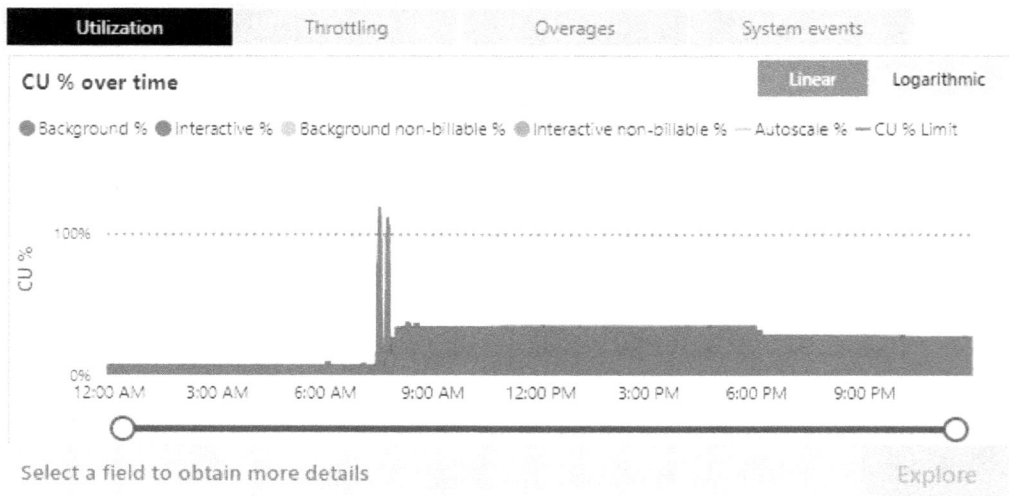

Figure 13.17 – The Utilization visual showing an overage

If we change this visual to the **Overages** button and use the slider to zoom in on the overage time period, we can see Fabric spreading the overage as **Burndown %** once free resources are available in that 24-hour smoothing period in *Figure 13.18*:

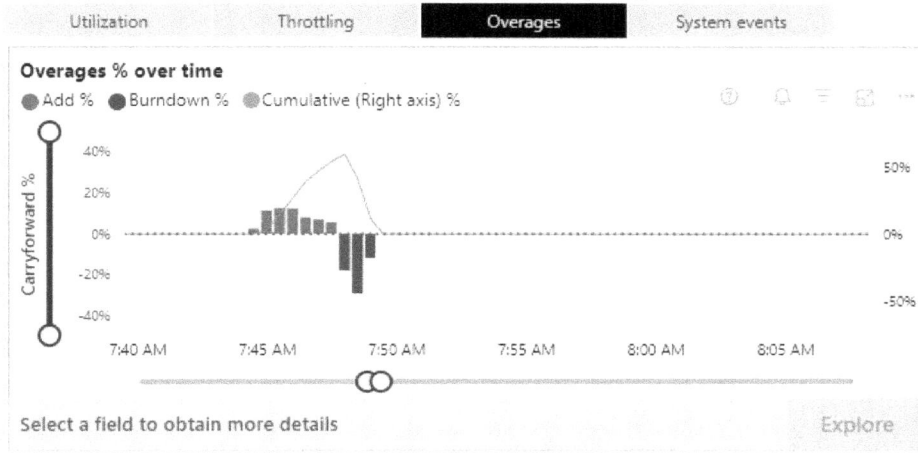

Figure 13.18 – Overage visual with Burndown %

In this example, there was the processing of semantic models and viewing reports (interactively) that used more than the 60 CUs available for the capacity. *Figure 13.19* shows the **Add %** that was needed to complete the processing:

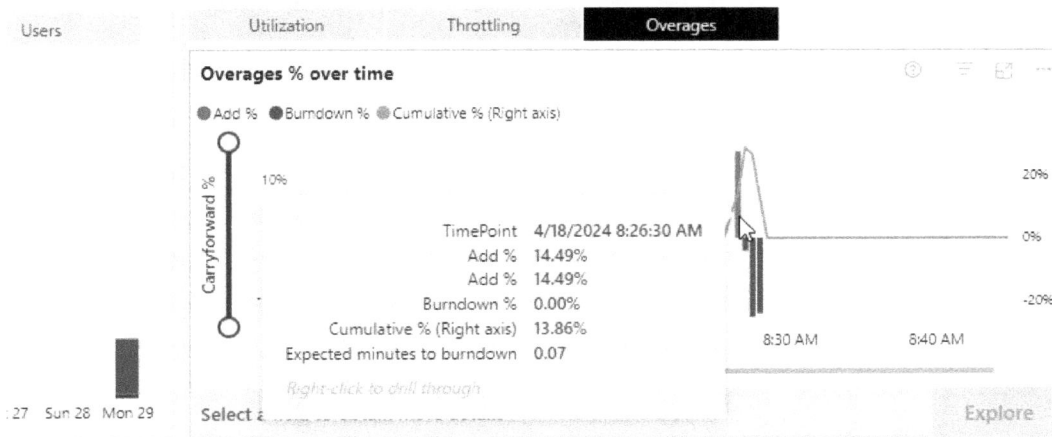

Figure 13.19 – The Timepoint Add% and expected minutes to burndown

Another option is to display details about the system at that time. Here, we right-click and drill through to the **TimePoint Detail** report like *Figure 13.20*:

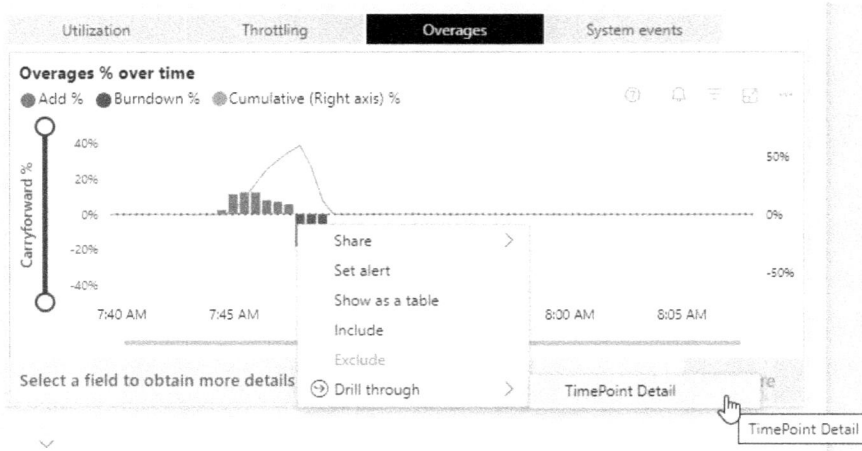

Figure 13.20 – The drill through menu

The details will show the rows that are using Interactive operations versus background operations with a matrix visual. In this case, the sum of the two, interactive and background operations, is above the CU capacity, which is displayed in the upper right of the detail page in *Figure 13.21*:

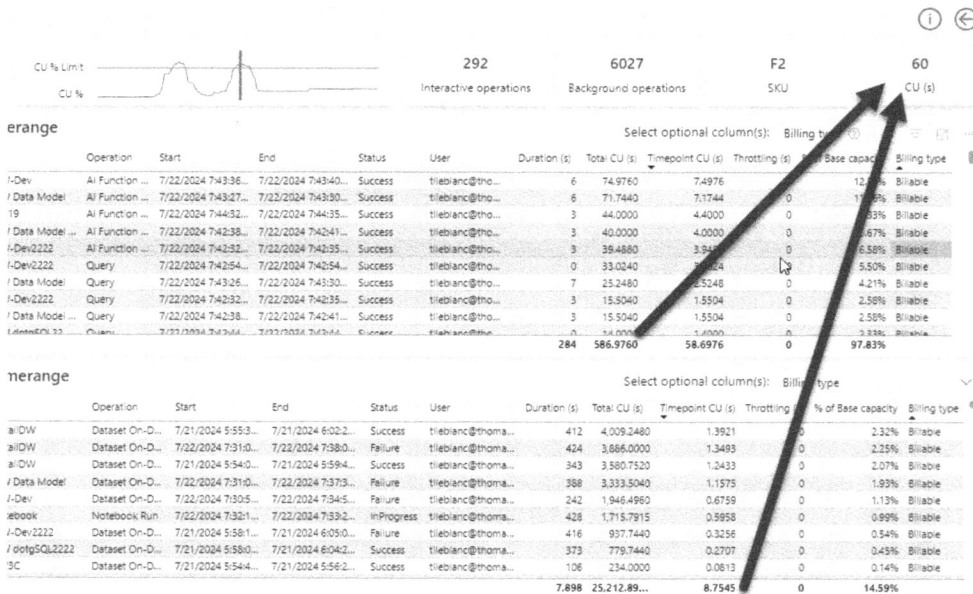

Figure 13.21 – The TimePoint Detail report of overage

As we can see in *Figure 13.21*, the **Rundown table for timerange** visual shows **Add %** to be 14.44% overall, with a breakdown in the matrix of the resources that need extra capacity. The same drill-through shows the burndown process for this overage. *Figure 13.22* shows this and the minutes to burndown in the **Burndown table for timerange** visual:

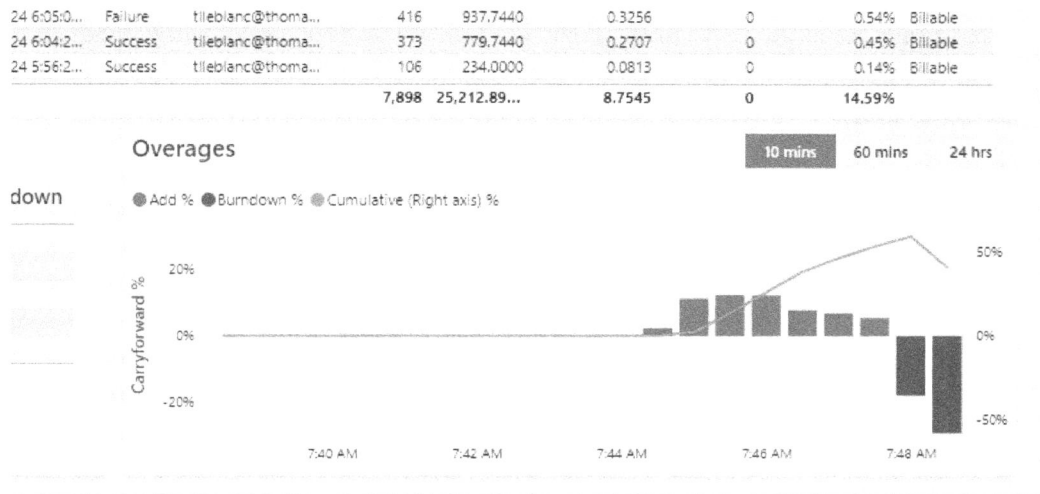

24 6:05:0...	Failure	tileblanc@thoma...	416	937.7440	0.3256	0	0.54%	Billable
24 6:04:2...	Success	tileblanc@thoma...	373	779.7440	0.2707	0	0.45%	Billable
24 5:56:2...	Success	tileblanc@thoma...	106	234.0000	0.0813	0	0.14%	Billable
			7,898	25,212.89...	8.7545	0	14.59%	

Figure 13.22 – The burndown percentage for the previous overage

Since this morning's process was using additional CUs and needed more resources to complete other activities, the capacity was changed from F2 to F4. The next day, there were no overages, as shown in *Figure 13.23*:

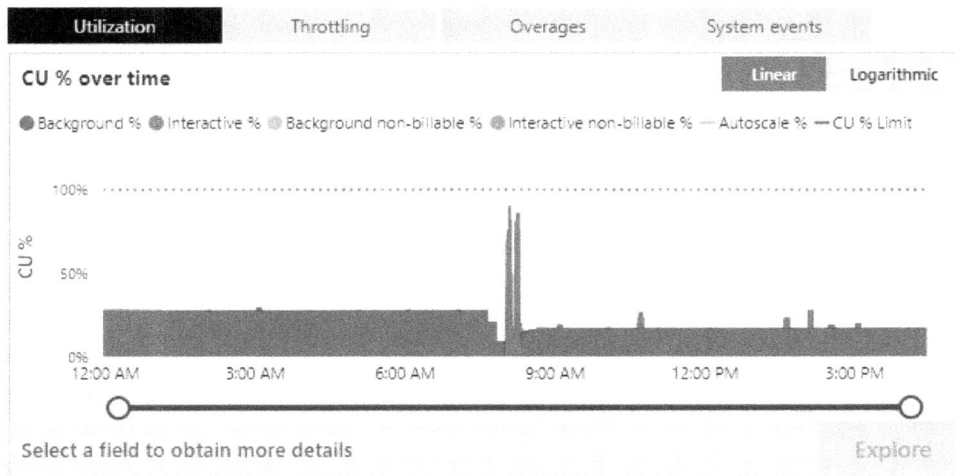

Figure 13.23 – F4 and no overages

The **TimePoint Detail** reveals useful granular information, as shown in *Figures 13.22* and *13.21*. It displays about an hour of capacity activity with the selected time point in the middle, which is shown as a vertical bar. Observe that **Interactive Operations for timerange** is separated from **Background Operations for timerange**. The interactive operations are scoped to the hour, while the background operations are from the previous 24 hours, since they all contribute to the load. The **% of base capacity metric** tells us what proportion of the total capacity was used by the operation. We can also see how long it took and whether any interactive delay was added, listed as **Throttling** in the report.

Performance delta

The **Item (x days)** visual on the main page of the report can help with tracking performance degradation. In *Figure 13.24*, the Performance delta of a DirectQuery report shows that the semantic model has a **-26** delta in performance in red.

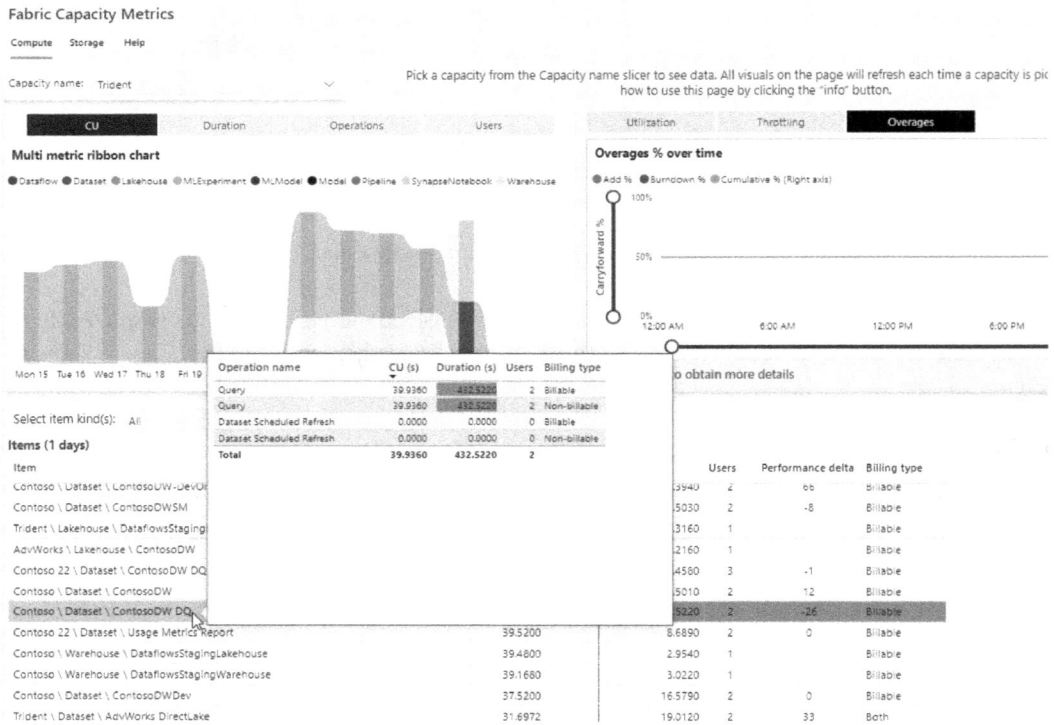

Figure 13.24 – A performance delta in a DirectQuery report

Hovering over the semantic mode will show a report tip that the duration was high in two queries coming from the **ContosoDW DQ** DirectQuery report. Since this could be an issue from the source system, a DBA might need to be engaged to investigate the source system while we investigate the report. Microsoft does not specify what the number represents, only that a lower value is highlighted in red, -10 to -25 is yellow, and greater than -10 shows no color. If the number is positive, this means that the performance of the report is improving over time.

The next section talks about some other artifacts using resources.

Notebook in capacity

There are many artifacts other than semantic models and reports that can affect resources. *Figure 13.25* shows that notebooks have a higher usage than semantic models. These notebooks should be moved to their own workspace, and capacity if possible, to help separate the resource utilization between Power BI artifacts (semantic models and reports) and the newer Fabric artifacts (Lakehouses, Warehouses, notebooks, and pipelines):

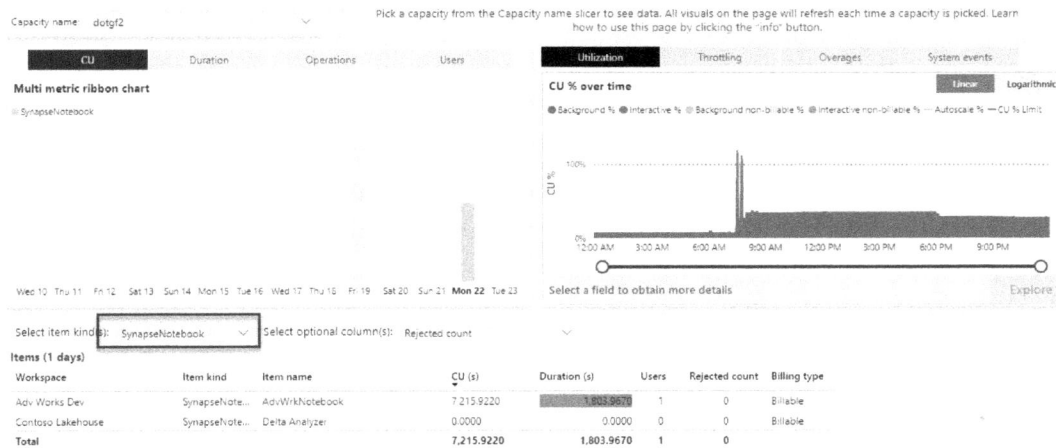

Figure 13.25 Notebook resource grabbing in utilization

At this point in our analysis, we would expect some collaboration between capacity admins and content owners to determine whether the throttling and overage are impacting users and to what extent. If users were impacted and we saw background operations contribute a lot, we could look at the scheduling refreshes at different times to lessen the total smoothed background activity and reduce the chance of an overload occurring. Fabric has helped with this issue with additional capacity and burndown, but it is still an issue with a capacity and should be mitigated before it affects end users and SLAs.

Let's summarize this section with some guidance on the steps you should take when you see overloads in a report:

1. Begin by identifying the largest artifacts that contribute to overloading, with an emphasis on those that are used by a higher proportion of users.

2. Look at the trends for the artifacts to see whether the problem is isolated or periodic. Also, check whether there is a visible increase in activity, users, or overloaded minutes over time. Gradual uptrends are an indication of organic growth, which could lead to a decision to scale up or out.

3. Investigate the periods of high load to see what other activity is occurring on the capacity. You may be able to identify interactive usage peaks in the same periods across different semantic models. You could move some busy artifacts to a capacity with more available resources, choose to increase the capacity's size, or enable Autoscale (if you are using Premium).

> **Note**
> Fabric and Embedded A SKUs are **Platform as a Service** (**PaaS**) services that are purchased and billed through Azure. They support native integration with Azure Log Analytics. This integration is an alternative source of capacity activity tracking and provides near-real-time traces and metrics, which are similar to those available from Log Analytics from Azure Analysis Services. There is no associated reporting, so you will have to query and report the data in Log Analytics yourself. Also, you will bear additional Azure costs and maintenance using Log Analytics. You can find out more about setting this up at `https://learn.microsoft.com/en-gb/power-bi/transform-model/log-analytics/desktop-log-analytics-overview`.

Next, let's summarize this chapter.

Summary

In this chapter, we came closer to the end of our journey of performance optimization in Power BI. We focused on the reserved capacities that are available as Power BI Premium, Embedded, and Fabric offerings. We learned that you could purchase and license the offerings differently, but that they share more functionality across SKUs. This means that the same performance optimization guidance applies to capacities consistently.

We introduced Fabric capacities that are set to replace Premium as of the printing of this book. We learned that there are still improvements that Premium brought to the table that are improved in Fabric when using large semantic models. After that, we looked at capacity settings such as query timeouts and refresh intervals, which you can use to prevent expensive operations from severely affecting the capacity.

Then, we discussed how capacities have different ways of evaluating capacity load. The memory limits we listed by capacity and options for scaling were discussed, such as Autoscale with an A SKU resource for Premium, as well as how Fabric uses reserved capacity for overages. For the overage situations, examples were given to demonstrate options for adding capacity without incurring a fixed cost. The 30-second evaluation cycle was discussed. It was also shown how the sum of activity during a 24-hour time frame can be smoothed so as not to incur overages.

We concluded the chapter by learning about monitoring, starting with alert emails to administrators. The newer template app from Microsoft for monitoring, Fabric Capacity Metrics, was covered in detail, with examples of overage and burndown of the extra capacity used. With the app, we can show how the main resources can be watched over time for opportunities to increase capacity if needed, as we learned. The artifacts were shown in a matrix visual with the relevant metrics to watch even with an ability to drill through to time-based usage.

In the next chapter, we will detail some of the performance needs with the new artifacts related to using a Fabric capacity.

14

Performance Needs for Fabric Artifacts

In the previous chapter, we looked at how to manage and monitor **capacities**. In this chapter, we will look specifically at the new artifacts in **Fabric** capacities that were not in Premium capacities. Fabric was created by Microsoft to simplify the modern data warehouse. All artifacts created are constructed to either relieve you of managing infrastructure or improve the performance of data warehouse development.

This chapter will give an overview of **OneLake**, Fabric's data storage, which is like OneDrive for data. The **warehouse** or **lakehouse** gives a container for tables or files plus coding areas. Inside each container is a default semantic model for Power BI to report the data. Alerts have been integrated into the streaming resource to help with real-time requirements. Data science people will have OneLake to consume raw, curated, or dimensional data.

The whole point of Fabric is to improve performance by consolidating common data warehouse tasks into one environment to satisfy the needs of anyone in the corporation who needs data to perform an analysis. The warehouse or lakehouse resource is a **software-as-a-service** (**SaaS**) container for handling workload management, table concurrency, and storage management. This structure relieves users of the administration of physical infrastructure. Fabric does not remove the best practices around dimensional modeling or proper data types for modeling. The best practices expressed in the other chapters of this book still apply to Fabric artifacts.

In this chapter, we will cover the following:

- Fabric artifacts
- Using **Direct Lake** for data sources
- Monitoring Fabric resource consumption
- Tips for enhancements

Fabric artifacts

Fabric is a new capacity type for Power BI. If you want, you can run the same Power BI semantic models, dataflows, and reports in a Fabric capacity as you run in a Premium capacity. So, what's the difference? The difference is Fabric is adding analytics, data warehousing, and streaming resources to the capacity.

What are these additional resources? Here is a list as of the printing of this book:

- **OneLake**: Microsoft has made a point with Fabric that storage is in one place and one structure. The storage is built behind the scenes on Azure Data Lake Storage Gen2, which is Microsoft's answer to big data. This also separates the processing of compute from data storage. All organizational data is stored in one unified location. Additionally, shortcuts can be created for other data sources to be used in OneLake without having to copy the data.

- **Lakehouse or warehouse**: The containers of data and code can be one of two types, or both can be used together. The main separation between the two is a warehouse, which is for those who are used to working in a relational database such as SQL Server. Most of their work is coding in T-SQL and stored procedures, whereas a lakehouse is for developers who are used to working with data lake files or table structures with programming languages such as Python.

- **Delta table**: All data structures saved in Fabric are stored in a Delta table. This ACID-compliant format has parquet files at the root storage level. A transaction log is added separately from the parquet files (data) that gives the structure a table with concurrency. Parquet files are the latest column-store, compressed format for big data. The parquet file type is optimized for performance with analytical reporting.

- **Azure Data Factory (ADF) / Azure Data Pipelines**: When performing **extract, load, and transform** (ELT) operations, ADF is the place for orchestration. Here, you can chain executions together from various objects such as notebooks, dataflows, and API calls. ADF requires a Spark engine to be engaged while debugging the flow. There is a heavy use of a Spark engine for dataflows within ADF, which is why some developers prefer notebooks to ADF.

- **Notebooks/Spark engine**: Though you can use dataflows to import data from API calls or ingest XML files, the efficiency of notebooks running on a Spark engine can speed up imports. The use of open-source libraries helps simplify tasks and the amount of code that must be written. Over and over, we have seen pySpark or SparkSQL exceed the performance of dataflows in getting data formatted and stored for Power BI semantic models.

- **Power BI**: These are not new to capacities, just included with Fabric capacities. The main resources are semantic models, reports, and dataflows. Best practices for Power BI resources are talked about in a majority of the chapters in this book.

> **Note**
>
> As of the printing of this book, streaming services and alerts are still in **public preview**. Due to the nature of changes in artifacts from public preview to **general availability (GA)**, they have been excluded from this chapter because they can change before GA. In their current state, they consume resources and could affect performance. Monitoring the use of these features is necessary and can be tracked the same way as described in this book for other artifacts.

All these artifacts need a serverless compute resource to execute a task. In Fabric, all the compute services are within a capacity. The capacity is tied to a workspace and you can only have one capacity for a workspace. So, if you want to separate compute resources, you will have to create multiple capacities and assign them to different workspaces. This is OK because Fabric data can be shared between workspaces and thus between capacities. Permissions can even be given to a semantic model in one workspace to a role or user without giving the user any access to the workspace. *Figure 14.1*, shows the separation of storage from compute while organizing by the persona:

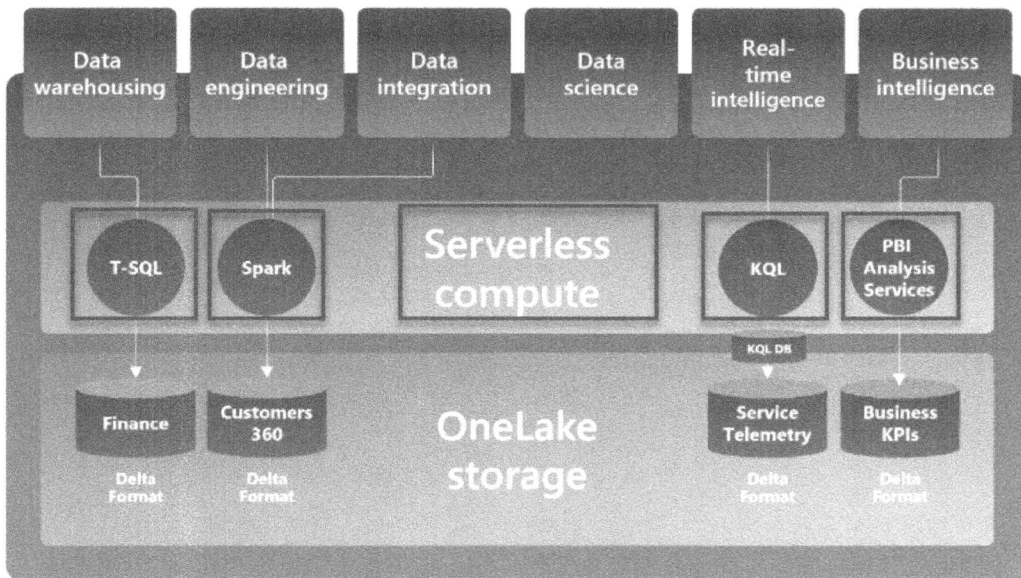

Figure 14.1 – Fabric personas drilling down to compute and storage

Figure 14.1 shows the persona of Fabric at the top. For the data warehouse persona, T-SQL is the serverless compute used to access the data in OneLake Storage. The data engineering persona uses a Spark serverless compute to access data in OneLake. Each persona will have various serverless compute while accessing the data in OneLake. Even though they use different compute, the data is still in the same storage area.

So, how does this affect performance? Well, all these new resources need compute, and this is usually from a Spark engine. This engine will use resources in the capacity that can affect Power BI semantic model refreshes, queries, and report renderings. So, you must monitor and determine the capacity needed to support Power BI artifacts as well as artifacts from Fabric. Using Fabric artifacts can be turned off in **Admin portal**. *Figure 14.2* shows **Tenant settings** for this:

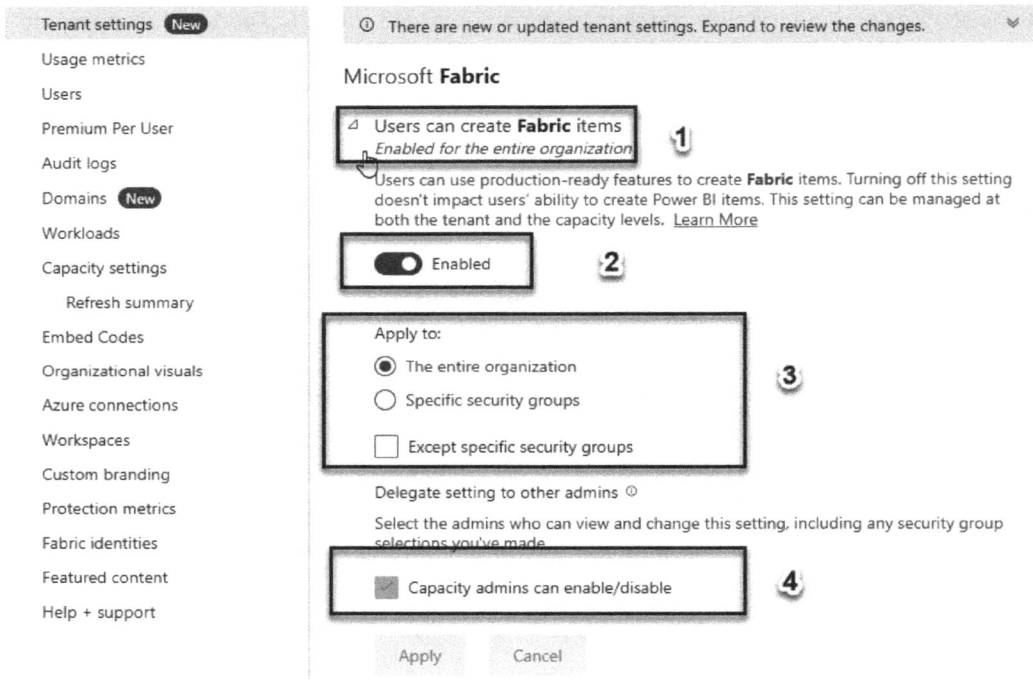

Figure 14.2 – Admin portal – User can create Fabric items

Here is an explanation of each setting in *Figure 14.2*:

1. This is the item in **Tenant settings** of **Admin portal**. You can search for it in the upper-right hand of the screen.

2. An administrator can toggle the setting on or off.

3. Applying this setting can be for **The entire organization** or a specific set of users and/or **Specific security groups**. There is an option to exclude security groups only: **Except specific security groups**.

4. These features can be given to **Capacity admins** to turn on or off at the capacity level instead of the tenant level (all capacities).

Next, we will look at the details of these Fabric artifacts, starting with Delta tables.

Delta tables

Delta tables bring a data warehouse structure to the data lake. With an open-source format file structure, Delta tables use parquet files with a transaction log. This brings **data manipulation language** (**DML**) statements (INSERT, UPDATE, DELETE) to data lake storage. So, all tables stored in a warehouse or lakehouse are Delta tables. This enables the default semantic model in each type to have a single storage structure for reporting. *Figure 14.3* shows the Fabric Explorer displaying the underlying parquet files and transition log for a Delta table:

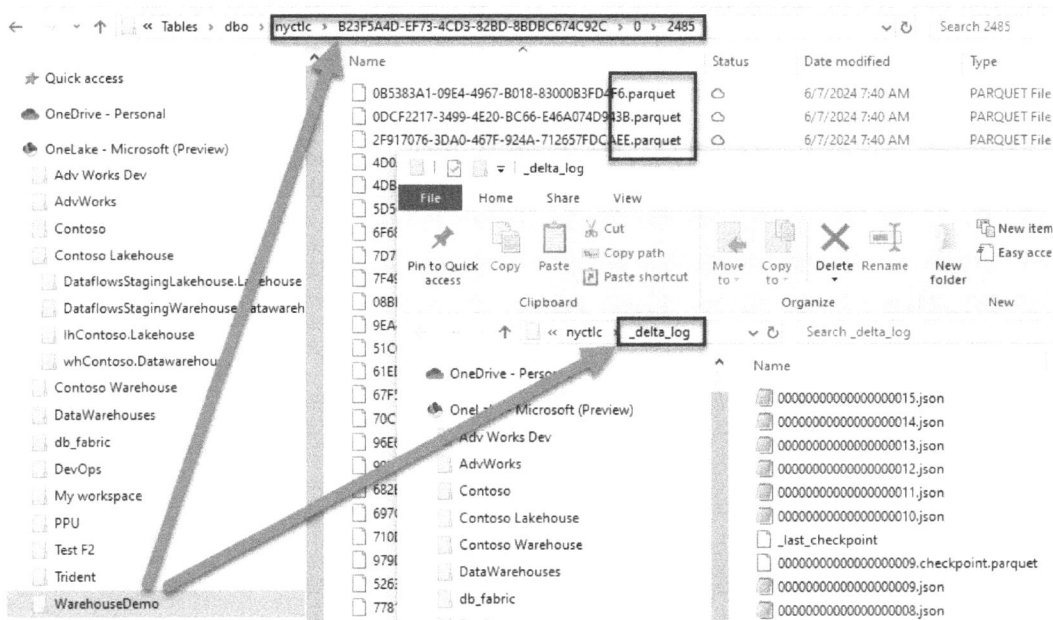

Figure 14.3 – Warehouse container for tables and related objects

There are two main benefits of Delta tables, the first one being its open-source structure, as most programming languages can read and write to this format, and the other is since it is the common format in Fabric, SQL, as well as Python, can be used to access the data for analytical reporting as well as manipulation of the data. The end user does not need to know the details; they just use it in Fabric. Each parquet file is immutable, which means the underlying files cannot be updated, so the changes invoked are placed in a new file and the transaction log directs the reader of the data to the proper files.

As a user of Fabric, you do not need to understand the internals of Delta tables to use a warehouse or lakehouse. Just understand that all tables created in Fabric are Delta tables. By default, a semantic model is created to use those Delta tables in each lakehouse or warehouse. The column-store structure of parquet files is what helps analytical reporting such as Power BI with aggregations and filtering as well as parallel processing queries. The performance gains by using this structure help alleviate infrastructure tuning for data warehousing.

On that note, an essential aspect of data warehousing is the differences between a lakehouse and a warehouse.

Warehouse or lakehouse

A warehouse or lakehouse is a container for tables and files used in the default semantic model for analytics. A warehouse looks like you are in SQL Server Management Studio or Azure Data Studio managing tables, schemas, views, and stored procedures such as a relational database. There are options in the interface to launch ingestion tools such as dataflows, pipelines, or notebooks. *Figure 14.4* shows this view with 1 for ingestions, 2 for a new report, and 3 for managing tables:

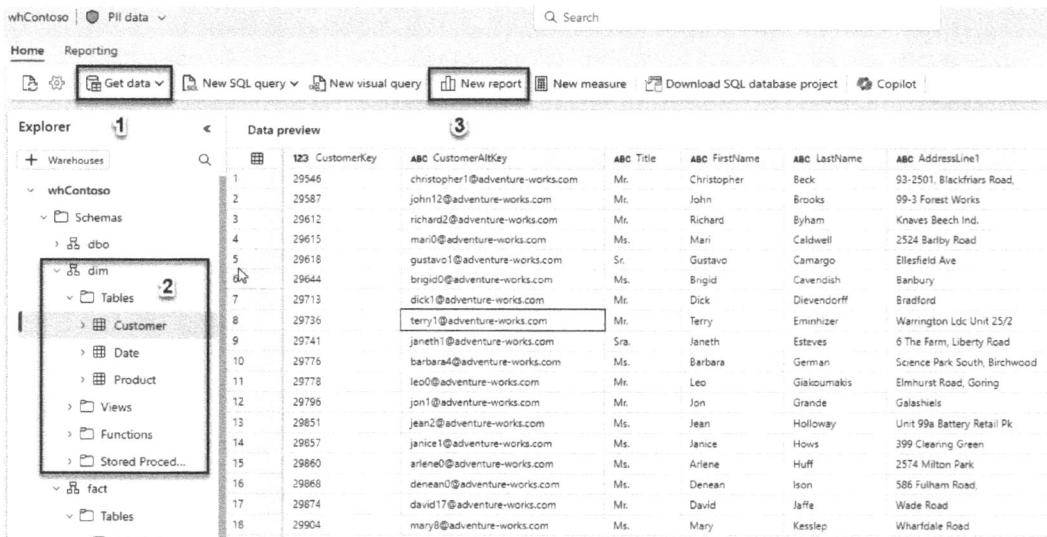

Figure 14.4 – Warehouse container for tables and related objects

All these objects can affect performance and count toward the **capacity units** (**CUs**). A CU is set by the capacity size; for more detail, see *Chapter 13*. All these artifacts are mentioned to help understand that planning to use a capacity depends on all resources.

In the past, when using on-premises resources or even individual cloud resources, each artifact would have its own resources allocated and managed. Fabric removes the managing of multiple resources but does not remove the fact that the processing must be accounted for. So, when planning, Microsoft gives you the option to start a 60-day trial (F64) Fabric capacity. This trial can be used to run simulations of workloads and monitor to find how the artifacts will affect the capacity for planning your capacity size. There is also an option for pay-as-you-go where you can pause and resume the capacity. Always start small and increase as you monitor.

Next, let's look at the Spark engine as far as performance is concerned.

The Spark engine

Most compute in Fabric comes from a Spark engine. In notebooks, it is obvious because, when running the code, you see the Spark engine ramp up. The other processing in Fabric uses Spark as a behind-the-scenes engine.

One main goal Microsoft has for Fabric is to have Spark servers on standby to be used by a capacity thus reducing the wait time for a Spark engine to be allocated. Things will start faster. Any current user of Synapse can attest to issues with starting a new Spark pool. Fabric is trying to eliminate this wait. *Figure 14.5* shows the monitoring in the Fabric service that drills into the Spark engine from a notebook:

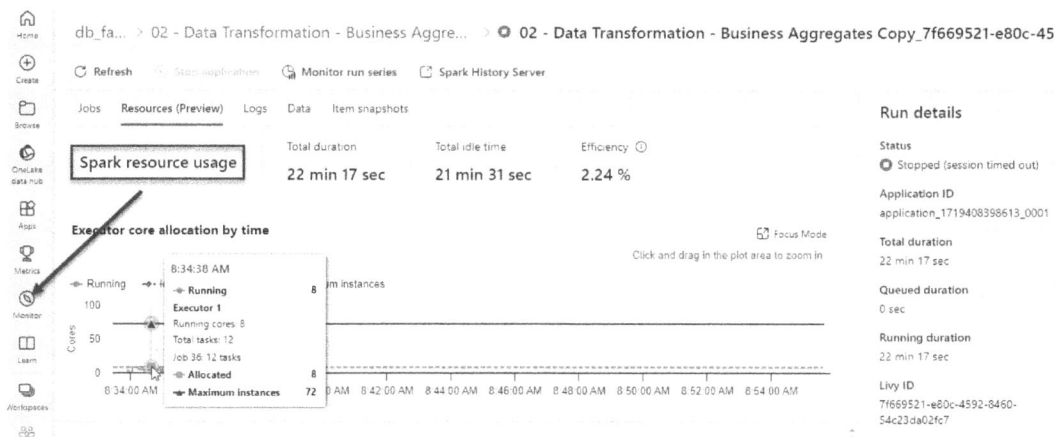

Figure 14.5 – Spark resource for a notebook run

Having discussed the Spark engine, let's transition to the default semantic model that uses Delta tables in Fabric.

Using Direct Lake for data sources

In *Chapter 5*, Direct Lake semantic models were introduced along with performance tuning in Import Mode and DirectQuery. It is now the third option for a semantic model. The performance of these different types of semantic models is created for a specific scenario. In the case of Direct Lake, the option is for large data volumes. For best results over Import Mode, as of the printing of this book, there is a need to have 100s of millions or billions of rows and 100+ GBs of data for Direct Lake to exceed the performance of Import Mode. We expect Microsoft to improve on this performance since Fabric was made GA in November of 2023.

The other requirement for using Direct Lake instead of Import Mode would be near real-time data in the model. Direct Lake is the replacement for DirectQuery on big data sources. Import Mode requires a data refresh when new data is available. Direct Lake does not need a data refresh because the connection is to the Delta tables in the warehouse or lakehouse. Even though data can be in-memory, the access to data is disk-based.

To see the options for Direct Lake, *Figure 14.6* displays the property for a Direct Lake model to switch between **Automatic**, **Direct Lake Only**, or **DirectQuery Only**:

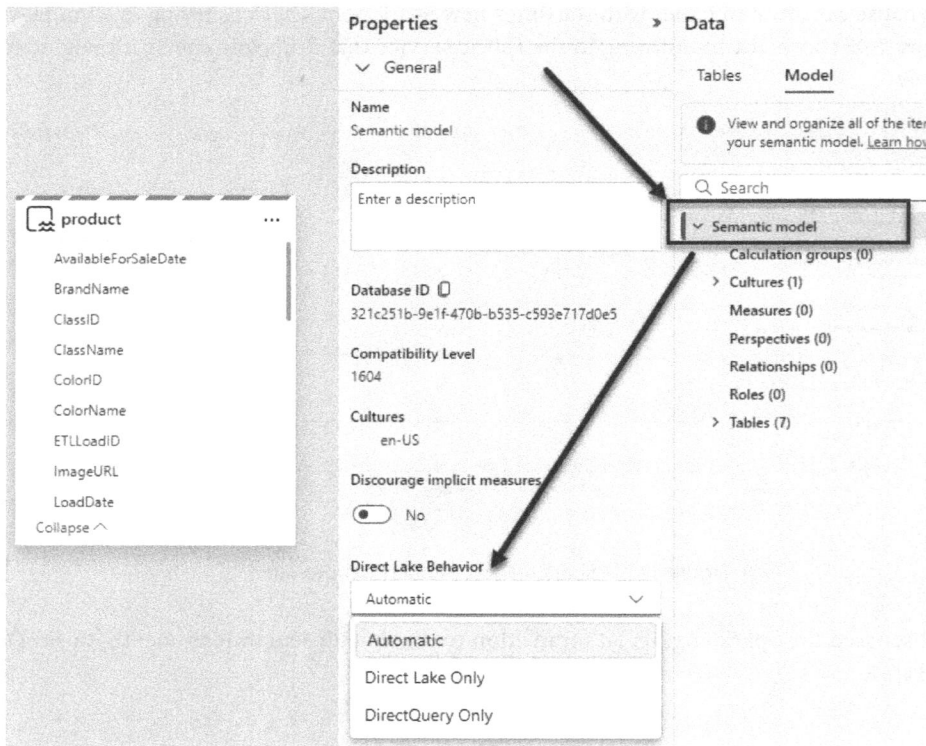

Figure 14.6 – Direct Lake behavior

In this figure, there are three options. The default is **Automatic**. This means Fabric handles the use of Direct Lake over DirectQuery. A switch to DirectQuery over Direct Lake can happen when the queries in the report using this semantic model exceed a limit. For instance, an F2 capacity has a limit of 300 million rows. If the query needs 310 million, the model "automatically" switches to DirectQuery over Direct Lake. This means the use of memory for queries cannot happen since the number of rows exceeds the capacity limit. The other two options force the model to use **Direct Lake Only** or **DirectQuery Only**.

There are two caches for Direct Lake – one for in-memory and the other for disk. So, even though there is no import mode, Direct Lake still takes advantage of caching data. The in-memory cache is to help with I/O operations, while the disk cache helps when data is not in memory. The caching relies on previous queries to cache data that was used in the query. So, while the first one to three queries of the day may seem slow, subsequent queries that read the same or similar data will benefit from the cache. Caching is transparent to the user.

Now that we know what new Fabric artifacts are present, let's move on to how to monitor these artifacts with existing Power BI artifacts.

Monitoring Fabric resource consumption

The main monitor help for the printing of this book is the **Microsoft Fabric Capacity Metrics** app. This is a Power BI template app you can install to monitor a Premium and/or Fabric capacity. The template app is explained in detail in *Chapter 13*. The details allow 30-second periods to be examined for all resources and the main measurement is CUs.

Figure 14.7 shows the list of `SynapseNotebook` resources used in a time slice of Fabric:

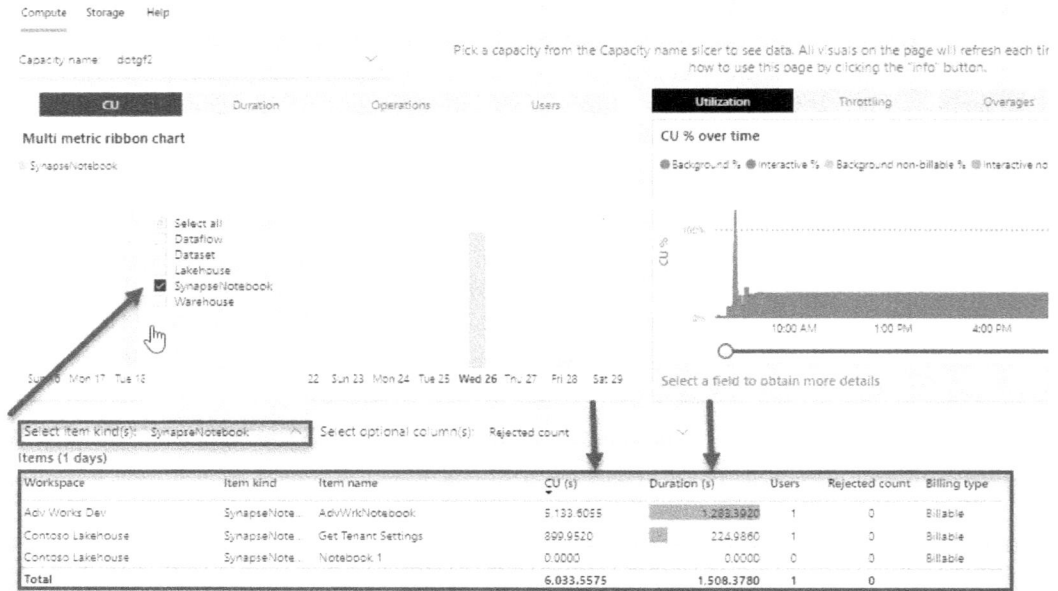

Figure 14.7 – Specific Fabric resource in monitor solution

Other resource types include `Dataflow`, `Dataset`, `Lakehouse`, and `Warehouse`. All these resources will show CU usage as well as durations for execution, queries, or data refreshes. The term "dataset" is referring to a semantic mode. The template app has not updated the header of this column yet.

To help you understand how to monitor resource consumption in real time, let's look at a system function to return information about column usage.

Measuring the hotness of data

There are system queries you can run to find the level of usage of data from a semantic model. The following code has a temperature column from a query. This indicates how often it is used, and, if it is lower than others, it can be evicted from memory when memory is needed by other queries or processes:

```
Select COLUMN_ID, SEGMENT_NUMBER, ISPAGEABLE, ISRESIDENT, TEMPERATURE,
LAST_ACCESSED from SYSTEMRESTRICTSCHEMA ($System.DISCOVER_STORAGE_
TABLE_COLUMN_SEGMENTS, [DATABASE_NAME] = 'AdvWkrDW')
```

`DATABASE_NAME` is where you specify the semantic model name. This example looks at the `AdvWrkDW` model and finds the temperature of each column. *Figure 14.8* shows the temperature of model columns from the `AdvWrkDW` semantic model:

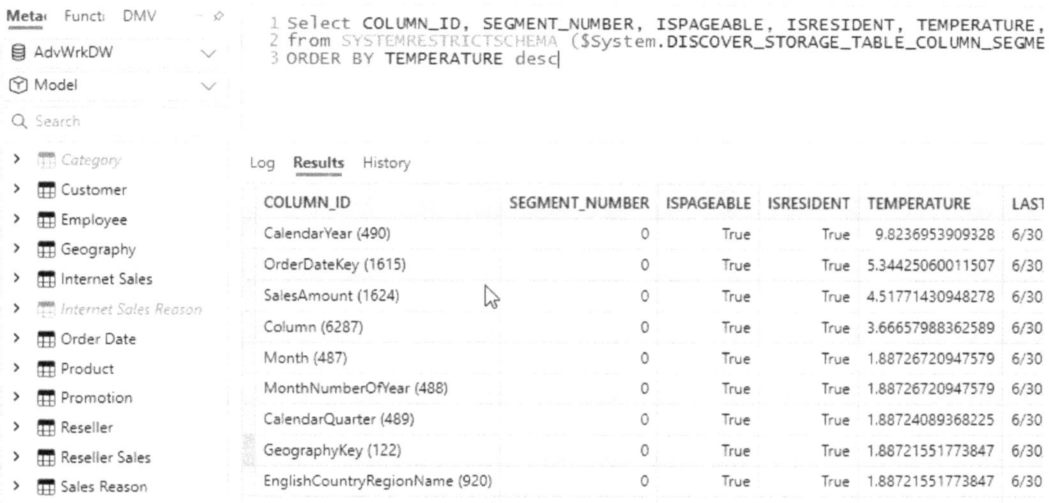

Figure 14.8 – The SYSTEMRESTRICTSCHEMA system function

The temperature for `CalendarYear` is higher than `EnglishCountryRegionName`. The data for the `EnglishCountryRegionName` column would be evicted from memory before `CalendarYear`. This also means that `CalendarYear` is queried more often. There is also a column named `ISRESIDENT` in which `True` means it is in-memory.

Let's look at some tips for enhancement performance for new Fabric artifacts.

Tips for enhancements

There are various options for handling performance with new Fabric artifacts. These can range from improving the model to using different capacities. One thing to keep in mind is that Fabric is a new capacity that will continuously have new features and improvements to the existing resources. There is always a monthly update that needs to be reviewed to understand the new features. Some of these would need to be turned on or off in the Admin portal.

First, let's look at load balancing.

Load balancing

Each function can be placed into its own capacity. That helps with resource contention and monitoring. Instead of creating one F32 capacity for all the work, you can separate it into multiple capacities. An F16 can be created for data warehousing where moving data is centralized. Dataflows and notebooks can use this capacity for processing lots of data and curating the data into a reportable structure. The semantic model can be on an F8 capacity for model processing and the reports can be on an F8 as well. If a company decides to use pay-as-you-go, the capacities can be paused and resume when needed. This ability can save money to not have a capacity running when it is not being used. Since semantic models can be shared between workspaces, there is no issue with a report being in a capacity different than a model. Since there are shortcuts, data can reside in a lakehouse in one workspace while the curated layer can be in another.

Next, we will look at a new feature for dataflows.

Dataflow copy fast

Dataflows offer a no-code or low-code experience through a graphical user interface. This easier process of moving data does come with a performance expense. Microsoft has been working hard to improve this performance gap. The latest is the copy fast improvement to Dataflow Gen2. It is a behind-the-scenes mechanism that mimics the pipeline copy activity from Synapse. This provides scale-out capabilities without having to switch this function to Azure Synapse. One prerequisite is for large files, such as CSV files of at least 100 MB. You can read more about this new feature here: `https://learn.microsoft.com/en-us/fabric/data-factory/dataflows-gen2-fast-copy`.

Let's continue this area with the on-demand loading of data.

On-demand loading

This feature was added before Fabric, but it allows the data to reside on disk while only the data needed for queries are in memory. Since the data is structured in parquet files, they are optimized for column storage and compression, which makes analytical reporting (aggregations) faster. Fabric has added this performance enhancement for users of data warehousing.

> **Note**
> Since the Delta tables are stored in parquet files, this structure is optimized for analytical reporting. It is not a good structure for row-by-row analysis of data. This is a standard report method that data from a relational database is structured better for. You are not going to get the same performance improvement for standard reporting as you will get for analytical reports on large datasets.

Let's look at the data size next.

Loading data in large chunks

Delta tables work best with loading data in large chunks. One or two rows at a time are not going to work well with this structure. Multiple small files will hurt the performance of Delta tables. The structure is meant for millions of rows. Parquet files created for Delta tables will show the most bang for the buck when the sets of data inserted are very large. In a Delta table, no data is updated in a previously created file by a change to a row. A new file will be inserted with the changes and the transaction log for the table will indicate to the data reader what files to load.

Lastly, let's look at maintenance that can help with too many files related to Delta tables.

Vacuum and Delta table structure

There is a maintenance option for optimizing Delta table structures once more data is added or updated. The command is called **Optimize** and comes from the Apache Delta table open-source functions. This function will try to optimize the number of files for the Delta table structure. This is like performing regular maintenance on table indexes in a relational database. It should be scheduled and monitored over time.

Here are some examples of using Optimize:

```
OPTIMIZE factSales VORDER;
```

```
OPTIMIZE factOrders WHERE predicate ZORDER BY InvoiceDate,
SalesOrderNumber;
```

The first example uses the ORDER optimization for the entire table. The second example uses the ZORDER to optimize the table file structures by the InvoiceDate and SalesOrderNumber columns in the table.

Let's summarize this chapter.

Summary

In this chapter, we learned about how Fabric improves performance overall with a data warehouse and analytical reporting. To begin with, we went over the additional artifacts in Fabric. We discussed the overarching concept of OneLake while talking about Delta tables. We also discussed data movement with notebooks and dataflows. In addition, we touched on the Spark engine as the ready-to-run serverless compute for most processing in Fabric.

Next, we looked at Direct Lake as a source for semantic models. Since the main data structure is Delta tables, the warehouse and lakehouse have a default semantic model with all Delta tables created in the container. We learned that Direct Lake mode is used only for very large datasets and that Import mode is still the best for small and intermediate semantic models unless near real-time reporting is required. We learned that Import Mode still can be used and should be if not looking to analytically report large data sets (big data). Microsoft has intentions of improving this.

Finally, we discussed monitoring with a main template app called Microsoft Fabric Capacity Metrics. We learned where a resource can be selected to help look specifically at that CU usage. At the end, we explored ways to enhance parts for the different artifacts and showed how these improve performance and why.

In the next chapter, we will learn how to optimize the process of embedding Power BI content in custom web applications.

15

Embedding in Web Apps

In the previous chapter, we talked about the new Fabric artifacts that will impact performance. The chapter started with data integration topics that need a spark engine that stores data in the Delta table format for Direct Lake access. The discussion ended with the monitoring tool used to measure performance with Fabric.

In this chapter, we will learn how to optimize for embedding, a capability that extends the reach of Power BI. This allows developers to use the Power BI APIs to embed reports, dashboards, or tiles into their custom applications. There are many possible uses for this, with popular choices being serving analytical content within company intranets, public-facing websites, or even commercial applications.

Embedding is technically possible with any Power BI capacity, so you don't need to buy Premium, Fabric, or Embedded to try it. However, for this to work properly at scale, you need to purchase reserved capacity to get around the limits of shared capacities, such as a limited number of embed tokens. Hence, the material in this chapter is relevant to the Premium, Fabric, and Embedded capacities. We will not cover Publish to Web, which is intended for mass distribution and behaves differently.

We will discuss what embedding involves, why there are special considerations, and how to make sure the Power BI content is loaded into the external applications as quickly as possible. We will also learn how to monitor Embedded content to identify areas that are slowing you down.

In this chapter, we will cover the following topics:

- Improving embedded performance
- Measuring embedded performance

Improving embedded performance

Embedding content in external applications gives organizations more flexibility in how they deploy and consume Power BI. There are different deployment costs and licensing considerations that will affect which type of capacity you purchase. Microsoft effectively provides reserved capacity offerings that are catered primarily to *externally* sharing content versus *internally* sharing content. However, the embedded functionality and mechanisms that are used to surface and optimize content are the same. Hence, the advice that will be provided in this chapter can be considered as generally applicable. If you would like to learn more about embedding licensing and distribution models and which capacity type is best for you, please check out the following documentation: `https://docs.microsoft.com/power-bi/developer/embedded/embedded-faq`.

Embedding content using APIs is an alternate way to expose where you don't use Power BI's web frontend. This can be seen in the diagram in *Figure 15.1*:

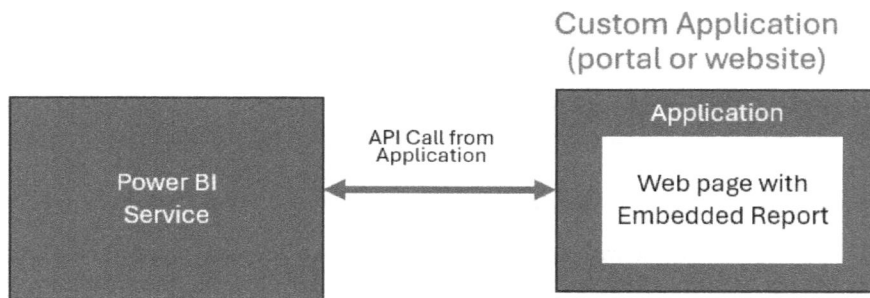

Figure 15.1 – Embedding Power BI content in other applications

In this configuration, users are interacting with the external application and not directly in the Power BI or Fabric service. Once the content has been initialized within the external application, performance is not affected by that application, unless it is also competing for CPU on the client.

> **Note**
>
> When you're embedding content, you should optimize it the same way as you would any other Power BI content. Follow all the guidance we have provided around data modeling, loading, report design, and so on. It is also important to perform capacity planning and sizing using the methods described in *Chapter 13, Working with Capacities*.

However, there are considerations regarding how the application is configured with Power BI and how it interacts with the Power BI service. Next, we will learn why embedding is different from viewing in the service and how we can speed it up.

When we embed Power BI content in another application, we are adding another layer of processing and latency. When we view a report on the Power BI portal, under most conditions, the Power BI application is already bootstrapped. This means that the core application code and dependencies have already been loaded.

However, when we load Power BI on-demand within our applications, this may not be the case. There may also be some overhead and latency between your application and the Power BI services. This includes time taken by your application before it even calls Power BI, where users can see other content already. This has the effect of exaggerating the delayed experience of loading Power BI content. Therefore, the advice we will give focuses on minimizing the embedding overhead.

The following list provides guidance and rationale for optimizing Embedded scenarios:

- **Consider application location and architecture**: The bi-directional arrow shown in *Figure 15.1* represents communication and data transfer between Power BI and your custom application. You should minimize communication latency by placing the custom applications as close to the Power BI home region as possible. This includes ensuring the number of network hops is minimized and sufficient bandwidth is available between Power BI and the custom app. Do keep in mind that visuals are executed on the client side, so if you have users in different geographic locations, some may have a different performance experience for the same content.

- **Keep SDK packages and tools up to date**: The Power BI team regularly updates both client tools and services, as frequently as once a month. These updates often contain new features, but they do contain performance improvements as well. When you deploy an application with embedded content, it is easy to continue updating the content without looking at the embedding mechanisms. To avoid missing out on performance improvements, we recommend using the latest SDK, API versions, and authoring tools such as Power BI Desktop. The SDK can be found at `https://www.nuget.org/packages/Microsoft.PowerBI.Api`, while the client libraries for embedding can be found at `https://docs.microsoft.com/javascript/api/overview/powerbi`.

- **Preloaded dependencies**: The Power BI Embedded API provides a method called `powerbi.preload` that allows you to load core Power BI dependencies on demand. This is useful when you have a custom application that displays Power BI content, as you can improve the first load experience. You can do this by calling `powerbi.preload` when you initialize the application, but before your users reach areas that display the Power BI content. This will load JavaScript files, CSS stylesheets, and any other artifacts to cache them locally. When the application needs to show Power BI content, it can avoid fencing the dependencies first. Additional information about preloading can be found here: `https://docs.microsoft.com/javascript/api/overview/powerbi/preload`. Use preload only when the Power BI content is on a different page of the application. It is best to bootstrap the iFrame when possible, as described in the next point.

- **Bootstrap the iFrame**: Embedding uses an HTML construct called an **iFrame** to host Power BI content. An iFrame is used to embed one HTML document within another and is typically used to expose external content that's served from a different web location or server. For example, you could use it to embed the Google search home page into a section of your website.

  When you embed content using powerbi.embed, you need a report identifier, an embedded URL, and an access token. Not all of these are immediately available, depending on the application's design and user journey. When you call the powerbi.embed method, the iFrame is prepared and initialized before the content loads. However, it is possible to perform this initialization earlier using powerbi.bootstrap(element, config). You must provide it with an HTML element and an embedded configuration object as parameters. When all the required parameters are ready, you can call powerbi.embed, passing in the same HTML element that has been already initialized. This is a great way to prepare for Power BI content to be displayed in the background while the user is doing something else in the application. Depending on the application's architecture and configuration, this can save some precious seconds, making a big difference to the user experience.

- **Use embed parameters effectively**: The second parameter in powerbi.embed(element, config) allows you to set options that control what features are enabled in the embedded content. The properties of the configuration object that affect performance are as follows:

  - EmbedURL: This property is the URL of the content you are embedding and is assigned to the src attribute of the iFrame. Avoid generating this URL yourself. You can obtain the best URL from the service using the Get Reports, Get Dashboard, or Get Tiles APIs.

  - **Permissions**: This property determines which operations you grant the person viewing the content. Use the Read permission if the user does not need to create content or copy or edit the report. This avoids initializing UI components that are not needed. Similarly, only set the minimum permission level that's needed if they require editing rights.

  - **Slicers, filters, and bookmarks**: These are separate properties in the configuration that allow you to set the context for the content. By design, Power BI tries to cache visuals to speed up report content while queries are executed in the background. This cached result considers the report's context set by slicers, plus more. However, if you are embedding and supplying this context via the code, the cache is not used. Therefore, if you have a default starting context for an embedded report, you should publish the report with that context already set. Then, you can call the embed method without context to take advantage of the cache.

- **Change reports efficiently**: A custom application allows you to build interesting functionality, such as a custom navigation UI that controls which Power BI report a user sees. A user could simply click a button or a link to replace the current report, without reloading the page. If you implement something like this, ensure that you reuse the iFrame. When you call powerbi.embed, use a different configuration but pass it the same HTML element.

- **Use a custom UI to reduce slicer complexity**: You can reduce the complexity of reports by removing slicer visuals from the report canvas and setting them in the embedded report configuration object described earlier in this list. This lets you capture a lot of different slicer and filter selections and pass them all at once while you're loading the initial embedded report.

- **Throttle the custom application to prevent misuse**: Users can double-click custom report links or navigate between reports in the custom app very quickly, causing many calls to be issued to Power BI's backend. You can limit this kind of behavior in your application by setting a short duration within which to ignore a user action that occurs too soon after the last one. A good rule of thumb here is about 100 ms.

- **Handling multiple visuals**: Many reports contain more than just visuals. You can embed a page containing multiple visuals as it was designed within a single iFrame. However, you may need to combine and embed multiple reports or even individual tiles in your custom application; each would need an iFrame. Initializing an iFrame is relatively expensive, so you should try to have as few as possible. Here are some options:

    - **Consolidate reports**: If possible, consolidate data and visuals from separate semantic models and reports. This will allow you to embed the content in one iFrame.

    - **Use a dashboard to combine disparate content**: A Power BI dashboard is designed to contain report tiles from different reports and semantic models that have no technical relationship with one another. If you need to embed tiles from different reports into your application, consider putting them in a dashboard and embedding this instead of all the individual tiles. This reduces the load to a single iFrame. You can also embed individual tiles from dashboards instead of reports. These are more efficient than report tiles and will load faster. Consider this option when you do not want all the tiles appearing together in your application and you don't want to use multiple iFrames.

- **Use a custom layout**: The embedded configuration has a `layoutType` property that can be set to `customLayout`. The latter allows you to define a page's size and visual layout, which will override the defaults. It even allows you to hide visuals you do not want to see. It is also useful to rearrange visuals so that they can be viewed on mobile devices. More information on setting a custom layout can be found here: `https://docs.microsoft.com/javascript/api/overview/powerbi/custom-layout`.

Now that we know how to optimize embedding scenarios, let's learn how to gauge embedding performance.

Measuring embedded performance

When you embed Power BI content in your applications, it is recommended that you measure the embedding activity to understand the performance profile. The methods we have described in this book can help you measure and resolve the performance of the Power BI artifacts themselves, but they do not tell you what is happening in your application and whether there is any inefficiency when it is communicating with Power BI and loading content. For example, the embedded Power BI report may execute queries and render visuals within two seconds, but the user experiences a longer total wait time due to the embedding overhead. Before we learn how to measure the embedding overhead, we will introduce a recommended practice.

When you are performance-tuning your embedded content, it is very important to obtain a baseline of performance without embedding. This will help you set the appropriate range for the best case in performance, as well as help you identify any issues unrelated to embedding. You can optimize their semantic models, DAX, and so on, independently and in parallel to the embedding optimization. Just be sure to optimize the embedding code in your web application using the same Power BI content all the time. This way, you can ensure that any improvements are from the embedding changes, and not from Power BI content changes.

When you embed Power BI content, the system generates events to help you track and optimize embedding behavior. To learn more about capturing embedded events, please see the following documentation: `https://docs.microsoft.com/javascript/api/overview/powerbi/handle-events`.

Next, we will describe the relevant events and how they can help with performance tuning:

- **Loaded**: This event fires when a Power BI report or dashboard has been initialized. Loading is complete when the Power BI logo shown in *Figure 15.2* is no longer visible:

Loading your report...

Figure 15.2 – The logo and progress bar that are shown when a report has been initialized

- **Rendered**: This event is raised after the report visuals have completed any work and displayed their results on the screen.

- **VisualRendered**: This event is fired for every visual. It is not enabled by default and needs to be enabled by setting `VisualRenderedEvents` to `true` in the embedding's configuration. This allows you to track the speed of each visual, as well as rank the visuals and focus on the slowest ones. This information can also be gained from the Desktop Performance Analyzer and is a good way to compare the performance of content that's deployed to production versus in development.

Now, let's learn how to use events to understand where delays are occurring. We suggest using a combination of the Power BI events we described in the previous list, plus the events that you manually generate in the custom application. This will give you a complete picture of all the activities. *Figure 15.3* shows a timeline representation of a user action in a custom application. In this example, we assume that a user has clicked a button in the custom application (not a Power BI report), which makes the calls to load a Power BI report that contains two visuals (A and B):

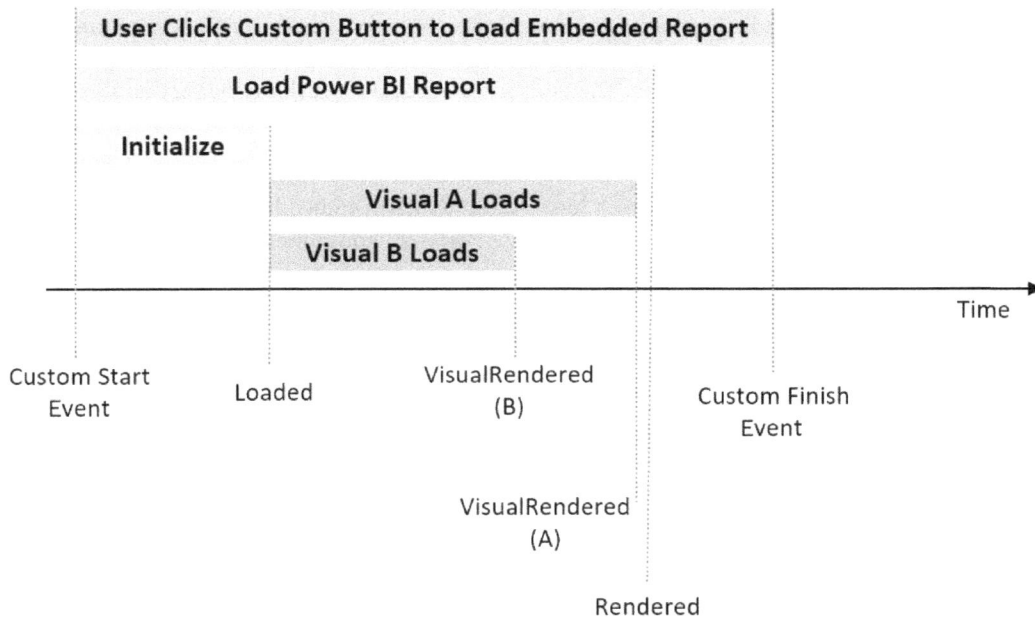

Figure 15.3 – Timeline of embedded activity and event generation

The diagram in *Figure 15.3* shows a **custom Start event** and a **custom Finish event**. These represent the entire user action from the time they clicked the custom button to the time the custom web app finished its work. There may be other work besides loading the report, which is why we have included a gap between the **Rendered event** and the custom Finish event.

Once you have captured these events, you can subtract the timestamps to work out the duration of any component. Then, you can compare this to the results of the service, as well as in Performance Analyzer, to see whether there is a substantial difference.

Now, let's summarize what we've learned in this chapter.

Summary

In this chapter, we conclude our Power BI optimization journey by learning how to embed content efficiently. We learned that reserved capacities that are sold allow developers to embed content in external applications. This allows them to build their own user experience that's been enhanced by analytical content. When they do this, they avoid using the Power BI user interface, and users access reports through the custom application.

Then, we learned that embedding involves communication between the Power BI service and the custom application via APIs. The Embedded SDK allows developers to authenticate, load, and then place content inside the custom application. This adds some overhead, which can be very noticeable if there is significant latency between the application and Power BI. However, we have highlighted that you can – and should – optimize your Power BI content separately from the embedding mechanisms.

We learned that it is important to use the latest tools and SDKs when embedding. We also introduced the API methods that can be used to load or initialize Power BI components ahead of time. This reduces the initial load time for content by having dependent assets such as JavaScript and CSS files loaded. We also looked at configuration settings such as minimal permissions, which can speed up content by only loading the necessary UI components.

Finally, we learned that when a custom application needs to load content, it uses an iFrame. We discussed how every separate piece of content uses an iFrame and you should minimize the number of iFrames used. The suggestion is to consolidate content to load faster. We learned how to measure performance through events. The application would use and monitor custom events with Microsoft events to look at performance. This gives a full picture and allows you to understand the total duration from a user's perspective between report initialization, rendering, and ready for input.

Congratulations! You have completed your Power BI optimization journey and should be ready to tailor and apply what you've learned throughout this book to your everyday job. We will close with a reminder that performance management should be a discipline that is ingrained into every stage of your development life cycle. You can achieve great results and maintain good designs with a bit of planning and strong collaboration between stakeholders with different roles and skill sets.

Index

‹packt›

packtpub.com

Subscribe to our online digital library for full access to over 7,000 books and videos, as well as industry leading tools to help you plan your personal development and advance your career. For more information, please visit our website.

Why subscribe?

- Spend less time learning and more time coding with practical eBooks and Videos from over 4,000 industry professionals
- Improve your learning with Skill Plans built especially for you
- Get a free eBook or video every month
- Fully searchable for easy access to vital information
- Copy and paste, print, and bookmark content

Did you know that Packt offers eBook versions of every book published, with PDF and ePub files available? You can upgrade to the eBook version at packtpub.com and as a print book customer, you are entitled to a discount on the eBook copy. Get in touch with us at customercare@packtpub.com for more details.

At www.packtpub.com, you can also read a collection of free technical articles, sign up for a range of free newsletters, and receive exclusive discounts and offers on Packt books and eBooks.

Other Books You May Enjoy

If you enjoyed this book, you may be interested in these other books by Packt:

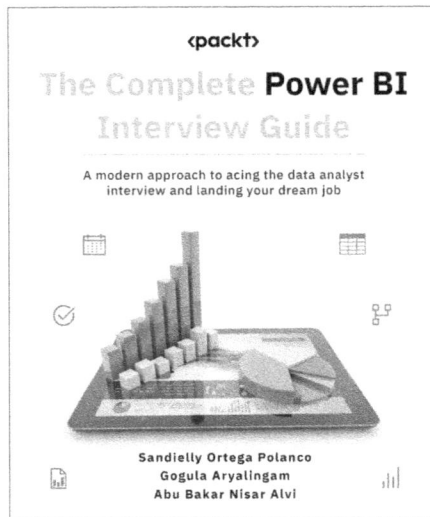

The Complete Power BI Interview Guide

Sandielly Ortega Polanco, Gogula Aryalingam, Abu Bakar Nisar Alvi

ISBN: 978-1-80512-067-4

- Elevate your profile presentation with standout techniques
- Navigate the Power BI job market strategically for job hunting success
- Cultivate essential soft skills for career growth
- Explore the complete analytics development cycle in Power BI
- Master key Power BI development concepts in core areas
- Gain insights into HR interviews, salary negotiations, and onboarding procedures

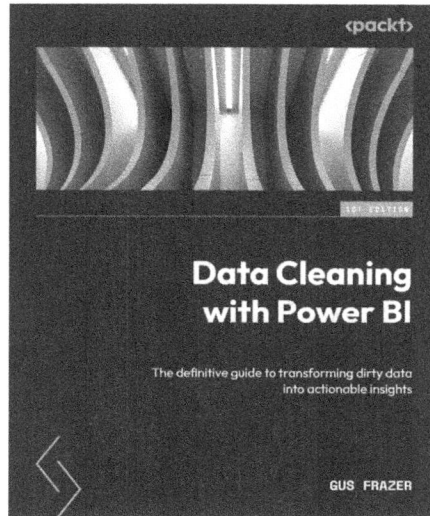

Data Cleaning with Power BI

Gus Frazer

ISBN: 978-1-80512-640-9

- Connect to data sources using both import and DirectQuery options
- Use the Query Editor to apply data transformations
- Transform your data using the M query language
- Design clean and optimized data models by creating relationships and DAX calculations
- Perform exploratory data analysis using Power BI
- Address the most common data challenges with best practices
- Explore the benefits of using OpenAI, ChatGPT, and Microsoft Copilot for simplifying data cleaning

Packt is searching for authors like you

If you're interested in becoming an author for Packt, please visit authors.packtpub.com and apply today. We have worked with thousands of developers and tech professionals, just like you, to help them share their insight with the global tech community. You can make a general application, apply for a specific hot topic that we are recruiting an author for, or submit your own idea.

Share Your Thoughts

Now you've finished *Microsoft Power BI Performance Best Practices*, we'd love to hear your thoughts! Scan the QR code below to go straight to the Amazon review page for this book and share your feedback or leave a review on the site that you purchased it from.

https://packt.link/r/1-835-08225-4

Your review is important to us and the tech community and will help us make sure we're delivering excellent quality content.

Download a free PDF copy of this book

Thanks for purchasing this book!

Do you like to read on the go but are unable to carry your print books everywhere?

Is your eBook purchase not compatible with the device of your choice?

Don't worry, now with every Packt book you get a DRM-free PDF version of that book at no cost.

Read anywhere, any place, on any device. Search, copy, and paste code from your favorite technical books directly into your application.

The perks don't stop there, you can get exclusive access to discounts, newsletters, and great free content in your inbox daily

Follow these simple steps to get the benefits:

1. Scan the QR code or visit the link below

https://packt.link/free-ebook/978-1-83508-225-6

2. Submit your proof of purchase
3. That's it! We'll send your free PDF and other benefits to your email directly

www.ingramcontent.com/pod-product-compliance
Lightning Source LLC
Chambersburg PA
CBHW081049220326
41598CB00038B/7036